Economic Growth and Democracy in Post-Colonial Africa

Economic Growth and Democracy in Post-Colonial Africa

Cabo Verde, Small States, and the World Economy

Edited by
João Resende-Santos and Aminah N. Fernandes Pilgrim

LEXINGTON BOOKS
Lanham • Boulder • New York • London

Dedicated to an historic figure in post-colonial Africa, Scholar, Dilpomat, Beloved Family Man & Friend André Corsino Tolentino 1946–2021

Published by Lexington Books
An imprint of The Rowman & Littlefield Publishing Group, Inc.
4501 Forbes Boulevard, Suite 200, Lanham, Maryland 20706
www.rowman.com

86-90 Paul Street, London EC2A 4NE

British Library Cataloguing in Publication information available

Library of Congress Cataloging-in-Publication Data

Names: Resende-Santos, João, 1966- editor. | Pilgrim, Aminah N., 1974- editor.
Title: Economic growth and democracy in post-colonial Africa : Cabo Verde, small states, and the world economy / edited by João Resende-Santos and Aminah N. Fernandes Pilgrim.
Description: Lanham : Lexington Books, [2022] | Includes bibliographical references and index.
Identifiers: LCCN 2022001775 (print) | LCCN 2022001776 (ebook) | ISBN 9781793653833 (hardcover) | ISBN 9781793653840 (epub)
Subjects: LCSH: Economic development—Cabo Verde. | Democratization—Cabo Verde. | Cabo Verde—Economic conditions. | Cabo Verde—Politics and government—1975-1991. | Cabo Verde—Politics and government—1991- | Cabo Verde—Foreign relations.
Classification: LCC HC594 .E26 2022 (print) | LCC HC594 (ebook) | DDC 338.96658—dc23/eng/20220214
LC record available at https://lccn.loc.gov/2022001775
LC ebook record available at https://lccn.loc.gov/2022001776

Contents

Introduction

Economic Growth and Democracy in Post-Colonial Africa: Cabo Verde, Small States, and the World Economy

Aminah N. Fernandes Pilgrim
and João Resende-Santos

This volume is a comprehensive academic analysis of the political economy of Cabo Verde (Cape Verde) from the time of its independence in 1975 to the present.[1] The volume brings together some of the most accomplished scholars and policy practitioners on the subject matter of Cabo Verde's political economy. The tiny West African island state has emerged as a relative success story in post-colonial Africa, achieving both good levels of human development and freedom. The Cabo Verdean case of comparative political and socio-economic success within post-colonial Africa is under researched and has been largely ignored by scholars, especially in the English-speaking world. Sadly, a distorted view of Africa continues to prevail—what literary giant Chimamanda Adichie called "a single story"—especially in the media but within academia as well. This has led to a persistent misconception of an imagined, singular post-colonial African experience of unmitigated failure, poverty, political breakdown, and coup d'états, economic ruin, societal disengagement from the state, and corruption. While it must be acknowledged that Africa has had its share of failures, and the continent continues to lag behind the rest of the world, exceptions exist, and these stories must be told as well. The recent Covid-19 pandemic demonstrated exceptions within the continent to global patterns and crisis response. The continent has had cases of sustained success in human development, human freedom, good governance, and credible institutions, such as Cabo Verde, Botswana, Mauritius, and others attest.

This volume provides an analytical narrative on one of post-colonial Africa's more positive experiments in economic development and democracy. As the first-ever scholarly work in English on the subject, the nine chapters examine the political system, economy, and foreign relations of Cabo Verde. Providing readers with first voice scholarship, the chapters compiled here represent primary research and primary sources written by leading specialists—many of them former diplomats—within each field represented here. Their work is based on privileged access to resources, information, and leaders. Thus, the collection offers an original, broad survey of the principal topics in the country's post-independence political economy. Bringing together rigorous but accessible scholarship, historically sensitive and information-rich analysis, the volume introduces the general public, policymakers, university students, and other young people—especially second- and third-generation Cabo Verdean descendants in the global diaspora—to the nature and evolution of Cabo Verde's post-independence political and economic performance.

Nine inhabited tiny islands strewn across the eastern mid-Atlantic, often not even recorded on most wall maps, Cabo Verde may be considered a relatively insignificant small state in the world system, but it is also a microcosm of many historical and contemporary global transformations. It is an unusual and unexpected country. The principal transshipment point in the brutal and dehumanizing Atlantic slave trade, Cabo Verde is one of the modern world's first creole societies. In many ways, Cabo Verde became the first Caribbean country, the first multicultural/multiracial society mixing African, European, and Asian that would eventually spread westward across the Atlantic. For millions of blacks in the Americas, it was a warehousing and transit point for their tears, blood, and suffering. At the same time, Cabo Verde is the origin of the first *free* Africans to emigrate to the United States, as the large numbers of Cabo Verdeans hired on the eighteenth- and nineteenth-century whaling ships made New England their new home. These tiny islands became a safe haven for Jews fleeing persecution in Europe, especially during the Inquisition. Roughly the size of the state of Rhode Island in the United States, Cabo Verde's role in many global transformations has been disproportionate to its micro scale.

Today, it has emerged as a popular tourist destination and enjoys wide international visibility largely as a result of its world-famous singer, the "barefoot diva" Cesária Évora. While scholars have largely neglected it, the archipelago has become a well-known and popular vacation destination for nearly a million European tourists annually. It is emerging as an unexpected pioneer in the use of renewable energy sources, leading all of Africa today by generating over 20 percent of its electricity for renewable sources. If democracy is a word rarely associated with the African continent, Cabo Verde stands as one of the world's vibrant democracies. Similarly, if today's globalizing world is becoming ever more a place of mixing and cross-fertilization of cultures, races, ideas, and traditions, Cabo Verde also stood at the vanguard of creolization. An African country sharing similar global transformations and historical processes as the rest of the continent, there are also elements of exceptionalism to Cabo Verde's history. Aside from its geographic positioning and creole society, it is also among the rare African countries to emerge from colonialism with a more or less functioning state and administrative elite, as the Barros chapter featured here shows. And despite centuries of colonial rule and brutality, and an utterly frail country at independence in 1975 that few believed would be viable, it emerged as a socio-economic and political success story in post-colonial Africa. Indeed, Cabo Verde's post-independence relative success and the recent challenges faced in its new development phase tell us as much about the country itself as they tell about the much larger question regarding the prospects and limitations of small states in the world system.

Cabo Verde today stands at a fork in the road. As such, this is an opportune moment for this volume to examine the road traveled as the country looks ahead into its next phase of development. Cabo Verde is confronting an array of domestic and external challenges that it has not faced since the early days of independence in 1975. The future is uncertain. The challenges are daunting, as discussed further below.

Development has become more difficult after graduation. Economic hard times, shrinking job prospects, and social distress have gripped the country and sapped people's optimism and self-confidence. Given its recent successes, this is unfamiliar terrain for its people and this generation of political leadership. Since 2008, the economy has barely managed to grow beyond 1 percent annually—disorienting for a country that averaged nearly 6 percent annual growth in the previous two decades. The country avoided disaster, however, managing a respectable 2.2 percent annual growth rate during 2009–2018, largely because of strong remittances and tourism inflows. However, this modest growth was largely due to recovery after 2015, with the economy struggling with anemic, above-zero growth since 2009. Moreover, given the country's many structural constraints, as discussed in this volume, the economy remains unable to generate the necessary employment and entrepreneurial opportunities for its citizens, both low skilled and even university graduates. Structural unemployment and the urgent need to create jobs continue to be the biggest policy and governance challenges. Like most Small Island Developing States (SIDS), the country has very few other viable options to spur growth and create jobs.

The road ahead is full of many challenges but also opportunities. The country is endowed with numerous strengths, such as its relatively good governance, social peace, an increasingly known tourist destination, and vast global diaspora, including many returnees who have invested in the infrastructure and digital economy of the nation. Good governance and sound macroeconomic management helped it navigate through the post-2008 crisis years. It is an African country closely integrated into the European Union (EU), the source of nearly 90 percent of its tourists, foreign aid, trade, foreign investments, and remittances. The country has been working steadily to become a mid-Atlantic "hub" for international services, such as air, cargo, and transshipment. With both the United States and the EU, it has been extending security and intelligence cooperation to protect the country's vast maritime borders and combat international criminal trafficking.

Forty-five years after independence, Cabo Verde remains a small, resource-poor, structurally vulnerable country that lacks the sufficient productive base and internal sources of growth to feed its own people or provide them the jobs and living standards necessary. Unlike the period of 1975, and the nearly four decades of robust economic growth that followed, Cabo Verde today can no longer rely on the same sources of growth and development that it enjoyed in the past nor on the same external circumstances. It is a small island state in an increasingly integrated, highly competitive world economy and a post-development aid international system. Its most important source of growth and development in the post-independence years, foreign aid, has all but disappeared. As a newly promoted middle-income country, it can no longer rely on cheap external financing, such as concessional loans, to finance growth and job creation. Foreign direct investments (FDIs) have dried up since the 2008 global financial crisis, and its growing public and external debt severely constrains its ability to spur growth. Its fastest growing industry and symbol of success, tourism, continues robust quantitative growth in arrivals and balance of payments accounts, but it is mostly foreign owned and remains largely disconnected from the rest of the economy. Closures of the country's borders due to the 2020 pandemic revealed the vulnerabilities of the tourism economy. Standing at the crossroads in a post-pandemic world, today, Cabo Verde must find a new model of development.

THE AIMS OF THIS VOLUME

To understand where Cabo Verde is headed, we must understand where it came from. This book examines Cabo Verde's political and economic development during the first forty-five years of its independence. As Cabo Verde confronts the challenges ahead, it is an opportune moment to examine its economic and political performance since 1975 in order to understand the scope, sources, and limits of this past performance, to explain where the country is today, and to illuminate the way forward as the country enters its next phase of development. The book's primary objective is to provide a scholarly analysis of the nature and sources of Cabo Verde's economic and political trajectory since 1975. By doing so, the book offers a more balanced perspective of the post-colonial experiences of African countries, as well as providing lessons on policy, institutions, and governance that can inform future lawmaking, as well as be generalized to other small countries in the region and beyond.

As the first academic book in English that analyzes Cabo Verde's political economy since 1975, the volume brings together some of the most widely respected experts on the economy, politics, society, and foreign relations of Cabo Verde. Each of their chapters offers analytical narratives on various aspects of the country's political economy since 1975. To date, there is no scholarly volume, in any language, that focuses solely on the Cabo Verdean political economy. Cabo Verde's rich cultural and literary traditions have received much more scholarly attention, with publications in English, Portuguese, and other languages of the diaspora. The first books in English, such as Basil Davidson's *The Fortunate Isles* (1989) and *No Fist Is Big Enough to Hide the Sky* (1981), and works by Patrick Chabal (2003), Richard Lobban and Marilyn Halter (1993), introduced the English-speaking world to the newly independent micro state, its liberation struggle, the leader Amílcar Cabral, and the Cabo Verdean diaspora. More recent works in English have been dedicated to identity and diaspora issues. A number of stand-alone studies in academic journals have addressed some aspects of recent political economy. Much more research attention has been paid to the so-called "miracle" of Mauritius and to Botswana, even though Cabo Verde outperformed Mauritius in terms of economic growth. Cabo Verde consistently ranks in the top, along with Mauritius and Botswana, across indicators such as growth rates, human development, transparency, democratic rights, poverty rates, good governance, gender politics, and political stability.

Not only is the small West African country an example of robust human development, Cabo Verde has been free of the many ills that have marred the post-independence experience of many other countries—contested politics, internecine warfare, anti-system forces, kleptocratic leadership, or democratic reversals visible in many countries. It made the dual transition from one-party rule and central economic planning to multiparty democracy and free markets in a rather routine and uneventful fashion, without schism, without reversals. Why? Quick and easy explanations, such as the absence of ethnic cleavages in Cabo Verde, are both incorrect and unsatisfying. How does a resource-poor, tiny country that no one believed would be viable after independence beat the odds and outperform bigger, resource-rich countries?

The book aims to inform both the general public as well as students and academics. The idea for a general volume has its origins in discussions among a small group involved in the creation of a research institute devoted to Cabo Verdean Studies at Bridgewater State University in New England, home to the largest concentration of Cabo Verdean-Americans in the United States. The purpose of the institute was to foster scholarship on Cabo Verde, promote international collaboration and exchange and community engagement, and raise awareness among the country's global diaspora. Through the institute and scholarly works like this volume, we were particularly interested in reaching the large numbers of youth and university students in the diaspora. These young people display an interest in the homeland of their parents and grandparents, especially as they struggle with their own cultural identity, but have little or no basis of knowledge about the country of their forebears.

Each of the chapters in this volume addresses critical aspects of Cabo Verde's experience since 1975. Written by some of the best people around, each chapter provides a succinct but comprehensive analysis of the structure and essential features of its economy, political system, and foreign relations; chronicles the major economic, social, and political transformations and performance from 1975 to present; investigates the factors and sources contributing to this economic, social, and political performance, as well as the scope and limitations of this performance; and assesses the major challenges ahead.

This introductory chapter examines some of the common themes in the volume and identifies some of the critical issues in Cabo Verde's political economy. The chapter by Corsino Tolentino, a highly respected scholar-diplomat, repositions the long-standing debate about Cabo Verde's peculiar historical-geographic situation in between Africa and Europe. Cabo Verdeans themselves have long grappled with this issue of belonging, identity, and positionality. A historic figure and one of Cabo Verde's most renowned diplomats, Tolentino reflects broadly on the issue of Cabo Verde's place in the world. Rather than repeating the stilted debates of whether Cabo Verde is an African country, European or something else, or debates about whether it should tie its destiny with Europe or Africa, the chapter steps back and takes a broader, longer view of a small island country being shaped by both forces of globalization and regionalization since its discovery in 1640. As a small island state in the mid-Atlantic, Cabo Verde's history, cultural identity, and economic evolution have been intimately intertwined with its geographical position at the crossroads of global flows of people, goods, cultures, and knowledge. In many ways, Cabo Verde is a product of its crossroads position. In the past and as today, this positioning has given rise to endless debates and agonizing self-reflection as to "who" Cabo Verdeans are in terms of their cultural-psychological identity, "where" Cabo Verde is located, and to "where" it should anchor its economic and political relations.

Anyone who wants to understand Cabo Verde more fully, and the global experience of Cabo Verdeans in the modern world, must begin with an appreciation of the nature and structural limitations of its tiny, resource-poor economy. It is the poverty of its economy over the centuries, its bouts of periodic droughts and devastating famine, that scarred the national psyche but also drove the global emigration of its people. In "Evolution and Macroeconomic Management of the Economy in Cabo Verde," the reader is introduced to the main characteristics of the Cabo Verdean economy, its evolution since 1975, and the main challenges to growth and human development it faces. The chapter by Rocha, a scholar and practitioner as senior administrator in the central bank, offers an expert analytical narrative of the evolution of Cabo Verde's economy since 1975. The chapter gives special emphasis on the two determining components of its economic performance, macroeconomic policy and the external sector. Rocha traces the major structural changes in the economy, from the centrally planned economic model of the one-party regime, to the structural transformation to an open, market-based economy beginning in 1991. The Rocha chapter offers an informative account of the main structural features of Cabo Verde's economy—its insularity, micro size and discontinuity of its domestic market, its narrow productive base, hostile climate and soil conditions producing periodic drought and family, and its utter dependence on the outside to import everything. As such, the chapter concentrates on macroeconomic policy (trade and monetary policy especially), external factors such as foreign aid, emigrant remittances, and today the rise of tourism. The chapter underscores the reality of a country whose economic growth and well-being of its people are shaped by forces beyond its control.

Roselma Évora's "The Political System, Transition to Democracy, and the Challenges to Democratic Consolidation in Cabo Verde," offers an accessible and critical examination of the country's political system. Évora is one of Cabo Verde's most astute and accomplished scholars of the country's democratic governance and political system. Author of the most widely read and cited books on Cabo Verde's democratic transition, in this chapter, Évora turns her attention primarily to the question of democracy's consolidation and quality. The chapter provides an informative analysis for students and the general audience interested in learning about Cabo Verde's political system. It traces the evolution of the political system since 1975, and then examines the key aspects and developments in democratic governance since 1991. The chapter examines some key challenges faced by Cabo Verde's democratic governance, especially civic participation, party politics, and the institutional deficiencies of the democratic process.

Cape Verde's most consequential foreign relations since independence is the bilateral relations with its former colonial ruler, Portugal. In general, Europe dominates all aspects of the country's global relations. In "Cabo Verde's Relations with Europe," former foreign minister Victor Borges examines Cabo Verde's most important global relationship and forcefully challenges the long-standing debate about the country's place in the world.

Another of Cabo Verde's scholar-diplomats, Borges is one of the rare individuals in public life, combining vast professional experience with deep intellectual capacity and breadth of knowledge. Borges offers a broad overview of Cabo Verde's relations with Europe since independence, examining both the political and economic dimension, as well as the social-cultural dimensions. The chapter is a valuable chronicle and interpretation of these relations, but its additional value added is the insider, first-person perspective. As minister, he was the chief architect of Cabo Verde's push to establish a Special Partnership Agreement with the EU, which became a framework for development assistance, as well as broad bilateral relations covering numerous areas of cooperation. The chapter underscores the depth and reach of bilateral relations, or rather Cabo Verde's extensive economic, as well as social connections to Europe and the country's broad reliance on Europe for nearly all its trade, financing, tourists, remittances, and diplomatic support. As such, Borges addresses head-on the debate over whether Cabo Verde is part of Europe or Africa and whether the country should anchor its relations with one or the other. Borges rejects the stifling either-or option. At the same time, he lays out the compelling reasons why relations with Europe merit the high-level political and diplomatic attention, especially in view of the absence of realistic alternatives that can substitute the country's reliance on Europe.

Tourism has emerged as the most dynamic and important part of Cabo Verde's economy. Today it accounts for nearly a quarter of the economy. More tourists visit the islands annually than the resident population. The industry has infiltrated national life and touched even remote rural communities, even though it is an enclave tourism industry largely concentrated on two islands. A chapter on tourism, therefore, is an essential part of any book examining Cabo Verde's political economy. The Bernardo chapter provides a careful, thorough examination of the evolution of the tourism sector, its main features, and the many challenges the sector poses. Based on field research, the chapter offers a critical examination of the impact, positive and negative, of tourism on the economy and society. Importantly, the chapter traces the evolution of government policy and strategies to develop the tourism sector and to manage it. The second half of the chapter examines the many risks and negative impacts, including the high leakage rate, the disconnect between this outward-oriented, foreign-controlled sector and the rest of the national economy, and the growing popular dissatisfaction with the sector due to some of its negative social and cultural impacts.

As alluded to above, Cabo Verde is partly exceptional in the context of post-colonial Africa because it inherited from colonial rule a functioning state and mobile, heterogeneous political elite with administrative experience. The chapter by Crisanto Barros provides a forceful, superbly researched analysis of state formation and the historical evolution of Cabo Verde's political class.

The analysis is breathtaking in scope and unrelenting in its reinterpretation of state formation, the post-independence period, and democracy. Barros directly challenges the widely shared view that the Cabo Verdean state emerged with independence in 1975. Indeed, he traces its origins to the early nineteenth century, thus making Cabo Verde's post-colonial experience quite different from that of other African countries that emerged from colonial rule without functioning institutions or very fragile ones. In one of the most compelling studies of political sociology, Barros traces the evolution of the country's political-economic elite. The analysis shows the socio-economic profile and historical transformation of the elite, the role of education (rather than economic class or race) in its composition and upward mobility, its internal circulation, and the increasing interpenetration of the political class, public administration, and the market economy. This latter focus compels our rethinking of democratic governance in Cabo Verde.

Abel Djassi Amado, a bright young scholar and superb researcher, examines the historic bilateral relationship between Cabo Verde and the United States. Even though Cabo Verde's relations with the outside world are anchored in Europe, its relations with the United States have deeper, more fascinating historical roots and a transnational dimension that makes U.S.–Cabo Verdean relations exceptional in the context of Africa. Cabo Verdeans were present in the United States long before the American Revolution, and in 1818 their homeland became host to the first U.S. consulate in Sub-Saharan Africa. This transnational social-cultural dimension—of migration, return, circulation of people, ideas, goods, culture—is sui generis in the context of U.S.–Africa relations with the possible exception of Liberia. Aside from the trans-Atlantic slave trade, Cabo Verde–U.S. relations are intimately intertwined in the transformative whaling industry out of New England. The United States became home to the oldest and largest Cabo Verdean diaspora communities in the world. Amado traces the evolution of U.S.–Cabo Verdean relations, focusing primarily on recent developments. The chapter examines the pattern of relationship between the United States and Cabo Verde in the past couple of decades, as bilateral relations intensified greatly. Specifically, it studies the securitization of the current U.S.–Cabo Verde relations. It argues that in the wake of 9/11 terrorist attacks, the U.S. policy toward Cabo Verde, as in the case of U.S.–Africa policy, in general, has become more focused on security and military issues. The securitization of diplomatic relations has been channeled mainly through two political military institutions, namely the Millennium Challenge Account and United States Africa Command (Africom).

Little more than three decades after independence Cape Verde's development progress was internationally recognized and validated. Its removal from the list of Least Developed Country (LDC) was a big milestone for the young country. The process was contentious, however, as many inside and outside the country worried about the implications of graduating from the list. The chapter by Djalita Fialho, "Cabo Verde and the United Nations," looks at the country's three decades of experience as an LDC and the role of international development assistance. The chapter is especially compelling in the context of developing countries and the limits and possibilities of foreign aid. In 2007, Cabo Verde became only one of four graduates of the LDC list of forty-seven poor countries. Cabo Verde's experience offers insights into the challenges of development in the current international system, as well as the limits of international aid as an instrument for global economic convergence and catch-up. Its experience also offers lessons about the impact of LDC graduation, and the development challenges and opportunities LDC graduates face as a lower middle-income country navigating the world economy without the special and differentiated support they received because of their LDC status. From the standpoint of its composition and paucity of graduates, the LDC category is less about the individual countries and much more about development in the current world economy. Fialho is an expert of Cabo Verde's experience as a member of the LDC, the United Nations grouping and classification of the world's poorest countries to prioritize international development assistance and special treatment. She has also written extensively on Cabo Verde's "graduation" from the LDC group. Poor, destitute, and facing famine, a major priority at independence in 1975 was the mobilization of foreign aid. Foreign aid along with migrant remittances were critical to the country's very survival. One of the most significant steps taken was to include Cabo Verde in the LDC group, ensuring special and differentiated development support that financed the socio-economic performance that eventually transformed it into a middle-income country by the mid-2000s. The chapter offers a richly detailed, extensively researched account of the LDC experience, bilateral relations with the United Nations system, and the politics and impact of LDC graduation.

Finally, political scientist Terza Alice Silva Lima-Neves's "Gendering the Cabo Verdean Diaspora: Kriolas and Development" examines the role of leading women in the diaspora, whose work has shaped the country's economic development since the time of independence. Broadly, the Cabo Verdean case is a window into the patterns, limits, and possibilities of global migration, diaspora, and African development. Specifically, this chapter draws attention to an overlooked but critical dimension to the role of diaspora communities in development. This chapter makes the case for gendered perspectives and analyses in the study of Cabo Verde's diaspora and development. Although there is a wide range of research on the role of the diaspora in the development of this small archipelago of ten islands located on the West African coast, as a unique and fascinating case, most discourses have focused on the diasporic population in its entirety. Limited attention has been given to the impact gender plays on migration, diaspora community building, and development at home.

THE UNLIKELY COUNTRY: FROM POVERTY TO MIDDLE-INCOME STATUS

In 2016, Cabo Verde held another national election, and citizens again will go to the polls in 2021 to elect a new government and head of state. The country has held regular, competitive elections uninterrupted since 1991. What stands out from these elections is how routine and uneventful they have been, even with all the partisan hyperbole and vociferous party militants. Elections and transfers of power have been routine and peaceful despite the severity of the 2008 global crisis and the many socio-economic challenges facing the country. While there are plenty of worrying aspects and trends in Cabo Verde's democratic governance, the routineness of its politics and state institutions stands out. It is also a testament to how far the country has come since 1975.

The current period of slow growth, anxiety, and social malaise stands in sharp contrast to a development performance that made Cabo Verde one of Africa's most successful post-colonial cases. The country's robust performance prompted the United Nations in late 2007 to remove Cabo Verde from the list of LDC. Cabo Verde's development performance, as discussed in this volume, was neither one-dimensional nor simply a temporary growth spurt. The evidence shows sustained social, economic, and political progress across the four decades after independence. Poverty, slums, income inequality, gender discrimination, political favoritism, bureaucratic inefficiency, pollution, disaffected youth—all these and more are visible in Cabo Verde today. Nonetheless, on balance, the country managed to achieve a measure of progress that eluded many post-colonial developing countries. This development performance, imperfect and incomplete, is all the more noteworthy because Cabo Verde is a micro state in the world system: one with all the structural handicaps to development but lacking the scale and natural resources to feed its own people or sustain improved living standards (figure I.1).

Based on all widely used international comparative indicators on social, economic, and political performance of countries, Cabo Verde is a comparative success story among African and developing countries. In the last two decades, it has emerged as one of the fastest growing economies in Africa, and ranks among the most stable democracies in the world. Cabo Verde consistently ranks in the top, along with Mauritius and Botswana, across indicators such as growth rates, human development, transparency, democratic rights, poverty rates, good governance, and political stability.

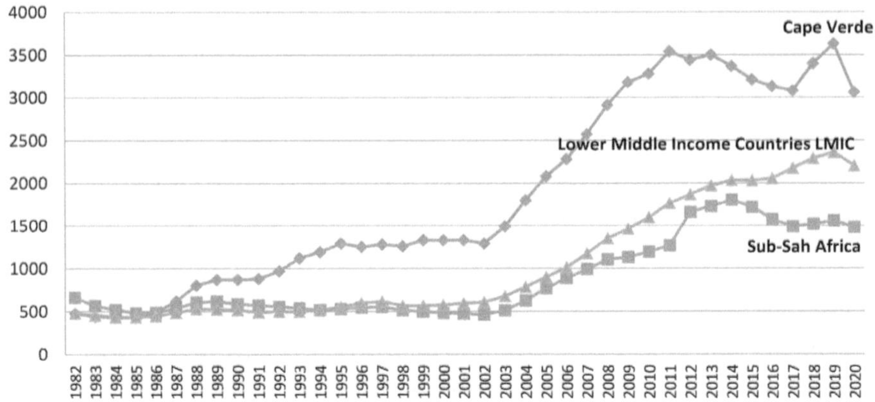

Figure I.1 Comparative GNI per Capita Income Trends, Current USD, Atlas Method. *Source*: Created with data from World Bank, World Development Indicators, DataBank, 2021.

Several other studies have examined in detail the scope and sources of the country's growth performance (AfDB 2012). A quick summary of its development performance in the past four decades reveals a number of salient features. First, Cabo Verde's successful performance was multidimensional and holistic. Cabo Verde is an economic, social, and political success story. Indeed, as Amartya Sen reminds us, true "development" has to mean much more than narrow measures of aggregate growth (Sen 1999). Development must encompass expanding human capabilities and freedoms. Not only did its growth performance earn its middle-income status in a shorter period of time than any other non-oil exporting country in Africa but it achieved political success, as a stable multiparty democracy, endowed with credible institutions and comparatively good governance. Second, the country has enjoyed a durable social peace and stability, free of strife, disruptions, fissures, and anti-systemic forces that plagued so many post-independence countries in different regions of the world.

Third, Cabo Verde's development performance is a case of doing a lot with little; a case of managing vulnerability and structural weakness. As emphasized by several chapters in this volume, Cabo Verde's has multiple structural impediments to growth and development. It is an externally vulnerable and dependent country. Foreign aid and emigrant remittances, as discussed in this volume, were vital resources for growth and development. Cabo Verde was not the only small, poor, and vulnerable post-colonial to be dependent on external generosity. Yet it employed these resources effectively to foster development and managed its smallness and vulnerability relatively well. A critical, but overlooked, aspect of this managing vulnerability is the country's handling of its foreign relations—its ability to navigate around the perils and traps of a world system characterized by power inequalities, Cold War competition, regional wars, and shifting alignments. It fostered good relations broadly, avoided becoming a Cold War battleground, and thus received development aid from a variety of sources. Finally, another feature of Cabo Verde's post-colonial trajectory is that its development performance has been policy-based; that is, the result of reasonably good leadership and development policy stewardship rather than on resource (human, capital, material) inputs.

Cabo Verde's broad-based positive performance since 1975 places it consistently among the top performers in Africa and the LDCs, as shown in figure I.1. During the 1991–2010 period, Cabo Verde averaged a 6 percent GDP growth rate annually, which was far higher than the Sub-Saharan Africa regional average of 3.5 percent, and even surpassed the 4.5 percent average of Mauritius, the model of successful economic performance and transformation in the region, based on World Bank data. Growth rates peaked as high as 11.9 percent and 10.1 percent in 2005 and 2006, respectively.[2] As expected from a small, externally dependent island economy, however, growth performance has been volatile and often displays erratic annual swings. Expectedly, the 2008 global economic crisis, especially the protracted recession in the Eurozone economies, was a severe blow to the island country's growth performance. The ensuing economic contraction has been visible. Revised GDP figures showed a sharp decline in real GDP growth from 6.7 percent in 2008 to 1.8 percent in 2014, for an average annual growth rate of 2.1 percent during 2008–2014, based on data from Cabo Verde's central bank. Interestingly, growth was evident even during the period of one-party rule, which is often viewed as a period of gloom and misery. Although little noticed, the country's strong growth performance dates back to the centrally planned economy of the 1980s, with average GDP growth for 1982–1990 of 5.2 percent, based on World Bank data. Indeed, Cabo Verde averaged a robust 7.2 percent annual GDP growth rate during 1981–2014 (figure I.2).

Robust economic growth resulted in improved living standards. Cabo Verde has a relatively high Gross National Income (GNI) per capita income of $3,450 in current USD for the Africa region in 2018 (figure I.1). Even though per capita too contracted and has remained stagnant since 2008, this figure is much higher than the average ($2,244) for the Lower-Middle-Income peer countries and much higher than the average ($1,506) for Sub-Saharan Africa.[3] Cabo Verde is one of the three small island economies in Sub-Saharan Africa that have outperformed most of their much bigger and resource-rich countries on the mainland. It is among the top ten in the region and the third highest behind the Seychelles and Mauritius when we discount

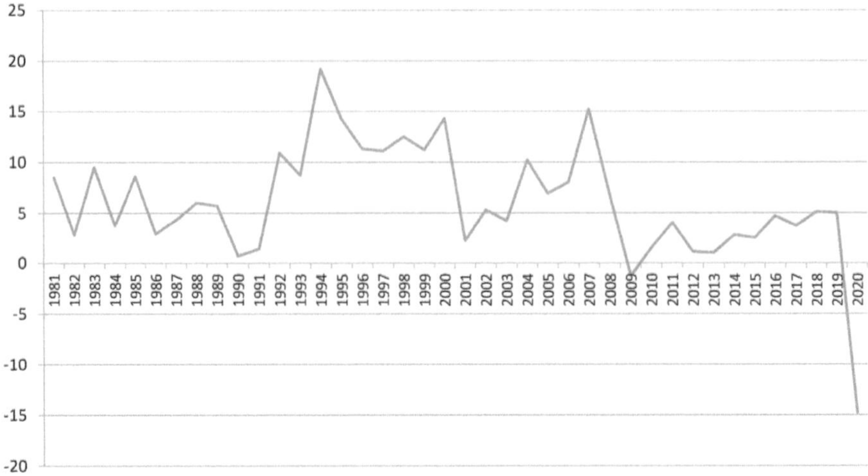

Figure I.2 Cape Verde Annual Growth Rates. *Source*: Created with data from World Bank, World Development Indicators, DataBank, 2021.

the mineral-rich countries of Equatorial Guinea, Gabon, Botswana, South Africa, Angola, and Namibia. While GDP per capita growth in the West Africa region had been stagnant for the majority of the continent during much of the past three decades, Cabo Verde's per capita GDP grew consistently during the post-independence years. Per capita income grew by nearly 300 percent from 1991 to 2014.

The living standards of the population improved consistently since 1975, displaying a real commitment to investing in human capital. Today it ranks among countries in the medium level of human development. Cabo Verde is among the top ten in the human development index (HDI) in all of Africa in 2011, including North Africa, the sixth highest in the Sub-Saharan region (UNDP 2018). Under the revised calculations of the HDI, Cabo Verde's HDI of 0.654 is much higher than the regional average of 0.537 for Sub-Saharan Africa and roughly equal to the average for SIDS and all developing countries. In all, Cabo Verde was deemed to have satisfied most of the Millennium Development Goals. The country has one of the lowest poverty rates in the region. Poverty remains an issue, especially in rural areas, but poverty rates declined 10 points between 2001 and 2007, when the last national survey showed the rate at 27 percent. Currently, the poverty rate is estimated to be about 25 percent in 2011, based on government data. This is a much slower rate of decline, but still positive news given the global economic crisis since 2008.

The country has made good progress in human capital, especially in the area of education. Cabo Verde typically devoted sizable resources, roughly 10 percent of GDP, to health care and education. Universal primary education has been achieved, with over 90 percent enrollment. The overall national literacy rate, for people 15 years old and higher, is 86.5 percent, and 97 percent among the young people (15 to 24 years old), based on data from the National Institute of Statistics (INE). As in many Africa countries, Cabo Verde has a relatively young population, with nearly 50 percent under 25 years old. Cabo Verde has one of the highest school enrollment figures in the world, including female enrollment. The gender disparity has been diminishing and rapidly so in favor of women who saw a jump of 15 percent between 2000 and 2010. The country's investment in higher education in the last decade, with the opening of the country's first universities, has benefited primarily women who dominate enrollment. Female enrollment in all levels of post-secondary education in Cabo Verde accounts for almost 57 percent of total enrollment; the gender gap in favor of women is even greater at the undergraduate (four-year bachelor's degree) level, where female students comprise 60 percent of enrollment. This is very positive for gender advancement as high paying jobs in the new economy demand a more educated and higher skilled workforce.

Cabo Verde has made progress on gender equality and social inclusion, though serious problems persist. Patriarchal cultural norms and gender discrimination, especially in the workplace and management levels, persist all over the world, including in the established democracies. Cabo Verde is no exception. However, women enjoy full rights and opportunities for social mobility and participation in national life. There are no legal, policy, or institutional barriers. Gender-biased cultural norms have eroded. Much work lies ahead, especially in terms of combating rising socio-economic disparity, sexism, and patriarchy, opening up more opportunities for women, especially in the business management and the political system. At the highest levels of government authority and decision-making, women have been heavily represented since 2001, with nearly half of cabinet-level posts occupied by women. Female representation in parliament lags, and the main political parties have been slow to recruit, train, and mentor female candidates. The 2019 Law on Gender Parity will make a significant difference in female participation in governance and law making.

As noted, Cabo Verde's comparatively strong performance since independence has been broad-based. It is a stable, multiparty democratic with relatively good governance. Cabo Verde was the first country in Africa to make the transition to democratic rule during the democratization wave sweeping across Africa and the rest of the world in the early 1990s.[4] As discussed in this volume, democracy in Cabo Verde today faces many challenges. Nevertheless, the country receives high marks for its democratic governance. Cabo Verde was ranked twenty-third among the world's democracies in the 2017 *Democracy Index* calculated by the *Economist* magazine; the rank is among the democracies considered "flawed" in some form and includes the United States, Japan, Portugal, Italy, and Mauritius (Economist 2018). Cabo Verde also performs well in the Freedom House indicators of 2018, ranking in the ninetieth percentile among the most-free countries in the world. As in many other comparative social and political measures, it occupies the top three positions in Africa alongside Mauritius and Botswana. As the Évora chapter explains, holding democratic elections is easy. Consolidating, sustaining, and deepening democracy is hard. Cabo Verde celebrates its sixth national democratic elections in 2016 at a time of retrenchment and erosion of democracy worldwide. Cabo Verde's three decades of routine democratic elections, political stability *with* sharply competitive partisan politics, and peaceful, matter-of-fact transfers of power stand in sharp contrast in a continent that failed to sustain the democratic momentum of the early 1990s, where elections and transfers of power have been traumatic. The rule of law remains durable. The judiciary is independent, even if highly inefficient and slow. The legal and law enforcement authorities do not hesitate to prosecute economic or political elites.

The country is also among Africa's top performers in good governance. Good governance is not the same as democracy. It is a measure of institutional quality, effectiveness, and accountability; a measure of the degree to which governance and decision-making are based on the rule of law and institutionalized procedures. Good governance is what sets apart Africa's good performers from its bad performers, not whether or not they hold democratic elections.

Cabo Verde has consistently ranked high among African countries in comparative good governance indicators, such as the widely used Ibrahim *Index on Good Governance* and the World Bank's *Worldwide Governance Indicators*. It ranks far above the regional average, and trails only Botswana and Mauritius. On indicators such as control of corruption and voice and accountability, based on the World Bank's 2012 *Worldwide Governance Indicators*, Cabo Verde performs above the regional average, and it is ahead of countries such as Mauritius, Seychelles, Comoros, and São Tomé and Príncipe, as well as Ghana, Senegal, and Nigeria. It has consistently ranked in the top three best governed countries in Africa, according to the Mo Ibrahim Foundation's annual Ibrahim Index of African Governance. In 2015, it ranked second with a score of 74.5, behind Mauritius (79.9) and far above the Africa average (50.1). Good governance is often narrowly defined as clean, or transparent, governance. Cabo Verde has consistently ranked as one of the least corrupt countries in Africa, according to Transparency International's *Corruption Perceptions Index*, ranking fortieth as least corrupt country in the world and trailing only Botswana in the Africa region.

The importance of good governance is not limited to the absence of corruption. Rather, its importance lies in the direct and indirect connection to human development and human freedoms. As argued here and in other works, good governance is the single most important factor propelling Cabo Verde's post-colonial relative success. If Cabo Verde's comparative development success has been based on reasonably good policies and leadership, not on abundance of natural resources or national self-sufficiency, then reasonably sound stewardship and management of the state and public finances were necessary. Foreign aid and emigrant remittances were vital resources without which the newly independent micro state would not have survived. Yet these, once they arrived, had to be put to effective use to spur economic growth and human development. The relationship between good governance and human development is not coincidental.

Discussions with key post-independence leaders indicate that, from the beginning, the leadership was concerned with creating credible institutions, deepening rule of law, minimizing personalism and personality cults, and institutionalizing politics. The early post-independence years, specifically the period of one-party rule, saw episodes of human rights abuses, cases of mild repression, intimidation against dissent, and other exuberance by militants. For the most part, these were neither systematic nor characteristic of state-society relations. Political prisoners were unknown. Mass human rights abuses unknown. Unlike in many other countries, guerrilla leaders successfully made the transition from armed combatants in "the bush" to civilian political leaders; militarism was subdued; and civilian supremacy characterized civil-military relations. In fact, while political pluralism did not exist during the time of one-party rule, dissent and open debate were common and tolerated inside the ruling party. Indeed, this pluralism inside the ruling party gave rise to the democratization that followed in 1991. If many post-colonial countries fell prey to civil wars, state repression, patrimonial rule, and power struggles, Cabo Verde escaped these ills.

Politically, building credible institutions have been the common thread spanning the decades since independence. Cabo Verde has not feared or shied away from deep reforms and restructuring of its economy or governing institutions. The country has proven to be adaptable and flexible in adjusting to changed conditions and to adopt radically different courses of action as the situation demands. In fact, what is noticeable about Cabo Verde as a post-colonial case in Africa is its willingness to adopt and sustain major reforms. Today, it is a country in the midst of continual reforms for over three decades. Since the structural reforms of the early 1990s, the country has not stopped. Its society and political system, from the very beginning of its post-independence journey, was open to reform. Unlike so many other countries whose politics or leadership is hostile and resistant to reforms, Cabo Verde embraces reforms. Pragmatism, not ideological purity or personal agenda, has guided decisions. The country did not hesitate to initiate a serious market-oriented reform process in the late 1980s, even under the one-party system, as the economy began to stall. Today, the most important cluster of reforms involves public administration.

Decades of state modernization reforms are introducing improvements in public administration, strengthening macroeconomic management, and transforming the relationship between the government and citizens. These reforms have a long way to go. Yet their impact is noticeable. State modernization reforms, especially in the area of public financial management, have substantially strengthened the country's macroeconomic management capacity. A new generation of reforms has been focusing on revenue collection efficiency and a national planning system, including debt management and public investment management systems. Beginning in the 1990s, state modernization reforms resulted in one of Africa's most successful cases of indigenous technological innovation—Cabo Verde's homegrown electronic government platform. There are two important products of this reform effort. One is the integrated public financial management system introduced in 2002 for central and municipal governments, the integrated system for budget and financial management (SIGOF). The other electronic government product is the one-stop-shop platform that allows the public sector to deliver quickly and efficiently the most common public services requested by citizens. The *Casa do Cidadão* (House of the Citizen) and its virtual counterpart, www.Portondinosilha.cv, have greatly reduced the time, cost, and administrative burdens that citizens and businesses face. Cabo Verde is among the global leaders in this area of electronic government. Today in Cabo Verde, citizens can quickly obtain common public services, such as birth certificates, in a matter of a few minutes and at a very low cost. Equally impressive has been the Empresa No Dia (Business in a Day) program, where entrepreneurs can register and license their business ventures within twenty-four hours, as well as obtain many other services. Additional streamlined services continue to be integrated into the electronic government platform, including one-stop-shop services for customs administration and foreign investments. The country is preparing to launch full electronic voting and is able to report today national election results within three hours.

The benefits of the state modernization reforms to society, the economy, and good governance are many. The improved efficiency in public administration, the reduced costs and time involved in common tasks and procedures, all result in quantifiable savings for government, citizens, and businesses. Electronic government strengthens good governance by improving the efficiency of managing public finances but also enhancing transparency and making corruption more difficult. Frustratingly long lines, confused and antiquated bureaucratic practices, and paper-bound procedures still persist. State modernization, like electronic government, is a work in progress. An overlooked but critical aspect of this electronic government infrastructure is that it has entailed a vast back-office integration.

However, we should note the worrying recent trends in the country's good governance indicators, which have eroded slightly since 2012. Moreover, it is proper for us to question some of the methodologies used to score and classify countries. For example, a corruption index based on perceptions may not necessarily reflect actual practices and experiences. Disconcerting headlines on major corruption scandals in public administration over the last decade—from a major drug trafficking and money laundering sting operation involving some public officials and business leaders, to a major profiteering collusion involving the sale of public lands in the capital city—erode public confidence. Cabo Verde may not be a country where it is routine and normal for citizens to have to pay bribes to police officers or public officials. Cases of bribery exist, and certain areas of public administration, such as customs and municipal planning, are widely regarded as problem areas. Cabo Verde is not a case of institutionalized corruption. Its achievements in electronic government have greatly diminished opportunities for corruption. However, favoritism, clientelism, and arbitrariness are rampant in public administration.

In addition, as discussed in this volume by Évora and Barros, a number of serious problems persist, including low civic participation and confidence, corruption in public administration at the national and municipal levels, and questionable practices by the political parties during election campaigns. Observational evidence suggests these corrosive electoral practices and micro corruption, mainly involving vote buying, are widespread. Demands for institutional reforms involving decentralization and "regionalization" have been frequent, indicating the need for some constitutional changes in a number of areas. One such area may be to rethink electoral design, representation and how elections are conducted, as intimated in the Évora chapter. Since the transition in 1991, elections have produced super majorities where one political party or the other has dominated all branches of government. There are advantages to one-party dominance, such as policy continuity, governance efficiency, and stability. Yet these come at the cost of accountability. The parties are able to colonize the state machinery and all branches of government, facilitating their hold on even the ostensibly independent institutions and agencies of regulation, adjudication, and oversight. The electoral design, particularly the closed-list proportional representation, results in a situation where elected representatives in the legislature are more beholden to the party leadership that selected them than to their local constituencies in the various islands. More troubling is the growing incestuous relationship between public administration, the political parties, and the private sector, and the increasing "revolving door" between economic and political elites. A careful reading of the Barros chapter in this volume reveals the corrosive effects on democratic governance—but also socio-economic equality—of this interpenetration of the public sector, party politics, and the market.

FACTORS BEHIND THE SUCCESS

Scholars in different fields of study have spent a long time examining the factors behind a country's political and economic successes and failures. There is a vast and interesting literature, with an equally vast set of arguments and findings. Development theories are many, both mainstream and unorthodox. Today's neoliberal economics points to free markets and the "right policies" of a minimal state, deregulation, privatization, and trade openness. Dependency theory and World Systems theory, in sharp contrast to the neoliberal view, point our attention to the power inequities and unequal exchanges in the global capitalist system that generates development in one part of the world while simultaneously generating underdevelopment and poverty in another part. Post-colonial critical theory, especially the theory of neocolonialism, reminds us of the degradation, exploitation, and brutality of imperialism and centuries of colonial rule for countries in Africa and elsewhere. Vicious, predatory and dehumanizing, centuries of slavery and colonial oppression did not just retard African development, but their corrosive cultural, psychological, political and economic effects persisted long after formal independence. The new institutionalism literature in development theory draws our attention to the importance of political and economic institutions in creating an enabling or adverse climate for development to take place. Some of this literature is even sensitive to the lasting effects of colonial legacies (Acemoglu and Robinson 2012). While all these theories offer us many insights, development theory has yet to provide us conclusive, consensus answers on the causes of economic development.

It is not the purpose of this volume or introductory chapter to examine this debate. Likewise, it is not our purpose here to offer a comprehensive assessment of all the factors behind Cabo Verde's post-independence performance. One aim of this volume is to spark more research interest and appeal to a new generation of scholars to examine more deeply and critically the Cabo Verde case. The individual chapters in this volume offer compelling insights into specific factors and areas. They examine Cabo Verde's post-independence trajectory and uncover the complex interplay of internal and external factors that shaped its development since 1975. In this section, we point to a few important clues and directions in assessing the trajectory of Cabo Verde's political economy.

At independence in 1975, no one inside or outside the barren archipelago would have selected these famine-prone islands as a candidate for development success. Many in Cabo Verde and its diaspora opposed independence, some out of fear that the islands were too small and too poverty stricken to survive on their own. These fears were well-founded.

Notwithstanding the many failures along the way, and the many daunting challenges ahead, Cabo Verde succeeded against all odds. Uncovering the critical success factors driving a country's development may be even more challenging for cases like Cabo Verde, not just a post-colonial country but a micro island state utterly deprived of the internal material means to satisfy even the basic needs of its population. Cabo Verde's irreducible structural debilities and unalterable external dependency means that its development was, is, and will always be a function of external forces. These forces, in turn, are translated through domestic conditions, institutions, policies, and conscious decisions taken by real people at all levels of society.

A stylized narrative of Cabo Verde's development trajectory might highlight four critical ingredients behind the country's relative success since 1975. The four broad factors are as follows: getting the politics right, prudent macroeconomic management, emigrant remittances, and international development support. These critical success factors have been discussed elsewhere (AfDB 2012). The important policy question today is whether these same ingredients of past success are relevant or available for the country's next phase of development. As discussed in this volume, Cabo Verde today is a tourism-based economy. Tourism receipts have become the largest source of external financing for the economy, accounting for nearly a quarter of GDP. As such, tourism and the tourism-focused FDIs that began pouring into the country by the mid-2000s had a transformational impact on the structure of the economy and its growth performance. Yet Cabo Verde's relative development success predates the rise of tourism and has foundations further back in factors that are still relevant today.

As alluded to above, getting politics right has been the single most important, overarching factor, whether broadly in terms of social peace and political stability or in terms of relatively good governance. Cabo Verde's relative development success has been policy-based. As such, this draws our attention to institutions, governance, politics, leadership, and state-society relations. It has been tempting for many people to cite ethno-linguistic and religious diversity or homogeneity, as the critical determining factor in the post-colonial trajectories of African countries. Cabo Verde's cultural, linguistic, ethnic, and religious homogeneity are seen as determining in explaining its social peace and development success. Yet success and failure in Africa and elsewhere in the world do not seem to correlate with ethno-cultural diversity. From Botswana, Mauritius, to Belgium and Switzerland, to India and Singapore, many of the world's political and socio-economic success cases have their share of ethno-cultural, linguistic, and religious diversity. Natural resources—their paucity or abundance—likewise do not seem to be determining.

If political instability, crisis of the state, governance failures, and institutional fragility and breakdown are common features associated with development failures or poor performance, these political and institutional factors set apart cases like Cabo Verde in the post-colonial context. These political-institutional factors have been critical to the post-1975 story, including pragmatic leadership, credible institutions, relatively clean and good governance, political stability, and a broad political consensus around development strategy. Political stability has been enduring, including the absence of anti-systemic forces, rebellions or armed opposition, repression, or institutional manipulation by incumbent elites, even during the period of one-party rule. The one-party regime not only ceded power peacefully in 1991, it initiated the opening internally and willingly went through the process ending in its demise. Corsino Tolentino, an author in this volume, was the lead negotiator for the regime during the transition talks.

Whether in terms of development planning or foreign relations, the pragmatism of Cabo Verde's post-independence leadership has often been cited. Cabo Verde's political leaders had their share of bad decisions, incompetence, and mismanagement. Barros examines the political class. The overall pattern since 1975 has been a reasonably good political leadership that was constrained by the rule of law and that managed reasonably well the state, public policy, and public finances. Pragmatism and good governance made possible the sound macroeconomic management that has characterized development performance since the early years. Even during the period of one-party, credible institutions, sound macroeconomic management, and good governance were pursued. The importance of this prudent, pragmatic, and non-ideological leadership can be seen during the Cold War years. Not only did the leadership astutely avoid becoming a Cold War battleground, the combination of a careful non-alignment policy and effective use of foreign aid earned the country early on an important capital—international credibility—that it could leverage for decades.

There is an additional political factor often obscured but significant, namely policy stability and continuity despite alterations in power and changing electoral fortunes of the dominant political parties. A close reading of the Rocha chapter will show this implicit policy continuity. If disruptive swings between alternative development models, deep policy reversals, and unpredictable policy changes characterize many developing countries, Cabo Verde has been a case of relative continuity in both development models as well as macroeconomic policy, in addition to social policy and foreign policy since 1991. Despite their heated rhetoric and partisan exaggerations, the two dominant political parties have steered the same policy and development course since 1991. This policy stability and continuity is another critical capital for an externally dependent micro state—bolstering the confidence of foreign investors, aid donors, and its global diaspora.

As an externally dependent micro state, Cabo Verde could not have survived without two vital sources of external financing: foreign aid and emigrant remittances. Both aid and remittances have declined in their shares of GDP, today accounting for roughly 10 percent, respectively. Historically, remittances and foreign aid have been the dominant inflows, accounting for as high as 80 percent of the country's GDP (World Bank 1985) (figure I.3).

Despite its graduation to lower middle-income country status, Cabo Verde remains dependent on foreign aid or Official Development Assistance (ODA). Cabo Verde remains one of the top largest recipients of foreign aid in the world in terms of aid per capita and the top recipient in developing Africa. Unsurprising, the top aid per capita recipients in the world are primarily the small island states in Africa, Asia-Pacific, and the Caribbean.

Total development assistance from all donors totaled $245 million in 2013, dropping to $113 million in 2016.[5] Foreign aid today accounts for roughly 7 percent of the country's GNI based on World Bank calculations (World Bank 2021). As noted, foreign aid has been experiencing long-term structural decline relative to GDP as the economy has grown. As noted, historically foreign aid accounted for a big portion of the country's GDP. Foreign aid peaked at roughly 48 percent of GNI in 1984 and 55 percent in 1986 and averaged 40 percent during 1980–1989 (World Bank 2021). During the 1990s, average

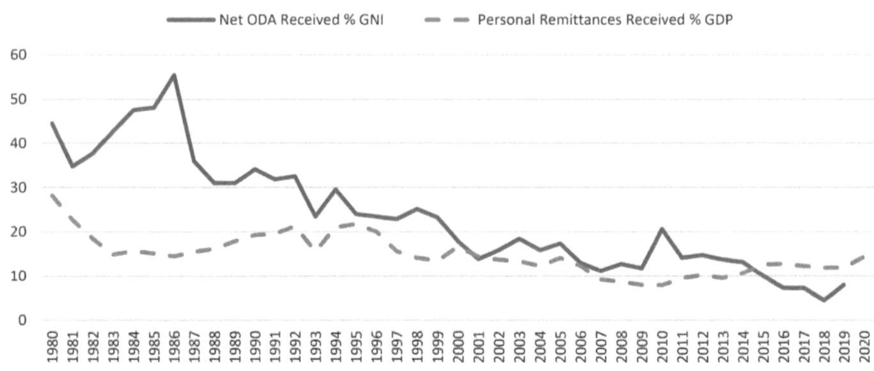

Figure I.3 Evolution of Foreign Aid and Remittances in Cabo Verde's Economy. *Source*: Created with data from World Bank, World Development Indicators, DataBank, 2021.

annual foreign aid inflows accounted for 27 percent of the economy. Most of the country's aid comes from bilateral sources, Portugal the top aid donor. Cabo Verde's top foreign aid donors have been the European countries. The top multilateral donors have been the EU and the international development association of the World Bank Group that funds the poorest countries.

Remittances have been a historical lifeline, even before independence. Emigration defines the history and society of Cabo Verde (Challinor 2008; Batalha and Carling 2008; Halters 1993; Carling and Akesson 2009). For centuries, its people fled poverty and famine in search of a better life in the Americas and Europe. Its large diaspora population, estimated to be twice the size of the resident population, has been a vital economic resource for the island country. The chapters by Lima-Neves, Borges, and Fialho highlight the historical and economic significance of Cabo Verde's diaspora and the goods and money they send back home. Of course, while this book's focus is on political economy, the country's global diaspora are sending back much more than monetary remittances and goods, such as medicine, clothing, vehicles, and the like. They are also sending non-monetary remittances, in the form of cultural influences, ideas, values and attitudes, voting and political participation, knowledge, social networks, and a broad range of transnational social relations. Historically, monetary remittances from emigrants have been a major source of external financing for the economy (Resende-Santos 2016). The economy's ability to avoid a more painful contraction after the 2008 global crisis was, in part, thanks to remittances. We saw a similar strong remittances response to the social and economic crisis triggered by the 2020 global pandemic.

As with foreign aid, remittances from Cape Verde's emigrants have been in long-term decline in terms of their shares in the economy. For most the decade and half after independence, remittances ranged between 40 percent and 25 percent of GDP. The World Bank estimates that remittances accounted for over 40 percent of GDP during 1978–1982 (World Bank 1985a, 29). Today, officially recorded remittances account for roughly 10 percent of Cabo Verde's GDP, according to both BCV and World Bank data. Strong remittance inflows in the last several years have pushed its share of GDP to 14 percent, but it is uncertain whether this surge is transitory or indicates a deeper trend. Cabo Verde's diaspora remitted roughly $244 million in 2020, averaging $200 million during 2010–2020, according to the World Bank. Data from Cabo Verde's central bank show strong and sustained annual increases in the absolute value of remittances since 2010. Cabo Verde's diaspora responded positively to the impact of the 2008 and 2020 global crises on the homeland, consistent with findings in much of the literature on remittances as countercyclical. As the Borges chapter shows, most of Cabo Verde's remittances, over 70 percent, comes from its Europe-based diaspora.

These official data on remittances do not tell us the whole story behind the significance of emigrant remittances to the economy and people's well-being in Cabo Verde since even the colonial days. First, as is often pointed out in the literature, the official data do not capture the monetary remittances from unofficial or informal channels. We have no way of knowing the extent and value of these unofficial remittances. An unknown but presumably significant portion, as high as 50 percent of official figures, is transferred through informal channels (Rocha, Tolentino, and Tolentino 2008). Second, the official data may not fully capture the economic or financial value of the non-monetary forms of remittances, such as goods remittances. There is no better symbol of migration and sentimental attachment to the homeland by the Cabo Verdean diaspora than the *bidón*—converted oil drums and large barrels that emigrants fill with goods to send back to family and friends in the homeland. A passerby at any of the many shipping warehouses in the United States or Europe would be stunned by the volume of goods shipped monthly to Cabo Verde. These monetary and non-monetary remittances have been crucial to households in terms of income, food security, access to health and medication, education, and even entrepreneurial activities. Third, not captured in official data is the significance—from the standpoint of recipient households—that remittances are typically less volatile than other financial flows, such as FDI. In addition to displaying counter cyclical patterns, remittances become timely and predictable for households. Finally, Cabo Verde's emigrants are also investing in the homeland, becoming an important constituency of foreign investors even if they are not viewed or treated as such (Resende-Santos 2016). The diaspora has been depositing their savings in the country's commercial banks, investing over $500 million in special, higher-yield savings accounts and providing a critically needed source of liquidity for banks to provide credit to the economy.

A LONG WAY TO GO STILL

Cabo Verde today is a changed society. For the 1975 generation, very little in the country today is recognizable. The face of Cabo Verdean society would be unrecognizable for those who had celebrated independence in 1975, as Évora notes in her chapter. If in 1975 there were only two high schools, one international airport, few roads and hospitals in the largely agrarian society, no one in 1975 could have imagined a country today of multiple international airports, high rise office buildings, widespread mobile technology use, glittery modern hotels, paved roadways, urban sprawl and urban slums, and a popular tourist destination on the global mass tourism circuit. Diaspora visitors do not find anything recognizable when returning to their hometowns. Even for residents, the pace and scope of social, cultural, economic, and technological transformation has been dizzying. Modernization is always in-motion and disruptive. Urbanization, literacy, technology, tourism, immigration and emigration, among other forces, have profoundly changed society. The changes are not limited to tourists and foreign-born Cabo Verdeans deported from the United States and Europe back to a country with which they have little if any cultural, linguistic or familial ties. If in 1975 Cabo Verde was a country of emigration, today it is also a country of immigration as a result of the free movement of people in the West African region. Cabo Verde today is home to large, semi-permanent communities of Chinese and West African immigrants, along with Lebanese, Italians, and other Europeans who have become residents. Whereas the Lebanese and the Chinese, the embodiments of transnational entrepreneurs in today's world economy, constitute the primary commercial class dominating the retail industry in the country, West African immigrants have become the primary source of cheap labor and ambulatory vendors in the informal economy. For the most part, these immigrant communities are alien, isolated, segregated, and, especially for the West Africans, live on the margins.

One dramatic but expected transformation in the country's political economy is the changing urban-rural mix. Rural exodus has been a major social, economic, and policy challenge, including the pressures created on urban planning and infrastructure. If in 1975 Cabo Verde was an agrarian society based primarily on subsistence agriculture and fishing, by 2010 the country was 62 percent urban and with much greater inter-island mobility. A combination of urbanization, emigration, and generational transitions has resulted in the depopulation of rural areas, and consequently a substantial change in the rural political economy. The rural economy, based on traditional farming and livestock, is both fading and failing. The consequence is greater pressure on urbanization, unemployment, food security, public services, and so on.

In other words, Cabo Verde is a changing society, but not all these changes have been for the better. Its relative success is undeniable, but it is also incomplete. Its socio-economic and political progress since 1975 is well documented, but so too is the fact that the country today faces a number of social, economic, and political problems. Success is both partial and has often come at a price.

As noted earlier, the list of challenges is daunting, both in terms of the long-term development challenges as well as the practical public policy and macroeconomic challenges. A separate study is needed to examine these more carefully and thoroughly. Cabo Verde remains a highly vulnerable and externally dependent micro state. Its options are few in fostering growth and human development. Its characteristics translate into serious structural impediments to growth and development. At the same time, Cabo Verde faces the same hurdles and limited options that all middle-income developing states in the present world economy. As is visible in the data, the country has to transition from being an economy heavily dependent on aid and remittances to a country that has to walk on its own two feet now. In the present world system, the record is weak of countries successfully navigating upward in the development ladder. Moving from lower-middle income to upper-middle and high income has been exceedingly elusive, and mounting evidence suggests a "middle-income trap" for countries like Cabo Verde.

The individual chapters in this volume, while assessing the country's performance since 1975, underscore some of the critical challenges confronting its people in this next phase of development. In this section, we cite a few of these short-run challenges, albeit intimately linked to the longer term development challenges. For example, the biggest public policy issue facing the country today is job creation. Structural unemployment may be inescapable for such a micro-economy, particularly one without the productive base and where its most dynamic sector, tourism, has weak backward and forward linkages to the rest of the economy. Job creation is intimately tied to the country's longer term prospects for diversifying the economy and fostering new growth sectors, including creating more links to the tourism value chain. In the meantime, the unemployment situation is serious, especially among young people between 15 and 24 years old whose unemployment rate has been around 30 percent. Graduates from the country's universities struggle to pay tuition but only to face unemployment or underemployment. Aside from the long-term hurdle of economic diversification to solve the jobs problem, the country's high risk public debt and limited resource mobilization base leaves very little fiscal room to address unemployment and other social services.

Poverty and income inequality persist, especially the latter which appears to be worsening. As noted above, Cabo Verde has made substantial progress in the areas of education and poverty alleviation. However, poverty remains a big challenge, especially rural poverty. A national poverty rate of 17.8 percent, based on an extreme poverty calculation of $1.90/day by the World Bank, translates in absolute terms into nearly 100,000 people in poverty. If we calculate the poverty line at $3.10/day, this translates into nearly 200,000 Cabo Verdeans living in poverty. The government's 2015 survey indicated a national extreme poverty rate of 10.6 percent, down from 29.7 percent in 2001 (INE 2015). However, closer inspection of the data reveals an absolute poverty incidence rate of 35.2 percent and nearly 50 percent for rural areas, where the extreme poverty rate is over 20 percent. As in many other countries, poverty disproportionately impacts the rural areas, as well as women. Regional disparities are big, with some islands and municipalities experiencing high levels of poverty. The survey shows islands like Fogo, Brava, Santo Antão, and interior Santiago suffering from high levels of poverty. Naturally, the combination of poverty and unemployment fuel the high rates of both rural exodus and the depopulation of the peripheral islands like Brava, Fogo, and Maio.

Likewise, there is a growing underclass in the major urban areas of the country. Data is non-existent, but observational evidence suggests that slums are a major feature of the capital city, Praia, as well as São Vicente and the tourist islands of Sal and Boa Vista. The rise of slums is only one manifestation of a much bigger problem in Cabo Verdean society and political economy—growing wealth and income inequality. Observational evidence suggests a much bigger problem in terms of the concentration of wealth, social mobility, and access, as well as the social divide evident in the spread of gated communities, closed condominiums, and walled-off mansions.

Tourism will necessarily be at the center of the country's next phase of development. In 2019, over 800,000 tourists, overwhelmingly from Europe, came to Cape Verde spending a week for sun and beach. For good or ill, Cabo Verde today is a highly tourism-based economy. Small island states of Africa, mid-Atlantic, the Pacific, Mediterranean and Caribbean have a natural comparative advantage in tourism. Their insularity, tropical climate, and natural endowments make them attractive destinations. Since it is largely a private sector and foreign investor initiative, in addition to requiring low skilled and low technology, tourism becomes an easy and potentially lucrative industry for small island states to adopt. As discussed in this volume, the tourism industry has brought many economic and other advantages. Aside from being the biggest sector, it has generated much-needed employment opportunities. The government estimates over 37,000 total jobs created, or roughly 20 percent of all jobs in the country by 2014 (INE 2015). Tourism satisfaction rates, previously low, have been high in recent years. Given the generous fiscal incentives for the industry, the extent of direct tax revenues is unclear but certainly, the mass consumption by the industry generates substantial revenues from sales taxes (figure I.4).

Nevertheless, there is no guarantee that tourism can be the "motor" for the economy. It is Cabo Verde's biggest industry, but it is also an industry whose characteristics limit its positive contribution to economic growth and development, as well as increase the country's external vulnerability. The more than 800,000 tourists visiting the islands in 2019 generated more than $500 million for the industry, yet it is unlikely that much of that money stayed inside Cabo Verde or had the multiplier effects on the economy we would expect from that amount in such a tiny economy. Empirical research is needed on the economic (and non-economic) impacts of the industry, but experience from other similar cases suggests the economic impact is limited. First, it is the familiar enclave mass tourism model, built around all-inclusive resorts and packaged tours, concentrated on the two islands of Sal and Boa

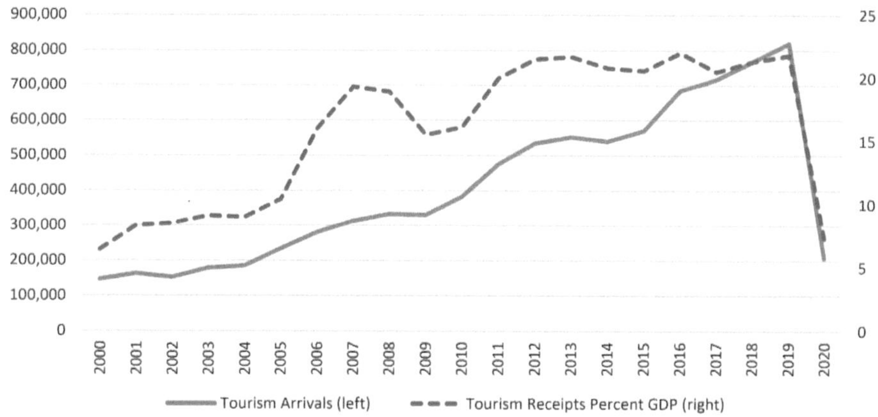

Figure I.4 Cape Verde Tourism Arrivals and Tourism Receipts Share of GDP. *Source*: Created with data from Banco de Cabo Verde (BCV), Balança de Pagamentos. Tourism arrivals data from Instituto Nacional de Estatísticas (INE), Estatísticas do Turismo, 2021.

Vista. Together with its foreign ownership, this model of tourism is known to have a more limited economic contribution to the national economy. Second, the industry is highly concentrated in multiple ways: the dominance of two tour operators, demand market reliance on Europe for nearly all its tourists, it lacks product diversification in a highly competitive global circuit with high substitutability. Third, largely as a result of the model as well as Cabo Verde's limited productive base, the industry suffers from a high leakage rate. That is, like the country, it imports everything it consumes. As such, the tourism industry in Cabo Verde is weakly integrated into the national economy. These and other characteristics increase Cabo Verde's risks to external shocks, as revealed in the 2020 global pandemic when its tourism industry contracted by over 80 percent (figure I.4). As the Bernardo chapter reminds us, along with experiences from other countries, there are numerous negative, non-economic impacts. As such, the major development challenge ahead is the need to diversify the economy, both in terms of fostering new growth sectors and fostering greater linkages between the tourism and non-tourism economy.

Among the biggest impediments to economic growth and diversification is the country's infrastructure, a persistent development bottleneck. From roads, to ports, to telecommunications, energy, to inter-island transportation. Infrastructure is limited in scope and in quality as well as high cost. Inter-island air and maritime transportation continues to be a serious problem and source of frustration for residents, diaspora visitors, tourists, and investors. All small island countries face a steep cost for their insularity. Cabo Verde's geographic fragmentation into nine inhabited islands is not only a serious development impediment, but it makes the country a high-cost place for infrastructure and doing business. In essence, geographic discontinuity means that an already micro-sized economy is actually nine tiny island markets with low- and high-cost connectivity among them. Poor and high-cost inter-island transportation is perhaps the biggest growth bottleneck, standing in the way of economic diversification, linkages to the tourism sector, local entrepreneurship, and even international investments outside the tourism enclave.

In this next phase of national development, Cabo Verde must rely much more on its internal resources while managing to do the most with little. In other words, it has to use its limited resources much more efficiently. As such, governance and public sector administration become determining factors—from macroeconomic management, fiscal policy and public finances, investment evaluation and implementation, to public services delivery. Good governance and credible institutions are real and substantial gains since 1975. A notable feature of Cabo Verde's development performance, especially after 1991, has been its consistency and willingness to engage in deep, sustained reforms, in the economy as well as public administration. Yet the country faces a number of deficits in terms of public administration and regulatory environment, as such a drag on public finances and business activity. Notwithstanding nearly three decades of ongoing state modernization reforms, public administration continues to be slow, inefficient, and archaic. Modern, computerized processes exist alongside antiquated paper-bound procedures; indeed, often, completion and certification of the modern, virtual procedures depend on the slow-moving, inefficient paper-bound procedures. Excessive centralization in the capital, where online procedures and services must get approval and clearing, further limits the potential gains of electronic government in the other islands and municipalities. For an open economy highly dependent on trade and goods remittances, customs procedures remain frustrating, inefficient, and byzantine. Cabo Verde is a private sector–led economy today. Growth, job creation, innovation, and entrepreneurship have to come from the private sector, not the public sector. Yet the country's private sector is small and weak as well as constrained by an economic, institutional, and regulatory environment that makes doing business costly. Another worrying trend in public administration is the frequency of cases of fraud and corruption, including at the municipal levels. Favoritism and influence-peddling are sources of open public complaint.

Another major challenge for Cabo Verde is its growing external debt. As of 2021, Cabo Verde's public debt level is becoming unsustainable. In 2008, the country's external debt burden stood around 51 percent of its GDP. In 2018, public debt reached 124 percent of GDP, roughly 75 percent of it external debt, according to the International Monetary Fund (IMF). It is approaching 150 percent of GDP. Since this implies a much heavier burden to service that debt, fewer resources are available to finance domestic needs and foster growth. Micro states like Cabo Verde, with limited productive capacity and sources of revenues, cannot sustain high debt levels. Aside from the macroeconomic pressures a large external debt imposes, a practical effect of having to serve its external debt is the reduced fiscal capacity to foster growth, create jobs, combat poverty, and fund social services. Further internal borrowing by the government will crowd private sector investment credit and further dampen economic activity.

Another issue that merits closer scholarly and policy attention is external security. A small island state with inadequate national security resources, Cabo Verde has a vast maritime territory it is unable to control, monitor, and defend. It is also part of a wider sub-region that continues to suffer from bouts of political instability, illicit trafficking, and international terrorism. The risk for Cabo Verde is not a direct harm to national or human security, or even contagion. The real risk posed by these external security challenges is the impact on investor confidence, on its tourism industry and tourist confidence, its diaspora engagement, as well as the potential for inducing corruption and domestic crime.

First, Cabo Verde has become a major transit point in illicit international trafficking, especially the trans-Atlantic drug trade. This is a sensitive and unpleasant subject, and much national and international efforts have been focusing on combating this problem inside Cabo Verde and its maritime territory. The frequency of cases such as the February 2019 seizure of ten tons of cocaine in the port of Praia has sparked growing concern by the United States, the EU, and the United Nations. Domestic drug consumption exists, especially in the major urban areas, but it has not yet emerged as a major social or public health concern. Cabo Verde is a transit point, not a market. The danger presented by international drug trafficking, and the associated money laundering and organized criminal networks, is the possible contamination and corruption of the political system and law enforcement agencies. A handful of such cases have emerged. Cabo Verde has a vast, undefended maritime frontier and lacks domestic resources to monitor and protect its vast territory. As such, the country has developed extensive security, law enforcement, and intelligence cooperation with the United States and the EU. Security cooperation has been increasing steadily since the late 2000s, as the Amado chapter discusses, with nearly half of U.S. aid today consisting of military and law enforcement assistance.

Despite its privileged geographic segregation from the continent, Cabo Verde will always be vulnerable to sources of instability and uncertainty emanating from a wider sub-region. That is, Cabo Verde will always be guilty by (geographic) association. Current trends are not favorable. Notwithstanding its many recent progress and the positive development of many individual states in the North Africa, Sahel, and West Africa greater region, it is a sub-region characterized by multiple sources of instability. The sub-region has become a proverbial arch of instability, not only emanating from the multiple state crises but also transnational violent actors. The sub-region continues to be plagued by governance instability, democratic breakdown, and episodes of political violence. By the third quarter of 2021 alone, there were already four military coup d'état and attempted coups. West Africa and the Sahel have emerged as a hotspot for international terrorism. The problem of international terrorism in this part of Africa is not limited to transnational actors like Boko Haram, Al-Qaeda in the Islamic Maghreb, the Islamic State, and al-Shabaab; there are numerous local armed groups, militias, and gangs, as well as the many drug and human trafficking networks. Finally, this is a region also where disease pandemics are chronic. The 2013–2015 Ebola outbreak in neighboring countries was an alarming reminder of how vulnerable Cabo Verde is to such pandemics, but also how vulnerable its key industry is to such developments outside its national borders. Tourism arrivals declined during 2012–2015. Given the nature of these porous borders, weak and failed states, extended ungoverned spaces, unchecked illicit cross-border trafficking, and the multiplication of organized transnational non-state actors, the growing capacity of these actors to network across the region as well as globally, Cabo Verde's sub-region will be a source of risk as it transitions into its next phase of development.

THE NEXT PHASE OF DEVELOPMENT AND THE CHALLENGES AHEAD

The next phase in Cabo Verde's development path will be much harder than the post-1975 phase. The challenges are many. It can no longer rely on many of the same ingredients, such as foreign aid and large amounts of monetary remittances, that fueled past success. The chapters in this volume directly or indirectly discuss these challenges ahead. History and comparative experience are not on Cabo Verde's side. The biggest risk ahead for Cabo Verde is not political breakdown, development reversal and depression, or social upheaval—although history and even recent global events remind us that no country is immune to such fates and sudden ruptures. The biggest risk is stagnation, what development economists refer to as the middle-income trap. Achieving lower middle-income status, as Cabo Verde has done today, may be historically and comparatively easier. However, between 1960 and 2008, of the 101 middle-income countries that existed in 1960 only 13 countries were able to break into the high-income category. Comparative experience and basic economics tell us that the transition to upper income is much more difficult.

Cabo Verde goes into its next phase of development with all its many development handicaps, diminished external sources of support, and few viable options for growth and development as a small island state. Today the country is in the middle of a transition from LDC to middle-income status. As the Fialho chapter makes clear, graduating from the LDC category comes with certain risks and disadvantages. Cabo Verde will lose access to the development aid, non-debt financing, and other preferential treatment afforded to LDCs. Put differently, graduation means that development becomes more difficult, not easier. Its two major sources of financing growth and jobs creation in the economy—donor assistance and monetary remittances—are in long-term decline. Globally, development aid is shrinking. The outlook for monetary remittances is likewise pessimistic because of generational turnover in the diaspora, and the fact that opportunities for emigration are closing as host countries adopt anti-immigration policies. Cabo Verde, like other micro states in the Pacific and Caribbean, are heavily dependent on migration and foreign aid, but these flows are increasingly unreliable as sources of growth and poverty alleviation. Like these other island micro states, and all small states, Cabo Verde's development options are few, given their structural impediments to growth.

The previous four decades since independence were, by and large, familiar territory in terms of economic development policy. The next four decades represent unchartered territory. The challenge over the next four decades is transforming the economy from an aid- and remittances-dependent economy to one based on new sources of growth, economic diversification, and efficiency. In other words, the transformation challenge is to build a twenty-first-century economy, one based on the required institutional capacity, human capital, knowledge resources, and innovation drivers essential in today's global economy. In the first phase of its development, Cabo Verde had the luxury of gauging its progress and competitive position by comparing itself with neighboring countries in the West Africa region. Going forward, it now has to compete with South Korea, Chile, Singapore, China, and other larger, resource-rich middle-income countries.

One urgent but uncertain issue along this road ahead is the role of its global diaspora. Cabo Verde's emigrants have played a critical role historically in the country's development. Considered twice the size of the resident population, there is compelling policy and theoretical reasons to engage this issue. Paradoxically, we know very little about this diaspora, including factual information of its true size, demographic and social composition, behavior, and ties to the homeland. It is a heterogeneous diaspora in terms of composition and geographic spread. It is also among the oldest diaspora for countries in the global South. More research is badly needed, especially on the political economy dimension. Data on remittances and emigrant savings deposits, in addition to observation evidence on emigrant investments and return migration, seem to point to a strong engagement of the diaspora with the homeland. Yet we have no data on who or which parts of the diaspora are engaged, nor what the nature, determinants, and motivations of this behavior are. The broader literature on migration warns of "remittance decay" and the loosening of bonds to the homeland as time and generations pass. Increasingly restrictive immigration policies in the global North make even more urgent this issue for Cabo Verde. The major policy challenge is how to continue to harness this diaspora as a development resource.

NOTES

1. In 2013, Cabo Verde officially changed its name to "Cabo" Verde instead of the translated name of "Cape" Verde. Both names are used by the authors given the historical record and common usage.
2. In 2007, the National Institute of Statistics (INE) changed its national accounts methodology. As a result, GDP figures have altered and longitudinal calculations must be treated with care.
3. The World Bank, *World Development Indicators* (WDI), 2019, in current USD. The World Bank estimates $7,330 for GNI per capita calculated on the basis of purchasing power parity (PPP) in current international dollars in 2018. The central bank (BCV) estimated GDP per capita to be $2,466 in 2013. Data by the IMF shows a GDP per capita of $3,578 in 2018. It is important to note discrepancies in per capita income data (as well as other national accounts and financial data) among various international agencies as well as Cabo Verdean authorities.
4. Cabo Verde was the first country in Africa to hold democratic elections during the so-called Third Wave of democratization, making the transition from one-party, non-democratic rule to multiparty electoral democracy based on universal suffrage. Cabo Verde's parliamentary elections on January 13, 1991 were quickly followed a week later by elections in São Tomé e Príncipe, and a month later by the more widely known case of Benin. Benin had already been undergoing political liberalization since 1989. Botswana stands as Africa's oldest and uninterrupted democracy since its independence in 1966. After decades of national liberation struggle, Namibia held internationally supervised elections in 1989 for a National Assembly, but gained formal independence only early 1990. Throughout Africa's post-independence years, as early as the 1960s, there were occasional elections in various countries but which did not result in stable, consolidated democracies.
5. Organization of Economic Cooperation and Development (OECD), Development Assistance Committee (DAC), *Development Finance Statistics* (Paris: OECD, 2018). Note that there is discrepancy between Cabo Verde's central bank and international

agencies on data for net aid received. For example, the central bank reports net "external assistance" received to be CVE4.19 billion escudos, roughly $52 million calculated with a dollar exchange rate of CVE80 escudos. The figure is less than 3 percent of GDP. See BCV, *Boletim de Estatísticas Janeiro 2016.*

REFERENCES

Acemoglu, Daron and James Robinson. *Why National Fail: The Origins of Power, Prosperity and Poverty.* New York: Crown, 2012.

African Development Bank (AfDB). *Cape Verde – A Success Story.* Tunis: AfDB, 2012.

Batalha, Luís and Jorgen Carling, eds. *Transnational Archipelago: Perspectives of Cape Verdean Migration and Diaspora.* Amsterdam: Amsterdam University Press, 2008.

Carling, Jorgen and Lisa Akesson. "Mobility at the Heart of the Nation: Patterns and Meanings of Cape Verdean Migration." *International Migration* 47 (3), 2009: 123–155.

Chabal, Patrick. *Amílcar Cabral: Revolutionary Leadership and People's War.* London: Cambridge University Press, 1983.

Challinor, Elizabeth Pilar. "Home and Overseas: The Janus Faces of Cape Verdean Identity." *Diaspora: A Journal of Transnational Studies* 17 (1), 2008: 84–104.

Davidson, Basil. *No Fist Is Big Enough to Hide the Sky: The Liberation of Guinea-Bissau and Cape Verde, 1963–74.* London: Zed Books, 1981.

Davidson, Basil, *The Fortunate Isles: A Study in African Transformation.* Trenton: African World Press, 1989.

Halter, M. *Between Race and Ethnicity: Cape Verdean American Immigrants 1860–1965.* Urbana: University of Illinois Press, 1993.

Instituto Nacional de Estatísticas (INE). *Estatísticas do Turismo.* Praia: INE, 2021.

Resende-Santos, João. "Cape Verde: Rethinking Diaspora in Development Policy." *International Migration* 54 (2) 2016: 82–97.

Rocha, Carlos M., A. C. Tolentino and N. C. Tolentino. *A Importância e o Impacto das Remessas dos Emigrantes em Portugal no Desenvolvimento de Cabo Verde.* Lisbon: ACIDI, 2008.

Sen, Amartya. *Development as Freedom.* New York: Anchor Books, 1999.

United Nations Development Program (UNDP). *Human Development Report 2018.* New York: UNDP, 2018.

World Bank. *Cape Verde: Economic Situation and Prospects*, Vol. 1. Washington, DC: World Bank, 1985.

World Bank. *World Development Indicators (WDI).* Washington, DC: World Bank, 2021.

Chapter 1

Revisiting State-Building and the Challenges of Democracy in Cape Verde

Crisanto Barros

Cape Verde's transition from authoritarian to a democratic political regime has been considered to be exemplary by most scholars of the Cape Verdean political system since the basic requirements for its institutionalization resulted from a solid agreement between the two major political forces—The African Party for the Independence of Cape Verde (PAICV) and the Movement for Democracy (MpD). This finding seems to induce many scholars to infer the process of construction of the Cape Verdean democratic state only from the political injunctions of the late 1980s and early 1990s and from the division of the political field made by these two major protagonists.

In this chapter, we intend to explore some interpretative clues regarding the process of the construction of the Cape Verdean democratic state. In so doing, we consider, on the one hand, the long-term historical aspects that were the basis for its construction, namely, the existence of a rational bureaucratic state, the formation of a political-administrative elite, the building of a sense of nationhood, the affirmation of an incipient public sphere, and the emergence of political parties, whose borders cannot be separated only by the advent of independence and, much less, by political openness in 1990. On the other hand, it is our intention to compare some implications that arise from the interpenetration between politics, public administration, and the market, inasmuch as a strategy to finance the political-partisan legitimization process and its effects on the changing nature of political careers.

The Cape Verdean liberal-democratic political system embodied in the 1992 Constitution, and revised over the last few decades, is based, as in other contemporary democracies, on the validity of the main rules of the democratic game, namely, the guarantee of inviolable individual liberties, popular sovereignty expressed through free and regular elections, mediation of political struggle through the civic actions of citizens and party organizations, the autonomy of civil society, the formal independence of the courts and public administration governed by the rule of law.

Most studies on the Cape Verdean political system in the post-independence period focus their analysis around the process of political transition in 1991 from the one-party authoritarian regime to democratic pluralism (Fonseca 1976/1999; Koudawo 2001). Other studies have emphasized the configuration of governance systems and the process of formation and reproduction of political elites, as well as issues related to the formation of national identity (Anjos 2002; Costa 2009; Fernandes 2002; Furtado 1997).

In this chapter, we intend to explore some interpretative clues regarding the process of nation-state-building and the consolidation of Cape Verdean democracy. In so doing, we take into account, on the one hand, the long-term historical aspects that underpinned its construction—namely, the construction of the rational bureaucratic state, the formation of a political-administrative and intellectual elite, the gestation of the public spheres, and the structuring of a feeling of nationhood—all of which whose borders are not at all delimited with the advent of independence. On the other hand, we intend to compare some transformations that have occurred with the consolidation of the national state and the institutionalization of the mono- and multiparty regimes, and their implications both in the configuration dynamics of the political and administrative elites and in the relationship between the party, the state, market, and civil society.

For the purposes of this chapter, we use the concept of democracy in its procedural sense, that is, as a form of political practice that accepts the possibilities of social subjects, within the framework of constitutional norms, to create new rights, to institute them and to reproduce them according to their historical needs (Lefort 1991). In this sense, the modern democratic state is, by its nature, a plural and polyarchical social construction that accepts the challenge of the imperfection of every political-social reality (Bobbio 2004; Dahl 2003).

THE FORMATION OF THE NATION-STATE AND A POLITICAL-ADMINISTRATIVE AND INTELLECTUAL ELITE

The rise of the modern Cape Verdean rational state, as defined by Weber (2001), emerged at least a century and a half before the proclamation of the national independent state in 1975. With the victory of the liberals in Portugal, the Constitutional Charter of 1822 was introduced, consecrating the ideals of the "One Nation, Indivisible" (*Nação Una e Indivisa*), as an antidote to the drifts of disintegration of the empire opened up with the independence of Brazil. In addition, it signals an assimilationist project that apparently integrated all the citizens of the empire of the continent and the overseas colonies (Miranda 1976; Silva 2009).

In this context, a set of legislation is enacted that changes the nature of political-bureaucratic institutions, in order to impose public authority and, at the same time, regulate a social sphere resulting from the failure of slave production structures. The Administrative Code of Mouzinho da Silveira, dated May 1832, was inspired by French legislation, which revoked the Philippine Ordinances and introduced a new regulation of the formation, composition, and competence of administrative bodies (Correia 1994). This code establishes, according to Lopes (1996), new principles of separation of administrative, civil, and judicial powers. The spirit that presided over the administrative reform of 1832, implemented in the empire and also in the provinces, was aimed at rationalizing the organization of the state sphere, delimiting the boundaries between the various powers hitherto intertwined, preventing the different political-administrative subjects from usurping powers belonging to the other social bodies. Hence the effort of this code to delimit the specific spheres of competence of the various administrative bodies ensured the rationalization of the workings of state structures.

The modern Cape Verdean state that results from the liberal reforms of the decade of the 30s of the nineteenth century, as in other Western countries, is based on the principles of liberty, equality among individuals, the separation of political bodies and the rule of law. The reforms proposed to combine two important aspects of the liberal ideology in the colonial context. In the first place, centralization through the central and dispersed services of the state as guarantors of the nation's interest—a condition to control the process of accumulation—and decentralization through local power, giving political initiatives to the citizens (i.e., illustrious men and landed elites), creating the bases for the crystallization of a legitimizing local elite for colonial domination.

According to the aforementioned administrative code, the overseas territories became provinces under the direction of a mayor with authority over the islands and their dependencies (Guinean Coast); divided into two regions (Leeward and Barlavento), commanded by subprefects and councils under the management of the purveyors (Andrade 1996; Correia 1994). With the consolidation of the victory of the liberals after 1834, a new administrative code was granted which sought to overcome the inconveniences found in the application of the previous code and to introduce a system of organization that reconciled local interests with those of the central administration.

Thus, the juridical-political design inserted in the administrative code of 1836 stipulated that the archipelago should be governed by a governor-general with the authority over the whole territory, and the councils fell under the double political-administrative direction. First, the chamber was elected by the assembly of municipal voters. Second, a representative in the administration of the council was an administrator appointed by the central authorities. At the lower level (parishes), governance was under the authority of a regent, appointed by the civil governor, on the proposal of the council administrator.

This code represented an attempt by the Kingdom to modernize and extend its capacity for political-administrative control over the whole territory, whose political sovereignty, as Valentim Alexandre (2004) warns, was more nominal than real, with local governments at the mercy of local elites. In addition to this code, according to Correia (1994), in the period from 1850 to 1870, a complex legal-administrative structure is established which legitimizes and regulates the organization of the overseas colonies in accordance with the political objectives of the Metropolis, culminating, in the case of Cape Verde, with the publication of its Organic Charter in 1869 (see Alexandre and Dias 1998).

In the meantime, this Organic Charter, despite maintaining the main aspects inscribed in the administrative code of 1842, introduced a greater degree of decentralization, in the spirit of liberal regeneration, albeit under the contingencies of the crisis that plagued the Metropolis (Alexandre 2008). In this context, the central government promotes management in the colonies in order to ensure greater efficiency in the management of scarce resources for local economic development. As Morais asserts:

> The Government of the Metropolis began to be concerned with the establishment of a sound and productive administration in the colonies, determining that in each of the governments of the overseas provinces there would be a governor-general to whom all the authorities established therein, and regardless of denomination, the choice for the position should always be of an individual with practical experience gained in some of the careers of public administration. (Morais 1969, 73)

However, the implementation of a new organizational model included in the administrative code resulted in major difficulties. First of all, the low salaries practiced and the successive delays in their payment discredited public administration, especially the municipal government; making it largely dependent on the goodwill of the local oligarchies who, in the face of the state's ineffectiveness in this matter, made patronage and nepotism legitimate governance practices. In addition, officials, mostly illiterate or with low levels of education, never studied the code or, in general, any other written norms issued by the general government, making their application on the basis of their ignorance and/or interpretation according to their own personal interests.

According to Rodrigues, the practices of corruption were phenomena so common that numerous measures, including forcing officials to take an oath of fidelity to the crown and the saints (Rodrigues 1998, 257–261).

The degree of degradation of the functioning of the municipal councils was such that Governor Caetano Alexandre de Almeida e Albuquerque, in his report sent to the overseas minister in 1872, openly confided to him the following:

> For the municipal administration, I have the honor to draw your attention to the fact that it is in a remarkable backward state, and although it is a proposal that departs completely from all liberal principles, I do not hesitate to do so. In the current circumstances of this province, what would be most advantageous for the regular running of the municipal affairs would be to replace the chambers elected by municipal commissions, retaining only the chamber in the capital of the province, where the greatest degree of sophistication allows this guarantee. [. . .] With this organization, we would have a municipal administration run by scrupulous and select men, instead of those that currently compose almost all the councils left from the suffrage of a people unconscious of their rights. The aberration of the constitutional principles, which is evident in this proposal, loses all its importance once your Excellency kindly considers that most of the municipalities of this province would constitute no more than an insignificant parish if there were the continuity of the territory among them. . . . [the Boa Vista municipal chamber was dissolved] because its councilors not only neglected their duties but also prevented any regular functioning of the administration. . . . From the municipality of Santa Catarina it also came to my attention that "that the income of the chamber was collected in private coffers, and that with it the councilmen and the treasurer negotiated, instead of applying them, as they should have, to the advantage of the municipality itself. (In Report of the Overseas Provinces for the year 1872)

Notwithstanding the exaggerations of this narrative, situated and besieged by the interests of those who pretend to defend the reins of central power, it nevertheless points to the difficulties of asserting a rational bureaucratic state in Cape Verde in which the administration was still largely beholden to the interests of local oligarchies to whom the representatives of the central government admonished the excesses practiced, but on whom they depended to guarantee solid domination in the islands.

Late in the decade of the 1880s, a set of laws was once again enacted which sought to perfect the administrative organization in the archipelago, making it more effective and efficient. In the preamble of this new administrative organization of Cape Verde, the legislation, despite extolling the level of Cape Verde's advancement, considers that the claim of similar status as that of Madeira and the Azores—the status of adjacency and autonomy—is not feasible because not even the revenues generated covered the expenses that such an undertaking required, and there were no elements of scientific education in the province to give effect to such a project. However, it recognizes that the islands were able to enjoy a greater degree of decentralization, which is why the government now takes full responsibility "for the acts of its administration and provides it with the means to exercise its leadership, aided by the intervention of the elements of popular election, from which the interests of the population are derived" (see Supplement to No. 4 of the Boletím Oficial da Província de Cabo Verde 1893; see Lopes 1996).

It should be emphasized, however, that the decentralization principle advocated for Cape Verde and for other Portuguese possessions in Africa also represented a strategy of cost containment by the Metropolis, itself entangled in indebtedness to modernize its economic infrastructure (Alexandre 2008).

The rejection by the authorities of the Metropolis of the autonomy pretensions of the Cape Verdean political-administrative elites was not merely a financial and/or civilizational matter, as implied in the justification drawn up in the legislation, but of a political nature. The political fractures that led to the independence of Brazil and the humiliation to which the Kingdom had been subjected with the English ultimatum of 1890 had contributed decisively to a reevaluation of the African continent.

It should be noted, additionally, Portugal needed large financial resources to reorganize its internal productive structure, which was unbalanced in relation to flourishing industrial capitalism and, at the same time, to reconvert its antiquated administration in Africa that were not industrious and profitable due to the blockade imposed by the British armada on the slave trade.

However, the possibility of a major overseas attack was overshadowed not only by the financial inability of the public treasury but also because the Kingdom did not have an entrepreneurial bourgeoisie capable of taking on the risks that a productive investment would entail. It should also be noted that an important part of the metropolitan bourgeoisie was made up of former officials converted to economic activity, owners of the old slave economy, and liberal professionals, accustomed to easy profit, who did not visualize the African continent—seen as a land of exiles—a safe market for easy exploration (cf. Vaquinhas and Cascão 1998).

The claim for adjacency status in the late nineteenth century was only possible because the Cape Verdean political-administrative elite considered themselves sufficiently learned to claim the command of the political-bureaucratic machine of the modern provincial state. Thus, at the end of the same century, when Portugal awakened to the actual occupation of its possessions in Africa, the Cape Verdean state carried a relatively structured bureaucracy in its main population centers, with the local population being under the control of the agents of the administration and the local elites.

EMERGENCE OF A POLITICAL-ADMINISTRATIVE ELITE

The Cape Verdean political-administrative elite that emerges and is affirmed throughout the troubled nineteenth century bears very different characteristics from the old weakened (but not annihilated) political and economic elite of the late eighteenth century led by Marquis de Pombal. In the first place, this elite is largely dependent on the administration of the expanding state whose loyalty and subservience are necessary requisites for securing a certain wage and insertion in the circles of power. Second, these are groups of elites from multiple geographical origins. Many of them were not born at the place of origin of their ancestors, but where their parents, at some point in their professional career, played some part in the bureaucracy or engaged in various businesses. For example, Luiz Loff Vasconcelos, whose relatives are from Brava, is born, however, on Maio Island (Barros 2012). Similarly, Raul Barbosa, a native of Boa Vista, having been a merchant and administrative officer in the municipality of Praia, was the son of Sebastião José Barbosa, a native of Fogo Island (Oliveira 1998).

This new elite that emerged throughout the nineteenth century seems to be the result of networking of officials who move to different islands to perform administrative functions and landowners/businessmen in search of new business opportunities arising in these places. In addition, the political, economic, and religious instability that characterizes the archipelago in the first two quarters of the nineteenth century, provoking the seasonal installation of the governor and bishop on the islands of Brava, Fogo, Boa Vista, and São Nicolau, contributes to a great spatial circulation of the native elite.

Another characteristic that seems relevant is that, since education in the early nineteenth century was still in the hands of families and the Catholic clergy, the acquisition of the cultural capital required for access to state administration depended almost exclusively on the family's economic conditions. These people, who had the landed capital to ensure their monopoly of political and administrative positions, given the existing feudal system, had in their mode of family reproduction an effective strategy for controlling the main public offices. This was the model on which the reproduction of the important local families was based that made family self-reproduction a decisive character in the process of access to positions in public administration. As Charles (1987) reports in his study of the French elite in the nineteenth century, the model of reproduction of notables, embedded in the very unequal possession of economic, political, and social capital, weakened as ownership of knowledge (education) capital ceased to be reproduced in the family circle.

The decline of traditional Cape Verdean families throughout the nineteenth century due to the vicissitudes of the disintegration of the slave economy contributed to the appropriation of education becoming a critical factor of upward social mobility.

In the next part, we will analyze, in a long-term perspective, the schooling process of the Cape Verdean elites and the difficulties of their reproduction during the last two quarters of the twentieth century.

FROM SCHOOLING RESTRICTED TO ELITES TO ITS EXPANSION TO THE POOREST POPULATIONS

The expectations of Cape Verdeans to participate in the management of the colonial state gained greater momentum during the second half of the nineteenth century, with the creation of formal institutions of education. Their creation was within the framework of a set of liberal reforms introduced in Portugal in which education was envisioned as a fundamental pillar in the process of building a modern society, that is, a liberal society, free from the hierarchies of the old regime. Thus, with the regularization of public education in the archipelago from 1845, after a few decades of struggling with enormous weaknesses, there was a resurgence of primary schools (elementary and primary) that were to be installed first on the island of Brava and later in Praia.

From the late 1860s onward, new educational measures were promulgated with the aim of rationalizing the education system and its expansion in the main municipalities where the most favored classes resided and clamored for education services. Thus, in light of the new regulatory provisions of 1869, the education system now included elementary primary education and secondary education, with primary education being compulsory for children aged nine to twelve years. However, given the extremely precarious subsistence social conditions to which a majority of the peasantry was subjected, schooling was practically restricted to the intermediate and upper strata of Cape Verdean society, made up of the landowning whites. It should be noted that it is no coincidence that the island of Brava, where most of the white population of the archipelago was established, has become the epicenter of the educational system during the first two quarters of the nineteenth century.[1]

The dynamics of the educational system gained a new impetus with the institutionalization of secondary education which, after an ephemeral opening in Praia in 1860, regrouped in São Nicolau with the creation of the seminary high school after 1866. This seminary inaugurated the formation of students for civilian occupation in the school year 1873–1874, a strategy of the Catholic clergy to seize a larger share of state funding.[2] From this period until its closure by the Republicans in 1917, the seminary high school became the main academic and cultural center of the country. It contributes decisively to the increase of the priesthood for the archipelago and other colonies, as well as individuals who, after completing the preparatory course (3 years), competed for the exercise of intermediate functions in public administration in areas such as teaching or in economic-entrepreneurial activities (Lopes 1996; Neves 2008).

The opportunities that were inaugurated with the development of the high school are taken advantage of differently by the different social strata in Cape Verde. Thus, it is the families of the upper and middle strata of São Nicolau who benefit, for the most part, from the opening of the high school, despite the fact that students from poor family backgrounds—probably from São Nicolau—likely received scholarships to attend this institution.

At the end of the nineteenth century, the geography of schooling availability in Cape Verde was extremely asymmetric, with the Boa Vista, Santo Antão, São Nicolau, and São Vicente islands offering schooling opportunities relatively higher than the national average, contrasting with the islands of Santiago and Fogo, where the mass of the free peasant population was still completely isolated from the nascent cultural and educational environment.

The privileged distribution of the school network in the northern region of the country favored the construction of a social imagination that visualizes in the schooling process an important instrument of upward social mobility. This tendency consolidated in the course of the twentieth century with the construction of the national high school of Cape Verde in Mindelo in 1917. It should be noted that students from Santo Antão, São Vicente, and São Nicolau represented 67 percent of those enrolled in the last year of secondary education when the demographic weight of these islands did not exceed 39 percent of the national population, which shows a huge disparity in terms of access to schooling (Barros 2012).

From the decade of the 1950s, a long process of alteration of the profile of the educated population in Cape Verde began. This change has to do, partly, with the alteration of the strategies of legitimization of two important actors, namely, the Church and the colonial state. In the late 1940s, the Catholic Church undertook a series of actions in rural areas, favoring the inclusion of many poor peasant families in the schooling process. This dynamic of inclusion of the most disadvantaged strata gains new contours with the re-politicization of the functions of the late colonial state as a consequence of the pressures of the politico-military movement of national liberation, as well as the actions of international organizations. Thus, the poorest strata are also targets of state public assistance policies, both in terms of employment in the public works and in access to schooling.

There is a certain tendency to delimit the construction of the independent national state as a unique and decisive device in the process of widening social opportunities, namely, education for the poorest sectors of Cape Verdean society. This demarcation, as shown by Correia e Silva (2001), is not at all sustainable, empirically. The late colonial state that precedes the independent national state is embryonic as a social welfare institution, implementing social regulation measures, improving conditions of survival of the mostly poor population who were historically vulnerable to the vicissitudes of subsistence agriculture. That is why, since the 1960s, the severity of the droughts did not translate into high levels of mortality. The reports on the implementation of development plans often refer to the increase in appropriations "due to the need to absorb available labor—as a result of the crisis caused by insufficient agricultural crops due to droughts" (Relatórios Planos de Fomento 1959–1964, 1965, 1971). Thus, these plans were, in some way, cushions that decompressed the social imbalances resulting from the prolonged droughts, having an increasing impact with the massive emigration of the rural population, especially to Europe from the decade of the 1950s.

The national state, forged since 1975, is itself a hostage to this welfarism dynamic, as it was said in popular jargon, which, however, gains new contours in terms of the expansion-differentiation of the administrative apparatus, caused both by new functions derived from the acquisition of sovereignty (driven by the idea of creating a new man) and by the deepening-expansion of social regulation (Afonso 2002; Correia e Silva 2001).

If it is credible that the actions of the late colonial state in the area of education contributed to the expansion of primary and secondary education in the 1960s and 1970s, it is not at all consistent from the empirical point of view that this expansion is due exclusively to its policies alone. In fact, the actions were undertaken by the leaders of some Catholic religious congregations in the 1950s and 1960s, namely the Spiritans in Santiago, the Salesians in São Vincente and the Capuchins in Fogo, Brava and S. Nicolau, and the Adventist and Nazarene organizations, predate at least a decade or more the vigorous educational actions of the late colonial state.

In Santiago, especially in the interior, where the majority of the population resided, it was the creation of the parochial schools, especially under the leadership of the Swiss priests Louis Allaz (in Santa Catarina) and Cyr Crettaz and the Portuguese João Eduardo Moniz (both in São Miguel), which allowed the peasants to have access to basic education and, above all, to see schooling as a possible way of social advancement.

In the islands of Fogo and Brava, the Capuchins from Italy, especially Father Camilo Torassa, whose vigorous action resulted in the emblematic

Maternal School of St. Francis of Assisi in San Filipe, created conditions for the peripheral population of this municipality to attend basic schooling (cf. Testimonies of priests, former teachers, and students of the parochial schools in Santiago, Maternal School in Fogo, and the Salesian School in São Vicente).

In São Vicente, where urban concentration is more intensive and the population less dispersed, the expansion of primary education to the poor is due to the combined efforts of state social action and the Church; first through the orphanage, and later the Salesians, with the pioneering action of Father Filipe and the creation of the student home and the primary and vocational schools. Thus, the exponential increase in enrollments in primary education in the 1960s and 1970s is, to a large extent, a subsidiary of the actions taken by religious institutions, rightfully speaking, driving the first cycle of expanding schooling opportunities for the majority of the population.

The hypothesis formulated by Correia e Silva (2001), according to which the late colonial state is the instrument for the expansion of primary schooling opportunities in Cape Verde, can only be endorsed if we also consider the impact of the educational and social actions undertaken by the clergy and religious congregations. They believed that their actions on the ground could help change the lives of the many people abandoned to misery and uncertainty. Therefore, for the fringes of the popular classes, the first routes to elite status started with the extension of primary education and, contrary to what is believed, not just with the expansion of secondary and higher education. For segments of the middle and upper strata of urban centers, primary schooling had already been acquired by the second half of the nineteenth century, and these are at least a century apart.

In relation to secondary education, the inflection point for the gradual change of its social profile in the high schools of Mindelo and Praia, results from the combination of several factors from the end of the 1950s, with a differentiated impact according to the social strata of the students and the strategies of individual families.

For the upper and middle strata living outside the high school area, up to the 1950s, the expansion of access to secondary education took place through private schools and/or tutors led by former graduates of the São Nicolau seminary high school and the Gil Eanes High School. The impact of the private tutors' phenomenon, because it has not yet been the subject of in-depth studies, is generally underestimated. In fact, it historically constitutes a concomitant and parallel mechanism to the regular public education system that contributes significantly to the increase of the schooling population. Thus, when one affirms that until the end of the 1980s there were only two high schools, what is meant effectively by this? In fact, if we take as a criterion the instructional practices in place in formal and informal private institutions, we cannot restrict the universe of students based only on the official secondary schools.

The pioneering experiences of private tutoring probably date back to the second half of the nineteenth century. However, this practice became widespread and, in the course of the twentieth century, there has been an increase in the flow of graduates from the high school seminary high school and the national high school who tutor full time or as a supplement to their teaching activities.

In Fogo, one of the best-known tutors was Madame Irene Barbosa, the mother of Gilda Barbosa, a former student at Gil Eanes, and a former high school teacher at Adriano Moreira. A mathematics graduate, she claimed that her maternal grandmother, Aninhas, was one of the teachers in São Filipe around 1900. Irene Barbosa, after completing primary school, and with no secondary school nearby, dedicated herself to self-learning. According to her, the thirst for knowledge was so great that "all available means, within and outside the family, were sought to continue studying" (Barbosa 2007).

In São Vicente, several interviewees report that former students, and later high school teachers, offered explanatory classes to prepare the young people for the entrance exams and the final exams at the end of the year. Among them are Olavo Moniz, Guilherme Chantre, and Augusto Pirico.

In Santiago, particularly in the urban centers of Praia and Santa Catarina, private lessons and/or explanations were regular activities of teachers such as Leão Gomes de Pina, Hugo dos Reis Borges, and Augusto Barreto, both former seminarians. This process gained new momentum in the capital since the 1940s, with the return of high school graduates from Gil Eanes as Alfredo Veiga, Filinto Correia e Silva, Júlio Teixeira, Orlando Mascarenhas, among others (Barros 2012).[3] Tutoring in its various forms deserves a separate study in order to understand its full nature and extent.

For students coming from the lower strata of the interior of the archipelago, access to secondary school is extended with the construction of the São José seminary in Praia, the construction of the hostel and dormitory of the Salesians in Mindelo, becoming authentic bridges to secondary education establishments.

In addition to these institutional spaces, it is worth noting the important role played by the extensive family and kinship networks that facilitated the reception of students from the poor fringes in the urban centers which, however, acquired greater consistency due to the effects of incomes from emigration. The remittance of foreign exchange and goods increases the stability of the income of the poorest families, often more exposed to the vulnerabilities of agricultural production and seasonal employment in the public works created by the state, improving the conditions of affording schooling beyond just the costs of school fees.

In short, if the expansion of secondary schooling opportunities is consolidated and expanded to the middle and upper strata only with the creation of the second high school in Praia, it should be pointed out that for the majority of rural students this enlargement was made possible as a result of Church actions, family networks, the effects of the remittance of emigration, as well as the late colonial social state.

With the structuring of the national state, access to higher (college) education—initially all abroad—has gained a completely different dynamic through the institutionalization of student financial aid programs. This arrangement represented a decisive mechanism facilitating the higher education of disadvantaged families, once practically excluded from higher education. It also extends training opportunities to the middle, urban, and rural strata who were also dependent on state support. Among the top public administration officials, three out of four have benefited from this financing mechanism.[4] The effects of this program of higher education abroad built by the national state are not limited to obtaining the human capital of the graduates. Importantly, it fosters a relevant social capital for those who historically have been disconnected from the most privileged social networks in urban spaces, with important implications in the definition of the professional trajectory of these students.

In sum, the heterogeneity of the social profile of the Cape Verdean political-administrative elite over the last half-century is a tributary of the long process of widening schooling opportunities to important fringes of the masses. In fact, one of the hallmarks of the process of affirming and consolidating the Cape Verdean democratic state is that it takes place in and with the important presence of political and administrative leaders from the popular classes (Barros 2013; Furtado 1997).

Another important element to understand the long process of democracy-building in Cape Verde is the historical existence of several public spaces within which narratives compete for national and state projects.

BUILDING A PUBLIC SPHERE AND SENSE OF NATIONHOOD

Since the end of the second half of the nineteenth century, the embryo of the political, journalistic, and literary public spheres, as Habermas (1984) put it, began to emerge in the country, in the context of contradictory liberal reforms in the Portuguese empire.[5] From the outset, between 1840 and 1926, liberal political reforms allowed local elites to compete in elections for the local chambers or for representation in national bodies (Correia e Silva 2004).

The expansion of primary education and especially the institutionalization of primary school, on a regular basis from 1845 onward, the creation of the seminary of São Nicolau and the national high school in Mindelo in 1917, endows this elite with symbolic resources to mediate the relationship between the nascent Cape Verdean civil society and the leaders of the colonial state. A significant number of publications in the unofficial part of the official bulletins, in newspapers, periodicals, and leaflets, give rise to a certain cultural effervescence in the main urban centers.

The construction of a sense of a Cape Verdean nation, as an imaginary community of belonging (Anderson 2005), finds its roots in the affirmation and consolidation of the Portuguese/Cape Verdean languages and in the diffusion of Catholicism. In the first phase, at the end of the nineteenth century, the native elite believed that the extension of the political rights of citizenship resulting from the liberal emancipatory movement would be enough to remove the various forms of discrimination to which it was subjected in the higher sphere of the administration in Cape Verde and in the Metropolis.[6] This is because this native elite considered itself a Luso-Cape Verdean citizen, forging a kind of creole regionalism (Fernandes 2002).

In a second phase, between the end of the nineteenth century and the dawn of the twentieth century, as the hope of full integration in the empire disappears, a long process of discursive refocusing begins, in which the native elite begins to speak not only *to* the Metropolis but also *for* the Cape Verdeans of whom they consider themselves legitimate representatives.

Thus, the construction of a national otherness (talking to and for the neighbor) is one of the crucial factors for the consolidation of a sense of nationhood that, however, gains new contours due to the symbolic struggles during the twentieth century around the Cape Verdeaness enunciated by the *claridosos* and reexamined by the Pan-Africanist generation (Anjos 2002; Fernandes 2002).

However, when national identity is mentioned, it is necessary to put it into perspective. In a society marked by the dispersion of its population and the lack of domestic market integration, there are, in fact, few conditions to affect otherness, without which identity lacks the identification of the recipients in all its extension. The meetings and disagreements that manifest themselves within the mobile and mingling populations in urban spaces (Praia, Sal, and Boavista) have been exposing new identity tensions, some of them of a racial nature (Furtado 2012; Lobo 2012; Rocha 2011).

In short, in our view, the central question is whether this long process of consolidation of the nation-state, of formation and renewal of a political-administrative elite, of the constitution of literary and journalistic public spheres, contributed decisively to the deepening of the ethos of bureaucracy and plurality, discursive bases on which the various forms of post-independence political domination were erected.

A positive response to this inquiry leads us to believe that some sense of "stateness," nationality, a plurality of symbolic references, and diversity of political-administrative elites would not have been a post-independence invention, let alone an invention after the political opening in 1991.

In this sense, it should be pointed out that what emerges from independence in 1975 and political openness in 1991 is not so much the bureaucratic dimension of the national state, even though it is less complex; nor the formation of a political-administrative elite; much less a feeling of nationhood, even though it is "re-signified," especially by the *claridosos* and the generation of Amílcar Cabral. What emerges after independence, above all, are the entry of new political actors, especially the mass parties (PAIGC/CV and MpD), and a new juridical-institutional reengineering, which allowed these actors to legitimize their project of a new society.

Hence, the challenges of consolidating democracy in Cape Verde depend on the way in which mediation between the party, the state, and civil society has been operating rather than with the construction of the elementary requirements of its functioning—the rule of law, the public sphere, plurality of political elites available for political competition.

FROM MONOPARTISANISM TO MULTIPARTYISM: BREAKS AND CONTINUITIES

In Cape Verde, the political cleavage in the post-independence period is undoubtedly marked by the emergence in the political arena of PAIGC, a party movement, as the main protagonist that mobilizes the majority of national politicians in the process of affirming an independent state.

The victory achieved by this party in an election without competitors, at the end of the first five-year period of the 1970s, put it in a position of transcendence compared to other embryonic political forces. It is this teleological bias that allows the party to arrogate itself as the leading political force of the state and of society, making its immanence a specific transcendence (Fetjo 1993; Kriegel 1984). Indeed, what really gains new contours with national independence are, on the one hand, the preponderance of the party over the state and, on the other hand, the tentacular domination over society through mass organizations that, in a micro-society context, tends to take on contours of total domination.[7]

However, the total and hegemonic party is not necessarily a party that holds all power in a society nor in full control of the source from which it results. As Foucault (1994) warns, however much politics may be totalizing, political power is never total, capable of nullifying all the free will of those who submit to it. Thus, the need for continued expansion of the state bureaucracy—as a sine qua non for ensuring the legitimacy of the PAIGC/CV society project—created within it conditions for the emergence of a plethora of new cadres. The source of power and legitimacy of these cadres came from other spaces of consecration and not only from the party. It is in this arena that schooling (knowledge) capital sanctified by the diploma (Bourdieu 2001; Saint-Martin 1993), acquired generally in institutions of medium and higher education, is able to impose itself in the face of the monopoly of political capital that the party's elders embodied (Furtado 1997).

Thus, if the party possessed mechanisms to accommodate and regulate, albeit tense, the process of renewal of the party and government leadership, and the mechanisms to protect civil society through mass organizations, the same cannot be said in relation to the process of legitimation at the level of the state bureaucracy. In it, the element of legitimacy, because it was based on schooling capital, was not at all controllable by the party. It is not by chance that significant fringes of officials came to support the emerging opposition party Movement for Democracy (MpD) which, in certain respects, indicates that this party was largely the result of an implosion within the state bureaucracy (see the signatories to the Political Declaration of March 14, 1990).

In this case, what is important to underline here in order to understand the logic of structuring the mass mobilizing authoritarian regime in Cape Verde during the one-party rule years is the consolidation of a narrative based on a political culture of the sole and indivisible protagonist as a strategy to safeguard, allegedly, the historical legitimacy, national unity, and the greater interests of the Cape Verdean nation.

The transition to democratic rule has been widely regarded as consensual since the basic requirements for its institutionalization have come from a strong agreement between the two major political forces—the PAICV and the MpD (Evora 2004; Koudawo 2001; Lima 1992, 1997). As Lins and Stepan (1999, 21) argued:

> A democratic transition is complete when a sufficient degree of agreement has been reached on political procedures for an elected government; when a government comes to power as a direct result of the free popular vote; when that government has, in fact, the authority to generate new policies; and when the Executive, Legislative and Judiciary branches, created by the new democracy, do not *de jure* share power with other organisms.

The uninterrupted holding of elections at different levels (municipal, legislative, and presidential) resulting in the alternation of the rulers indicates the stabilization of the new regime.[8] Lins and Stepan (1999), in their analysis of the transition and consolidation of democracy in southern Europe and Latin America, recognize that the process of democratic consolidation requires some additional conditions, among which the following stand out: (a) behavioral (whereby democracy becomes a benchmark for all political actors and none of them seeks to subvert that belief); (b) attitudinal change (where democracy becomes a single game for society); and finally (c) constitutional (insofar as all actors in the political community resolve their conflicts according to normative precepts).

Modern democracies, as Duverger (1985, 1986) and Sartori (1982) have argued, revolve around political parties. They would be non-functional without the organizations that group citizens, transform their interests and efforts into projects and programs, and select and support candidates in electoral contests. However, if the existence of the political party is vital to the functioning of democracy in a mass society, it is no less true that the form and nature of how it mediates its relationship with the political system and with society, in particular, can, under certain conditions, become antidemocratic, to the point of degenerating into a "party-docracy." With this inversion, the specific interests of party militants are transformed into general interests and popular sovereignty, in a kind of self-sovereignty by a delegation of the popular will (Boutin et Rouvillois 2004; Gaxie 1977).

After the institutionalization of the basic conditions that propelled the political transition to democracy in the 1990s, after 1991 the process of consolidating democracy operated again around a party movement, the MpD. Legitimized by two booming victories in the 1990s, and anchored in a mobilizing discourse of mission—under the banner of Freedom and Competence—as a slogan for change, this party set the tone for the dynamics of the new system set up.

Instead of a one-party system that had been in place for the first decade and a half after independence, a single party now backed by a qualified parliamentary majority had considerable powers to shape the state and society in the light of its new ideals. Indeed, the party system resulting from the dynamics of the political system instituted with the Second Republic comprises, in our view, the ingredients of a predominant system, thus distorting the principles of separation and constraints of power in the political system.

Evora (2004) evokes a legal-constitutional argument that provides guarantees of political competition to counteract the ruling party in Cape Verde. According to her, the democratic political system of Cape Verde is characterized as being minimalist because it is based exclusively on the formal and procedural aspects. Now, if Cape Verdean democracy is minimalist, it is because there is, in fact, something inherently maximalist in it. This is precisely what should be explained, otherwise, the political system will be analyzed only in the light of its utopias.

Sartori (1982), in his consistent theoretical effort to adapt the universal dimensions of his theory of party systems to concrete historical situations, proposes the dominant party concept as a "subtype" that explains the distortion of the pluralistic (multiparty) competitive system. This predominance is characterized by the fact that one of the competing political forces has such unequal resources that it can compete and, at the same time, conform the rules of the game to its benefit in order to stay in power. In the Cape Verdean case, the party system that existed between 1991 and 2000 had typical characteristics of a dominant party system, since the MpD had in fact enormous powers: to grant a new constitution and other ordinary laws, to replace the old insignia (the national flag) of the Republic, to appoint the entire administrative body of the state and its business sector, to influence the chain of decision-making through the alignment resulting from the electoral process of the principal organs of sovereignty (government, parliament, Presidency), to promote and finance associations of civil society that were related to them, etc.

The signs of a two-party system begin with the divisions within the MpD, following the political struggles to choose the new leadership in 1999 and stabilize with the victory by an absolute majority of the PAICV in 2001. With this new political rebalancing, the opposition plays a more active role in the construction of the decision-making process and greater control in the dynamics of the functioning of the state, as well as its relationship with civil society.

The spectacle of the "one," which was exorcised during one-party rule, is returned to the political system through the back door. In fact, the new multiparty framework is born and develops around a messianic and Manichean polarization, in which the "new ones" of the dominant pole (those of the good, the liberators, and competent) exercise the old guard of the previously dominated pole (those of evil, oppressors, and incompetents). One of the dilemmas of the MpD in the early days of its mandate lay in the institution of a liberal-democratic regime (a regime government, as it was called at the time) and in the adoption of strategies and devices to guarantee its continued political legitimation. In its relationship with civil society, it was not long before the party movement set in motion strategies, sometimes explicit and other veiled, to create a business class tied to it, to co-opt civil society associations—NGOs, community associations, trade unions, among others, and thus reproducing the same logic of tentacular action on civil society. Instead of mass organizations of the party/state, formally free organizations emerge, but under strong influence and dependence on the party/government providing public resources in its most diverse forms.

Another way through which one can analyze the challenges of the consolidation of democracy in Cape Verde has to do with the nature of the interpenetration between administration, politics, and the market. It is an unpopular topic whose understanding is important for scrutinizing the trajectory of the new wave of politicians as well as the effects of their practices on the functioning of the democratic political system.

Interpenetration between Administration, Policy, and Market

The relationship between public administration and politics in contemporary societies—far from entailing a separation as advocated by Weber (2001) in his studies on the rationalization of the modern state—is, in fact, an interweaving dynamic. Contrary to what this German sociologist predicted, bureaucratic institutions became politicized and increasingly led by politicians (Aderbach 1982), and institutions under the umbrella of politicians (parliament, government, parties) themselves became bureaucratized, and their decisions depend to a large extent on the technical support of specialized employees (Suleiman 1995). Thus, a supposed disassociation between these two dimensions—because they have profoundly different, sometimes antagonistic logics of action—have little explanatory potential for the functioning dynamics of states in contemporary Western societies.

The structural conflict between administration and politics arises from the fact that, on the one hand, "administration is considered in liberal democracies as an instrument of politics inasmuch as it is a representative of the popular will" (Cruz 1999, 325) and, on the other, respecting the principle of equal and impartial treatment of citizens. There thus arises a contradiction between the principle of representative government of a majority that implements its program—and the administration must accept its political guidelines—and the liberal principles of the American and French revolutions in which equality implies the renunciation of partisan treatment.

In this context, the existence of senior leadership positions aims at reconciliation within public administration between the political and bureaucratic rationalities of the modern democratic state, however, constantly subject to the need for political legitimation. The tensions between public administration and politics are extremely complex and vary according to the historical experiences of nation-states. Weber (2000) believed that the consolidation of parliamentary democracies would pave the way for the dominance of political rationality over administration, opening the door for competition between political parties to become more and more conflict-driven to control these bureaucratic posts rather than for the objectives for which they were created (Suleiman 1995).

Similar to the Weberian perspective, Bourdieu (2001), when analyzing the process of secularization of political action, points out that:

> The more advanced the process of institutionalization of political capital, the more it tends to subordinate the conquest of ideas to the conquest of the posts; and the more the party militants, bound only by their dedication to the cause, retreat to the benefits of prebendalism (using public resources for their own benefit and the benefit of other party supporters), clients that become connected

to the apparatus in a lasting way for the benefits and the gains that it guarantees them. (195)

In this sense, the colonization of public administration by the party responds to a vital necessity of the functioning of the parties based in part on the return of material and symbolic benefits to militants and supporters as a way to seduce them for the political-electoral competition. Therefore, the understanding of the logic that governs the process of interpenetration between politics, public administration, and the market must be inferred from the struggles of the political parties for control of state resources.

The osmosis between politics and top public administration is very accentuated and constitutes one of the historical features whether in both socialist and single-party systems or in liberal democracies—where the alleged autonomy of the political arena should prevent this relationship. This interpenetration between public administration, politics, and the market endows senior officials with a multi-positioning as a result of the appropriation of various kinds of capital (Birnbaun 1975; Timsit 1986).[9]

In most Eastern European countries, the changes in the political system in the late 1980s and early 1990s did not translate into the renewal of existing elites. On the contrary, most cases served to harness the power of the old elites who, while recycled into the new political framework, maintained the reins of state control and the opportunities attached to it. The young cadres from the most diverse social strata, with the exception of those who passed through the political filter of the ruling party, had few opportunities to access important positions of the state apparatus.

Party, the State, and Public Administration in Cape Verde Post-Independence

In Cape Verde, the modalities of separation and interpenetration between the political and administrative arenas take their specific shape as a result of the way the political-administrative system has developed since the second half of the nineteenth century to this point. However, for the purposes of this chapter, our analysis will focus on the national state shaped in the light of the emancipatory ideology of independence for which the PAIGC was the main actor.

With the institutionalization of the one-party system, in the mold of the so-called "popular democracies" (Fetjo 1993; Kriegel 1984), the interpenetration between party, state, and administration is genetically structural. At the dawn of independence, in order to guarantee control over public administration, the government obliges that the officials swear in the act of taking office their fidelity to the people and to the party.

Thus, the legal text of 1976 reads:

> I swear, on my honor, to devote my intelligence and my energies to the service of the people of Cape Verde, performing with loyalty the duties of the function for which I was appointed, with full fidelity to the objectives of the African Party of Independence of Guinea and Cape Verde. (See paragraph 2 of Article 7 of Decree nº 4/76 of 10 January)

In addition to this ritual of bureaucratic party baptism in public administration, the party itself needed to expand its internal bureaucracy to meet the needs of consolidating its political legitimacy. As Gramsci (1988) observed, lasting domination requires, beyond the control of instruments of political coercion, the construction of an active consent of the dominated—a hegemony.

It is in this context of conditioning the structures of the party to the country's development that the party creates its own private structure with a budget allocation set by joint decrees of the ministers of economy, finance, and the prime minister. The party bureaucracy includes a part of the officials in public administration and party militants who, hitherto, were absorbed in the civil service (see Decree Law nº73/84 of July 23).

At the end of the 1990s, with the introduction of the first measures leading to the adaptation of the current political system to a new and more competitive political framework, it was decreed that the private structure of PAICV staff would be terminated and placed at the disposal of the General Directorate of Public Administration.

Thus, Law No 96 / III / 90 from the parliament stipulated, essentially, the following:

1) Officials who are in situations contemplated in this law, while awaiting placement in the services and bodies of the Public Administration, will provide services in places determined by the Secretary of State for Public Administration, after hearing the public departments concerned (Article 4 (1)).
2) The placement of the other employees hired and salaried by the PAICV, referred to in the preceding article, present in the departments and agencies of the state, will be carried out in accordance with their educational and professional qualifications, experience, and time of service previously provided and in accordance with the financial resources and human resources needs (Article 6 (1)).

With the political opening in 1990, profound changes in the political system were introduced. Among the banners of the new party was eliminating partisan influence and interference in public administration, a principle consecrated in the constitution which stipulated that:

> (1) access to and professional development in the civil service is based on the merit and ability of the candidates, demonstrated as a result of a public call for candidates and (2) public administration workers and other agents of the state and other public entities may not be benefited nor discriminated against by virtue of their political-party affiliations or the exercise of their rights as established in the constitution and law. (see Article 263 (1) and (4) of the 1992 Constitution; Silva 2010, 224)

However, the withdrawal of political prerogatives of the party over the state and society in the constitution is not, in itself, as we will explain below, a guarantee of the lack of partisanship of the state bureaucracy, at least as far as high-level positions are concerned. Indeed, the major challenge of the new party that largely shaped the Second Republic was to remain faithful to the idea of establishing a new liberal-democratic political regime and, at the same time, to consolidate its political legitimacy.

The process of recruiting the directors of the public administration, historically, has been done through the nomination process. The difference between the system in place during the colonial period and that of post-independence lies in the fact that the choice of senior directors in the former usually falls on career officials, while in the second case there is a slight reduction in that requirement.

In the post-independence period, the changes introduced in the process of recruiting the senior officials to aim to reinforce the discretion of the governing party, while safeguarding the academic requirements in a flexible way (see Decree Law 9/81 of February 11, Decree Law Decree Legislative nº13 / 97 of 1st of July, Decree Legislative nº4 / 98 of 19 of October). Indeed, the suppression of the constitutional provision which gave the party a political monopoly over the state in the framework of political reforms in the 1990s did not go hand in hand with significant changes in relation to the recruitment and selection criteria of the ruling party.

Some excerpts of narratives from in-depth interviews of personalities who have held high positions of leadership in a number of key institutions point to the fact that what has been and is at stake is the political control over public administration as a guarantee of political control of the dominant parties over the critical structures of the state sphere. This is how one of our interviewees put it.

> In 1979, a first level of the PCCS (Plan of Positions, Careers and Wages) was outlined, the impact of the selection was delineated since it was free but within

> certain categories. But it fell in 1981 because of a specific situation of someone who was from a mass organization of the party who was appointed to one of the ministries. This man attended some higher education and would be appointed advisor. But he could not be a mere advisor because to be an advisor he would have to be in category C, and besides, he was not a career public servant. And because they wanted to appoint him, they revoked the regulation of 152/1979 by the Decree-Law of 1981. From that time forward, it remained open until today. (Interviewee)

The rationale for the change to which the interviewee refers reads as follows: "Members of the special staff are regulated by a service commission, by free choice of the entity to which he/she depends and is made by executive order and does not require the approval of the Tribunal of Auditors" (see Article 1 of Decree Law no. 9/81, of February 11).

The government, under the baton of the party, wished to have free hand in relation to the process of filling the leadership positions under the special staff arrangement, a way in which certain political decisions could not be hampered either by public administration procedures or by the Tribunal of Auditors as a supervisory body. Throughout the period of the single-party regime, the government's intention to have discretionary power in the process of recruiting top management had, on several points, friction with the young cadres who worked in the design and formulation of the public administration reform. They were attempting to reserve an important role for education capital and professional experience in the provision of senior officials, which in fact came to pass with the approval of the statute for senior staff in the late 1980s.

Thus, the aforementioned statute establishes that:

> Level I and II officials shall be appointed from among individuals of proven professional and civic standing, graduates with university education conferring a bachelor's degree or, not being university graduates, are from civil servants whose category corresponds at least to the letter D of the Civil Service classification table. (See Article 3 of Decree Law no. 31/89 of June 3, Supplement to the Official Gazette of Cape Verde No. 22)

While it was true that this provision limited access to senior positions to holders of higher education at the undergraduate level, it would subtly open margins for the appointment of career staff without a university education, creating loopholes for some discretion on the part of those responsible for nomination. When we question some of the former top management leaders with long experience in executing and making laws in the context of the evolution of the recruitment criteria in the course of the one-party and multiparty system, they said:

> To be frank I do not yet see a substantial change in appointment criteria beyond those objective requirements. The question of merit only in marginal situations has a bearing. We continue to practice as we did before. [. . .] Often not just for political trust, but confidence in the person. I know several situations in which personal trust prevails, for even though that person may not be very attuned to the political thinking of the regime, but having full confidence that the choice offers guarantees of loyalty and personal trust, the person is chosen. In general, political trust remains dominant both in the governance of the MPD and in the governance of the PAICV. (Interviewee)

This same perception was given to us by another former senior director with a different trajectory in the state bureaucracy. He bluntly states the following:

> Any government, that is, has the pretense of remaining in power. And it thinks that in nominating people if adopting only the criterion of competence, it might be destabilized. As such, there is a concern that you can have a fifth column in the civil service. Do you see? As such, the tendency is to be dealing with trusted people. And there is another aspect as well. Sometimes there is what is called in Portugal "jobs for the boys." Sometimes you have to reward the good party militant, the guy who helped me in the campaign, or the brother of the leader. So political trust is mixed a bit with certain nepotism. It is evident that the brother of the minister who is appointed director general, of course, is also of political trust. He is a man of confidence. But the two things then, you see, are all a web of connections (*parede de meias*). Because this is the reason for nominating people, people of your confidence. It means the government wants to surround itself with people who in fact will guarantee its permanence. Therefore, they want to be in power as long as possible and think they need to nominate, I would not say a peon, but at least yes-men (*esteiros*). This is the logic of the trust system. (Interviewee)

It seems to be consensual among the high-level officials interviewed that, in fact, political considerations weigh decisively in the choice of public administration officials, notwithstanding the objective orientations established in the law in terms of the demand of an academic profile. As another interviewee confided:

> The general directors have always been politicians in Cape Verde. I am one of the few people who do not fight this because it is part of the DNA of the State of Cape Verde. . . . Therefore, the prime ministers who say no, it is for the English to see. (Interviewee)

In truth, among the recruitment criteria, the political trust to which the interviewees refer is nothing more than a process of rewarding positions to party militants and friends for the social and political capital invested in the political-electoral battles that precede the formation of the governments.

RECONVERSION TO THE MARKET

In the research we conducted in 2011, regarding the emergent socio-political conditions of the post-independence Cape Verdean political-administrative elite (Barros 2012), we found that more than half (53.4%) of the officials in public administration carried out professional activities in the private sector for private and international organizations, which reveals an important phenomenon of circulation toward other sectors, especially for the market.

The positions held in these institutions are largely concentrated (46%) in high management positions and intermediate positions, denoting a repositioning to a place of status and usufruct of earnings with relative horizontal proximity to the previously held positions. It should also be noted that a significant proportion (12.3%) has a consultancy role and 10.8 percent in teaching in private institutions and positions in non-governmental organizations.

Among the officials who performed other functions in private institutions, 73 percent concede that they are party activists, evidencing an important interweaving between public administration-politics-market. Likewise, 54.9 percent confirm that they have been nominated or selected to political office, also revealing that the acquisition of political capital represents an important variable in this process of circulation. As for the officials who held positions of leadership in public administration, 54.4 percent were in the private sector. It should be noted, however, that of those who occupied positions in the private sector, 90 percent held positions of leadership in the public sector.

Apparently, this circulation to the private sector, state-owned enterprises, and other organizations is due in large part to two concomitant phenomena. First, given the high level of interpenetration between the administration and party political militancy, the alternation in the country's governance provides opportunities for the entry of new leaders, which is a type of Cape Verdean style spoils system. The leitmotif of this entanglement is the attribution of positions to party militants as a way of rewarding the political capital invested during the "political sowing," which results in dethroning the former and impelling them to seek other opportunities in the private market, otherwise, they would be relegated to lower levels of the bureaucracy to languish and stagnate.

In the wake of the growth of the private sector, with the liberalization of the economy since the 1990s, in a country where the specialized resources and skills were/are relatively scarce, new opportunities opened up for the reconversion of officials from public administration to the private market.

This rotation of the political-administrative elite results from the accumulation of diverse kinds of capital, namely, political, social, and informational throughout their professional trajectory, favoring, seasonally, the occupation of multiple positions, thus diversifying its sources of accumulation of material and symbolic goods. It is a game of musical chairs, as Augé warns: "which the actors move away temporarily only to return to the game even more presently, repositioning, sometimes in multiple ways by splitting their administrative, political, economic responsibilities" (2005, 161).

This process of disappearance and seasonal reappearance of officials according to the "political season," occupying positions at times in politics, sometimes in public administration, other times in the private sector responds to the functional needs of diversification of opportunities for accumulation in order to guarantee the sustainability of their lifestyle and socio-political status acquired during the exercise of political-administrative power.

It should be noted that in the last decade the new niches of accumulation, certainly more attractive, have to do with the rapid expansion of the tourism sector and, to a lesser degree, the financial sector where dozens of former high political and administrative officials position themselves as entrepreneurs, managers, lobbyists, etc.

The trend toward the reconversion of former senior officials in public administration to the private sector operates in a context where regulation is still incipient. The legislation on incompatibilities provides that "senior officials are prevented, during the exercise of their functions and up to one year after their termination, from acting as arbitrators or experts in any proceeding in which the state or other legal person is a party" (see Article 34 of Decree Legislative No. 2/95, of 20 June).[10]

Yet what is the spirit of this diploma? When delimiting the incompatibility of the leaders only to the questions related to arbitration and expert opinion, in truth, but unspoken, adduced from the reading between the lines of this regulation, is that everything else is permissible, being left to the mercy of each leader the ethical-moral judgment regarding their options after the exercise of their public functions. Thus, the lack of precise and comprehensive provisions for disciplining incompatibilities is probably due to the fact that the ruling elites are not prepared to regulate a system which, in essence, limits the scope of their personal accumulation possibilities. It should be noted, however, that with regard to newly established regulatory agencies, the provisions on incompatibilities are more precise and verifiable (see Law 20 / VI / 2003 of 21/04/03: Legal Regime of Independent Regulatory Agencies).

CONCLUDING THOUGHTS

From the re-reading of the process of consolidation of the Cape Verdean democracy during the past two decades, it seems relevant to point out the following:

First, some pillars on which the post-independence political systems were erected—such as the existence of a rational bureaucracy, a sense of nation-state, a political-administrative and intellectual elite capable of managing the state and mediating the discursive process in the construction of projects for society, an active journalistic and literary public sphere—were not post-independence constructions. These have gained new meanings and have been the object of deepening in the light of the political projects of the politically dominant social forces.

Second, one of the great achievements in the post-independence period, from the point of view of the affirmation of democracy, is the emergence of the mass parties that allowed them to channel and congregate interests of the popular strata and to accommodate them in their programs of governance. Since 1991, the institutionalization of the liberal-democratic regime has accelerated this process. The parties have been forced to look more closely at the demands of the electorate and to incorporate within them a growing number of political leaders from the most disadvantaged social strata and the new emerging middle class, as a result of the rapid expansion of the state. One of the most notable effects of the insertion of new actors in the national political scene has to do with the fact that the social demands of the populations of the rural and urban peripheries are made by political subjects often originating from these localities when, in the recent past, they were subsumed in the narratives of the elites living in the urban centers of Praia and Mindelo.

Third, the transition from a single-party regime with an authoritarian nature to a multiparty regime of a liberal-democratic nature did not represent or result in the discontinuity of the preponderance of the political party over the state sphere, effectively weakening the counterweights that drive the dynamics of separation and the interdependence of the organs of sovereignty. Thus, the logic of the party/state, prevailing during the mobilizing one-party system resurfaces subtly, however, no less intense and vigorous, within the framework of the multiparty regime.

This logic tends to remain since it responds to a structural and functional need of the parties to appropriate state resources (central and local) as a strategy for financing the process of political-partisan legitimization and, as a result, a form of rewarding militants with material and symbolic goods according to the "political seasons."[11] In fact, the partisanship of public administration, far from being a deviation from the new times, is, on the contrary, a strategy of lubrication of the party machine without which the parties are obliged to make an immeasurable effort to alter the process of political legitimation, which up until now they have not been willing to do so.

Fourth, the specific historical conditions that gave the two major political parties (PAIGC/CV and MpD) enormous political power contributed decisively to becoming, on the one hand, omnipotent at the state level, to the point of transforming the state, in certain aspects, in its "seasonal property" and, on the other, ubiquitous in civil society to the point of maintaining a clientele relationship with it. As a result, we are faced with an increasingly servile society, to use the expression of Suzano Costa (2013), strongly dependent on the state that, through its support and financing programs, guarantees the conditions of operation and reproduction of associations inhibiting and limiting the autonomy of these in the definition of their interests. It should also be noted that "state-dependency" also affects intellectual circles where the broad freedom of expression and cultural production is totally inhibited by the tacit commitment not to call into question the foundations of state power on whose shadow they depend to carry out their personal and professional activities. The realization of a certain "intimacy in the shadow of power," as Coutinho (1980) observes regarding the Brazilian experience, is at the cost of self-censorship in the relationship between citizens and the state.

The information provided in 2015 by the two largest parties (MpD and PAICV), in the framework of their internal elections, indicate that about 55,000 militants are part of their ranks which represents at least about 30 percent of the national adult population. In principle, this high rate of *creole* political militancy should be reflected in greater participation of people in civil society organizations. However, the results of a series of four opinion surveys on the Quality of Democracy and Governance in Cape Verde in the last decade show that the rate of civic participation in civil society associations is still low (12%) and, when it happens, is limited to religious and sporting organizations.[12] This gap between the growth of political militancy and civic participation probably shows that investment in political capital is mainly aimed at securing the personal and professional advantages of citizens in a context in which the parties constitute one of the most important channels of social mobility.

Fifth, the intertwining of party/state has been provoking a profound change in the status of citizenship. Citizenship, which should be an expression of individual equality, freedom, and autonomy, tends to become a kind of partisan-citizenship, since the exercise of full rights of citizenship requires, at the outset, a party political mediation, without which ordinary citizens are, in practice, sub-citizens. In these conditions, anyone who is not a "partisan" and dares to be an active citizen immune to the webs of subjective control of militants and sympathizers is an "agitator," as they say in popular jargon.

In this sense, our "big man" is not a superman who turns his economic and religious resources into political resources according to the classic formulation of Marshall Sahalins (1966)—but a "Big Party," an organization that does not necessarily lead the state and society directly, but directs them "invisibly visible."[13]

Sixth, the intensification of the interlocking of politics, public administration and the market, as well as being an important means of individual and family wealth accumulation and party financing, tends to contribute to changing the nature of the political career. Thus, if in a first phase (1975–1992), characterized by the operationalization of the emancipatory utopias both around the building of the independent national state and around the democratization project, a kind of political-ideological elite emerged, today it is reasonable to wonder whether, in a second phase, we are not seeing a wave of professional politicians. "They live for politics on the condition that they live in politics," as Bourdieu (2001) warns, in some cases leading to the emergence of a fringe of "business-man" (entrepreneurial) politicians whose borders of simultaneous circulation between political spaces, public administrative, and business are, in fact, very tenuous.

These metamorphoses of politicians, however, occur at a time when the model on which the process of development of Cape Verdean society was based—recycling of public aid and remittances of emigrants—seems to show signs of contraction and exhaustion in a context of great instability and uncertainty of the cycles of capitalist accumulation in Europe on which the Cape Verdean economy is dependent.

Faced with these structural challenges, the reaction of the important part of the political elites has been the search for the re-foundation of the state, a sphere outside of which their conditions of survival seem to be painful and uncertain. In this perspective, the demand for regionalization by segments of decadent elites who formed part of the "predestined" orphans under the third republic, who had been the notables in the first and second republics, all of them marginalized by the political effects of independence and the institutionalization of new political competition after the 1990s, can be understood as the last gasp of this modern Cape Verdean political-administrative elite born and created around the dependence of the expansion of the economic and social political functions of the state of which it is the creator and creature.

NOTES

1. Brava was the only island in the archipelago whose white population was larger than the black population, called "color." The white population there represented 71

percent of the white population in Cape Verde (cf. Statistical map of 1872, Overseas Historical Archive).

2. The seminary training curricula included the Preparatory Course, which was subdivided into primary and secondary education. The first covers the elementary stage and the second to complement. The complementary phase lasted six years, covering sixteen seated disciplines in areas such as languages, classical literature, rational philosophy, law, economics, politics, physicochemical sciences and mathematics (Lopes 1996, 221).

3. Leão Gomes de Pina was one of the great protagonists of institutionalizing secondary education in the capital, having established a private school in the 1950s which, however, did not last long (Carvalho 2010).

4. These findings were taken, as explained previously, from a survey of public administration officials. The *Official Bulletin* No. 39 of September 8, 1979 and September 27, 1980, in which are listed a significant number of scholarship recipients who, after graduation, returned to the country to occupy high posts in public administration.

5. João Nobre de Oliveira, in his work on the Cape Verdean Press, conducts an exhaustive investigation of more than six dozen publications and numerous public spaces through which ardent debates were channeled among the native elite, discussing diverse questions of public interest and more (Oliveira 1998).

6. According to Silva, the social reference that corresponded to the expression "citizens of the overseas," in fact, did not concern the native population as a whole, but it had as its right recipient the Portuguese-descendant settlers, especially in the initial case of the Americas. In relation to the African and Asian territories, citizenship was applied to a (very restricted) group of elites of native origin, mixed or not and, in principle, Christianized. However, the delimitation of this group of overseas citizens was uncertain and ambiguous in its criteria. It should be noted that according to this author, outside the group of citizens were the populations as Indians and slaves, as well as the freedmen, although located in an intermediate zone. (Silva 2009, 430).

7. In the Cape Verdean case, the totalitarian dimension of political domination is characterized by the intensive vigilance and control of individual action by the friend, acquaintance, neighbor, godfather, compadre, companion who is often also a militant, deputy, minister, public administrator, etc. The transposition of this logic of social control into the space of political struggle transforms the social relation into a political relation. That is, the boundaries between the political and the social become very tenuous, limiting, in this way, the margin of individual autonomy.

8. The legislative elections of January 1991 resulted in the overwhelming victory of the opposition party, the MpD, obtaining a qualified majority of more than two-thirds of the seats in parliament. In the presidential elections, candidate Mascarenhas Monteiro, supported by the MpD, was elected president of the Republic. In that same year, in the municipal elections, the MpD and Independent Groups supported by it conquered the majority of the municipalities. This same trend was repeated in the 1995 legislative and presidential and local elections of 1996. In 2000, the PAICV, after a decade of wandering in the desert, returned to victory, conquering the majority of the municipalities. The same trend is confirmed in the 2001 legislative session in

which the absolute majority of the MPs elected to the National Assembly are seized. The former prime minister, Pedro Pires, supported by the PAICV, is elected president of the Republic. In the municipal elections of 2004, the MpD, reconquer most of the chambers, but it did not obtain the same success in the legislative elections of 2006. The PAICV reinforces its majority in the parliament and the candidate supported by it reflects itself in the presidency of the republic. Already in the municipalities of 2008, the leaders supported by the MpD maintained its dominion in the majority of the municipalities. In 2011, the PAICV renewed, for the third consecutive time, its majority in parliament.

9. In the former European east, with the overthrow of state socialism in 1989, they are, in general, the old elites of the communist party, who oversaw the private sector and became chiefs of companies. Thus, in Hungary, the reconversion of its elite takes place during the 1980s. As Romsics (2006) notes, "by benefiting from the advantages attached to its position and thanks to the technique of appropriation used in the course of economic transformation, 4/5 of the economic elite and manager of the old regime maintains its place to this day" (276). In Sub-Saharan African countries, the process leading to the independence of the former colonies has allowed parties forged in the liberation struggle to play a crucial role in shaping the new elites. They had a high political capital that allowed them to take over the state and thus to benefit from the best opportunities for the accumulation of economic, symbolic and cultural capital (Daloz 1999).

10. Article 32 of the aforementioned decree establishes that there are high public positions: Governor and vice governor and the administrators of the Bank of Cape Verde, the high authority against corruption, Head of the Civil House of the Presidency of the Republic, the Ambassador, Counselor of the President of the Republic, The President of the National Assembly and the Prime Minister, the Secretary-General National Assembly, the Presidency of the Council of Minister or Ministry, President of the Public Institute, public foundation or any other form of personalized service, public manager and member of the administration of any anonymous society, exclusively or majority-owned of public capital appointed by a public entity, as long as he or she performs full-time executive functions, director general or equivalent, others whose appointment, based on the principle of free designation by the government, is based, by law, on reasons of special trust, the full-time member of an independent entity provided for in the constitution or in law (Legislative Decree 2/95 of 20 June).

11. "The waters" is a popular term used in Cape Verde to designate the rainy season in which there is a good amount of precipitation.

12. We refer to a series of four opinion studies on the Quality of Democracy and Governance in Cape Verde conducted by Afrosondagem in 2002, 2005, 2008 and 2011.

13. In Cape Verde, for historical reasons related to the dynamics of the configuration of its socio-economic structure, most of the great men and families succumbed in the course of the decadence and decomposition of the slave system (Correral e Silva 2001; Cabral 2001). The most favored social classes that have resulted are the ones who establish relations with the state as a stable and safe anchorage to reproduce the

conditions of their existence. That is why, in our view, "super-personalization" in the process of political and bureaucratic domination was not affirmed in Cape Verde, at least within its elite. This Cape Verdean feeling averse to "super-personalization" is reported to us by the Governor of Cape Verde, Carlos Alves Rozadas. He says in the annual report sent to the Overseas Ministry: "It is certain that career managers in continental Africa have not given good proof here because they have been embroiled in a complex of superiority which is not in line with the ways of being of the people of this land" (see Report of the year 1950, 355, Overseas Historical Archive).

REFERENCES

Aderbach, Joel et al. (1982). *Bureaucrats in Western Union*. Cambridge, MA: Harvard University Press.

Afronsondagem (2011). *A Qualidade da Democracia e Governação em Cabo Verde—Dados comparativos das últimas quatro sondagens 2002, 2005, 2008 e 2011*. Praia: Afronsondagem.

———. (2015). *A Qualidade da Democracia e da Governação em Cabo Verde*. Praia: Afronsondagem.

Alexandre, Valentim (2004). "O Império português (1825–1890): ideologia e economia." In: *Revista Análise Social*, Vol. XXXVIII (169), pp. 959–979.

———. (2008). *O Império Africano*. Lisboa: Edições Colibri.

Alexandre, Valentim and Dias, Jill (1998). *O Império Africano: 1825–1890*. Lisboa: Editorial Estampa.

Anderson, Benedict (2005). *Comunidades Imaginadas: reflexões sobre a Origem e a Expansão do Nacionalismo*. Lisboa: edições 70.

Andrade, Elisa (1996). *As ilhas de Cabo Verde: da descoberta à independência (1460–1975)*. Paris: L'Harmathan.

Anjos, José Carlos (2002). *Intelectuais, Literatura e Poder em Cabo Verde*. Praia: ICL.

Augé, A. (2005). *Le Recrutement des élites politiques en Afrique subsaharienne: une sociologie du pouvoir au Gabon*. Paris: L'Harmattan.

Barbosa, Gilda (2007a). "Meio século de professorada I." In: *Terra Nova nº365*. Agosto-Setembro.

———. (2007b). "Meio século de professorada II." In: *Terra Nova nº366*. Outubro.

Barros, Crisanto (2012). *Génese e formação da moderna elite político-administrativa cabo-verdiana*. Tese de doutoramento defendida na Uni-CV/UCL, 403 p.

———. (2013). "A ascensão dos pobres a posições de elite político-administrativa no contexto do Cabo Verde pós-independente." *Revista de Ciêcnias Sociais*, Vol. 49, nº1, nºonli da Unisinos-Brasil.

———. (2013). "Notas sobre recrutamento da elite político-administrativa cabo-verdiana pós-independência." In: *ENTRE ÁFRICA E A EUROPA: NAÇÃO, ESTADO E DEMOCRACI EM CABO VERDE*. Organizados por Sarmento e Costa. Lisboa: Editora Almedina.

BAUQUET, Nicolas (2004). "Partis uniques, totalitarisme et démocratie," in *Partis politiques et démocratie: Inséparables mais incompatibles?* Direction de Boutin, Christophe et Rouvillois, Frédéric. Paris : Editeur L'oeil F.x. De Guibert.

Birnbaun, Pierre et al. (1977). *Les sommets de l'Etat: essai sur l'élite du pouvoir en France*. Paris: Editions du Seuil.

———. (1978). *La Classe dirigeante française: dissociation, interpénétration*. Paris: PUF.

Bourdieu, Pierre (2001). *Poder Simbólico*. Algés: Editora Difel.

Cabral, Iva (2001). "Política: ascensão e Queda de uma Elite Endógena." In: *História Geral de Cabo Verde*. Vol I. Luís de Albuquerque e Maria Emília Madeira Santos (Coord). Praia: Edição IICT e INIC.

Cardoso, Humberto (1993). *O Partido Único em Cabo Verde: Um Assalto à Esperança*. Praia: Imprensa Nacional.

Charle, Christophe (1987). *Les élites de la République: 1880–1900*. Paris: Edition Fayar.

Correia e Silva, António (1997). *O Processo Cabo-Verdeano de Transição para a Democracia*. Lisboa: Tese de Mestrado do Instituto Superior de Ciência e Tecnologia de Lisboa-ISTEC.

———. (2001). "Nascimento do Leviatã Crioulo Kultura." In: *Revista de Estudos Cabo-verdianos*. Número Especial, Setembro, pp. 27–37.

———. (2001a). "Sociedade Agrária Gentes das Águas: Senhores, Escravos e Forros." In: *História Geral de Cabo Verde*. Vol I. Luís de Albuquerque e Maria Emília Madeira Santos (Coord). Praia: Edição IICT e INIC, pp. 275–358.

———. (2004). *Combates pela História*. Praia: Editora Spleen.

Correia, Cláudia (1994). "A Administração Colonial Portuguesa entre os Séculos XIX–XX." In: *Repertório Numérico Simples do Fundo*. IAHN.

Costa, Daniel (2009). "O Papel do Chefe de Estado no Semipresidencialismo Cabo-verdiano: 1991–2007." In: Marina Costa LOBO e Octavio AMORIM NETO (Orgs.). *Semipresidencialismo em Países de Língua Portuguesa*. Lisboa: ICS: Imprensa de Ciências Sociais.

Costa, Suzano e Sarmento, Montalvão (Org.) (2013). *Entre África e a Europa: Nação, Estado e Democracia em Cabo Verde*. Lisboa: Editora Almedina.

Cruz, José Maria Teixeira da (1999). *A Função Pública e o Poder Político: as situações na Alemanha, em França, a Grã-Bretanha, nos Estados Unidos da América e em Portugal*. Vols. I e II. Tese de Doutoramento, ISCSP—UTL. Lisboa

Dahal, Robert (2003). *Um Prefácio à teoria Democrática*. Rio de Janeiro: Zahar Editores.

Duverger, Maurice (1985). *Os Grandes Sistemas Políticos*. Lisboa: Editora Almedina.

———. (1986). *A tecnodemocracia*. Rio de Janeiro: Editora Paz e Terra.

Évora, Roselma (2004). *Cabo Verde da abertura política e a transição para a democracia*. Praia: edições Spleen.

Daloz, Jean-Pascal and Chabal, Patrick (1999). *L'Afrique est Partir: du désordre comme instrument politique*. Paris: Económica.

———. (1999). (dir). *Le (non-)renouvellement des élites en Afrique subsaharienne*. Paris: UMR.

Fernandes, Gabriel (2002). *A Diluição da África*. Praia: INBL.

———. (2006). *Em Busca da Nação*. Praia: IBNL.

Fetjo, François (1993). *La fin des Démocraties populaires; Les Chemins du Post-Communisme*. Paris: Seuil.

Foucalt, Michel (1994). *Dits et Ecrits*. Vols I, II, III, IV. Paris: Galimard.
Furtado, Cláudio (1997). *Génese Reprodução da Classe Dirigente em Cabo Verde*. Praia: ICL.
Furtado, Clementina (2012). *As migrações da África Ocidental em Cabo Verde: atitudes e representações*. Tese de doutoramento defendida na Uni-CV e na Universidade Livre de Bruxelas.
Gaxie, Daniel (1977). "Économie des partis et rétributions du militantisme." *Revue française de science politique*, Vol. 27 (1), pp. 123–154.
Habermas, Jurgen (1984). *Mudança Estrutural da Esfera Pública*. Rio de Janeiro: Biblioteca Tempo Universitário.
———. (2012). *Teoria do Agir Comunicativo*. Vols 2. São Paulo: Martins Fontes.
Koudwao, Fafali (2001). *Cabo Verde e Guiné Bissau: Da democracia Revolucionária à Democracia liberal*. Bissau: INEP.
Kriegel, Anne (1984). *Le Système Comuniste Mondial*. Paris: PUF.
Lefort, Claude (1991). *Pensando o político: ensaios sobre a democracia, revolução e liberdade*. Rio de Janeiro: Editora Paz e Terra.
Lima, Aristides (1992). *Reforma Política em Cabo Verde, do Paternalismo à Modernização do Estado*. Praia: Grafedito.
Lins, Juan e Stepan, Alfred (1999). *Transição e Consolidação da Democracia: a experiência do Sul da Europa e da América latina*. Rio de Janeiro: Editora Paz e Terra.
Lobo, Andréa (2012). *Tão Longe e Tão Perto. Famílias e movimentos na ilha da Boavista de Cabo Verde*. Praia: Edições Uni-CV.
Lopes Filho, João (1996). *Ilha de São Nicolau Cabo Verde: Formação da sociedade e Mudança Cultural*. Vols. I e II. Praia: Secretaria Gerald o Ministério da educação.
Lopes, José Vicente (1996). *Os Bastidores da Independência*. Praia: Instituto Camões.
Movimento para Democracia (1990). *Programa Político*. São Vicente.
———. (1992). *Documentos da III Convenção Nacional*. Praia: INCV.
———. (1997). *Moção de Estratégia e Estatuto*. Praia.
Ministério do Ultramar (1950). *Relatório do ano de 1950*. Carlos Alves Roçadas, p. 355.
Miranda, Jorge (1976). *As Constituições Portuguesas* (1822, 1826, 1838, 1911, 1933, 1976). Lisboa: Livraria Petrony.
Morais, Humberto Nascimento (1969). *Cabo Verde na Política Ultramarina (evolução Social e Promoção Política)*. Dissertação de Licenciatura. ISCSP da UTL, Lisboa, pp. 1–156.
Neves, Baltazar Soares (2008). *Seminário Liceu de S. Nicolau: contributo para a História do Ensino em Cabo Verde*. Porto: Editora do Centro de Estudos Africanos da Universidade do Porto.
Oliveira, João Nobre (1998). *A Imprensa cabo-verdiana entre 1820–1975*. Macau: Fundação Macau.
Rocha, Eufémia (2011). *Mandjakus são todos os africanos, todas as gentes pretas que vêm de África: xenofobia e racismo em Cabo Verde*. Dissertação de mestrado defendida na Uni-CV.
Romsics, I. (2006). "Les élites hongroises et le changement de régime." In: *Le Communisme et les élites en Europe centrale*. Paris: PUF.
Rosenfild, Denis (1984) *Qual é a questão da democracia?* São Paulo: editora brasiliense.

Sahlins, M. (1963). "Poor Man, Rich Man, Big Man, Chief; Political Types in Melanesia and Polynesia." *Comparative Studies in Society and History*, Vol. 5 (3), pp. 285–303.

Sartori, Giovanni (1982). *Partidos e Sistemas Partidários*. Rio de Janeiro: Zahar Editores.

Silva, Cristina Nogueira (2009). *Constitucionalismo e Império: a cidadania no ultramar*. Coimbra: Editora Almedina.

Silva, Mário (2010). *As Constituições de Cabo Verde e textos históricos de direito constitucional cabo-verdiano*. 2ª Edição. Praia: Imprensa Nacional de Cabo Verde.

Saint-Martin, Monique (1993). "Introduction." In: *les éllites: formation, reconversion, internalisation*. Colloque de Stokholm, pp. I–XII.

Suleimn, E. and Miendras, H. (1995). *Le Recrutement des élites en Europe*. Paris: La Découvert.

Timsit, G. (Dir.) (1986). *Les Fonctions Publiques en Europe de L'Est et de L'Ouest*. Paris: Editions du Centre National de Recherche Scientifique.

Ultramarino, Arquivo Histórico (1872). *Mapa estatístico de.* Portugal: Lisboa.

Vaquinhas, Irene Maria and Cascão, Rui (1998). "Evolução da Sociedade em Portugal: a lenta e complexa afirmação de uma civilização burguesa." In: *História de Portugal*. Vol. 5. (Coord) Mattoso, José e (dir) Torgal, Luís Reis e Roque, João Lourenço. Lisboa: Editorial Estampa, pp. 379–419.

Weber, Max (2001). *Economia e Sociedade*. Brasília: UnB.

LEGISLAÇÃO

Código Administrativo (1842). In: *Colecção de Leis e outros documentos oficiais. Lisboa*: Imprensa Nacional.

Decreto nº 14/77 de 5 de Março.

Decreto-Lei nº152/79 de 31 de Dezembro.

Decreto-Lei 9/81 de 11 de Fevereiro.

Decreto-lei nº73/84 de 23 de Julho.

Decreto-Lei nº31/89 de 3 de Junho.

Decreto-Lei nº31/89 de 3 de Junho, Suplemento ao Boletim Oficial de Cabo Verde.

Decreto-Lei nº15-B/90, de 30 de Março.

Decreto-Lei nº 10/93 de 8 de Março.

Decreto-Legislativo n.º 2/95, de 20 de Junho.

Decreto-Legislativo nº13/97 de 1 de Julho.

Decreto-Legislativo nº4/98 de 19 de Outubro.

Lei nº 20/VI/2003, BO Nº 13, I Série, de 21/04/03 que define o Regime Jurídico das Agencias Reguladoras Independentes

Lei de Organização Política do Estado (LOPE). In: SILVA, Mário (2010). As Constituições de Cabo Verde e textos históricos de direito constitucional cabo-verdiano. 2ª Edição. Praia.

Suplemento nº 4 do Boletim Oficial de Cabo Verde de 1 de Fevereiro de 1893.

Chapter 2

Cabo Verde in the World

André Corsino Tolentino

This chapter has two parts. The first is to demonstrate how the Portuguese invented Cape Verde and the Cape Verdeans created the sovereign state. The second part discusses the situation of the state in the face of the phenomena of regionalization and globalization.

FROM THE INVENTION OF THE TERRITORY TO THE CREATION OF THE STATE

It is said that God created the universe and Portugal invented Cape Verde. All Christians, Jews, Muslims, Hindus, and others, who suffice proof of faith, myth, or legend, agree with the first statement, which is the domain of beliefs. But who will accept the assertion that Portugal invented Cape Verde? This subject is more terrestrial and recent. And it has been the subject of history, here understood as knowledge resulting from the investigation of the action of the human being at the intersection of time and space.

The arguments are presented by developing the following topics: (a) the European expansion of the fifteenth century gave new directions to globalization, notably through the settlement of the Atlantic islands of Madeira, the Azores, the Canaries, and Cape Verde; (b) the royal charters of 1466 and 1472 are episodes of the struggle between Cape Verde and Portugal for the domain of commerce in the western strip of the African continent; (c) the slave trade is situated on the paths of domination and, later, on the liberation of Africa; (d) the emergence of the PAIGC in the independence of Cape Verde; (e) of the Law of Political Organization of the State (LOPE) to the 1980 Constitution; (f) the two phases of the transition from colony to democratic state: from the single-party regime (1975–1990) to the multiparty regime (1991–2010).

European Expansion and Globalization

The word "globalization" is recent and dates back to 1944 when the American publisher Merriam Webster first entered it to define the tendency for certain phenomena to expand across the globe. However, the dynamics are older than the word, and it has come to mean the increasing interconnection of human communities. Globalization scholars agree that the voyages of Christopher Columbus (1492) from the west and Vasco da Gama (1498) from the east reached a domain of lands and oceans never before seen and gave rise to European maritime empires.

In the case of the Cape Verde Islands, occupation of the territory began in the fifteenth century and lasted until the nineteenth century, over more than 400 years (1462–1893), as can be seen below, with the approximate year of the beginning of the settlement in parentheses: Santiago (1462), May (1490), Fogo (1493), Brava (1545), Santo Antão (1548), Boa Vista (1620), São Nicolau and Sal (1893). At this point, the reader will note that: (a) the settlement of the nine inhabited islands resulted from a slow process of human fusion or creolization, which took more than four centuries; (b) the complexity and slowness of the process simultaneously explain part of the human diversity of the islands and national resilience; (c) the date of settlement or occupation is approximate and, in general, does not coincide with the date of conquest; (d) like Christopher Columbus and Vasco da Gama, the Italian António da Noli and the Portuguese Diogo Gomes drove globalization forward.

Cape Verde and Portugal Fighting for Trade Control

Portugal found the islands some 500 kilometers from Cape Verde, the westernmost part of the African continent, where Dakar, now the capital of Senegal, is located. In fact, what for the economy was called Cape Verde is neither a cape nor green, but Portugal led the formation of a nation there. The country should be called the Cape Verde Islands, on its own, and to avoid confusion with the Senegalese, who still say and write: *La République des Îles du Cap-Vert.* Looking back, how was this creation possible if the rain had always been rare and natural resources never plentiful?

The European maritime empires began with the militarization of the eastern routes by land and sea. In this odyssey, Portugal played a pioneering role. And in 1444 it reached the west coast of the African continent. In 1460, it took over the islands of Cape Verde and in 1462, King Afonso V donated the island of Santiago to the Italian António de Noli, who tried to install some Portuguese families in Ribeira Grande, then the seat of the southern part of the island of Santiago, and nowadays, Cidade Velha, today designated a World Heritage Site.

A few years later, the second beneficiary of the royal donation, Diogo Gomes, took over the northern part of the same island, based in Alcatrazes, a town near the current city of Praia. Alcatrazes and the domain of the north succumbed shortly after its institution. At that time, in the fifteenth century, the island of Santiago was synonymous with Cape Verde. The archipelago had a geographical position whose benefits contrasted with the adversity of the climate and the scarcity of natural resources, the main reason for being of any colonial enterprise. Between expanding Europe, Africa in the process of being occupied, and the Americas under European control, Cape Verde's strategic utility as a fulcrum for globalization seemed clear. And it was with this vision that the kingdom of Portugal tried to compensate the residents in the islands with exclusive benefits.

In a letter from the king of 1466, the residents of the island of Santiago were granted the exclusive right to trade with the coastal strip from Sierra Leone to Guinea, with the exception of Arguim in Mauritania, which was considered a territory reserved for direct trade with the kingdom of Portugal. The main goods exported from Santiago de Cabo Verde to the coast were cotton, horse, and cloth. The main imported merchandise were slaves for use on the islands and for re-export to the Iberian peninsula (Portugal and Spain), Central, and South America, the Caribbean, and North America. The economy took advantage of the slave trade and prospered for a short time. Consequently, the concepts of international trade and gateway have always characterized Cape Verde's relations with the African and European continents.

Already in 1472, new royal letters imposed a drastic reduction in the benefits granted to the colonists living on the island of Santiago. The great difference was that which separated the exclusive right to general trade attributed through the royal charter of 1466 and the right to trade restricted to goods produced on the island of Santiago, weak in agricultural products and almost nil in manufacture. This was the first battle for the domination of the geostrategic space waged and lost by the Cape Verdeans against the Metropolis.

So far we have spoken of the actions of the Portuguese and the Europeans, saying, therefore, only a half-truth about the settlement, creolization, and identity of the Cape Verde Islands. The other part of the truth, which will certainly influence the reader's perception, is related to the slave trade, which played a crucial role in the formation and affirmation of Cape Verdean society.

From the Slave Trade to the National Liberation Movements

"Slave trade," "slave trade across the Atlantic Ocean," and the "transatlantic slave trade" are expressions used to invoke the same reality involving the use of millions of enslaved Africans in the production of coffee, cocoa, tobacco, sugar, cotton, and ores, such as silver and gold, in American and European lands. The slave trade constituted a dominant part of what became known as the triangular trade promoted by the colonial empires and which included the following regions and commodities: Europe (manufactured goods such as firearms, powder, iron, alcohol, and textiles), Africa (slaves, ivory, gold, and silver) and Americas (coffee, cocoa, tobacco, sugar, and cotton).

The temporal coincidence of the settlement of Cape Verde with the slave trade between the fifteenth and nineteenth centuries shows the importance of this period and of this phenomenon in the formation of the Cape Verdean nation. In 1731, the population of Cape Verde was about 30,000, distributed as follows: whites (2.62%), mestizos (29.74%), freed slaves or former slaves (51.28%), and slaves (16.36%). In little more than three centuries, Cape Verdean society evolved from a model of slave society based on a racist hierarchy of whites, mestizos, freed blacks, and slaves to a nation of citizens, admittedly one of the most integrated in the world at the beginning of the twenty-first century.

Put in the context of globalization, the history of Africa is the continuation of the resistance of the peoples to the usurpation and the logic of invasion and domination. In saying the same thing differently, when circumstances allowed, Africans adopted and made their own philosophical, ideological, and action principles of the most universal societies to reach independence and continue to advance. Resistance was translated into the invention of languages, solidarities, cultures, and practices that led to the independence of Africa in a relatively short period. National liberation movements were part of this intellectual and moral baggage of humanity.

From the PAIGC's Emergence to the Independence of Cape Verde

The creation, consolidation, and defense of the African Party for the Independence of Guinea and Cabo Verde (PAIGC) was the most original and difficult task that Amílcar Cabral and his companions conceived and fulfilled. The assertion that it was not born out of anything and was not a perfect organization is a truism. It resulted from the fusion of several movements of resistance and nationalists, and the leadership was made up of men and women who by being exceptional, did not stop being human. Bringing together what was most advanced in the elites of the colonies of Guinea and Cape Verde, the PAIGC managed to lead the two peoples to national independence.

The PAIGC had included in its program the consultation of the people of both colonies to ascertain whether they would voluntarily unite in a transnational state in the context of African unity, but this objective was made unfeasible by the evolution of events and a new situation was entirely assumed. The unilateral proclamation of the State of Guinea-Bissau was prepared before Amílcar Cabral was betrayed by the contradictions in the process of national liberation of the peoples of Guinea and Cape Verde. Even today the interpretation of the circumstances of his murder has not revealed a definitive explanation of what really happened.

It is documented that the intention of Amílcar Cabral and PAIGC, which he created and led, was to unite the anti-colonial forces of Cape Verde and Guinea to achieve independence and development in the context of the struggle for national liberation and African unity. The union was instrumental and had two sequential objectives: national liberation and the sovereign decision on the conditions for the exercise of individual freedoms. Regional integration against colonial oppression and social injustice were crucial. In addition, Amílcar Cabral was aware of the history of Cape Verde and the role of emigration and transnationalization. He saw in the union of the peoples of Cape Verde and Guiné-Bissau two complementary realities: their belonging to the African region and the inter-regional bridge that Cape Verde could play.

In fact, parts of the story are known, even if not in its entirety. It is known, for example, that the colonial government wanted to arrest or eliminate the leader of the PAIGC, but this is not new, it is intuitive. It is also in the public domain the existence of internal contradictions in the PAIGC to which the project of union was not strange. These contradictions merit further discussion. For example, the issue of Cape Verde's anchorage in Africa or Europe is much more complex and needs to be more deeply and broadly discussed than it has been until today. Also, it is known that the coexistence of Guineans and Cape Verdeans in the context of the national liberation struggle had high and low moments and that the relationship between the freedom fighters of the two national communities evolved in a line with several points of incomprehension and discomfort. In short, it was a PAIGC leader who executed Amílcar Cabral. All these factors contributed to the puzzle that still today is the unexplained tragedy. It is true that there is a lack of concrete knowledge of who had ordered the assassination of Amílcar Cabral and, therefore the motivations of the crime.

Those who are familiar with the process of winning national independence in Guinea-Bissau and Cape Verde agree that the strategy of combining the resources of the populations and the forces of resistance was great. The articulation of the action of all the movements of national liberation of the old colonies with the progressive organizations of Portugal was an important condition of the liberating process. And it was not by chance that 1975, the year of all the independence of the Portuguese colonies of Africa, happened one year after the events of April 25, 1974 in Portugal, which coincided with the intensification of the socio-political movement that would lead to the democratization of Brazil with the election, in 1985, of President José Sarney. The end of the Portuguese dictatorship is symbolized by the change of April 1974, and this was historically considered as a common result of the peoples who, in 2014, formed the Community of Portuguese-Speaking Countries (CPLP).

Whatever the risks of any national independence, to combine the advantages of an armed struggle for liberation, as happened in the territory of Guinea-Bissau, and independence without a violent shot in the islands was a unique phenomenon with multiple consequences. Among them, the reader will note: (a) the strengthening of Cape Verdeaness based on the shared management of the diversity of the islands; (b) the rise of self-esteem of all Cape Verdeans residing abroad; and (c) the growth of socio-economic well-being indicators, despite geographical, economic, demographic, social, and political constraints. We could add relative social peace, the absence of armed groups, and the supremacy of civil authorities. Part of the success of the state and society in Cape Verde is due to the strategy of unity for peace drawn up by Amílcar Cabral.

From the Colony to the Sovereign State

In Cape Verde, based on the agreement between the PAIGC and the Portuguese government resulting from April 25, 1974, elections were held on June 30, 1975, with characteristics of a referendum, whereby 88.3 percent of the citizens registered on the electoral roll voted, with 92 percent expressly agreeing to the lists submitted by groups of 300 voters in each constituency. This information is especially relevant for those who think that there should have been a referendum on the independence of Cape Verde or who argue that there was no alternative to the PAIGC. On the one hand, the United Nations (UN) had resolved in 1961 that the principle of national sovereignty is not negotiable. On the other hand, there were groups of people who understood that Cape Verde was an atypical case, and therefore there should be an express consensus on national independence or any other form of political organization in the territory. The numbers indicate that there was a general election and a constituent assembly was formed even if, for the sake of consistency, that word was never officially used. It should be noted that the electoral law provided that 300 voters could submit lists of candidates for deputies in each constituency and that this was the legitimizing basis of the power used by the PAIGC.

The 1974 agreement between the Portuguese government and the PAIGC expressed the possible compromise, and there was the election of the deputies to the National People's Congress (ANP) in the form of a referendum. Another issue was related to the rule of law, and it was fulfilled. The same session of the ANP that proclaimed the state adopted the Law of Political Organization of the State (LOPE), a pre-constitution, which established that to matters not covered by it, as long as they did not contravene the principles of national sovereignty, that Portuguese law would apply. The principle prevailing that an imperfect law is always preferable to not having any law.

However, in 1980, the constitution enshrined the one-party political regime that was to last until 1990 or fifteen years after independence. Thus, the islands of Cape Verde have moved from colony to democratic rule of law in two phases: (a) in the first, the rule of law, with a single-party regime, from 1975 to 1990; (b) in the second, the democratic rule of law, with a multiparty rule, starting in 1990. The multiparty regime took shape in the parliamentary elections of January 13, 1991 and has been consolidated through the alternation of political power by the Movement for Democracy (MpD) and the Cape Verdean African Independence Party (PAICV), heir to the PAIGC. It is recalled that the institutional separation between Guinea-Bissau and Cape Verde happened with the coup d'état of 1980 in Guinea-Bissau. The PAIGC of Cape Verde considered that the coup was incompatible with the peaceful resolution of political conflicts and created the PAICV.

CAPE VERDE BETWEEN REGIONALIZATION AND GLOBALIZATION

The originality of the Cape Verdean nation in Africa, the youthfulness of the newly independent state, and the complexity of the processes of regionalization and globalization made some political choices difficult. However, any coherent government has to face simultaneously two dynamics: on the one hand, for more than fifty years, regionalization and globalization are dominant in international relations and, on the other hand, the forces of globalization and regionalization often come into conflict.

Regionalization and Globalization: Conflict and Cooperation

In the first part of this work, we saw the meaning of globalization. Now it is the turn of regionalization. Revisiting these concepts, what will be the most reasonable choices for Cape Verde? And how to measure changes in regionalization?

Since World War II, regional integration has been a hallmark of international relations. Once again, the movement started from the old continent where it faces the challenges of the construction of a united Europe. Regional integration is a more or less complex and slow process during which initially independent actors agree to unite vision, efforts, and resources, reducing their degrees of sovereignty, to belong to a whole that, as a rule, will be worth more than the sum of the parts. Depending on the nature of the objectives, these actors are profit-making and non-profit-making states and private sector organizations.

The more than 190 UN Member-States are integrated into geographic blocs with greater or lesser political weight, and there is a general tendency for each geographical and economic unit to become a region. So, it seems that we will have Africa, Asia, Central and South America, North America, Europe, etc. With regard to these trends, what do we mean by region, regionalization and globalization? Well, region implies geographical proximity and identification of common political and social characteristics and ambitions. In the case of direct interest to Cape Verde, the Economic Community of West African States (ECOWAS) is a grouping of fifteen contiguous and nearby states united in the ambition to create an economic community. It defines itself as a sub-region, the Africa region being formed by a variable number (today five) of sub-regions comprising the continent and the islands. Therefore, I think it is incongruous to talk about our continent when it would be more correct to speak about our region or simply about Africa, which means the continent and the islands.

The Economic Community of West African States (ECOWAS), in English, was founded in Lagos, Nigeria, on May 28, 1975, shortly before Cape Verde was born as a sovereign state on July 5, 1975. The objectives were peace, trade, cooperation, and the development of its members. Cape Verde was greeted as a member as soon as 1976, less than a year after independence. As for Mauritania, it has remained a member since its founding until 2002. In 2014, the fifteen member-states are Benin, Burkina Faso, Cape Verde, Côte d'Ivoire, Gambia, Ghana, Guinea, Guinea-Bissau, Liberia, Mali, Niger, Nigeria, Senegal, Sierra Leone, and Togo. In surface and population, Nigeria is the largest and Cape Verde the smallest member-state. Other Cape Verdean particulars are its archipelago profile and its character as a source of emigrants and a recipient of immigrants.

The ECOWAS and the African Union are groups of continental and island countries that share geography and other specificities. Etymologically correspond to regions, the one belonging to it. And regionalization? Regionalization is the process of economic, social, and political integration of states geographically contiguous or proximate, as in the case of islands, through cooperation.

The concept of globalization is now lacking. Let us remember that a pragmatic definition would say that globalization consists of the increasing flows of goods, services, capital, people, and information across the borders of countries.

The observation on the conditions of increased regionalization and the efforts of the United States and the European Union (EU) to reach a Transatlantic Partnership on Trade and Investment (TTIP) suggest that these processes are twofold. In fact, the fall of the Berlin Wall and the collapse of the bipolar world of the Cold War period projected the United States and the world into the situation of a unipolar planet. The desired multipolarity remains postponed and dependent on new balances in the redistribution of political power.

Indicators of the Rhythm of Regional Integration

If it is possible to have a coherent regional integration policy and be proactive in globalization, Cape Verde will have to look specifically at ECOWAS without losing sight of its real size and propensity to defend the national interest through relations with other regions. Having established the principle that membership of ECOWAS is compatible with the constant progress of relations with countries in other regions and with their common institutions, and therefore with globalization, it is necessary to define strategies to resolve the difficulties arising from membership in ECOWAS. Naturally, it will be necessary to measure the pace and quality of integration through the operationalization of previously adopted indicators.

All countries that have a common economic integration project define the criteria and performance indicators in three domains: economic, institutional, and social. To assess the performance of any of the fifteen ECOWAS member-states, the task force will need to collect and process relevant information to respond to three categories of indicators.

Economic Indicators:

1) What is the growth rate of the commercial flow of goods within the bloc?
2) What is the growth rate of the commercial flow of services in the bloc?
3) What is the growth rate of the investment flow within the block?
4) What is the volume of products included in the Common External Tariff?
5) What is the degree of harmonization of monetary policy?

Institutional Indicators:

1) Nature of legislative and judicial bodies (parliament and court)
2) Legal disputes and conflict resolution mechanisms
3) Representation of the bloc in international institutions, etc.
4) Out of-Block Dispute Resolution
5) Creation of organs in each state to deal with integration issues

Social Indicators:

1) Circulation of tourists and university work
2) Education: legislation on equivalence and university standardization
3) Culture: cultural promotion activities of other member-states
4) Regional entities: entrepreneurs, workers, NGOs, etc.
5) Identity: degree of identification of individuals with the population of the block

These three sets of indicators will make it possible to measure the progress and partial or total setbacks of each state in the implementation of the common regional integration project. The simple observation of this example of the fifteen indicators proves the complexity of the regionalization process and allows us to perceive the specific difficulties of Cape Verde. The construction of a strategy and its operationalization are two major challenges for Cape Verdean diplomacy.

On this point, we must add that trade has declined among the fifteen ECOWAS member-states from an already very low percentage of national external trade. Except for Benin, Senegal, and Togo, ECOWAS member-states have as their main trading partner countries outside the sub-region. In general, ECOWAS trade is directed toward Europe. Cape Verde is no different. The average of 85 percent or more of Cape Verde's exports and imports has Europe as the main market, while the ECOWAS sub-region accounts for less than 2 percent of Cape Verde's foreign trade. However, the informal business relationship is significant. The monetary situation in the region is also complex. Information on the above-mentioned indicators is neither organized nor universally accessible.

A cursory analysis of Cape Verde's regional integration reveals enormous advantages and challenges. The objective of the fifteen member-states is to create an economic community. And the main questions remain unanswered: economic integration implies inclusive political participation; inclusive political participation involves the state and the nation; this means that a community is sustainable when the citizens of each state participate genuinely in its construction.

Cape Verde formally belongs to ECOWAS, the World Trade Organization (WTO), and the UN. The creation of the West African Institute (IAO), based in the city of Praia, was intended to be an instrument of strategic management of the processes of regionalization and globalization. However, the focus on African integration faces many risks in the future, as it is clearly contrary to maintaining the dependence of the EU and the desire for horizontal relations with the countries of all regions of the world.

In other words, Cape Verde and the majority of ECOWAS member-states have not yet reached the levels of sophistication necessary for the technical analysis of regional integration, nor have they established mechanisms for involving the different sectors of society in the debate. It is a question of good governance and democracy.

Cape Verde and the Possible Choices

The singular history of the emergence of the nation and the state of Cape Verde explains the hesitation at the time of great decisions about the future. However, the time seems to have come to increase the weight of reason and decide on the basis of cautiously defined national interests.

The world is becoming regionalized and we have seen that regionalization is coexisting with globalization, now in cooperation, now in conflict. Three hypotheses are possible: Cape Verde is Cape Verde, not Africa or Europe. This way of seeing has no reason to exist in today's world because Cape Verde cannot live in autarchy and the planet is regionalized and globalized. The second hypothesis that Cape Verde is an almost European nation does not stand up to historical and social analysis, because the arguments go against the principle of national sovereignty, which seems to be very dear to the people. The third hypothesis is that Cape Verde is an African nation with specific geographic, economic, social, and cultural characteristics, like all the nations of the world. What we think is desirable and viable is Cape Verde assuming definitively its status as an African state and maintaining its hyphenated nature between regions, peoples, religions, and cultures.

Let us mention three characteristics of the process of affirmation and prediction of the future: (a) the nation was invented just over half a millennium; (b) the Cape Verdean people resisted and created a democratic rule of law within the framework of national emancipation; (c) Cape Verdean society is open to other peoples and universal values. Being the most Western state in Africa, Cape Verde has grown in the islands, and in the world, through migrations.

The international relations Cabo Verde has created and grows range from Australia, Japan, and China to Chile, the United States, and Cuba, from South Africa to the EU. The ability to expand and deepen cooperation with other regions depends on the strength of regional integration and the effectiveness of its good neighborly policies. In addressing internal and external challenges, the mid-Atlantic situation between the Africa to which it belongs geopolitically, the America of complicity, and the Europe of the civilizational embrace, presents great potential, but still, there is a lack of education, science, technology, and human capacity, and institutional framework to mark the next phase of growth in the Atlantic. Cape Verde lacks the national option for African integration.

It has been demonstrated that the Cape Verde path is unique and that the challenges of sustainable development are enormous. The truth is that in just over half a millennium, a nation was born in Africa, created a state to serve it, spread throughout the world, and opted for freedom and social justice. Today it tries to reinstate its name between regionalization and globalization. However, regional integration, as well as the management of the globalization process, is directly related to the internal and external management of the national interest in the increasingly complex real world.

FURTHER READING

Almeida, G. *Cabo Verde: viagem pela história das ilhas*. Editorial Caminho, Lisboa: Editorial Caminho. 2003.

Belassa, B. *Theory of Economic Integration*. Homewood, IL: R.D. Irwin. 1961.

Cabral, Iva. *A Primeira Elite Colonial Atlântica. Dos "homens honrados brancos" de Santiago à "nobreza da terra." Finais do séc. XV – início do séc. XVII*. Praia: Livraria Pedro Cardoso, 2015.

Coutinho, Marcelo et al., Raio X da integração regional, Estudos e Cenários. http://observatorio.iuperj.br. 2007.

Haas, E. *Beyond the Nation-State. Functionalism and International Organization*, Stanford University Press. 1964.

Kuhnhardt, L. *Africa Consensus -New Interests, Initiatives, and Partners*. Washington, DC: Woodrow Wilson Centre Press. 2014.

Manji, F. & Bill Fletcher Jr. (editors). *Claim No Easy Victories – The Legacy of Amílcar Cabral*. Published by CODESRIA (www.codesria.org). 2013.

Nye, J. *Power and Interdependence: World Politics in Transition*. Boston, MA: Little, Brown. 1971.

Santos, Maria Emília Madeira et al. *História Concisa de Cabo Verde (Coord. e org.)*. Lisboa-Praia: IICT-IIPC. 2007.

Teodoro de Matos, A. Santo Antão de Cabo Verde (1724–1732), II RIHA. 1996.

Tholen, Berry, "Regional Integration Organizations, Legitimacy and Democracy," in *Closing or the Widening Gap?* eds. A. R. Hoffmann and A. van der Vleuten. London: Routledge, 2007.

Chapter 3

Evolution and Macroeconomic Management of the Economy in Cabo Verde

Carlos Rocha

Over the years, during the period since independence until today, Cape Verde has been identified as a country that has succeeded in the process of growth and socio-economic development, compared to the economic and geographical region where it is located (African Development Bank 2012).

The results achieved can be considered satisfactory if one takes into account not only the starting point—having been a colony—but also the constraints of a small island economy that is insular, open, and virtually devoid of natural resources, highly vulnerable to shocks, both external and internal, and has periods of prolonged drought. In fact, it is worth mentioning the country's characteristics: an archipelago with ten islands of volcanic origin, extending over 4,033 square kilometers, lying some 500 kilometers off the west coast of Africa, situated in a dry tropical zone under the influence of the Sahara Desert. With a current population of about 500,000 inhabitants, it does not have an attractive or unified market. This result of relative success can also be attributed to the way the country has been able to take advantage of the financial and technical resources made available to it by external and international partners. Good governance and healthy, sound macroeconomic policies have yielded notable economic development and social progress.

This chapter provides an analysis of Cape Verde's macroeconomic developments since 1975, with a focus on the nature and changes of growth models and the macroeconomic policies adopted. It is divided into three major sections, each analyzing the three main stages of macroeconomic evolution. In a very brief way it can be said that, after becoming independent in 1975, during the succeeding decade, the country followed a model of import substitution industrialization through the creation of public, state-run enterprises. This inward-looking strategy proved to be inefficient due to several constraints, namely low productivity, a very small domestic market, logistical problems, high subsidies that were needed for companies to produce, and management problems.

When international public aid began to decline in the late 1980s, the balance of payments began to show signs of concern. During this period, signs of economic imbalance and the exhaustion of the existing model of economic growth began to emerge but without a clear long-term development strategy. It was at that time that the main external financing flows (foreign aid, despite the maintenance of remittances) also fell. At the same time, the process of economic reforms called economic extroversion began, albeit timidly.

In the 1990s, with the political opening toward a democratic regime, the new government embarked on the path of economic liberalization. The goal was reforming the state enterprise sector, privatizing the state-owned companies, with a view toward transforming the economy into a privately run economy where the state would cease to be a producer and become only a regulatory agent.

During the decade of the 1990s, there were successes and failures determined by structural problems, namely the pressures exerted on the balance of payments created by the imbalances in the external accounts. Domestic debt was another major problem that needed to be resolved urgently because high-interest rates on the debt consumed a lot of budget resources. In recent years following the 1999 shock—high oil and dollar prices and drought—macroeconomic imbalances have been corrected while stabilizing inflation and maintaining an acceptable and less volatile pace of growth, although at a slower rate than in the past decade.

Support from bilateral and multilateral external partners, such as the World Bank and the International Monetary Fund (IMF), was crucial during this period by providing technical assistance and concessional lending that enabled the country to build infrastructure and internal management capacity. Support for the creation of the Trust Fund, which made it possible to reduce the burden of debt and its interest rates, was a major step forward. We cannot forget the stabilization achieved by the nominal anchoring of the national currency, the Cape Verdean *escudo*, to the Portuguese currency and later to the Euro with the support of the Portuguese Ministry of Finance.

However, the pace of economic growth has slowed down in recent years, even before the 2008 crisis, as a result of the depletion of the growth model and also reflecting the state of the external economies in which the national economy was anchored. History has shown that any stabilization process, however successful, has always been dependent on the occurrence of factors beyond the control of economic policy, whether external shocks (oil prices, public and private transfers), or internal shocks (drought), since a poor agricultural year almost always meant spending on emergency programs and public employment that absorbed a large chunk of budgetary resources. A highly open micro-economy with a reduced production base is always vulnerable to these external and internal sources of shocks. The critical role of remittances has been notable, but they have also declined in their share of external flows over time.

Toward the end of the first decade of this new millennium, the international financial crisis began, with repercussions at various levels—the real economy, financial sector, balance of payments—forcing the country to deepen the process of reform and transformation begun at the outset of the decade. The country has a structural feature in which it cannot go beyond its small size and archipelagic condition, which increases vulnerabilities. As such, it is technically considered that fluctuations in the domestic product of small island economies are mainly caused by external factors due to their vulnerabilities and openness to the external market.

It can be said that at this time the economy faces challenges resulting from a new international context, and one that needs to be overcome if some dynamism in economic growth is to be regained. Basically, there are two sets of issues that need to be addressed: reducing vulnerabilities (external and internal) and resuming economic growth. The first issue involves greater prudence in the management of public finances (a process already started in response to the reduction of concessional lending), better integration of the internal market (transport and intermodal connections), improving the external market with a view to increasing exports, and finally, diversification of sources of growth and reduction of dependence on tourism. The second issue involves a more active private sector that promotes growth and employment, involves more active integration into the world economy through attracting external investment for export, resolving the problems of transport, and finally reducing the burden of the state in the economy to give more space to the private sector. The private sector will need to build capacity by partnering with external partners to solve the problems of financing, technology, know-how, and access to export markets.

RESOLVING URGENT PROBLEMS AND ESTABLISHING THE FOUNDATIONS, 1975–1991 (POLITICAL OPENING)

Macroeconomic Situation

This section aims to describe and analyze the macroeconomic situation from independence to the time of political and economic opening in the early 1990s. Much of this analysis is based on other works (Rocha 1997, 2006).[1]

The choice of this period was, of course, a result of the structural change that occurred at the political and economic level, mainly, the paradigm shift in 1991 from a centralized economy dominated by public enterprises in the state sector to a market-based economy led by the private sector. This change, as it happened, was due to the fact that a more liberal political party came to power in 1991. Before going into detail about politics, let us briefly describe the main features of the economy in the early post-independence period.

Brief Characterization of the Economy

The Cape Verdean economy has some characteristics that end up conditioning the choices of economic policy. Among these characteristics, we will address four, namely: size, insularity, absence of natural mineral resources, and the structure of GDP.

1. *Dimension*: The economy is among the world's small island states, with a small open economy and very dependent on the outside, both from the point of view of the monetary flows for its development financing and the real flows of imported goods and services. An economy of this reduced size, for example, does not guarantee economic efficiency in the exploitation of infrastructure that must be duplicated in the main islands. It is also not attractive to foreign investment, except tourism.
2. *Insularity*: In addition to its reduced size, the economy suffers from double insularity as an island state and an archipelago. The physical and territorial disconnection of the country from the mainland and the fragmentation of the territory into nine inhabited islands, aggravated by poor maritime and air links, means that, in practice and in many situations, we no longer have one single economic space but nine micro spaces; in some cases, we confront the impossibility of movement of agricultural products from producing islands (Santo Antão, S. Nicolau) to the consumer islands (Sal, Boa Vista, tourist islands par excellence). These two characteristics have consequences, namely, high factor costs, the impossibility of economies of scale, and the impossibility of building a single internal market. On the other hand, there are no regular cargo connections between Cape Verde and the economies of the economic region where it is located—the Economic Community of West African States (ECOWAS), the main vehicle for free trade and economic integration in the region.
3. *Absence of Natural Resources and Poor Precipitation*: Besides the two characteristics mentioned above, Cape Verde lacks natural mineral resources and raw materials capable of making the country desirable for external investment. The only natural resources, with commercial

expression, exploitation, and export in scale, are fisheries resources but these are limited by the sustainability policy (recently, there have been efforts to exploit ornamental stones for export). Combining these three characteristics, the result is a difficult environment for industrial activity because factor costs are high, context costs are high, there are no economies of scale, and there are no local raw materials. The primary sector is basically one of subsistence.

4. *GDP Structure*: Although conditioned by the characteristics mentioned above, there has been a change in the structure of the economy and in its contribution to the national wealth. Let us look at this evolution.

Agriculture and Fisheries—In spite of employing around 55 percent of the population, it contributed only 17 percent to GDP in 1991, which shows the weakness and the low productivity of the sector (Associação Industrial Portuguesa 1992). Today the primary sector comprises about 8 percent of GDP. It is estimated that, due to persistent drought in the period 1982–1987, 90 percent of food requirements have been met through imports. Only in 1987, due to the abundance of rainfall, the local production was able to satisfy 25 percent of its food needs (AIP 1992).

Successive governments have worked hard to increase the irrigated area using techniques to retain rainwater and exploit underground water. Of the 39,000 hectares of arable land in the study period, only 2,000 were irrigated, and the rain-fed area was 11,000 hectares (AIP 1992). More recently, the new policy guidelines have been in the direction of the construction of dams on several islands for the retention of rainwater.

The main natural resources the country has are at sea, with an Exclusive Economic Zone of 700,000 square kilometers, where fish and lobster are extracted, which represent more than two-third of exports (Silvestre 1994). In 1990, fish exports accounted for 43 percent of total national exports (data from III Plano Nacional de Desenvolvimento, Relatórios Sectoriais 1992). By comparison, although it is not part of this review period, in 2014, fishing accounted for about 85 percent of total merchandise exports (BCV 2015). This sector was a major source of employment, as it employed 5,400 people directly, and 4,968 in pre- and post-fishing activities. About 86 percent of the fishermen practiced artisanal fishing, while the industrial fishery focused mostly on export.

In 1990, the agriculture, forestry, and fishing sector occupied 43 percent of the population for a production that does not reach 10 percent of the needs. About 54 percent of the farmland properties had less than 1 hectare of the area and less than 3 percent exceeded 5 hectares due to soil morphology (Silvestre 1994). The most important crops are maize, beans, cassava, bananas, common, and sweet potatoes.

Industry—Industrialization was a bet of the country from the first years of independence. The goal was industrialization that would replace imports, promote exports, and thus spare foreign exchange for the country. The government recognized industry as the engine of the economy because of the benefits it would bring to employment, growth, and foreign trade. These objectives were not achieved. For example, in terms of employment, industry represented an average of 6 percent of GDP but absorbed about 4 percent of total employment: 10.7 percent in public enterprises, 17.5 percent in mixed companies, and 71.8 percent in private companies (Silvestre 1994).

The internal obstacles to economic development do not permit diversification, concentrating the weak industrial apparatus in the areas of agri-food, fishing, building materials, ship repair, metal mechanics, clothing, footwear, furniture, paints, and pharmaceuticals. The sector was heavily dependent on the outside world, only on the input side because production is destined for the domestic market. But, on the other hand, the reduced size of the market has been a strong obstacle to industrialization, with the units installed working below the installed capacity.

In 1991, the industrial sector occupied 27 percent of the working population, and civil construction occupied most of the sector (III Plano Nacional de desenvolvimento 1992). The bulk of the industrial fabric was concentrated in the two main poles that are São Vicente and Praia, where 93.4 percent of the main industrial units were located. The extractive industry was not very expressive—salt and pozzolana—with manufacturing being the most important. With regard to productivity and employment, 900 new jobs were created between 1986 and 1990, bringing industrial employment to around 3,900, representing an average annual growth of 5.4 percent (Associação Industrial Portuguesa 1992).

Tourism—The evolution of tourism has been characterized by the qualitative and quantitative evolution of infrastructure and by the fact that, in the 1980s, it did not have the same importance that the government gives it today. In July 1990, there were forty hotel units with a total of 920 rooms and 1,600 beds. If the industrial activity is concentrated in Praia and Mindelo, tourism is concentrated on the island of Sal with about 42 percent of hotel capacity, followed by the island of Santiago with 25.5 percent and São Vicente with 16 percent. Recently, with the infrastructure on the island of Boa Vista, this island has become the main tourist destination.

During the early period, the occupancy rate was 67.8 percent in Sal, with the occupants being aircrews, European visitors, and emigrants. The number of visitors at that time was around 20,000 annually. In 2016, thanks to investments, the number of tourists has already exceeded 500,000.

Domestic Commerce—Since agriculture is scarce due to natural conditions and industry is incipient, needs have been met through imports. In 1990, the value of imports accounted for 54 percent of GDP. From independence to the economic opening, the distribution of food and necessities was exclusively controlled by the state-run company, the Empresa Pública de Abastecimento (Public Enterprise for Provisions [popularly known by its acronym, EMPA]).

ECONOMIC GROWTH AND ITS SOURCES

The first leaders of the post-independence country faced a Herculean task: to lead a new country, without financial or natural resources, without experience of governance, practically without technically qualified human resources, and a country without infrastructure. Hence the first six years after independence involved tactical governance of the country (emergency programs to solve basic needs of the population and financed by cooperation). The following years saw the first medium-term strategies: I and II National Development Plans, based on a model in which the state was the principal agent that promoted development focusing on the goal of industrialization based on the substitution of imports. It was notable that the first national development plans were contemplated six years after independence.

Thus, from 1975 to 1981, the situation the country found itself in was of profound backwardness: a weak productive structure, a subsistence agricultural sector, and a virtually non-existent industry, a desolate scenario that put into question the economic viability of the country. Nevertheless, the economy grew due to the flow of foreign aid resources from international cooperation, as well as remittances from emigrants. The high growth rate of the product is also justified by the very low starting point due to the delay in the period before independence. United Nations figures point to a growth of 2.1 percent in 1976 and 5.3 percent in 1980 (figure 3.1).

The social situation is a reflection of the poor economic performance, characterized by a population that in the pre-independence period was considered excessive, leading to high unemployment rates coupled with a situation of structural unemployment. This situation stems from the facts mentioned above, that is, a large part of the population (55%) is linked to subsistence farming facing long periods of drought.

With an incipient, reduced, and fragmented productive structure, and high unemployment, emigration was an escape valve that helped to alleviate the impact of population growth on resources, on unemployment, and, later on, a source of balance of payments financing. The size of the private sector at this time was meaningless and, as such, unable to create infrastructure or development projects; it concentrated primarily in the agriculture, fisheries, civil construction, and retail sectors.

Independence in 1975 was to be the opportunity for development and breaking the cycle of underdevelopment and poverty. Given the absence of

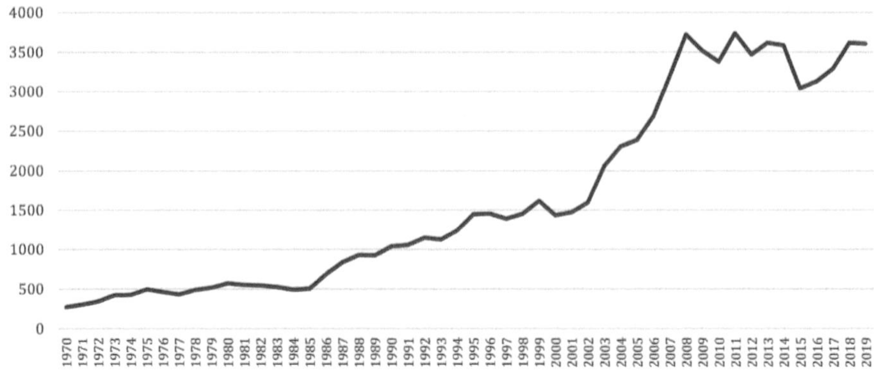

Figure 3.1 Cabo Verde GDP per Capita, in USD. *Source*: Created with data from United Nations, UNData, Statistical Division, 2021.

the private sector, the main actor would have to be the state to organize the economy, design and implement the development model, create infrastructure and mobilize resources. Due to this fact, the first years of the country were marked by the intense diplomatic effort in the mobilization of external resources. This was the reason why public aid was the main motor in that period. Between 1975 and 1981, the country mobilized about $242 million of foreign aid (Rocha 2006).

During this period, the economy had an economic structure dominated by the primary sector, hence large and frequent droughts meant serious economic and social problems. The strategy was to change the structure of the economy, while the primary sector lost weight in the product, and the tertiary and the secondary sectors continued to grow demonstrating that such a structural change was taking place (figure 3.2).

From 1982 to 1991, the first development plans emerged. However, while in conceiving the operation of the economy and its financing, there were no major differences compared to the previous period; the main difference with the plans arose with the introduction of deliberate planning which aimed to set a medium-term development path. The first development plan, I PND (1982–1985), aimed to solve the pressing problems of basic infrastructure and industrialization of the country, job creation, and poverty reduction. As conceived in the model itself, it was necessary to develop a highly protected and highly subsidized state-run business sector to enable the realization of economic and social programs.

The financing for the PND I (initially $450 million) was basically from bilateral and multinational international cooperation, as well as remittances from emigrants and some revenues from the commercial activity of the international airport on the island of Sal.

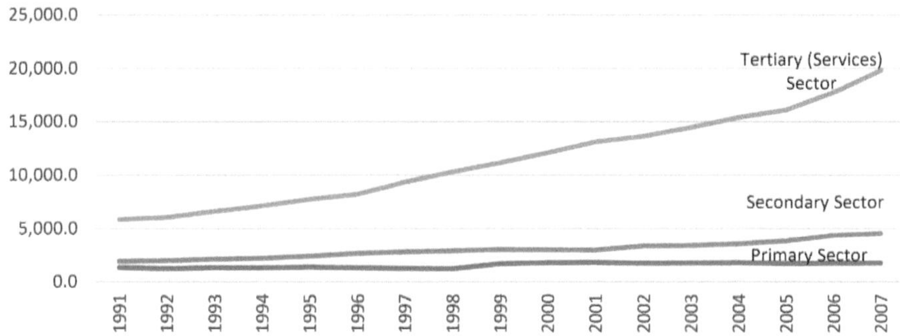

Figure 3.2 Structure of the Economy, Millions of ECV, 1980 Constant Prices. *Source*: Created with data from Banco de Cabo Verde (BCV), *Boletim de Estatísticas 20 Anos*. Praia: BCV, 2012.

Despite the unfavorable world context, the results were positive: moving from an average annual growth from 2.7 percent in the pre-independence decade to 6 percent (projected to have been 9.8 percent) in post-independence years. At the level of employment, the number of jobs created corresponded to half of the proposed target.

The Second National Development Plan (II PND 1986/1990) had as its main objective the consolidation of the gains from the previous plan. At the same time, it sought to reduce dependency on aid and sought to diversify the sources of growth. To this end, it chose four priority sectors: light industry, fisheries, tourism, and services. Growth prospects were not as ambitious as the previous plan, predicting growth of 4.5 percent and the creation of around 10,500 jobs per year. The completion of these projects under the plan required financial resources in the order of $503 million from the same sources as the previous plan.

A CRITIQUE OF THE STATE-OWNED ENTERPRISE SECTOR

The planners were aware of the multiple objectives that are often assigned to public enterprises, namely, promotion of employment, redistribution of income, as well as profit-making as productive economic entities. However, a negative effect was notable due to the intervention of other sectors and the lack of coordination between the activities of the companies and the plans of the state, that is, for the finance ministry, the goal would be profits, for the ministry of employment, it would be the reduction of unemployment. The implementation report of the II PND even concluded that the state enterprise group was something that did not exist but only companies supervised by different ministries.

Notwithstanding this criticism, the fact is that public and mixed enterprises were the instruments for the implementation of various government policies in activities and sectors such as tax collection, housing, the marketing of food aid, agri-food production, and livestock.

Balance of Payments

The I PND sought an investment of $450 million over the three years; funding was provided through private transfers (remittances) and public donations, guaranteeing the necessary balance of payments. The importance of external flows was evident. That is, 80 percent of the funding came from foreign donations. In the same period, these transfers grew at the average annual rate of 23.2 percent and contributed greatly to the positive balance of payments. It should be remembered that thanks to these sources, it was always possible—even though the trade balance was critical during the period—to have a balanced global balance of payments, allowing the accumulation of foreign exchange reserves and a level of national consumption higher than the wealth being produced.

Regarding the period during which the second plan was in effect, it was not possible to carry out all the investments, precisely due to the lack of funds to finance them. Several warning signs emerged showing the need to change the development model and to diversify funding sources. The current accounts balance became negative as a result of insufficient transfers in relation to the deficit in the balance of services and income. The productive base was not strengthened, and exports did not live up to expectations. What actually balanced the current account was the financial flows of remittances from emigrants and international development aid.

Monetary and Exchange Rate Situation

In terms of monetary and exchange rate developments, monetary policy was inconsistent in allowing the growth of the monetary mass/GDP ratio above 8.2 percent between 1986 and 1990 (IMF 1992). Put differently, in practical terms, the ratio indicates that the growth in the amount of money circulated was proportionally higher than the domestic wealth created, which could have adverse effects in terms of the increase in inflation and consequent internal loss of value of the national currency and/or the reduction of external reserves.

But it was a reflection of lax budget policy in existence because, despite the reduction of net external assets in 1989, the money supply grew more than expected due to the unprogrammed needs of the public sector.

This growth in the money supply—above the growth of reserves—led to an increase in liquidity in the market and consequently the growth of domestic credit by around 16.1 percent per year. In an open economy such as the import-dependent Cape Verdean economy, to meet domestic demand, increased lending increases imports and thereby puts pressure on foreign exchange reserves. It is recalled that at the time the exchange rate regime was not fixed but rather the value of the national currency quotation was made on the basis of a basket of representative currencies of external relations (remittances, imports, external debt).

Macroeconomic Management—Instruments, Institutions, and Policies

Fiscal and Budgetary Policy

During the initial phase of the process, soon after independence, the priority naturally was to meet the basic needs of the population and begin to build the state. There were certainly no economic policy instruments, including fiscal and budgetary instruments, not least because the country did not have sufficient qualified human resources. The precarious social situation justified some increase of expenditure in the First National Development Plan, mainly social expenditure to reduce unemployment. However, by the second development plan, there was a moderation in the growth of public expenditure, now limited to a growth ceiling of 4.1 percent—compared with 13 percent of the previous plan—which necessitated reforms in public administration, agriculture, and education in order to avoid budget overruns.

As a result, between 1976 and 1981 public expenditures, basically financed by international aid, grew at an annual average rate of 12 percent in real terms; the public sector alone contributed 48 percent of GDP. A decade later, specifically in 1986, the budget remained strongly oriented on the social front (education, health, housing, urbanization, and sanitation), consuming 22 percent of resources against 31 percent of productive sectors and 47 percent for supporting sectors, based on data from the implementation report of the II PND in 1986.

Monetary and Exchange Rate Policy

Prior to the creation of the central bank, Banco de Cabo Verde (BCV), in 1993, and the nominal anchoring of the national currency to the currency of Portugal in 1998, there was no strategic and operational framework to define monetary and exchange rate policy. Likewise, there was no concern with the definition of a strategic or operational framework for monetary policy in the context of that time, in the sense that monetary policy is understood today as an instrument of economic policy. Indeed, there was not a central bank but a monolithic system in which the same institution operated as a central bank, as well as a development and commercial bank. On the other hand, interest rates were administered and fixed according to the economic activity sector.

During the period of the second plan, monetary policy was essentially exercised by establishing the limits to the expansion of credit and its distribution in the economy would be determined according to the same plan. Interest rates were fixed administratively and used as an instrument of selectivity in the distribution of credit (Rocha 2007). The intermediate objective was, given the open nature of the economy, the stability of the exchange rate in order to achieve a controllable rate of inflation, with the main axes being the maintenance of a financeable deficit in the current account balance, price stability, and development of the national economy. Control of domestic liquidity would also ensure the objective of increasing reserves (BCV 1982).

IN SEARCH OF AN ANCHOR FOR DEVELOPMENT, ECONOMIC PARADIGM SHIFT—1992–2008

Macroeconomic Situation

The choice of this historic landmark has to do with the socio-political changes that were taking place in the world and which had internal repercussions. In fact, with the end of the Cold War and the collapse of the Eastern Bloc, the least developed countries lose a reference point from among various points of view, including the economic development model. Internally, until then the country had been governed by a single-party regime that came to an end, in the wake of these international events and democratic elections, promoting a change to a democratic regime. Thus, it can be said that the most important political event that marked this period (and which was decisive for what happened next) was the democratic transition—a pioneering and peaceful transition in Africa that would become a model for the rest of the continent. Following the 1991 elections, a new political party emerged and won. As a more liberal (center-right) party, its economic program has basically focused on the transformation of the economy into a privately based economy based on market principles.

The weaknesses of the existing development model based on recycling aid flows and remittances resulted in worsening debt, poor productivity, and low profitability of many public investments (along with the import substitution policy and other forms of protection that served to increase costs), as a consequence of the decrease of these foreign aid and of the poor performance of the national economy.

The new model adopted in 1992 was a market-based economy model, whose main vectors were the reinforcement of the role of the private sector as the direct and primary economic agent, the reduction of state intervention in the economy, openness to foreign investment, and the search for full and dynamic insertion of the country in the world economic system.

Among the targets for reforms were the banking and insurance sectors. In the real sector of the economy, the restructuring of the state-owned enterprises (privatization, reform, and liquidation) and the attempt to attract external investment were underway. It is from this context that a new paradigm is born and the search for a new anchorage.

Economic Growth and Its Sources

After a period of high growth with annual average rates of around 7 percent, the economy began to struggle with difficulties in the late 1980s and early 1990s, which eventually led to a slowdown in the rate of growth, from 6.6 percent during 1885–1888 to only 4 percent in 1989–1990.

Macroeconomic imbalances increased both internally and externally, resulting in accelerated domestic debt growth, increasingly negative domestic savings, aggravated public sector deficit, and rising inflation. All this is not unrelated to the reduction of funding in the form of international public aid to the economy. Prolonged droughts and the reduction of port, air, and maritime services contributed to the reduction of external capital financing flows of the economy (with the reduction of Sal international airport revenues accounting for much more along with the restrictive policies of emigration countries). Without external financing, the solution was to resort to internal credit with the central bank, accumulating arrears of debt that also had consequences for the level of inflationary pressures. It is worth noting that inflation went from 4.2 percent in 1987 to 10 percent in 1990.

At the external level, the balance had begun to show successive deficits since 1989, but also in 1990, as a result of increased imports of agricultural goods, naturally to cope with another year of low precipitation. The evolution of the external sector presented to the authorities one of the biggest constraints to growth due to the degree of openness of the economy and the poor performance of exports.

At this point in time, the state-owned enterprise sector could not help much due to its poor economic performance resulting from (a) the fall in the financial results of a well-protected sector and guided by a social objective; (b) the reduction of public investments due to a lack of external funds; (c) inadequate financial sector, unable to provide credit to enterprises and the whole economy at a cost compatible with needs; and (d) inadequate infrastructure for economic development, such as energy, water, and transport.

The III PND had positive results in terms of social sectors, infrastructure, and the creation of favorable conditions for business development. The targets for reducing unemployment were not achieved, and macroeconomic imbalances were further aggravated, notably the increase in public debt, the reduction of external reserves, and the widening of the current account deficit. It was not possible to reverse the external position because imports grew faster than exports (17.5% versus only 11.9%). As a result, it was not possible to escape from external transfers as a financing mechanism for the balance.

It can be concluded, however, that there was a gain in reversing the fall in the growth rate of the product. In fact, after stagnation in the previous period, the GDP grew at the annual average rate of 7.5 percent supported by large private transfers (remittances were 29% of GDP). This growth was also the result of previous bets on attracting foreign investment and promoting tourism. By 1990, the tourism sector accounted for 1.3 percent of GDP and employed 772 people in hospitality and 60 more in travel agencies, according to the III Plano Nacional de Desenvolvimento, 1992. Inflation was stabilized at 2 percent aided by the nominal anchorage made possible by the exchange agreement with Portugal.

In 2000, as a result of the expansionary fiscal policy, at a time when both fiscal revenues and external aid flows stagnated, the government deficit reached 19 percent of GDP. On the other hand, the 6.6 percent growth of GDP, influenced by imports, and in a context of negative inflation (-2.4%) combined with the increase in liquidity caused by fiscal policy, ended up having effects on the reduction of reserves and pressure on the exchange rate regime. Several factors contributed to the imbalances observed between 1999 and 2000, namely, the oil shock of 1999, the drought and bad agricultural year, and the assumption of the bad student debt portfolio during the banking privatization. This figure reached 1.2 percent of GDP in 2000.

Fiscal and Budgetary Situation

On the fiscal and budgetary side, there were two factors that affected economic performance and particularly the budget balance: the rise in the price of oil in the international market (subsidized domestically) and the government's takeover of student loans and scholarships which the central bank had granted to students for their higher education before the privatization of commercial banking. Worsening the situation, the year 1999 was one of drought. Budgetary expenditure thus increased by 68 percent between 1998 and 2000, leading to a widening of the deficit to 18.9 percent of GDP compared to 11 percent the previous year. The financing of the deficit was mainly due to the accumulation of external debt arrears, an increase in domestic debt, and privatization revenues that were diverted to the budget.

Monetary and Exchange Rate Situation

Once again, the increase in the money supply led to an increase in domestic liquidity, which, given the characteristics of the national economy, exerted pressure on reserves and deteriorated the country's external position. Thus, external reserves were reduced by 18.2 percent between 1993 and 1995.

As for the instruments, it was during this period that the process of interest rate liberalization began (the lending rates were liberalized in 1995) in order to move gradually toward the use of indirect monetary policy management instruments. However, credit ceilings remained the most widely used instrument. Another instrument used was the reserve ratio for commercial banks, which increased from 12 percent to 17 percent in 1995. The same coefficient was to be changed from 17 percent to 20 percent in 1996 but was reduced before the end of the year to 15 percent, but the incidence base was loosened (BCV 1996).

These developments in monetary policy cannot be separated from the measures taken to liberalize the external sector. The combined effect of the expansionary monetary policy and the liberalization of the external sector led to an increase in imports and a consequent deterioration in the external position of the economy. Liberalization presupposed a high stock of external reserves because reducing price pressures would increase the pressure on reserves.

Balance of Payments

The current account deficit improved moderately, from 13.7 percent of GDP in 1999 to 10.8 percent in 2000, due to the dynamism of exports and the slower growth of imports. This result alone, however, was not much better because of the negative effects of the oil shock on the deterioration of the terms of trade (more than 9% between 1999 and 2000) and in the state budget (table 3.1).

The current deficit as a percentage of GDP between 1999 and 2008 does not have a clear trend, initially improving after 2005 onward to grow again. Migrant remittances continued losing weight in GDP, but not because they have been decreasing in absolute terms, but because the rate of GDP growth has been higher than the rate of growth of remittances.

The debt service lost weight in this period under review, but due to the higher growth of GDP, because, as will be seen later in the following period, the debt skyrocketed for the reason already mentioned, causing the service of the debt to increase its weight in GDP.

There is a clear increase in external reserves during this period. It is recalled that following the adoption of the peg with the Portuguese *escudo* of that time, there was an increase of confidence in the economy which attracted more exchange revenues, both from investment and remittances.

MACROECONOMIC MANAGEMENT—INSTRUMENTS, INSTITUTIONS, AND POLICIES

With the end of the inward-looking, state-led model, indicated by the increase in internal and external imbalances and weak economic growth, a change in economic policy became imperative, accelerated by the political change of 1991 following the first free, democratic and multiparty elections in the country's history. The new, more liberal party took power in 1991 following

Table 3.1 Principal Macroeconomic Indicators

Rubric	1999	2000	2001	2002	2003
Current Deficit % GDP	13.72	10.86	10.62	10.35	10.23
Remittances % GDP	13.07	15.85	13.66	13.44	11.45
External Debt Service/ Total Exports	10.35	10.80	7.75	9.93	8.28
Liquid Reserves in Months Imports	1.50	0.99	1.54	2.01	1.83
Rubric	**2004**	**2005**	**2006**	**2007**	**2008**
Current Deficit % GDP	13.26	3.78	6.80	12.94	16.81
Remittances % GDP	10.13	12.47	10.82	8.83	8.20
External Debt Service/ Total Exports	9.15	8.05	5.95	5.09	4.48
Liquid Reserves in Months Imports	2.37	3.40	3.6	4.1	4.0
Rubric	**2009**	**2010**	**2011**	**2012**	**2013**
Current Account Deficit, % GDP	17.66	18.20	18.49	10.92	4.02
Remittances, % GDP	7.54	7.46	9.54	9.54	9.06
External Debt Service/ Total Exports	5.43	4.95	4.13	4.29	4.51
Liquid Reserves in Months Imports	4.2	4.2	3.2	4.0	4.9

Source: Created with data from Banco de Cabo Verde (BCV), *Boletim de Estatísticas 20 Anos*. Praia: BCV, 2012.

the outcome of the elections and eventually took steps to turn the centralized economy into a market economy, guided by private initiative. In the summer of 1992, the National Assembly discussed the privatization program, and in September the economic reform project began.

The new model started in 1992 is a model of the market economy, whose main vectors are the reinforcement of the role of the private sector as a direct economic agent, reduction of state intervention in the economy, openness to foreign investment, and the search for full and dynamic insertion of the country in the world economic system. The new model was consistent with economic transformations in other regions of the world at that time.

The Third National Development Plan (III PND) is the central document that marks the economic transformations, in the sense that it seeks to move from a centralized model in which the state was the motor of development, to a model based on the market, private initiative, and the active insertion of the national economy into the world system. It should be noted that, in this respect, the document is not totally original, since the II PND (1986/1990) argued for greater private initiative and openness to the outside world. What is new is the total rupture with the past, since the state intended to leave the productive functions, worrying more about the maintenance of a stable economic framework. The state gave place to entrepreneurs as the agents of the development process, guided by the market mechanisms through the attraction of the external investment and the reform of the state-owned enterprise sector (SOE), via liquidation or privatization.

The III PND advocates a model that gives precedence to the private sector and which should be based on improving productivity, improving factor costs, and improving the market. The state has designated the role of modernizing the economy through investments in infrastructure, modernizing society through a break with underdevelopment—participatory human development, better education, health and nutrition, the environment, and reduction of poverty.

At the institutional level, two reforms were introduced: in public administration and in education. The need for reform of public administration was evident because its functioning was an obstacle to business development and the pursuit of private economic activity, both because of the poor quality of its services and because of the high cost of bureaucracy. The challenges of the plan were to create measures to modernize the sector, streamline its structure, simplify procedures, that is, break with the existing model, and introduce innovation. Within this framework, the key to improving services would be human resources. A second vector, initiated during the second term of the government, contemplated the modernization of the public administration through the introduction of information and communications technologies (ICTs), mainly in the areas of public financial management. This was the beginning of what is now called e-government, as well as the establishment in 1998 of the State Administrative and Financial Reform project (RAFE), which later became the Operational Nucleus for the Information Society (NOSI).

Education reform was imperative for its adaptation to the development process. The objective was therefore to raise the qualification of the general population and to ensure the training of qualified staff, to equip them with the tools to accompany economic and social development. Training was also an essential component of employment policy aimed, in particular, at young people to enter the job market, including the massification of education, vocational education, and the construction of secondary schools in all municipalities. In 1992, a Commission for Higher Education was created.

The document, the Grand Options of the Plan in 1997–2000, was the second instrument guiding public policies during this period. Its elaboration must be understood in the context of the results of the III PND, namely, the persistence of macroeconomic imbalances already considered structural. For example, the rate of import coverage rose from 4.8 percent in 1990 to 2.6 percent in 1994 and 3.8 percent in 1995 as a result of an accelerated increase in imports, despite a slight improvement in exports. Economic liberalization coupled with expansionary monetary and fiscal policies led to increased imports, so the external position deteriorated by 12.7 percent.

It was in this context that the document Grand Options of the Plan was drafted, whose objectives were (a) to ensure internal and external balances, (b) to develop the market and private initiative, (c) to value human resources. Other goals were also established:

- GDP growth never below 5 percent;
- Maintenance of the public deficit below 5 percent;
- Promotion of public employment policies to reduce unemployment; and
- Improvement of national production and food security.

The plan consisted of five major programs: (a) public administration reform, (b) improvement of transportation infrastructure, (c) promotion of human development, (d) development of natural resources, and (e) strengthening of democracy.

INSTITUTIONAL FRAMEWORK FOR PRIVATIZATION

The III PND determined that the restructuring of the state-owned enterprise sector constituted one of the strategic axes of the government's economic policy. As such, it was enshrined in the government program, which stems from the choice of a model of economic and social development guided by market mechanisms and driven by the private sector. The reasons for the choice relating to the unsatisfactory or negative performance in some cases of this sector, both in terms of financial results and the quality/price of products and services provided to the public. At the legal level, the guarantee to private property and a definition of the basic rules of the institutional framework of the economic system are necessary to convey the trust for private investment. The privatization process is one of the measures that emerged as part of the reforms that began in 1986.

As we have already mentioned, the change in the economic system, and more precisely the change in ownership, necessarily involved a change in legislation. With a view to giving greater transparency and legitimacy to the process, the entire process of disposing of state assets was regulated by Decree Law no. 47 / IV / 92, of July 6, 1992 (Framework Law on Privatizations). It should be noted that the SOE restructuring process was managed by the Office for the Restructuring of the State Enterprise Sector (GARSEE), duly established by the legislative framework.

The framework law on privatizations in Article 2 defines the objectives of the procedure:

- Increasing the Efficiency, Productivity, and Competitiveness of the Economy and Enterprises;
- Reducing the State's Weight in the Economy and the Development of the Private Sector;
- Fostering Business Development and Strengthening National Entrepreneurship;
- The Participation of National Citizens, in Particular, Workers, Emigrants, and Small Shareholders in the Ownership of the Capital of the Companies.

Since privatization is an interconnected process and within a broader framework of economic reforms, the definition of these objectives must be consistent. That is why Article 31 determined that state revenues from privatization would be used, separately or jointly, only for:

- Business Development;
- Investment in the Area of Vocational Training; and
- Amortization of Public Debt.

Each enterprise to be privatized should have a specific treatment for determining the particular objectives (within the general objectives) and the most appropriate privatization modality. The specific objectives would be set taking into account the nature and sector of activity of the company, the size, and the economic and financial situation (III PND).

Privatization Policy, Legal Framework

Within the framework of economic reforms, the government's economic policy aimed at restructuring the SOE sector and reducing the state's weight as a direct economic agent. This restructuring process had two aspects: the privatization of public enterprises and state holdings in other companies and the reorganization of companies that remain in the public sector.

The III PND stated that

> the problem of restructuring the SOE sector should not be seen in isolation. On the contrary, it is part of a broader process of liberalization and general privatization of the Cape Verdean economy and society, of creating an environment conducive to the development of private enterprise. (III PND 1992, 75)

Included as one of the objectives of the process (and even though measures were being taken to establish a stable nucleus of shareholders to foster and develop national entrepreneurial capacity and ensure the normal functioning of the company), ownership diffusion is promoted through subscription mechanisms, with part of the capital reserved for small shareholders, in particular workers and emigrants.

Foreign investment was called upon to intervene through a rather favorable external investment law. It was necessary, especially in companies where the technological factor and know-how, in general, were decisive for the development of the company and the sector.

The privatization policy defined the objectives of the program, but in order to achieve those objectives, it was necessary to take into account:

- *The Mobilization of National Entrepreneurial Capacity*: the national business community should have a more active role, including leading the restructuring process in relevant aspects. But, unfortunately, this has not happened, mainly because of the many obstacles faced.
- *Access to Technologies and Know-How*: The III PND advocates that a stable nucleus should be created for companies where the technological factor and know-how are decisive, while the framework law on privatizations, in Article 5, defended the option of limited tender or direct sale, for the constitution of groups of national shareholders with business experience and technological absorption capacity, in joint ventures with foreign investment.

- *Raising External Financial Resources*: Taking into account the structural obstacles of the economy (lack of financial resources, technology, and small size of the geographically fragmented market), it was clear that external capital should be called alone or in partnership with the national private sector. Another aspect of the external resources that was called was emigrants' savings, for which Article 14 established benefits such as (a) deduction of the tax on the complementary tax of the dividends corresponding to the shares acquired; (b) guarantee of purchase of shares by the company within the limits fixed by law; (c) the right to one or more supplementary shares, free of charge.
- *Mobilizing Domestic Savings*: Namely, small subscribers and the general public. The same benefits considered in Article 14 of the framework law have been attributed.
- *Development of New Possibilities for Effective Employment*: It was inevitable that the entire restructuring process, not only of the SOEs and of public administration, would lead to worker dismissals in an economy with an already high unemployment rate. To create alternatives to alleviate unemployment, the government signed training protocols with the World Bank. Also encouraged was the creation of income-generating activities by those who left the public sector (promotion of self-employment).

Privatization Methods

The framework law provided, in Article 6, that the sale of the shares should be carried out, as a rule, by public tender or public subscription. Paragraph 2 of the same article stated that, by imposing a national interest determination, the alienation of the shares could be carried out by means of a limited tender or direct sale, with a view to the creation of a strong nucleus.

Article 8 defined public subscription as the launching of shares on the market where they could be purchased at the price fixed by any person, while Article 9 stated that the restricted tender would be open only to a limited number of specially qualified and pre-selected candidates, among which would be the comparative assessment, evaluation, and selection of purchasers. Article 10 defined direct selling as the award of the capital to be sold to one or more purchasers without a call for tenders. Article 12 also provided for capital reserve for workers, small subscribers, and emigrants.

For its part, the III PND maintains that limited tendering and direct negotiation should be used in special cases, where the economic and financial situation so determines or in situations where the transfer of know-how is decisive for the development of the company.

Methods Used

The methods used in the privatization of the various companies and participations varied according to the importance of the company, its economic and financial situation, the availability of local financial resources and the sector of activity.

Article 3 of the framework law provided that privatization, whether partial or total, should be carried out alternatively or cumulatively by the following processes: divestment of share capital, capital increase, spin-off, liquidation, and leasing or exploration contracts.

In practice, the following methods were used:

- *Alienation of Shares*: Shares held by the state were put up for sale at a fixed price and for a set period of time;
- *Sale of Assets*: This method allows the sale of all or part of the assets of the enterprise;
- *Break-up*: This method allows the reorganization of public companies in several units, which are then privatized separately (it was the policy followed in the telecommunications sector, where the state separated the postal services from telecommunications into two companies);
- *Direct Negotiation*: Consists in selling a public company through the direct negotiation with possible buyers (method followed for the sale of some hotel units);
- *Sale to Workers*: Consists of the acquisition of the company by the staff or employees and is used when the company is considered unsalable or difficult to sell, while still avoiding unemployment problems (restructuring of the poultry company acquired entirely by the workers); and
- *Operating License*: Business operating contract, as was the case for shipyards.

The Strategy Used

The strategy adopted to achieve the objectives envisaged implied the creation of a legal and institutional framework to legitimize the process, both from a legal and economic point of view. Basically, the process had two aspects: pre-privatization and privatization itself.

Pre-privatization entailed a more detailed knowledge of the SOE. It was carried out in three stages: the diagnosis of the whole sector through the studies already mentioned, the restructuring according to the data of the diagnosis, and, finally, the creation of economic-legal conditions for the development of the eventual private activity. For each company, an x-ray was taken, which included, besides other data, the number of establishments, corporate purpose, capital, net worth, turnover, employment volume, and a summary of economic and financial analysis. The restructuring involved the reduction of the excess workforce, redefinition of activities (such as the Arca Verde case, where it was recommended to withdraw long-haul navigation), and ceasing certain operations. The valuation of the assets of the companies was a necessary step because it allowed not only an idea of the value of the company but also to construct a reference for the appreciation of the proposals of purchase.

Privatization itself is the transfer of companies from the public to the private sector, culminating in the whole process already described. In summary, the privatization itself involved the launch of the public offering according to any of the methods described, evaluation of the purchase orders according to the defined criteria, final negotiation, and transfer of ownership.

Between 1992 and 2004, about four dozen state-owned enterprises were privatized. Privatizations took place in all sectors. The first privatization rounds focused on the energy, telecommunications, and banking sectors. Among the best-known companies privatized at that time were: Cabetur, the travel agency which was sold to workers, the beverage company Ceris, the pharmaceutical company Emprofac, SITA, Moave, the insurance company Garantia, the hotels Atlantico, Belo Horizonte, and Hotelmar, while the telecommunications company was divided into two entities, the Post Office that remains public today, and Cape Verde Telecom, which was privatized. Electra was also privatized, but due to structural problems, it was re-nationalized and subsequently restructured in 2014. Among the public companies not privatized at the time, but still remain candidates for privatization, are TACV, Enapor, and ASA—the aeronautical safety agency.

Fiscal and Budgetary Policy

Inherited from the previous model, the main objective of fiscal policy was to reduce the deficit by reducing current expenditure. Administrative reform aimed at reducing staff, mainly through early retirement and voluntary abandonment, a measure taken to rationalize expenditure in the context of a restrictive fiscal policy. In the SOE sector, the same would be achieved by liquidating and privatizing public companies, reducing the number of workers, and eliminating subsidies to loss-making companies. This objective, on the whole, was not achieved given the resistance as people preferred their job security.

On the fiscal side, the reforms aimed at combating tax evasion and avoidance, broadening the tax base, reformulating the entire tax structure by creating a single income tax, and improving the relationship between the tax authorities and taxpayers.

Monetary and Exchange Rate Policy

The country's financial system up to this point consisted basically of a credit institution with the function of the central bank and commercial bank—the BCV. There was also Caixa Económica de Cabo Verde, which was an independent public entity, which had the vocation of a savings institution and activity in the granting of credit, namely, housing.

The system was not very sophisticated or very demanding because it was appropriate to the economic reality, a mostly centralized economy and a private sector with little expression, while the public companies were financed through the use of the public resources through the central bank, generally with few restrictions.

The measures that would be implemented at the level of the real economy would have to be accompanied by changes in the financial system, which would support many of those measures. Thus, in 1990, the restructuring of the system began with the publication of Decree Laws 52-D/90, 52-E/90, and 52-F/90 of July 4, consisting of the BCV being discharged from the functions of commercial and development banking, the possibility of more commercial banks and the opening of the insurance sector to the private sector.

During the period of the development plan in place, monetary policy continued to focus on the priority objective of economic stabilization, taking into account the goals of price stability, defense of the fiscal balance, and economic financing (BCV 1993). Naturally, the reform of foreign exchange policy in this context was intended to facilitate the country's active insertion into the world economy. Due to global competition, this would only be achieved by increasing productivity and reducing costs.

The difficulty in managing monetary policy was evident, reflecting a cumulative increase in total domestic credit between 1993 and 1995 by 69.3 percent, as a result of the cumulative growth of money supply by 40 percent. Consequently, inflation rose from 5.8 percent in 1993 to 8.4 percent in 1995 (IMF 2001). In average terms, inflation averaged 7.2 percent between 1992 and 1995.

The year 1997 was marked by an expansionary monetary policy that worsened the external imbalance. This was evident in the growth of the money supply, by 12 percent, when the target was only 9.5 percent (BCV 1997), resulting in an increase in credit to the economy by 26 percent and total domestic credit by 20 percent. For a 5 percent product growth, the excess liquidity had repercussions on the level of inflation that was 8.6 percent (BCV 1997).

Faced with such imbalances, it was necessary to outline policies for adjustment. Thus, a more restrictive monetary policy was pursued in 1998, resulting in a growth of the monetary mass of only 1.8 percent, a growth of total domestic credit by 6.1 percent, and a reduction of 0.35 percent in credit to the state (BCV 1998), permitting credit to the economy. Despite this more restrictive policy, the GDP followed dynamism and grew almost 8 percent while inflation grew only 4.4 percent.

Another important result achieved was the reduction of external arrears from a balance of $38 million in June to $9 million in December. At the exchange rate level, the most important measure was the adoption of the new exchange rate regime that allowed the stabilization of – inflation fixed peg between the Cape Verde escudo and the Portuguese escudo. Changes were also made to the foreign exchange law in order to liberalize the current account and allow foreign accounts to be opened by resident nationals.

In 1999, the credit ceilings regime was definitively abandoned and the instruments of indirect control of monetary policy were used, through the variation of the monetary base. For this purpose, the intervention instruments were created, namely, intervention bonds and monetary adjustment instruments. In the same year, the reserve ratio was also changed. Other instruments of economic policy include the Stand-By agreement with the IMF, the exchange agreement with Portugal, and the establishment of the Trust Fund.

Other Measures and Policies

Within the framework of the economic reform package, a number of very important measures helped stabilize the economy.

(i) The IMF Stand-By Arrangement

In the context of the Grand Options of the Plan for 1997–2000, the government continued with the economic reforms. It was in this context that in 1998 it signed a Stand-By agreement with the IMF aimed at giving international credibility to the program. In fact, fiscal policies carried out between 1992 and 1995 led to a rapid increase in public expenditure, which was financed through increased domestic debt. The domestic deficit provoked more deficit of the external accounts and created the need for stabilization. Certain targets were established in relation to GDP growth (4%), inflation (3.5%), and the current account deficit (15.7%) of GDP As such, it was necessary to reduce the public deficit from 15.1 percent to 8.7 percent of GDP.

(ii) The Formation of the Offshore Trust Fund

For a micro-economy, foreign debt quickly becomes unbearable. As a result of successive debt financing through the issuing of securities, debt servicing reached 3 percent of GDP in 1997. This constituted an impediment to development, and it was, therefore, necessary to find a way to overcome this constraint. Subsequently, a process was initiated in 1998 to convert domestic debt into external debt under better conditions, including a lower interest rate. The process involved the establishment of a Trust Fund, aimed at eliminating the constraints arising from Cape Verde's high internal debt through the creation of a fund managed by the Bank of Portugal and funded by the proceeds of the privatizations, valued at $100 million, and from international donors by $80 million. The law required that domestic debt held by banks be converted into Consolidated Financial Mobilization Securities (TCMF), whose income would be indexed to the Trust Fund's international market yield.

The budgetary impact of the Trust Fund was initially very significant, with an evident reduction in debt service costs. Indeed, the value of the domestic debt interest rate declined from 2.9 percent of GDP in 1998 to 0.8 percent in 2000. Consistent with this behavior, the weight of domestic public debt interest on current expenditure fell from 14.2 percent in 1998, when they reached a critical level, to only 3.1 percent in 2000. From this year, an upward trend began again, so that in 2002, that percentage again reached the value of 9.5 percent.

Due to a number of problems (delays in donor disbursements, delayed privatization, misappropriation of funds to the state budget), the objective of reducing the domestic debt problem has not been fully achieved.

(iii) The Foreign Exchange Agreement with Portugal

One of the most significant measures in Cape Verde's macroeconomic policy in the post-independence era was the decision to fix the value of the Cape Verdean escudo to the Portuguese escudo, and later to the Euro. Thus, in 1998, the government signed an exchange cooperation agreement with Portugal, constituting yet another instrument for the stabilization of inflation and credibility of the economy. It aimed at strengthening foreign exchange reserves through an annual credit facility granted by the Portuguese Ministry of Finance up to a maximum amount of 44.9 million euros, to be amortized by December 31 of each year.

The agreement contained the following characteristics:

The connection of the Cape Verdean escudo (ECV) to the Portuguese currency through a fixed parity, which was later replaced by the euro;

- Guarantee of the convertibility of CVE by Portugal;
- Portuguese financial support through a credit line to strengthen exchange reserves;
- Adoption of the benchmarks of European Union member states in order to safeguard exchange parity.

The agreement would be followed by a Monitoring Commission for the Exchange Co-operation Agreement created for this purpose—COMACC. The Cape Verdean side would undertake to implement economic policy measures compatible with the safeguarding of exchange rate parity between the national currencies of the two parties, adopting as reference criteria those of the Member-States of the European Union.

Under COMACC, a Technical Unit for Macroeconomic Monitoring (UAM) is in charge of monitoring the functioning of the agreement and verifies compliance with the conditionality set forth in the agreement, keeping COMACC duly informed.

The agreement has been a success for both its direct and indirect effects. A direct consequence was that it anchored the country's inflation to the lower Euro area inflation and allowed internal currency stability. At the exchange rate level, risk and exchange rate uncertainties were minimized, a very useful factor in the attraction of investments and the contraction of external debt. Indirectly, it increased the confidence of all economic agents, especially foreign investors.

The results show that the agreement made it possible to stabilize the inflation rate and maintain the stability of the exchange rate regime, with financial support from the Portuguese Ministry of Finance. Soon after the agreement was signed, it was possible to verify the increase in remittances from emigrants.

(iv) Structural Adjustment Agreement with the World Bank

Like many other developing countries throughout the world, during the 1990s, Cape Verde was also a case of structural adjustment through an agreement with major international financial agencies. In this context, a stabilization program was created with support from the World Bank (WB) and the IMF that would be implemented between 2001 and 2003, with the objectives of (a) restoring macroeconomic balances, (b) alleviating the impact of the oil shock on the budget, and (c) to lay the foundations of sustained growth through structural reforms and poverty alleviation.

MANAGING THE INTERNATIONAL CRISIS 2008–2012 AND THE CHALLENGES OF A NEW CONTEXT

In 2008, a new international crisis unfolded, whose characteristics are widely known today. It was a turning point in terms of macroeconomic management since it was the year in which the country graduated to a middle-income country and the year in which it joined the World Trade Organization (WTO).

These two facts are extremely important because they help us to understand the macroeconomic management measures taken, mainly at the fiscal and budget level and also at the level of the country's infrastructure. Similarly, the country had already completed its adjustment program with the World Bank and was now only with the Policy Support Instrument (PSI) with the IMF.

Accession to the WTO, as the 153rd member, had consequences for trade, investment, and export policy, because much of the legislation had to be changed because it was not in line with the organization's dictates: elimination of export subsidies, amendment of the foreign investment law, amendment of the statutes of the free enterprise, and eliminations of other prohibited subsidies. Other measures included amendments to the Customs Code, regulation of the telecommunications sector and termination of monopoly, new legislation on foreign trade, revision of the legislation on the ecology tax.

The other milestone was the graduation of Cape Verde from the list of Least Developed Country (LDC) of the United Nations, to the category of a middle-income country. While, on the one hand, this has brought positive aspects, on the other hand, it posed several challenges, namely, in terms of development finance. In practice, graduation reduced the concessional financing window that the country had previously enjoyed as an LDC. Thus, the strategy was to use this transition period to maximize the benefit to build up the country's infrastructure, through a Program of Public Investments for social housing, ports, airports, roads, schools, health centers.[2]

It is in this context of international crisis, which also resulted in affecting foreign investments, that the country was governed and that now had to search for new sources of growth and respective financing. With regard to the post-crisis, diversification of sources of growth is crucial so that the economy gains resilience and reduces its vulnerability. This diversification concerns the primary sectors (agribusiness development) in order to enter more into the value chain of tourism and also to continue supplying the internal market. The secondary sector was to be the focus of external investment in the labor-intensive industries and where there are still comparative advantages. The services sector was to be invested in services that can be outsourced (BPO—business processing outsourcing).

Economic Growth and Its Sources

Central bank (BCV 2008) had projected real GDP growth of 5.9 percent in 2008, and as a result of the crisis, this rate was already 0.8 basis points lower than in the previous year. This development had to do with the reduction of domestic demand and external investment, namely, investment in tourism. In other words, although still unrecognized, and as a result of the slowdown in the world economy, the effects of the crisis would already be perceptible, since already in 2008 there was a reduction in the flow of external capital, namely, debt disbursements, external investment, and remittances.

The situation deteriorated further to the point where, in 2009, the economy went into recession, translating into a growth rate of -1.3 percent, compared to previous forecasts that projected it to reach +4 percent. (This evolution was not only a reflection of the international crisis but also a change in the methodology for calculating national accounts). Objectively, there was a contraction of domestic demand, deceleration of private consumption and investment. Another indicator of poor economic performance was the reduction of imports.

In terms of economic sectors, contributing a big part to the fall of the product was a sharp drop in agriculture and construction (resulting from the crisis in real estate) and a less favorable evolution of services. With private consumption practically stagnant (+0.4%), the increase in public consumption (+6%) remained as a way of sustaining the effects of the crisis and allowing some level of product growth, although, as we have seen, this was not possible.

On the demand side, the biggest drop was in investment, with a negative 9.3 percent rate as a result of a reduction in the backlog of orders in the construction and real estate sector. Confirming this reduction in private investment, central bank data also pointed to a reduction in bank credit for homeownership.

For its part, and as a countercyclical measure, as already stated, public investment increased by 6.3 percent, taking advantage of the window of concessional financing and with positive results in the real economy, as economic activity would recover slightly in 2010 with real GDP growth of 1.5 percent, also reflecting the global recovery. Despite being strongly influenced by the international scenario, domestic consumption and private investment were the drivers of this recovery. To justify this level of consumption, the credit granted was very decisive, having increased by 9 percent and placing bank loans at the level of 45 percent of disposable income of households. Thus, for example, private consumption recovered, reaching a growth rate of 4 percent against 0.4 percent of the previous year. On the other hand, public consumption registered a slowdown, but with real positive growth of 2.6 percent. This economic recovery benefited, according to the central bank, the increase in construction, to 4 percent from a decline of 5 percent.

In 2011, the economy grew somewhat robust, according to data from the central bank, at a rate of 4 percent, despite the deteriorating external environment. In fact, domestic demand was the driving force behind this growth as net external demand fell sharply. The contribution of domestic demand was positive, having accelerated, according to the same source, from 5.8

percent to 10.2 percent, driven by the dynamics of private investment and consumption.

Consumption is estimated to have seen real growth of 3.5 percent, still below the value of the previous year, and a possible explanation is the degradation of real disposable income of households. Let us open a parenthesis to highlight the fact that consumption has been increasing at a faster pace than disposable income, leading to household indebtedness and reduced savings. Central bank data point to a worrying fact: in one decade, household indebtedness rose from 15.1 percent of disposable income to 51.9 percent.

The other component of domestic demand, investment, grew 14.5 percent, driven by the gross fixed capital formation of transportation equipment and materials. Public investment had a contrary behavior, contracting 1.3 percent in real terms due, among others, to the delay in the execution of some projects (BCV 2011).

In 2012, anemic growth continued, with GDP growing by only 1.2 percent, in an international environment of uncertainties, against 4 percent in the previous year. Again, this growth result was greatly influenced by the sharp reduction in domestic demand as a result of the fall in private consumption and investment.

A number of factors contributed to the reduction of private consumption by 12 percent, namely, the fall in disposable income of families and the fall in remittances. Private investment also fell by 11 percent, according to data from the central bank, although this behavior can be understood by taking into account the end of major projects, namely, the wind farm, the introduction of 3G technology, and the conclusion of the West Africa Cable System, the submarine cable interconnection. By sector, tourism and construction were more dynamic but not enough to offset the decline in trade and manufacturing.

Tourism—Although tourism revenues increased by 7.8 percent (BCV 2008), this growth rate has already represented a slowdown, a consequence of the international crisis in countries that emit tourists (Portugal, Italy).[3] The same behavior occurs in 2009, namely, a 16 percent reduction in tourism revenues, notwithstanding the increase in inflows.

The following year, tourism contributed much more to the recovery that occurred, according to data from the National Institute of Statistics (INE), with an increase in tourism demand by 17 percent. As a result of this development, tourism receipts grew at a rate of 6.3 percent, but it should be noted that, following the crisis, there was a need to adjust prices to low demand. Thus, data points to an increase in tourist arrivals by 3.9 percent and 27.4 percent, year-on-year in the first and second semesters, respectively. The number of overnight stays, in turn, accelerated from 5.4 percent to 26.1 percent from the first to the second half (BCV annual report 2010). The United Kingdom continued to be the main emitter of tourists and the island of Sal as the main destination, followed by Boa Vista.

The dynamics of tourism continued in 2012, although with some slowdown in growth, according to official INE data. It is noted that foreign visitor arrivals, measured by the number of registered guests in the establishments, increased by 12.6 percent, compared to 27.4 percent in the previous year, and a possible explanation is related to the resumption of stability in North Africa, a competing market.

Despite the external crisis and the domestic economic recession, a major gain in macroeconomic policy was keeping inflation under control. Data indicate that in the period under analysis, a reduction trend in inflation was observed, rising from a peak of 6.8 percent in 2008 to 1.5 percent in 2013. The fall was most pronounced in 2009, also a year in which there was a recession.

In 2008, the consumer price index, according to data from the central bank, showed a clear upward trend, reaching 6.8 percent, up from the previous year. This upward trend was no longer observed in 2009, on the contrary, reduced to 1 percent. This lower inflation figure was certainly not unrelated to the reduction of the real product by a negative 1.5 percent.

In 2010, inflation accelerated slightly, reaching 2.2 percent, in line with the resumption of GDP growth. The increase was around 0.9 percent, compared to the previous value, and can be considered a comfortable value, reflecting, in essence, imported inflation. The following year, 2011, the rate continued the upward trend reaching 4.5 percent. The upward trend had started in April of the previous year, in line with the evolution of prices on international food markets (from 2.2% in 2010 to 5.2%) and energy goods (from 3.1% in 2010 to 9.2%). Of course, these increases at the international level were passed on internally to other goods and services—electricity, water, transport.

Reversing the upward trend of the previous year, annual average inflation was set at 2.5 percent in 2012, reflecting, of course, the downward trend in international prices, as well as a good domestic production of fresh food. In fact, imported inflation slowed down in 2012, contributing to the mitigation of consumer prices; energy goods grew by only 1 percent while food goods decreased by 7 percent in the international market. As a direct reflection on the national economy, passenger land transport prices, whose growth, according to the central bank, decelerated in average terms by 3.2 percentage points.

POLICIES, INSTITUTIONS, AND INSTRUMENTS

Monetary Policy

The effects of the crisis, as already mentioned, began to be felt in the balance of payments. This unfavorable balance of payments, coupled with the fact that the level of external reserves (which was a target under the PSI), is at a low level for a vulnerable country such as Cape Verde, there was a need to tighten monetary policy with restrictive measures, namely, to increase the lead rate by 25 basis points and then by a further 100 basis points.

In the following year, with the continued deterioration of the balance of payments, the central bank tightened monetary policy again, this time increasing the reserve requirement ratio from 14 percent to 16 percent, which would in theory make credit more expensive and more scarce, leading soon to fewer imports. Within the scope of the PSI, it was important to maintain the target of the adequate level of reserves to ensure the sustainability of the exchange rate regime. As such, in 2010, the monetary policy maintained the objectives focused on stabilizing the country's external reserves, in line with the targets of the same PSI, according to data from the central bank. Notwithstanding this restrictive policy, the monetary policy measures taken, aimed at the stability of external capital flows, contributed to the recovery that took place in 2010.

Naturally, as we have seen, economic growth has almost always led to the consumption of foreign exchange in the form of imports. That is why even in 2011 the central bank had to take more restrictive monetary policy measures to stabilize the country's foreign reserves, such as:

- Expansion of the incidence base for the creation of minimum cash requirements (DMC), including public sector deposits of 50 percent in July and 100 percent in December
- restricted access to the permanent transfer facilities, worsening the rate in an increasing proportion of the volume requested
- set a ceiling for the provision of funds to banks.

In addition, in December 2011, other measures were taken that came into force in 2012, namely, raising the cash ratio from 16 to 18 percent and raising interest rates. This more restrictive monetary policy was followed up in 2012 with the further worsening of central bank interest rates and the entry into force of the new DMC coefficient of 18 percent. The result was, in addition to the increase in external reserves and the containment of inflationary pressures, a slowdown in the growth rate of total credit: from 12 percent in 2011 to only 3.2 percent. With this contraction of credit and domestic consumption, the result was a less favorable performance of the economy.

On the side of remittances, its behavior was in line with what the literature predicts, that is, a growth trajectory continued despite the crisis in the host countries (Rocha, Tolentino, and Tolentino 2008). The differential of interest rates very favorable to emigrant deposits in Cape Verde made a big contribution.

Disaggregating credit, despite the liquidity available in commercial banks, financing to the private sector practically stagnated, even declining for individuals and for other purposes. Only credit for strengthening treasury and investment had positive growth.

Fiscal and Fiscal Policy

At the beginning of the crisis, budget and fiscal policy effects were not yet felt, so overall the fiscal deficit for 2008 was only 1 percent of GDP, considerably better than the previous year (1.5%). Contributing to this improvement was a more rigorous expenditure and a good performance in the collection of revenues. Disaggregating the components, it can be seen that tax revenues grew 13 percent as a result of the growth in current revenues, while expenses increased 11 percent (financed by 92% with external resources) compared to the previous year due to public investments in the country's infrastructure. Of the current expenses, the increase in personnel expenses as a result of new recruitments and the salary update in the public function stand out. The largest share of expenditure was for the social functions of the state (social security, health, and education).

As a reflection of the economic slowdown and fiscal policy easing, public accounts began to deteriorate in 2009. The overall public balance, being negative, was 6.8 percent of GDP, well above 1 percent of the previous year, while the primary deficit was 11 percent of GDP, compared to 4 percent in 2008, as a result of higher expenditures. Investment expenditure continued to grow, increasing by 9.6 percent, mainly for infrastructure projects.

On the revenue side, there was a strong reduction of 8.9 percent, and this was due to the reduction observed in current revenues (-8.3%) and in particular in tax revenues. As an example, value-added tax revenues decreased by 16.9 percent. This reduction was caused by the slowdown in economic activity and the reduction in consumption.

In the wake of public deficits, public debt began to show signs of concern, since it has a clear upward trajectory, but this would be expected, as a consequence of the use of concessional financing for the country's infrastructure. Thus, public debt reaches the figure of 72.8 percent of GDP, which, in gross terms, was an increase of 9.5 percent with respect to the previous year.

In 2010, and in the midst of the crisis, there was a strong boost in fiscal and fiscal policy, resulting in a considerable tax reduction initiated in the previous year, with a view to boosting domestic demand.

A deterioration in the fiscal position was expected, with the deficit at 12 percent of GDP, according to data from the annual central bank report. The situation was expected because the government issued a countercyclical policy, as discussed above, following the severe international financial crisis that had started in 2008. Thus, excluding interests on debt, the (primary) budget deficit reached 10.3 percent of GDP. This was considered a high value for a vulnerable economy with Cape Verde. With the reduction of foreign aid, there remains the increase of taxes or the accumulation of debts to cover the deficit.

Over the last few years, the combination of poor performance in tax collection and high capital expenditures has led to an increase in public debt to above 100 percent of GDP by the end of 2014—an increase of 50 percentage points since 2008. Although highly concessional, this high debt growth may jeopardize the sustainability of the debt.

On the revenue side, total revenues grew 3.1 percent, compared with a reduction of 5.4 percent in the previous year, a recovery considered good. Fiscal revenues grew by only 2.8 percent, a phenomenon greatly influenced by better collection efficiency, as well as the growth of economic activity itself. Total expenses increased by 18 percent compared to 2009, with a strong focus on investment expenses.

Taking advantage of the last windows of concessional financing as a low-income country, the government decided to invest in the country's infrastructure (with the multi-year Public Investment Program, PPIP), while maintaining the pace of economic growth. The PPIP was funded mainly by external loans and donations and was aimed at increasing the competitiveness of the economy in this phase of transition from a low-income country to a middle-income country. That year's budget had a strong social character and protection of the most disadvantaged, with a view to softening the effects of the international crisis, which resulted namely in reducing growth, reducing remittances, reducing foreign investment, and increasing unemployment.

The final result of the fiscal policy, in addition to the others already announced, translated into an expected increase in public debt that reached 77.6 percent of the economy, according to data from the central bank. If at the beginning of the crisis the country had budgetary space and room to borrow, 2011 marked the beginning of the phasing out of this expansionary fiscal policy materialized in the PPIP. The deterioration of the external environment and the reduction of donations created the need to contain operating expenses and improve tax collection (combating tax evasion and avoidance). We talked about operating expenses, but even investments were also reduced, as the value of the investment program in 2011 was 12 percent.

This containment effort, mainly on investment spending, was translated into a reduction of the budget deficit, including donations of 2.2 percentage points of GDP to 10.1 percent. Disaggregating this trend, the primary deficit declined by 3.1 percentage points to 8.4 percent of GDP, according to central bank data, standing at 1.6 percentage points below the overall budget deficit.

Total revenues of the central government, in contrast to the previous year, decreased by 4.9 percent, due in part to the drop in donations, particularly those destined for the investment program. Fortunately, the dynamism of economic activity was reflected in a significant increase in tax revenues of 12.3 percent, catalyzed by measures to reduce fraud and tax evasion. The single income tax also increased by 9.7 percent and value-added tax rose by 10.3 percent, which shows some economic recovery.

Total expenditure was reduced, as a result of the 18 percent reduction in the investment program, according to data from the central bank, but, contrary to what was desired, current expenditure increased, due to the increase in the salaries for teachers and doctors. Another item that had the same behavior was the social transfers, namely, for the municipalities.

The following year, 2012, was again marked by an expansionary fiscal policy: even though the state's budget projected, in anticipation of a drop in foreign aid donations, a reduction in investment spending and moderate growth in operating expenses, what we saw was an acceleration in the implementation of the PPIP, resulting in a deficit of 11.5 percent of GDP. Total central government revenues maintained the downward trend of the previous year by 7.6 percent, a natural consequence of the reduction of budget aid by about 36 percent. Tax revenues, in particular from value-added tax, decreased by 10 percent, while customs revenues decreased by 7 percent.

On the expenditure side, operating expenses grew by 3.4 percent, driven by higher public debt interest rates and higher social spending. Investment expenses, as we have seen previously, increased by 9.2 percent due to the acceleration of the annual investment program.

Balance of Payments

For a highly open and externally dependent economy such as Cape Verde, the evolution of the external accounts generally presents a trajectory that is contrary to the evolution of economic activity. In other words, there is a slight improvement in the balance of payments whenever there is an economic slowdown and a reduction in imports. From 2008 to 2009, the current account deficit was reduced from 14.9 percent to 12.3 percent, with a consequent strengthening of foreign exchange reserves to 4.4 months of imports. Some factors that underpin this positive evolution include the improvement of current transfers, despite the stagnation of emigrant remittances. The reduction in the price of oil also contributed positively, as it decreased from the average $98.5 in 2008 to the average $62 in 2009 (figure 3.3).

The financial flows of the economy had a negative trend: from 18.2 percent of GDP to 14.3 percent. Foreign investment flows fell by 5 basis points compared to 2008, notwithstanding the disbursement of foreign aid by 69.7

percent. Naturally, this situation led to the worsening of public debt: according to the central bank (BCV 2009), the debt ratio increased by about 50 percent.

Foreign trade in 2009 showed a very negative development, due to the slowdown in external demand, mainly in the Euro zone, the main market for the country's exports. Exports of goods fell by 18.4 percent, but imports also fell by 13.7 percent (BCV 2009), naturally as a consequence of the reduction of domestic demand and private investment.

As a result of the slight recovery, the external accounts showed a slight improvement in 2010, reflecting a reduction in the external financing needs of the balance. However, the deficit reached 12.5 percent of GDP, entirely financed by external capital, private external investment, and public debt. This good performance of the external accounts translated into an accumulation of reserves corresponding to 4.2 months of imports.

In 2010, the strength of remittances was evident, with a resurgence in the growth rate to 1.1 percent, after a reduction from 2008 onward. This evolution was very much determined by the positive evolution of U.S. remittances (+9.5%), favored by the appreciation of the U.S. dollar exchange rate and the stabilization of remittances in the Eurozone. The current account was affected (6% increase) by the behavior of international prices through imports, namely, fuel and food prices.

Finally, in 2010, the external accounts ended up reflecting the end of the implementation of the projects under the Millennium Challenge Account

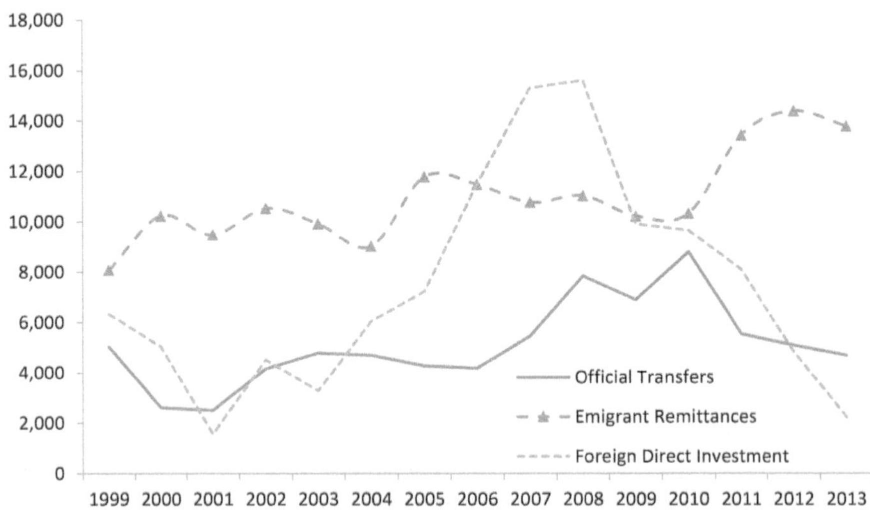

Figure 3.3 Balance of Payments, Million ECV. *Source*: Created with data from Banco de Cabo Verde (BCV), *Boletim de Estatísticas 20 Anos*. Praia: BCV, 2012.

(MCA-I), important support of the U.S. Government for the economic, social, and environmental development of the country.[4] The growth of the national economy always has a peculiarity, which is that it has a strong component of imports, which leads, along with robust growth, to some deterioration in the external position. Thus, in 2011, the economy's net borrowing needs, as measured by the current account deficit, increased, following the central bank, by 4.7 percentage points of GDP to 16.4 percent. According to the same source, this worsening reflected the increase in the rate of investment in the economy in a context of stabilization of the domestic savings rate.

The current account deficit increased to 18.4 percent of GDP due to strong import growth (23.3%), in line with the growth in global demand coupled with the slowdown in export growth. For its part, the capital account surplus decreased by 2 percentage points, partly as a consequence of the reduction of official foreign donations. The completion of the MCA projects largely explains this behavior. Emigrant investments also suffered a reduction, contributing to this behavior in the balance. Emigrant investments relate to the share of remittances in foreign exchange that are not reportedly earmarked for family aid but are intended for small investments.

On the external investment side, the situation was not favorable (a reduction of 21.6%), maintaining the downward trend that started in 2009. There has been a continuous reduction; 20 percent in 2010 and 0.8 percent in 2009. This evolution is the result of the international crisis and the consequent reduction of international financing for tourism real estate projects. On the services side, the performance of the balance was less positive, due to the behavior of the balance of air transport services, while gross tourism revenue grew by 26.4 percent, compared to 5.3 percent a year earlier, according to central bank estimates.

Remittances from emigrants, despite the international crisis and particularly in the Eurozone, remained resilient and had a very positive effect on current transfers. The balance of current transfers was marked by the increase in remittances (28.5%), which offset the reduction in foreign aid donations. Interestingly, the strong push for remittances came from Portugal and France. U.S. remittances declined by 1.1 percent (compared to a 9.5% increase in the previous year), in part explained by the depreciation of the dollar.

The external accounts performed very favorably in 2012, reflecting the reduction of the financing needs of the national economy by 27 percent. As a result, there was an increase in external reserves, which came to guarantee four months of imports, according to official data. Naturally, some factors contributed to the evolution of accounts, namely, more restricted access to financing by the private sector. Conversely, the public sector had more need and access to external financing in order to accelerate public investments.

It is worth mentioning the improvement in the trade balance due to the reduction of imports of goods by 8 percent and the increase in tourism revenues. Exports of goods fell by almost 6 percent, notably the reduction of supplies to air and sea shipping and a decrease in exports of fish and clothing to the Eurozone. In relation to services, its behavior was increased by 12.1 percent, driven by gross tourism revenues. On the side of transfers, official budget support from foreign donations has been reduced by 29 percent, although foreign aid to non-governmental bodies has maintained and disbursements for projects have grown by 52 percent, eventually balancing the situation. On the private side, there is also a reduction in remittances from Portugal, the United Kingdom, and Spain, curiously, countries where remittances had seen the most growth in the previous year. The evolution of the dollar exchange rate also influenced remittances, having increased from the US by 10 percent. Finally, foreign direct investments continued their downward trend, reflecting the restrictive conditions of access to financing. There was a slight improvement in net external demand in 2012, however, exports decreased slightly by 0.7 percent.

CONCLUSIONS

The major conclusion that can be drawn is that Cape Verde, considering its starting point in 1975, and the nature of its territory and the lack of resources, has until now been a country that has achieved relative success in economic, political, environmental, and social performance. Successive rulers have, over time, developed policies and created institutions to overcome external constraints and obstacles, as well as their internal vulnerabilities. This was the case soon after independence, in the first phase of development, and has thus continued with the political and economic change in the 1990s and now in the post-crisis years. The result was extraordinary gains in terms of the country's infrastructure, poverty reduction, and increased population literacy.

Of course, old challenges remain, and new challenges arise. This is how the country must prepare itself to meet the following challenges:

- The challenge of empowering and materializing an expanding and sustainable economic growth as a way to continue, using social policies, reducing poverty and unemployment, especially among the young.
- The challenge of diversifying the economy to find new sources of growth, widening the productive base for tradable goods, in order to have a more dynamic insertion into the world economy.
- The challenge of diversifying sources of finance for the economy in order to reduce vulnerabilities in this area, leading to more external investment flows, also reducing dependence on public aid for development.

- The challenge of having a "business-friendly and efficient" public administration, under penalty of maintaining an inefficient bureaucracy in the business environment, stifling growth.
- The challenge of having an integrated education system that is geared to the needs of a new development strategy that is defined and embraced, otherwise the country will continue to train people in areas where the market no longer needs.
- The challenge of market integration and unification, both in terms of the domestic market to give consistency to domestic production and enter the tourism value chain through agribusiness, but also integration into the regional and international economy in order to increase the size of the market.
- The challenge of increasing the overall productivity of the economy, starting with the workforce, in order to increase the competitiveness of the economy and the possibility of exporting more tradable goods.
- The challenge of maintaining public debt within the parameters of sustainability, without undermining development finance. It is a dynamic balance, that is, nothing can be guaranteed, requiring a constant exercise of adaptation.

These are challenges, and as such, with entail, some degree of difficulty and will require coherent policies. Economic policy should focus heavily on the creation of conditions and the basis of economic growth, given the structural situation of our economy. And this is why we must focus on the conditions of attracting foreign investment as a gateway into world markets, but also an opportunity for the national business class to have access to finance through the inflow of funds and know-how.

Given these vulnerabilities and emphasizing the reduced size of the economy, fiscal policy should provide some form of incentive if Cape Verde is to compete with other countries in attracting foreign investment. For its part, a budgetary policy must, of course, continue with the necessary rigor to avoid overruns and to take into account the already high level of indebtedness of the country, even though most of it is concessional debt and with very reasonable debt service conditions.

Monetary and exchange rate policy, with the current exchange rate regime that has guaranteed nominal stability of inflation, has been cautious and should continue to be so, aimed at guaranteeing the external balance and with sufficient external reserves to guarantee continued growth.

NOTES

1. Unless otherwise noted, all data used in this chapter are drawn from various sources and publications of the central bank, Banco de Cabo Verde (BCV).

2. The government created an ambitious program of public investments financed by concessional lending, with a view toward building up the country's infrastructure and maintaining aggregate demand, investment and growth. Even though it was a highly concessional financing, the risk to debt sustainability and fiscal consolidation resulted in the phasing out of the program.

3. This includes the entire local value chain—hospitality, transportation, food, fees and taxes. Constant balance of payments values.

4. The "Millennium Challenge Account" is a U.S. government program aimed at combating global poverty. For a country to be considered, it must comply with international standards of good governance, democracy and transparency in public administration. Cape Verde was selected twice to receive MCA funding. In 2005, the MCA grant amounted to $117.8 million, of which $110.1 million were financed by the MCC and $7.7 million by the Government of Cape Verde. The program had the following objectives: (a) the increase of agricultural production in three areas, namely, the Vale do Paúl in Santo Antão, an area of Fajã in S. Nicolau and the Mosteiros in Fogo; (b) integration of the national market and reduction of transport costs through the improvement of the rural road network, and expansion of Porto da Praia; (c) support for the development of the private sector through the promotion and public and private investment in priority development sectors, the reform of the financial intermediation system and the increase of competition in the access to Treasury bonds.

REFERENCES

African Development Bank (AfDB). 2012. *Cape Verde: A Success Story*, Country Research Report. Tunis: AfDB, June.

Associação Industrial Portuguesa (AIP). 1992. *Guia de Cabo Verde.*

Banco de Cabo Verde (BCV). 1987–2003. *Relatório do Conselho de Administração.* Praia: BCV.

International Monetary Fund. 1992. *International Financial Statistics*, Vol XLV, Number 1, January.

International Monetary Fund. 1993. *Balance of Payments Statistics. Yearbook, Part 1: Country Tables*. Washington, DC: IMF.

International Monetary Fund. 1996. *Cape Verde—Recent Economic Developments,* IMF Staff Country Report Nº 96/103, Washington, DC.

International Monetary Fund. 1998. *Cape Verde: Statistical Tables*, IMF Staff Country Report No. 98/31, Washington, DC.

International Monetary Fund. 1999. *Cape Verde:—Recent Economic Developments,* IMF Country Report Nº. 99/58, Washington, DC.

International Monetary Fund. 2001. *Cape Verde: Statistical Appendix*, IMF Country Report No. 01/175, October.

International Monetary Fund. 2005. *Cape Verde: Poverty Reduction Strategy Paper-Joint Staff Advisory Note*, IMF Country Report Nº 05/136.

Rocha, C. 1997. *Privatizações em Cabo Verde e crowding-in de uma classe empresarial, ISCTE.* Lisboa: Tese de Mestrado.
Rocha, C. 2006. *Estabilização Económica e política monetária em Cabo Verde.* Praia: Instituto da Biblioteca Nacional e do Livro.
Silvestre, Alda. 1994. Cabo Verde na rota da internacionalização, Grupo de Cooperação de Língua Portuguesa do Instituto de Ciências Económicas, 1ª Edição, Lisboa.
Tolentino, C., C. Rocha, and N. Tolentino. 2008. A Importância e o Impacto das Remessas dos Imigrantes em Portugal no Desenvolvimento de Cabo Verde, ACIDI.
United Nations. 2021. *UNData*, Statistical Division. New York: United Nations.
World Bank. 1996. *World Development Indicators.* Washington, DC: World Bank.
World Bank. 2003. *World Development Indicators.* Washington, DC: World Bank.

Chapter 4

The Political System, the Transition to Democracy, and the Challenges of Democratic Consolidation in Cabo Verde

Roselma Évora

Independent since July 5, 1975, the political history of Cape Verde must be a surprise to all those who at that time considered the archipelago inviable, "without the conditions even to be dependent let alone independent" (Editorial, *Jornal Noticias*, 1990). Forty-five years later, of which the last thirty years have been under a democratic regime, Cape Verde is today a benchmark for good governance and considered a model of consolidated democracy in Africa, where political instability and armed conflicts are frequent, leaving doubts about the future of democracy on the continent.

This chapter aims to analyze the nature and characteristics of the Cape Verdean political system. We begin by analyzing the fundamentals that define the birth of the independent state, seeing that our objective is to understand the possible factors that determined the successful implantation of democracy in the archipelago. On the one hand, the chapter aims to present the central aspects that define the political system, namely: the system of government, the electoral and political party systems, examining their role in the successful transition to democracy. On the other hand, we intend to present some evidence for democratic consolidation while also questioning the democratic consolidation from other dimensions, among them, that of political participation and the institutional efficiency of the decision-making process across the three decades of democracy.

Cape Verde today is a stable and vibrant multiparty democracy. It has a parliamentary model of democracy with a mixed, or dual, executive authority shared by a popularly elected president and a prime minister elected by the parliament. Democratic governance is decentralized, with twenty-two municipal governments directly elected by local populations. Suffrage is universal. Moreover, Cape Verde is among the few countries in the world that extend the right to vote to its diaspora population.

Cape Verde was one of the first countries in Africa to make the transition to democracy in the early 1990s, and it ranks today among the world's most successful democracies. Its democratic and governance performance has been notable. As in many other comparative social and political measures, it trails only Mauritius and Botswana. Cape Verde also performs well in the Freedom House indicators and it is one of the freest countries in the world (Freedom House 2020). The World Bank's Worldwide Governance Indicators also show Cape Verde's governance and institutional performance far above the average for Sub-Saharan Africa.

Cape Verde's strong comparative performance in democratic governance cannot be denied. However, as this chapter argues, Cape Verde's democracy faces several challenges and deficiencies. Its ranking in international measures has even experienced some erosion lately. The aggregate international indicators mask serious challenges, especially in terms of the quality of democracy, accountability, participation.

The text is divided into five sections. The first three sections analyze the conditions that determined Cape Verde's first successful transition—political independence, explore the peculiarities of the democratic transition, the evidence of consolidation of the democratic regime, and a subsection on the first democratic elections held in January of 1991.[1] The last two sections are presented in the form of questioning some parameters of democratic consolidation, based on central aspects of substantive democracy, bringing to the reader evidence that calls into question the quality of the Cape Verdean democratic regime.

FROM THE FIRST TRANSITION: THE FOUNDATION OF THE STATE AND GOVERNANCE IN THE POST-INDEPENDENCE PERIOD

Cape Verde's political success must be credited to a set of factors that came together in that archipelago, making that country a different case from most African countries, with regard to the configuration of the political system and the design of the decision-making process. What are the determining characteristics of Cape Verde's political system in the post-independence period, and to what extent do they reflect on the democratization process? This is the question that will guide us in the first part of this chapter.

Discovered around 1460 by Portuguese navigators, the colonization of the islands of Cape Verde resulted in the formation of a cohesive society, characterized by a strong ethnic, religious and linguistic homogeneity, different from the ethnic, linguistic and religious heterogeneity that we find on the African continent. The construction of this homogeneous society was possible because there was no native population at the time of its discovery, which during its colonization process resulted in miscegenation as the hegemonic pattern that prevailed.

> There were no people on these volcanic pieces of rock. As the Cape Verdean poet Jorge Barbosa used to say, "In the Islands lost in the middle of the sea/ forgotten/in a corner of the World [. . .] neither naked men/nor naked women/prying/ fearful innocents behind the vegetation." There was also no mineral wealth (silver, gold, or precious stones). It was needed to introduce everything in them: Europeans (some free, but many sentenced by the Portuguese Court) and Africans (enslaved), domestic animals, food crops and a production crop for the European market (the sugar cane). From the crossing of Europeans and Africans the crossbreeds were born, in a much deeper synthesis in Cape Verde. (Amaral 2005, 8)

The immediate result of this synthesis is the birth and unity of a nation before Cape Verde became an independent state. The solid national unity subsequently facilitates the consolidation of the state in the post-independence period. This element is crucial, because, as Bobbio (1994, 795) leads us to understand, national unity constitutes the natural foundation of political power and, in the Cape Verde case, national unity not only allows to facilitate successfully the rapid consolidation of the state but also explains the consolidation of a legacy of social peace that has always existed in the archipelago. This has not happened in the other Portuguese-speaking countries colonized by Portugal or in the African continent.

> Guinea-Bissau and Angola and the other on the Indian Ocean side, Mozambique; in them, the Portuguese found peoples organized in multisecular societies, in stages of historical changes. Paradoxically, in many cases outsiders sought to deny them their own stories. [. . .] Their ethnicities were not, as was later defined, of stable combinations of historical, political, economic and social invariants. If colonization was peaceful in the island territories, the same did not happen in the other three: the order was that of military conquest by weapons, technologically more advanced and destructive than those of the Africans, imposition of European civilization. (Amaral 2005, 9)

Having known no armed conflict throughout its history, not even to acquire its political independence in 1975, Cape Verde's first governing elite follows, nonetheless, the prevailing trend on the African continent, by implementing a single-party regime at the birth of the independent state.[2]

> The option for one-party dictatorial regimes and political monolithism in the former Portuguese colonies is evident even in the period of armed conflicts that were taking place in Guinea Bissau, Angola and Mozambique. In the final moments of the conflict, according to the Portuguese leader Mário Soares, it was evident the liberation movements were beginning to defend a position that indicated a hardening, in the sense that they did not want only the end of the war but the commitment, acceptance and the guarantee on the part of the Portuguese government that they would take control of governance in the post-independence period. (Lopes 1996, 355)

In the process of negotiating the independence of the Cape Verde archipelago, it was established that recognition of the country's independence required the formation of a transitional government that would have the responsibility to prepare for the election of a constituent assembly. Once elected, it would have sovereign powers to draft the constitution of the state of Cape Verde. The election of a constituent assembly was necessary because in the case of Cape Verde, in the words of Mário Soares:

> The principle of self-determination should be fully respected, but a consultation with the population about their own destiny should be organized because, where there is no armed struggle [. . .] it is necessary to allow freedom of expression for the populations so that they can freely express what they desire and organize themselves as they wish. (Soares 1999, 92)

The transitional government was made up, on the one hand, of ministers appointed by the Portuguese government and the other half by Cape Verdeans appointed by the PAIGC. An important aspect that should be highlighted was the almost unanimous victory of the only competing list of candidates in the election of the constituent assembly. PAIGC obtained more than 90 percent of the votes as shown in table 4.1. With this result, the party had the strength to implement the one-party regime.

Correia e Silva (1997, 20) emphasizes that, in the case of Cape Verde, it did not make sense to justify the implantation of mono partisanship as a necessary condition to preserve national unity, an argument widely used by the parties that led the independence struggles in other African countries. For that author, the monoparty regime in the archipelago is justified based on the discourse of historical legitimacy of the PAIGC, which considered itself responsible for the independence of Cape Verde. This recognition was even formalized by the international community, particularly the United Nations (UN) and the Organization of African Unity (OAU), which recognized PAIGC's right and legitimacy to govern Cape Verde after independence.

Table 4.1 Results of the National Constituent Assembly Elections (Single List of the PAIGC), June 1975

Electoral Districts	*Registered*	*Voters*	*Votes*			*Elected Deputies*
			Valid	*%*	*Invalid*	
Nossa. Senhora da Graça	14,818	13,257	12,731	96.03	526	5
Nossa. Senhora da Luz/São Nicolau Tolentino	4,492	4,228	4,106	97.11	122	2
Santíssimo Nome de Jesus/São João Batista	2,372	2,222	2,149	96.71	73	2
Santa Catarina	12,742	11,105	10,759	96.88	346	4
São Salvador do Mundo	3,685	3,362	3,173	94.37	189	2
São Lourenço dos Órgãos/Santiago Maior	8,403	7,491	6,923	92.41	568	3
Santo Amaro Abade	4,599	3,373	3,207	95.07	166	2
São Miguel	5,011	4,247	3,960	93.24	287	2
Nossa Senhora do Livramento/Nossa Senhora do Rosário	4,343	3,818	3,637	95.25	181	2
Santo Crucifixo/São Pedro Apóstolo	4,730	4,340	4,272	98.43	68	2
Santo Antônio das Pombas	3,069	2,650	2,532	95.54	118	2
Santo André	1,639	1,356	1,287	94.91	69	2
São João Batista	3,784	3,472	3,217	92.65	255	2
Cidade do Mindelo	12,699	10,721	10,409	97.08	312	4
Bela Vista	2,651	2,683	2,635	98.21	48	2
Monte Sossego	3,277	2,931	2,870	97.91	61	2
Nossa Senhora da Ajuda	3,624	3,315	3,257	98.25	58	2
Nossa Senhora da Conceição/Santa Catarina	6,244	5,377	5,230	97.26	147	2
São Lourenço	4,442	3,665	3,485	95.08	180	2
Nossa Senhora do Rosário/Nossa Senhora da Lapa	5,882	4,947	4,576	92.50	371	2
Nossa Senhora da Luz	1,485	1,320	1,015	76.89	305	2
São João Batista/Nossa Senhora do Monte	3,576	2,000	1,982	99.10	18	2
Nossa Senhora das Dores	2,518	2,256	2,196	97.34	60	2
São João Batista/Santa Isabel	1,639	1,367	1,227	89.75	140	2
Total	121,724	105,503	100,835	94.37	4,668	56

Source: Created with data from *Boletim Oficial de Cabo Verde*, Nº 26, 4 de julho de 1975.

With political independence and the acquisition of its sovereignty, Cape Verde acquired the element that it lacked to be considered a country with a state, in the modern sense of the term. It possessed the other two elements—people and territory—the people element being characterized by a solid national conscience, cohesive racial, religious and also regional unity, despite its archipelagic geography—which eliminated the demarcation of borders—aspects that in many African countries provoked situations of conflict and instability (Soares, 92). Cape Verde brought together the fundamental foundations of the state's sociological base that will contribute to good governance introduced after political independence.

Political independence represented for Cape Verde an advance for the modernization of the country, even though democracy was not the choice for the political system. In our view, Cape Verdean monopartism inserts itself in the cases of institutionalized one-party systems that emerged in contexts where there was a long autocratic period which, as Duverger (1970, 313) underlines, puts an end to the domination of a traditional aristocracy (colonial), allowing the emergence of a new local and national elite. In these cases, mono partisanship contributes to reducing the deep inequalities of the previous situation and improving the living conditions of the population.

In the post-political independence period, most countries in Africa are governed by authoritarian one-party regimes. Although there was variation among these regimes, with several distinct aspects among the single-party dictatorships on the continent due to cultural and historical aspects—results of the colonial legacy of each country—the literature identifies the predominance of two types of single-party regimes that prevailed on the continent (Gomidee 1997; Nwabueze 2004).

A very common type of monopartism was the neo-colonial bourgeois dictatorships. They were characterized by the concentration of power in the local bourgeoisie who, in most cases, were economic allies of the former colonial elite. In these dictatorships, the political power of the independent state functioned to preserve the status quo of a narrow elite, while the majority of the population remained on the sidelines and was excluded from state action. In these cases, political independence instead of providing well-being and improving the living conditions of the population meant frustration and disappointment:

> The masses had been led to expect that Independence would bring an immediate improvement in their conditions, and the non-realization of those expectations had, in turn, bred a mood of impatience and disillusion. Unless, therefore, improvement could be effected as speedily as possible, this mood of impatience and disillusion might explode into violence to endanger, if not destroy, the state itself. (Nwabueze 2004, 271)

A second type of one-party dictatorship that existed on the African continent had a clear socialist orientation as their distinguishing feature; however, this model was implemented only in a few countries. In our view, this was the one-party model established in Cape Verde. The aim of these dictatorships was to preserve the independence and guide the political action of the independent state to improve the social conditions of the population. The political elite that assumed control over the government in Cape Verde after independence identified its governance priority as solving problems and trying to respond to the principal social demands.

Thus, there is a commitment and an effort by the political power to improve the precarious social conditions inherited from the colonial period. This commitment is evidenced by the state's strong investment in social policies, particularly in the areas of education, health, and food security, which in Cape Verde's case contributed to a remarkable improvement of social indicators in the post-independence period. On the other hand, this choice prevented the birth of a neo-patrimonial system that became common in Africa, differentiating Cape Verde from other countries on the continent. In this sense, says Chabal, the particularity of Cape Verde's one-party regime is:

> Of these, the most convincing is Cape Verde which arguably never was neopatrimonial in the sense in which the rest of Africa has been since independence. (Chabal 2005, 27–28)

Another important characteristic of Cape Verde's one-party regime that should be highlighted is the civilian character of its system of government since the founding of the independent state. This choice reinforced, in our view, the archipelago's tradition of peace, which throughout its history has not experienced any armed conflict, not even for the acquisition of independence. The governance of the archipelago in the hands of civilians has given the military a secondary role in the political system and without any weight on decision-making.

In many African countries, the military became a strong institution and transformed into an important player in the political system in the post-independence period. Their weight and influence in the government systems and in the decision-making process determined, according to Ibrahim (1995), in many cases, that they became the crucial element and essential piece that determined the exercise and maintenance of power. In many African countries, the use of military force has also become the condition for reaching power.

The military's power in African single-party systems was consolidated, in part, due to the long period of armed conflict experienced in the colonial period. On the other hand, in some countries, the outbreak of civil war after independence, and permanent situations of social instability, contributed to reinforce the military's power, transforming it into an actor with a lot of power and significant weight in the government system and in the decision-making process.

The consequence of the strong power of the military in government systems on the African continent has produced in many countries, a social fabric marked by many instabilities that Ibrahim characterizes as follows:

> The African military has remained committed to the erosion of civil relations and the banalization of the culture of violence out of corporate self-interest, or rather, greed. Ever since the military realized that access to positions of power is a direct route to enrichment through the private appropriation of public resources, they have turned banditry into the means of the conservation of power. Although they have always claimed that the purpose of *coup d´états* was the fight against corruption, almost every military regime has turned out to be more corrupt than the regime from which it took over power. They have become the major segment of the power elite in most African countries, occupying the summit of the most powerful organizations in the polity and economy. (Ibrahim 1995, 123)

In the case of Cape Verde, the secondary role assumed by the military in the political system after independence reinforces the hegemony of civilian rules and social cohesion in the country. Throughout the fifteen years of a one-party regime, Cape Verde did not experience any military coup, and there are no reports of episodes of instability during this period, instigated or led by the military. In many African countries, the reality would be quite different. According to Essuman-Johnson:

> Civilian-style politics, with regular elections and peaceful change of government, have not been the norm in post-colonial Africa. Military-led coups d´état represent the typical way in which regimes were changed and rule by the military was as widespread as that by civilians. According to McGowan and Johnson (1986, 539–546), between 1956 when Sudan became the first country to achieve independence from colonial rule and 1985, 126 plots to overthrow African governments were reported; 71 were attempted and 60 coups were carried out in 40 out of the 45 independent African countries. (Essuman-Johnson 2005, 51–52)

Another crucial feature that contributed, in our opinion, to the good governance of Cape Verde in the post-independence period was the option for a constitutional configuration that establishes a parliamentary government system. In the design of the institutional framework established during the authoritarian period, the president of the Republic and the prime minister are responsible to the National People's Assembly (ANP). The constitutions that prevailed in that period established that the ANP was the supreme organ of the state's power, represented the nation and had the competence to decide the fundamental questions of the country's internal and external policy.

In the majority of African countries, the option for presidential systems of government proliferated after political independence, characterized by a strong concentration of power centered on the figure of the president. The strong centralization of power and the predominant choice for presidential systems were justified by the leaders of the African monoparty dictatorships as the fundamental condition for guaranteeing national unity and preserving the national interests of the newly independent countries (Fawole and Ukeje 2005; Gomidee 1997).

In the case of Cape Verde, the option for an institutional model based on the division of powers, with three decision-making bodies—president of the Republic, prime minister, National Assembly—was a reflection of the very structure of the single party that prevailed in this country and which indicated a decision-making process with the characteristics of a collegial decision-making process. This characteristic of the Cape Verdean single-party regime differs from the framework strongly centered on a single actor—the president of the Republic, existing in most government systems in other African countries with single parties that opted for presidential systems. The collegial character of the decision-making process in Cape Verde is evident in the composition of the unique Cape Verdean single party which, according to Hodges:

> The party is headed by a nine-member Supreme Council, including the President, the Prime Minister, the President of the National Popular Assembly, and six other senior party officials. [. . .] The governing party, which appears to have a genuinely collective leadership. (Hodges 1982, 160–161)

CAPE VERDE: THE TRANSITION TO DEMOCRACY AND SIGNS OF CONSOLIDATION OF THE DEMOCRATIC REGIME

In the democratic transition processes that took place in Africa in the early 1990s of the twentieth century, Cape Verde is presented in the literature as an example of transition made by reformers, just as it was, for example, in countries like Mauritius, São Tomé and Príncipe, and Zambia, etc. (Nwabueze 2004, 105). This classification considers the democratic transition of the archipelago as a result of the will of the ruling elite of the authoritarian monoparty regime, disregarding in our view the role of other forces and actors that were relevant in the process of democratic transition.

The political opening of the archipelago was partly one of the rare African cases where the democratic process was initially led by the rulers of the authoritarian regime. Rare because, in Chabal's words, openness to democracy was not necessarily a desire of the governing political class on the African continent:

> With few exceptions, African rulers did not welcome the introduction of multiparty elections. To them, it was the price to pay for continued financial assistance rather than the political modality that would make development more likely. (Chabal 2005, 20)

In the process of political opening in Cape Verde, it is also necessary to bear in mind that there was no visible evidence of popular dissatisfaction with the authoritarian political regime. This explains the absence of strikes, popular demonstrations, and protests demanding the end of the one-party regime, as has happened in several African countries. The social environment in the archipelago, which existed on the eve of the democratic transition, contrasted with the environment experienced in many African countries, particularly those in the Sub-Saharan African region portrayed by literature as a scenario of social instability.

Popular dissatisfaction with authoritarian rule existed not just in the minds and feelings of the masses. It was given practical expression in mass political protests in the form of street demonstrations, rallies, boycotts, strikes, violent riots, and other forms of popular action, of which there had been 400 occurrences in 39 countries in Sub-Saharan Africa in the five-year period, 1990–1994. The 400 protest actions were not driven essentially, not to say exclusively, by economic grievances; rather, while they were often fueled by economic hardships, especially hardships associated in popular perception with structural adjustment programs, they were all essentially political protests, in which the protesters were explicitly demanding an end to authoritarian rule, with its exclusionary and repressive practices. Composed of diverse social elements with varying interests, the protesters were temporarily united in the spirit of "a popular crusade to eject unpopular autocrats" (Nwabueze 2004, 50).

Absent popular pressure, and initiated by the leadership of the ruling elite, the democratic transition in Cape Verde, however, was not, exclusively, a transition made by reformers within the authoritarian regime. The process of opening up to the democratic regime in Cape Verde is, in our view, a case of a negotiated transition process. The democratic transition process initially contained reformist elements; indeed it was inside the authoritarian regime that the first steps of the opening process were triggered. However, the process subsequently took a particular dynamic and configuration with the emergence and rapid growth of the political opposition.

During the time of the single-party regime, there were some signs of instability within the governing party. In 1979, four years after independence, the ruling party suffered an internal crisis that indicated a shock to the regime and signaled weakness in the level of intra-party consensus. Cardoso (1993, 77–86) argues that the crisis of the ruling party in 1979 was an exacerbation of the conflicts that had existed internally and indicated the ideological divergences within it, which in turn stemmed from the fact that there existed within the party members who were in favor of political pluralism.

For the aforementioned author, those in favor of the institutionalization of a more open political regime clashed with the conservative and hierarchically better-positioned faction in the party leadership that had control over the government. The crisis of the ruling party in 1979 became known as the crisis of the "Trotskyists" resulting in the dismissal of ministers and the expulsion from the party of so-called "liberals."

Another problem within the single-party regime was the fragile circulation of the ruling class. The selection mechanisms for the party's leadership positions were authoritarian and, according to Cardoso (1993), they obeyed a rule based on a hierarchical classification of those who participated in the armed struggle and those who did not. Thus, the former, called "historicals," had the right to assume the highest positions within the party and within the state, regardless of competence. The rest were responsible for accepting and respecting this hierarchy and following the guidelines of the party leadership. In this sense, the question of meritocracy is completely set aside.

Furtado also presents evidence indicating that the leaders of the most important organs of the state and the government were recruited preferentially among the militants of the ruling party (PAICV) and, the dominant positions were directly related to the positions occupied in the party structure.

> The group formed by those from the armed struggle ended up imposing its hegemony, both in the party and in the government. Thus, with independence, key positions at the ministerial level are in the hands of the so-called "historical" or "combatants," and similarly in two other sovereign bodies, namely the National Assembly and the Presidency of the Republic. (Furtado 1997, 139)

The closed character of the regime and its weak capacity to allow the ruling class to circulate, contributed, in part, to its destabilization, even though there was no visible evidence of disapproval. The low social mobility in its midst, and the impossibility of party competition, weakened the Cape Verdean single-party regime and hid the divergences that existed within it, which formally could not result in the creation of another political party because it was prohibited.

With the constitutional prohibition of political pluralism, what we have is the coexistence within the same party of different and contrary ideas, as there are no channels to formalize these tensions.

It is also important to underline that with regard to the discourse and the legitimacy basis of the single governing party, it was essentially based on its achievement of Cape Verde's independence. However, there came a time when this reasoning became inadequate and alternatives were not created to support the maintenance of this legitimacy. It is then that the regime begins to show signs of exhaustion.

For Cohen (1991), the crisis of the one-party regime in Cape Verde, is visible when the ruling party makes efforts to introduce what they called "participatory democracy," through social organizations (whose objective was to bring people to participate in political structures of the party). However, according to that author, they did not have positive results, in part, because the organizations had neither legal nor material conditions to act with autonomy, which signaled isolation of society in relation to the ruling party.

At the end of 1985, the leaders of the single-party regime introduced some timid changes, showing signs that the political system was not going well and, in order to preserve power, some reforms were necessary. Thus, for the legislative elections of that year, the party introduced a novelty: the lists of candidates for the National Assembly would be presented and approved in advance by voters on the islands.[3] For Cohen (1991), the 1985 legislative elections can be understood as a demonstration of the decomposition of the one-party authoritarian regime since the abstention rate in those elections was very high.

The efforts of the leaders of the single party in trying to get closer to the populations of the islands, aimed to strengthen the regime, but which in our view, indicates that there was the perception of the void created between the party and society. This void, according to Correia and Silva (1997, 2), determined the liberalization measures, referred to by that author as "gradual decompression" whose objective was to broaden the social bases of the party which, however, eventually culminates in the political opening and bankruptcy of the single-party regime.

The bankruptcy of the one-party regime for the aforementioned author was especially evident on the economic level and, for many, it was as a result of this that they precipitated the opening of the political regime. Although we recognize the relevance of economic factors over political systems, they are, in our view, not the determining factors for political change in Cape Verde. Cape Verde's economic structure has always been very fragile, structurally precarious due, in part, to unfavorable agricultural conditions and the absence of natural resources. The country does not possess the conditions for the development of the industry, which is still very incipient and on a fragile basis. Because of these and other aspects, the Cape Verdean economy is very dependent on the outside.

The poor conditions of the economy were intensified by the development model adopted by the one-party regime. During the fifteen years of a single party, a development model based on the planned economy and strongly dependent on the state was adopted. The investment in the development of the private sector was neglected and little was done to create the basis for developing export-oriented activities. The economic structure was strongly subordinated to the state, which had control over the exploitation of the main economic activities and the rules of the market. The presence of the state was dominant in all sectors, through state-owned companies or by mixed companies with the state having the majority of the shares.

The fragility of the private sector led to a "swelling" of the public sector which resulted in the economy showing signs of stagnation and bankruptcy in late 1985. Party leaders began to realize that the model of the planned economy had negatively perpetuated the country's economic conditions that were naturally already structurally fragile.

Among the results of the fifteen years of the planned economy, we have the considerable increase of the external and internal debt, the deficit situation of many public companies, and the low productive capacity of the country. Another factor that contributed to the worsening of the economic situation in the late 1980s was the reduction in development aid by donor countries compared to the volume of aid made available in the first years after independence.

To change this scenario of economic stagnation, the government of the single-party regime launched a process of economic liberalization in 1988. It undertook a constitutional review allowing the alteration of the current legislation in order to create the legal conditions for a more open economy. In this constitutional revision, changes were introduced in the legislation that now allowed foreign investment and the operation of the private sector. In addition, the state ceded exclusivity and monopoly control over some sectors of the economy.

Correia e Silva (1997, 3) defends the thesis that this economic opening, promoted by the single-party regime, combined with greater demands from the population and more pressure against the regime, determined the conditions to abolish the monopoly of power.[4] For some Cape Verdean scholars, economic liberalization was responsible for the political liberalization.

> Liberalizing measures [in the economy] caused the expansion of civil society's expectations, which, far from being satisfied with them, will always demand

> more. Consequently, the process presents, throughout its course, an unbalanced dynamic. [. . .] To provide the country with economic viability, the regime opened loopholes in its doctrinal foundations. The government accepted that the State loses certain monopolies, puts an end to the price control system for essential goods and services and promotes the emergence of private companies, etc. In order to achieve the central objectives proclaimed by the regime's ideology (the fight against unemployment, the redistribution of income and the reduction of social inequalities) the government is obliged to yield in several aspects. . . . Consequently, the economic reforms impelled the government to adopt measures that circumvent aspects on which the legitimacy of the regime is based. (Correia e Silva 1997, 3–4)

Nonetheless, it is not only economic factors that are responsible for the end of the authoritarian regime in Cape Verde. It was only in February 1990 that the then head of the government, Pedro Pires, publicly declared the beginning of political reforms, the aim of which was to change the single-party regime to a multiparty system in order to allow other political associations to contest the next national legislative and municipal elections. The formalization of a multiparty system took place in September 1990 with the constitutional revision.

The political opposition, however, had already been born, according to Meyns (2002). A portion of the members of the opposition were dissidents from the then ruling party. The opposition managed to organize very quickly which allowed it to play a relevant role in the opening process. The growth of the opposition prevented the Cape Verdean transition from being exclusively controlled by the ruling elite. The opposition ended up having a role in defining the principles that established the rules for the holding of the first democratic elections to be held in January 1991 and also played a role in the design of the institutional framework for the democratic regime.

As such, we must not be naive in seeing the intention of the then political elite in power to want to reform the political system as the result of an intentional desire and an act of free will.

There is an acknowledgment on the part of the head of government of that period that external factors contributed to motivating the process of reform and political opening (Évora 2001). In Cape Verde, the role of the external scenario had implications for the regime change process. The country has always been very dependent on the outside, and we cannot forget also that African countries were under great pressure from donors to open up politically and embrace the principles of rule of law.

Since the late 1980s, there was already external pressure on the continent in favor of multiparty politics and the holding of direct elections as a condition for continuing development aid. In the case of Cape Verde in particular, the head of government of the authoritarian period came to recognize that despite the state's strong dependence on foreign aid, there was no demand for political openness on the part of any donor country. The absence of direct external pressure was justified, according to that government official, because Cape Verde did not have high levels of corruption, it had achieved good social indicators in relation to other African countries in the post-independence period, had positive results in governance, and also it did not have a violent and repressive regime with serious violations of human rights as was the case in many African countries. The country was not democratic but was considered to be well-governed.

The role of external forces was important because of the "contagion" effect on Cape Verdean leaders in the single party. The transformations that had been occurring in some African countries and in Eastern Europe prompted the ruling party to anticipate possible popular demands in favor of opening up. However, in Cape Verde, unlike other African countries, such as Benin and Côte d'Ivoire, which experienced strong popular protests, general strikes, and a lot of violence, Cape Verdean civil society was dormant. Cohen (1991) states that there were timid demonstrations made by students but that they were moderately repressed. Changes in Eastern Europe and the levels of violence in several African countries motivated the ruling elite to start the process of political openness.

Another hypothesis that can be considered is that political openness was also initiated due to the existence of false evidence that indicated that the ruling elite would remain in power in an eventual democratic system. This confidence came from two sources. On the one hand, throughout the fifteen years of the one-party regime, there was no evidence of dissatisfaction and discontent with the political class and with governance. On the other hand, a few months after the announcement of the political opening, the ruling party had a poll that indicated a positive popular approval rate. It may be that this generated comfort in the ruling class, producing a false belief of popular acceptance which resulted in illusory confidence that they would remain in power.

The silence of Cape Verdean society and the lack of evidence of discontent with the authoritarian regime are explained by the literature (Mainwaring and Share 1989). In authoritarian regimes, there do not exist legal and institutional channels for the free expression of the opinions of civil society or, when they do exist, they are usually a façade, and the regime's contestants are silent. The silence of society is interpreted by the political class as approval and they start to hold multiparty elections confident of victory.

THE FIRST FREE DEMOCRATIC ELECTIONS

The first democratic elections surprised the former political leaders with the resounding victory of the opposition party. In the other Portuguese-speaking countries in Africa, the parties that ruled the countries in the authoritarian period managed to preserve power. In Cape Verde, the holding of the first democratic elections resulted in the change of the governing elite and opened the opportunity to introduce changes in governance (table 4.2).

In many African countries, the democratic transition did not really mean a change in the ruling elite. The continuity of the old elite is explained by literature (Van de Walle and Smiddy 2000) by the following fact:

> The ex-single parties that made the transition to the multiparty regime continued to play an active role in the politics of most of the current African multiparty regimes. [. . .] In many cases, they are strongly institutionalized, benefiting from stable resources, the support of the State apparatus and its long-standing implantation. Indeed, its ability to remain in power after the transition is explained by its resources, its adaptability and, in certain cases, by real political support from the population. (Van de Walle and Smiddy 2000, 46)

The maintenance of power of the former African rulers in some cases was also due, according to some authors (Nwabueze 2004; Riley 1992), to the manipulation of the political opening process by the old political class that benefited from the strong support of the one-party structures, which guaranteed them the conditions to preserve favoritism in the first democratic elections. Keeping the former single parties in power with the holding of the first multiparty elections, the transition to democratic rule in many countries instead meant the preservation of the hegemony and continuity of the former ruling class that had held control of power for decades.

The first democratic elections held in Cape Verde in January 1991 gave the opposition party, the Movement for Democracy (MpD), a qualified majority in parliament, obtaining fifty-six of the seventy-nine seats in the National Assembly as a result of the 62.5 percent of the votes obtained. The former governing party, the African Cape Verdean Independence Party (PAICV), achieved only 31.6 percent of the votes, with twenty-three seats in parliament.

The victory of the opposition party in Cape Verde in the first elections is, in our view, the result of the triumph of the symbolic vote, consistent with Huntington's (1994) thesis that the victory of the opposition parties in the first free and democratic elections in most countries of the "third wave" of democratization, of which Cape Verde was part, were, above all, victories achieved with protest votes against the previous regime and motivated by a strong desire for change. According to that author, many of the opposition

Table 4.2 Results of the First Democratic Elections in Cape Verde, 1991

Electoral Districts	*Registered Voters*	*No, Voters*	*Deputies to Be Elected*	*Votes (%)*			
				MPD	*PAICV*	*Blank*	*Invalid*
Boa Vista	1,897	1,689	2	31.3	65.8	0.4	2.5
Brava	3,000	2,489	2	49.9	45.0	0.1	5.0
Maio	2,334	1,876	2	40.6	54.3	1.6	3.5
Sal	4,380	3,076	2	52.4	43.7	0.9	3.0
Nossa Senhora da Ajuda	4,033	3,694	2	29.6	67.9	0.4	2.1
Nossa Sra, da Conceição	6,916	5,857	3	36.9	59.6	0.2	3.3
São Lourenço	3,925	3,217	2	35.4	60.0	0.3	4.3
Praia Urban	27,548	19,117	12	59.7	36.9	0.5	2.9
Praia Rural	4,995	4,133	2	68.5	28.1	0.7	2.7
Praia Rural 2	2,849	2,116	2	52.0	40.1	0.6	7.3
Santa Catarina	14,608	10,206	6	72.9	19.3	0.5	7.3
São Salvador do Mundo	3,654	2,847	2	60.0	26.1	0.9	13.0
São Lourenço dos Órgãos	12,113	9,300	5	72.8	20.6	0.5	6.1
Tarrafal	11,604	8,147	5	68.9	24.9	0.8	5.4
Nossa Sra, do Livramento	5,084	4,325	2	72.2	21.4	0.3	6.1
Santo Crucifixo	5,702	4,730	2	80.9	12.7	0.7	5.7
Santo Antônio das Pombas	3,555	2,904	2	64.5	26.2	0.5	8.8
Santo André	1,842	1,408	2	72.5	18.2	0.9	8.4
Nossa Senhora do Rosário	5,944	4,695	3	54.0	31.1	0.6	14.3
Nossa Senhora da Lapa	1,153	916	2	61.0	29.5	0.9	8.6
Nossa Senhora da Luz	27,408	21,380	12	74.9	19.9	0.4	4.8
São João Batista	5,444	4,425	2	66.7	25.1	0.5	7.7
África	2,976	1,557	1	31.9	64.2	0.4	3.5
Americas	857	495	1	20.6	77.4	0.2	1.8
Europe	2,997	965	1	55.0	41.6	1.9	1.5
Total	**166,818**	**125,564**	**79**	**62.5**	**31.6**	**0.5**	**5.4**

Source: Created with data from *Boletim Oficial de Cabo Verde* nº 3 25 de janeiro de 1991.

parties, emerged and organized very quickly, started to channel the repressed desires of the population, becoming a channel for absorbing the frustrations of society that is reflected later in the polls of the first elections.

Table 4.3 shows the number of seats obtained by political parties in Cape Verde over twenty-five years of democratic rule (1991–2016). The electoral results of the parties provide clues for understanding important aspects of the democratic system that will be analyzed later. From the data in table 4.3, we can see that in almost three decades of democratic rule, Cape Verde presents evidence that indicates the stability of the party system that has assumed a clearly bipartisan characteristic. The results obtained by the two largest Cape Verdean political parties have enabled governance and the smooth implementation of political agendas, guaranteeing the fulfillment of the government's mandate as established in the constitution.

CHARACTERISTICS OF THE ELECTORAL AND PARTY SYSTEM IN CAPE VERDE

The consolidation of the two-party system in Cape Verde is the result of a number of factors that must be mentioned. At the time of the democratic transition, the political class opted for the proportional representation electoral system and the D'Hondt method for the election of the members of parliament. The magnitude of the constituencies, or electoral districts, has also been preserved. Most constituencies in Cape Verde are of low magnitude and a significant number of them elect only two deputies. Although in 2010 a revision of the Electoral Code was made, the constituencies are districts, with Cape Verde being considered a case of proportional representation system with one of the lowest averages in the world (Montero 2003, 165).

Silva (2007) considers the maintenance of the size of electoral districts in the democratic period as a reflection of a legacy of the authoritarian regime. For that author, the electoral legislation of the authoritarian regime established that, for each constituency, there would be one deputy for every 3,000 registered voters or with more than 1,500 registered voters when the amount did not reach 3,000. This rule determined a minimum of two deputies per district. Failure to change electoral rules during the transition process thus had implications for the configuration of the party system that emerged in the democratic regime.

Another feature of Cape Verdean electoral legislation is the election of deputies through a closed and blocked party list. This means that the voter will choose candidates previously chosen by the party, and they cannot

Table 4.3 Percentage of Seats in Parliament in the Democratic Elections in Cape Verde, 1991–2021

Year	*MPD*	*PAICV*	*OUTROS*
1991	62.5	31.6	—
1995	61.29	29.75	9.77
2001	30.19	47.85	9.16
2006	29.1	41.2	3.67
2011	41.71	51.98	4.3
2016	53.58	37.53	7.24
2021	52.7	41.6	5.5

Source: Author's calculations.

change the candidate's position on the list. The mandates (seats) for the parliament are obtained based on the D'Hondt formula.

An extensive literature recognizes that such a formula is the least proportional and favors particularly large parties to the detriment of small parties (Jalali 2007; Lijphart 2003; Nicolau 1996). Considering the electoral results up until today, we can conclude that the two major Cape Verdean parties have been favored by the D'Hondt method, controlling more than 80 percent of seats in parliament, as seen in table 4.3. Even when competing in a coalition, small parties perform poorly at the polls, resulting in an insignificant presence and with little relevance or weight in parliament. The closed fixed list also has an impact on political representation by gender as we will see later.

In addition to the aspects determined by the configuration of the electoral system, two other interconnected factors must be considered in order to understand the consolidation of the two-party system in Cape Verde. The first has to do with the fact that elections are publicly financed. Cape Verdean legislation allocates public financial subsidies to political parties, derived from the state budget, depending on the number of votes obtained by each party. The electoral results achieved by the two largest parties in twenty-five years of democracy indicate that the two main parties, PAICV and MPD, control public financing. Presumably, this means having more resources and more money to finance their operations and support the expenses of their election campaigns. This means that the two parties have better conditions, and therefore a greater advantage, and are better positioned during the period of electoral disputes to preserve their hegemony in power.

This financial advantage, combined with Cape Verde's dispersed island geography, made it possible for the two largest parties to consolidate their hegemony on all the islands, having party structures rooted throughout the national territory, which requires resources, making it difficult for small parties to have conditions to compete on equal terms and have little chance of being real alternatives for voters.

The two-party structure of the Cape Verdean parliament differs from the multiparty systems that emerged on the African continent with democracy. African democratic parliaments in the words of Van de Walle and Smiddy:

> The new African legislative assemblies quickly acquired a reputation for having an excessive number of parties represented in parliament. Among the sixty-eight elections for which data are available, fourteen assemblies were made up of ten or more parties, while the other thirteen had between seven and nine parties. The average number of parties represented in Parliament increased even between the first and second elections, from 6.3 to 7.2. [. . .] Thus, the system that emerges in a large part of the subcontinent is that of a large dominant party surrounded by a swarm of small, extremely volatile parties. Of the twenty-eight of the seventy elections that make up our sample, the second largest party in a legislature has never exceeded 15 percent of parliamentary seats. (Van de Walle and Smiddy 2000, 50–51)

Lopes (1999, 46) and Van de Walle (2000) maintain that the party system that emerged in Cape Verde in the democratic period produced a system with a party structure of a dominant party system because it allows a political party the possibility of obtaining more than 60 percent of parliamentary seats. In fact, this situation occurred in the first two democratic elections held in 1991 and 1995. However, in our opinion, considering only two elections is insufficient and precipitous to classify the Cape Verdean system as a dominant party system. For Sartori (1982, 224), we can only classify a dominant party system when, for at least four consecutive legislatures, a party remains in power and manages to achieve, throughout these four legislatures, consecutive absolute majorities, making it possible to speak of the stabilization of the party political system. In 2016, with the election of MPD, the hypothesis of Cape Verde being a dominant party system was undermined.

The legislative elections of 2001 and 2016, allowed the transfer of power, considered by authors as Huntington (1996) as an important indicator of democratic stability and evidence that the rules of the democratic regime are consolidated. For authors like Linz and Stepan, it means that the rules of the democratic regime have become "the only game in town when no significant political group seriously attempts to overthrow the democratic regime or to promote domestic or international violence in order to succeed from the state" (Linz and Stepan 1996, 15).

The alternation of political power is a relevant criterion to consider the stability of the democratic regime, particularly if we take into account that in eleven of the fifteen countries in Sub-Saharan Africa there was a boycott and non-acceptance of the electoral results by a political party in the period after the realization of the first inaugural democratic elections (Bratton 1998, 55).

Political alternation in Cape Verde has occurred regularly and is consistent with the principle postulated by Bratton, who argues:

> While elections and democracy are not synonymous, elections remain fundamental, not only for installing governments, but as a necessary requisite for broader democratic consolidation. The regularity, openness, and acceptability of elections signal whether basic constitutional, behavioral, and attitudinal foundations are being laid for sustainable democratic rule. (Bratton 1998, 52)

If, on the one hand, parliamentary majorities favor governability, the fact that the Cape Verdean two-party system is characterized by strong party discipline ends up having implications for the functioning of the legislature. As stated earlier, the system of choosing members of the National Legislative is through a closed, fixed party list. This means that the political parties have a constitutional monopoly on the presentation of candidacies; having the power to enumerate and determine the place of each candidate on the list. For this reason, the list is closed and fixed, and the voter cannot change the order of the list or add more names. It is in this sense that Silva stresses that the vote in Cape Verde is a list vote, more particularly of parties (Silva 2007, 287).

The election of members of parliament through the closed and fixed list results in a legislative power organized in a very centralized way, with a weak capacity for an individual legislative initiative by the deputies. Moreover, the behavior of deputies is conditioned to the guidelines of the parliamentary group that, as a rule, corresponds with the guidelines of the party leadership. In the event of an absolute majority in parliament, this means being dependent on the executive branch.

According to the literature, the two-party parliamentary system produces specific behavioral patterns in the legislature. The party that obtains the largest number of seats in the parliament defines the legislative agenda, resulting in the executive branch having control over the decision-making process in the legislature. It is not by chance that we perceive in the two-party parliamentary system, during the electoral campaigns, the fixation and the greater concern of the political parties in obtaining the largest number of seats, as it is the condition for the approval of the political agenda that they want to implement.

Based on the previous election results presented in table 4.3, we can also examine the behavior of the two largest Cape Verdean parties in the legislature in the period 1991 to 2006 and 2006 to 2019. These two periods indicate different moments and portray the period where one of the two largest parties, MPD and PAICV, held most seats and controlled the government. We can examine evidence of legislative initiatives of the two largest parties by comparing these periods, when one of them held the majority of seats and the control of the legislature, and when it lost the majority and passed to the opposition.

In our analysis, we examine only the legislative initiatives of the two largest parties, considering that, in the Cape Verdean party system, the electoral results obtained over more than two decades of democracy guarantee only two parties a position of relevance. For this delimitation, we assume the thesis defended by Sartori (1982), who considers that the strength of a party depends on its electoral strength, on the number of votes obtained in an election that is later converted into seats in parliament.

The barrier clause in Cape Verdean legislation states that a party must reach at least 5 percent of the votes in the legislative election to obtain seats in the National Assembly. In this sense, the results of the elections held from 1991 to 2016 allow the attribution of relevance to only two parties—MPD and PAICV.

On the other hand, the institutional structure of the National Assembly of the democratic period is entirely centralized in the parliamentary groups. The formation of a parliamentary group implies a minimum of five deputies per party, which means that in Cape Verde only two political parties have managed to form parliamentary groups. The evidence demonstrates differences that indicate that when the party has a majority in parliament and supports the government, it controls the legislative process and has greater legislative initiative. When the situation reverses and the party passes to the opposition, its legislative capacity is substantially reduced.

One of the classic functions of the legislative branch is its oversight capacity with respect to the acts of the executive branch. Rennó (2003), stresses that, in addition to the legislative initiative, members of parliament have the power to review and investigate the executive's activities. They may require the creation of parliamentary commissions of inquiry, for example. This oversight power is considered by literature to be an essential and vital condition for ensuring the principle of the separation of powers.

Lijphart (2003), however, maintains that the principle of the separation of powers and the activities of oversight over the executive branch is generally conditioned in two-party parliaments. This conditionality is more evident in cases where the executive holds the majority of the seats in parliament and is marked by strong party discipline, which contributes to one part of the legislative power omitting its oversight function. This function is delegated almost exclusively to the opposition party.

In the parliamentary rules of the National Assembly of Cape Verde, parliamentary control over the activities of the executive can be done using three types of control instruments: review and debate of the government's program; a motion of confidence or a motion of no confidence; and the classic parliamentary control exercised through subpoenas, questions to the government and parliamentary inquiries. But we can also consider other mechanisms of parliamentary control such as the debate of the State of the Nation, debates of the State of Justice, debates on issues of internal and foreign policy.

With regard to the parliamentary commissions of inquiry that are considered excellent tools for monitoring the activities of the executive branch in Cape Verde, the functioning of these commissions has not been efficient or relevant over the three decades of democracy. Fonseca explains the reason for this inefficiency when stating:

> In Cape Verdean constitutional practice, commissions of inquiry, since they consist of a majority of members from the parliamentary majority party that supports the government, have not produced results that translate into effective government oversight. (Fonseca 2001, 38)

Despite Cape Verde's democratic constitution bestows a great weight to the legislative branch and, in our opinion, the Cape Verdean government system is clearly parliamentary, but the low performance and behavior of the legislative in the democratic regime is conditioned by the results produced by the electoral and party systems. Such results have privileged the hegemony of the executive branch in the decision-making process since it benefits from absolute majorities that guarantee it the control of the legislature. The evidence indicates that, with the control of the majority of seats, the executive dominates and determines the legislative agenda, with the legislative branch acting almost exclusively as a formal voting body for executive proposals, deferential to the government, making the National Cape Verde a model of a reactive legislature.

A vast literature argues that democratic consolidation presupposes, among other things, the existence of an institutional model that ensures a balanced distribution of powers, in order to allow the functioning of institutional checks and balances. Several authors have also drawn attention to the fact that, in the formation of political decisions, which impact the lives of the citizens of a given community, the principle of the majority cannot be synonymous with the general will or with the general interest. In this line of thought and, being that the legislative power is constitutionally recognized as the power that represents the entire nation, the political system of the archipelago already signals the need for deep political reform in order to improve its performance and increase the efficiency of the power legislative as a condition for a higher quality of democracy that resonates with social reality.

THE EFFECTS OF THE CLOSED AND FIXED LIST ON GENDER REPRESENTATION IN CAPE VERDE

Democracies with different degrees of consolidation have as a major challenge the inclusion of historically marginalized minorities in the decision-making spheres. The issue of equality and equity between the sexes remains a focused debate and is on the political agenda of several governments. In this debate, several variables have been considered to explain the character of the country's decision-making and representation spheres. In this section, we intend to present the panorama of representation by sex in Cape Verde, highlighting especially the effects of the closed and fixed list on representation in national and local elected offices.

Cape Verde was recently considered an exemplary case of gender parity in the composition of its executive. In recent years, the composition of the government has been almost equal with a significant number of women occupying ministerial positions. We can take as an example, the months before the start of the 2011 legislative campaigns where nine of the sixteen ministers in the government were women. However, Costa (2012) warns us that government parity is sociologically misleading because it has little statistical weight in the national socio-political reality, on the one hand, and, on the other, because the positions depend on political appointment and not by direct election.

The Portuguese colonial legacy in Cape Verde contributed to the establishment of a patriarchal system that would result in the invisibility of women (Costa 2012; Coutinho 2013; Monteiro 2013) with a reflection in the decision-making spheres.

While the cultural aspects are of great importance to understand the panorama of representation in Cape Verde in terms of the gender dimension, institutional variables have been decisive. In our view, the effect of the closed and fixed list adopted by Cape Verde is a factor that has inhibited a greater presence of women in the organs of political power.

An extensive bibliography maintains that the electoral system of closed and fixed lists is the one that least favors the election of women in decision-making positions (Blasco 2010; Matland 2007; Osório 2010). Monteiro (2013) analyzes the political representation of women in the democratic period and concludes that women are underrepresented on the electoral lists and occupy secondary positions, which has perpetuated the inequality of representation by sex in the structures of power despite the author recognizing a timid advance. Over two decades of democracy, women represent only one-fifth of the seats in the national parliament, according to the data in figure 4.1. This inequality also exists in the sphere of local municipal power, which is constituted by a legislative branch (the Municipal Assembly) and an executive power (City Councils) that indicates a marked level of under-representation (figure 4.2).

Monteiro (2013) raises extremely pertinent questions in the research. When analyzing the biographical profile of representation by sex in decision-making spheres in Cape Verde, the author questions who are the women who are in politics in Cape Verde? The evidence indicates that they are women who come from a privileged social category of the middle class, favored by the family environment

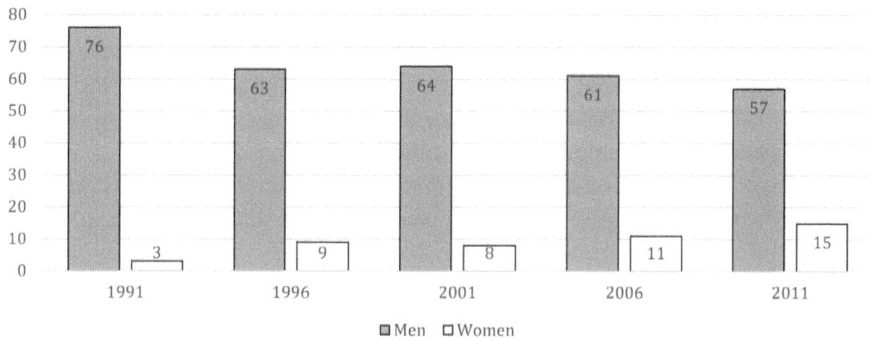

Figure 4.1 Distribution of Deputies in the National Assembly by Gender. *Source*: Based on data from Monteiro 2013.

of origin and, therefore, it is a top-down representation, far from being button-up. This means that as important as the challenge of promoting equal representation between the sexes in decision-making spheres, it is also imperative to invest in expanding the recruitment base to include the marginalized social strata representing the lowest social categories for an authentic transformation of the public sphere and a truly inclusive democracy (figure 4.2).

POLITICAL PARTICIPATION AND THE QUALITY OF DEMOCRACY IN CAPE VERDE

The crisis of representative democracy is at the heart of the debate in almost every country in the world. It reaches countries with different levels of democratic consolidation, including, in some cases, countries with long-standing

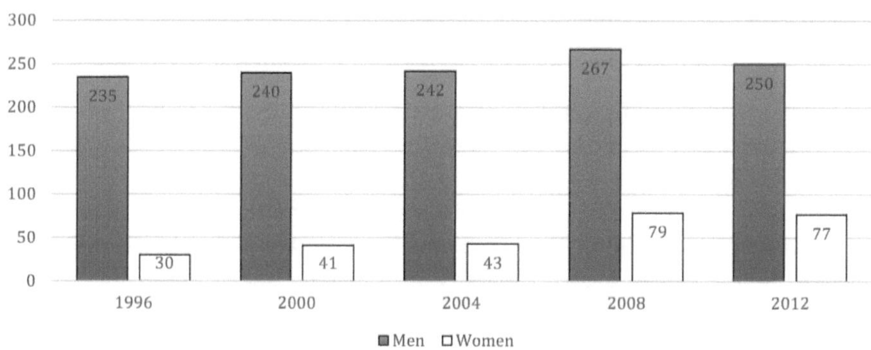

Figure 4.2 Distribution of Deputies in Municipal Assemblies by Gender. *Source*: Based on data from Monteiro 2013.

democratic experience. Part of this crisis is manifested particularly in the decrease in electoral participation. In the new democracies, it is already possible to find evidence that indicates a certain dissatisfaction with the functioning of democracy. What is the portrait of electoral participation in Cape Verde over the two decades of democratic rule?

The Cape Verdean constitution determines the election by universal and direct suffrage of the three levels of power: the legislative, the president of the Republic, and the municipal level. In thirty years of democracy, a total of twenty-three elections have been held since 1991: seven legislative elections, eight municipal elections, and eight presidential elections. The regular and normal holding of these elections has contributed to the strengthening of procedural democracy, guaranteeing, particularly over these years, governing stability.

Since voting is not obligatory, in an attempt to answer the question previously asked—how has been the electoral participation of Cape Verdeans—we seek to know the trend of political participation in the period of two decades of democracy at these three levels of government. To answer the question, we take into account the average vote in the elections held from 1991 to 2012, in national electoral circles, at the three levels of power. As for diaspora constituencies, created with political openness to allow thousands of Cape Verdeans living abroad to participate in the political life of the archipelago, it is important to underline that their right to vote is restricted to legislative and presidential elections (table 4.4).

The data indicates levels of electoral participation differentiated by election among Cape Verdeans, showing selective behavior in the three levels of power. Thus, considering that Cape Verde's government system is parliamentary, the global average of the total vote of national constituencies indicates that people participate more in legislative elections (71%), followed by municipal elections (65%) and less in the presidential elections (57.4%). This differentiated participation can be explained by some factors.

First of all, we must consider the weight and impact of each election and each power in the voter's life. As seen in other democracies, according to the literature, depending on the voter's interest and the type of election, the symbolic weight assigned by the voter for each election is different, resulting in higher or lower levels of participation.

The Cape Verdean constitution assigns quite significant powers and levels of competence among the three levels of power. Legislative elections subsequently result in a government that will have the resources to implement a very comprehensive public policy agenda and that will have a major impact on people's lives. They are generally policies that, in principle, meet the expectations and interests of voters in various fields, such as education, health, employment, security, sanitation, housing, etc.

Table 4.4 Average Electoral Participation by Districts, 1991–2012

	Total	*Legislative*	*Presidential*	*Municipal*
São Vicente	57.8	69.2	51.2	56.2
São Nicolau	63.9	70.9	57.0	66.2
Sal	60.7	66.6	51.5	66.4
Boavista	68.7	78.2	60.0	70.8
Maio	72.7	78.6	64.3	77.8
Santiago Norte	62.6	67.4	56.9	64.3
Santiago Sul	62.8	70.8	58.7	61.0
Fogo	69.5	73.7	61.1	75.9
Brava	67.4	72.9	58.2	73.5
National Total	**63.5**	**70.6**	**57.4**	**64.7**

Source: Created with data from PNUD 2013.

Similarly, for the election of local government bodies (local executive and municipal assembly), even though the volume of public resources are smaller and the powers of that level are reduced, local policies also have a considerable impact on the life of the individual and their interests at the local level. Contrary to presidential elections, which is also elected by means of direct and universal suffrage, its powers are almost exclusively of a symbolic character, limited particularly to the representation of the state at the external level. The president has limited powers and has neither the financial nor the formal resources to implement public policies that have an impact on the life of the citizen.

It should be borne in mind that the average number of voter participation at the level of the three constituencies in the diaspora (America, Africa, Europe, and the rest of the world) is significantly low when compared to national constituencies. In electoral circles abroad, it is the levels of abstention that stand out. The global average of electoral participation in the diaspora also varies between the two elections that the voter is entitled to participate in.

Of the elections held from 1991 to 2012, the global average participation of legislative elections in the diaspora is 39 percent, while for presidential elections, the participation is 30 percent. Although Cape Verde has a significant diaspora, a very small fraction is eligible, and even those with voting rights who participate in national elections are even smaller.

Taking the 2011 presidential elections as a reference, according to CNE data, only 8,306 voters were registered in the Americas circuit, and of these, only 4,412 voted. In Europe and Asia, 24,029 voters were registered, but only 5,743 voted. In the total number of registered voters in the Cape Verdean diaspora, with 36,945 registered, the abstention rate in the 2011 presidential elections was 66 percent. This diaspora participation profile does not change much in legislative elections.

Table 4.5 Average Abstention Rates in Diaspora Electoral Districts by Elections, 1991–2012

	Total	*Legislative*	*Presidential*
Total Diaspora	66.4	60.8	70.4
Electoral District			
Africa	48.8	45.2	51.4
Americas	57.5	49.7	63.0
Europe	77.0	72.0	80.5

Source: Created with data from PNUD 2013.

The low voter turnout in the diaspora can be explained by a variety of factors. We will particularly highlight two factors that we consider relevant. First, there is a recognition by national electoral authorities of the existence of constraints that interfere with their operational capacity in electoral circuits abroad. Such limitations have implications for the operationalization of their institutional efficiency in circles abroad, which ends up interfering in the periods when elections are held.

Among the constraints, they highlight an institutional deficiency in knowing and understanding the geographic and demographic aspects of the diaspora electoral circuits. This fact forces the electoral institutions to rely heavily on information from third parties, which results in the reduction of their capacity for control and efficient response in the period leading up to the elections and during the elections. In our view, these limitations have an impact on voter participation (PNUD 2013).

On the other hand, the main Cape Verdean political party officials justify the low electoral participation of the diaspora as a reflection of the low interest of the diaspora voter in national politics since it has a secondary impact on their lives and interests. The Cape Verdean voter residing in foreign constituencies are, according to these party officials, much more interested in the domestic politics of the host country as it is the one that directly affects them.

In diaspora constituencies, high levels of abstention significantly surpass the abstention rates of national circles, which have been varying in each national district and have fluctuated throughout these twenty-four years of democracy. Let us look at the overall abstention rates in the diaspora as shown in table 4.5.

CHALLENGES OF DEMOCRATIC CONSOLIDATION IN CAPE VERDE

If the election of a government by popular vote is considered an essential requirement of a democratic regime (Bobbio 2000; Bratton 1997), and if electoral participation is a condition for choosing a democratic government, the role of civil society is recognized by literature (Atwood 1992; Linz and Stepan 1999; Putman 2001) as an important and fundamental dimension for the consolidation of democracy.

Much research maintains that the existence of a strong and vibrant civil society encourages the exercise of a genuine democracy. If it is civil society that basically gives meaning to the democratic process, the surveys by Afrobarometer and other opinion surveys carried out in Cape Verde regularly have indicated that one of the weaknesses of the archipelago's democratic regime is the weakness of its civil society.

Empirical evidence has indicated a low level of participation by individuals in civic activities. The available data show that more than 80 percent of Cape Verdeans do not participate in activities of civic and political engagement, such as the mobilization for marches, protests, participation in associations. There is also a low level of communication with elected representatives, etc.

This evidence is, in our view, symptoms of anemic democracy. Authors such as Fonseca (1997), Furtado (1997), and Silveira (2005) argue that the weakness of civil society in Cape Verde is due, on the one hand, to the fact that it remains stuck in the authoritarian past that left a legacy of non-participation in matters public. On the other hand, a strongly paternalistic view of political power persists in Cape Verde, which limits the development and autonomy of civil society. In addition, the continuity of a strong centralization of political power contributes to amputating the autonomy of civil society, conditioning its flourishing.

Some authors have called attention to the fact that in many countries that had regimes of one-party dictatorship and political repression, that experience conditioned the development of a civic culture. They point out that civil society was mobilized by the mass organizations of the ruling parties, which subsequently after the political opening, disappeared, or lost their role and capacity to mobilize, in addition to having limited the autonomy of civil society. In many of the countries that had a single party, the post-transition period presents a reality where there is a weak presence of civil society in the public sphere as a result of its weak capacity for mobilization and loss of autonomy.

For Atwood (1992), the very structures of the decision-making process of many of the new democratic regimes continue to function in a strongly centralized logic, arguing that there is little effort by the political elite to promote the necessary changes to incorporate citizen participation in the existing institutional channels in order to increase the participation of society in the decision-making process.

One of the great challenges of Cape Verdean democracy is, in our view, to develop the civic dimensions of its democracy, a decisive aspect to promote more transparency in public management, confidence in democratic institutions, and greater satisfaction of Cape Verdeans with democracy.

CONCLUSION

Cape Verde is recognized as an example of democracy in Africa. By successfully making a negotiated transition, with the introduction of democracy, the archipelago consolidated aspects of its political system that have contributed to a history of peace and good governance over four decades since its political independence in July 1975.

Discovered without a native population, the colonization of the archipelago produced a strong ethnic, linguistic, and religious homogeneity, which determined the unity and solidity of the nation—conditions that contributed to the consolidation of the independent state.

The institutional choices made in post-independence, particularly that of a civilian government and a system of parliamentary government, reinforced the legacy of social peace and contributed to an exemplary process of democratic transition. Such aspects are reflected in the process of democratic consolidation that is evident in a number of dimensions, such as the successful transfer of power that took place a decade after the first free, multiparty elections, attesting to the acceptance of the rules of the democratic game by political actors which is still problematic in many other countries on the African continent.

Governing stability over three decades of democracy implementation was the result in our understanding, in part, of the two-party system that consolidated in the country, producing ample majorities that allowed the establishment of stable governments. However, the two-party system also resulted in a functioning of the legislative power with characteristics of a reactive legislative, conditioning the principle of separation and balance of powers, legislative oversight of the actions of the executive power with consequences in the degree of accountability and transparency, which are important aspects for the consolidation and quality of democracy.

Although the evidence indicates the solidity of the aspects of procedural democracy, the weakness of Cape Verdean democracy in our view is visible in the dimensions of substantive democracy, highlighting above all a weak civil society, with low participation in the decision-making process, reflecting in low or varying levels of electoral participation depending on the elected office. The evidence presented here indicates a trend of disenchantment and signs of declining participation in politics, even though the Cape Verdeans' preference for the democratic regime has been gradually increasing over these three decades.

NOTES

1. The concept of democratic regime used in this work is similar to the definition provided by Bobbio, who argues: "A democratic regime is understood primarily as a combination of rules of procedures for the formation of collective decisions which envisions and facilitates the widest possible participation of everyone interested" (Bobbio 2000, 22).

2. Cape Verde's political independence resulted from a binational project where the political party PAIGC (African Party for the Independence of Guinea and Cape Verde) claims the independence of the two countries achieved through armed struggle in Guinea-Bissau.

3. According to Cohen, the party's intention was to make the system more competitive and for this reason they decided to adopt a populist-based election model similar to that used by Frelimo in Mozambique to give an idea of being democratic.

4. Many political analysts tend to attribute and justify the transition processes in Africa as a result of economic factors and international pressure that they underwent in the late 1980s to change the economic system. The pressure led to the expansion of social and political forces that ended up culminating in the opening processes.

REFERENCES

Amaral, Ilídio Do. "Os Países Africanos De Língua Oficial Portuguesa Face Aos Desafios Do Século Xxi." In: Silva, Teresa et al. (Orgs), *Lusofonia Em África: História, Democracia E Integração Africana*. Dakar: Codesria, 2005.

Atwood, J. Brian. "Reflections on the Transition in Eastern and Central Europe." In: Garber, Larry and Bjornlund, Eric (Eds), *The New Democratic Frontier: A Country-by-Country Report on Election in Central and Eastern Europe*. Washington, DC: National Democratic Institute for International Affairs, 1992.

Blasco, Gemma Bardají. *La Representación Política En Disputa: Marco Conceptual Para El Análisis De Los Sistemas Electorales Con Perspectiva De Género*. Republica Dominicana: Un-instraw (Parte De Onu Mujeres), 2010.

Bobbio, Norberto. *O Futuro Da Democracia*. São Paulo: Paz E. Terra, 2000.

——— et al. *Dicionário De Política*. Brasília: Ed Unb, 1994.

Bratton, Michael. "Second Elections in Africa." *Journal of Democracy*, 9(3), July 1998, 51–63.

Chabal, Patrick. "Power in Africa Reconsidered." In: Engel, U., and Olsen, G. (Orgs), *The African Exception*. Aldershot: Ashgate, 2005.

Correia e Silva, António. *O Processo Caboverdeano De Transição Para Democracia*. Dissertação De Mestrado Do Instituto Superior De Ciência E Tecnologia De Lisboa—Istec, Lisboa, 1997.

Costa, Suzano. "Do Falocentrismo Estéril: Mulheres E Participação Política Em Cabo Verde," 2011. http://www.icieg.cv/article/410.

Coutinho, Ângela. "Mulheres Na «sombra»: As Cabo-verdianas E A Luta De Libertação Nacional." In: Silva, Carmelita, and Fortes, Celeste (Orgs), *As Mulheres Em Cabo Verde: Experiência E Perspetivas*. Praia: Edições Unicv, Vol. 4, 2011.

Duverger, Maurice. *Os Partidos Políticos*. Rio De Janeiro: Zahar, 1970.

Pnud. *Participação Política Em Cabo Verde Na Perspectiva Do Género*. Relatório Final Elaborado Por Évora, Roselma E. Ramos, Noemy, Praia, 2013.

Editorial, *Jornal Noticias*, Ano III, Nº 24, 1 Fev., 1990.

Fawole, Alade, and Ukeje, Charles. *The Crisis of the State and Regionalism in West Africa: Identity, Citizenship and Conflict*. Dakar: Codesria, 2005.

Fonseca, Jorge Carlos. "Os Partidos Políticos E A Sociedade Civil Em Cabo Verde." In *Ciclo De Debates: Direitos Humanos, Cidadania E Democracia*, Praia, November 1997, pp. 1–9.

Fonseca, Lígia. "Parlamento E A Função De Controlo Do Executivo." Comunicação Apresentado No Seminário: "O Parlamento No Sistema De Governo," Praia, 23–24 Março 2001.

Furtado, Cláudio. "Democracia Na África: Possibilidades E Limites." In *Ciclo De Debates: Direitos Humanos, Cidadania E Democracia*, Praia, November 1997, pp. 1–15.

———. *Gênese E Reprodução Da Classe Dirigente Em Cabo Verde*. Praia: Instituto Caboverdeano Do Livro E Do Disco, 1997.

Gomidee, Pierre-françois. *Les Systémes Politiques Africains. Les Nouvelles Démocraties*. Paris: Lgdj, 1997.

Hodges, Tony. "Republic of Cape Verde." In: Delury, George (Org.), *World Encyclopedia of Political Systems and Parties, Schagler Group, Vol I*, Cap 3, 2006, pp. 160–161.

Huntington, Samuel. *A Terceira Onda: Democratização No Final Do Século Xx*. São Paulo: Ática, 1994.

Ibrahim, Jibrim. "Democratic Transition in Africa: The Challenge of a New Agenda—Concluding Remarks." In: Chole, Eshetu, and Ibrahim, Jibrin (Eds), Chole, Eshetu, and Ibrahim, Jibrin (Orgs), *Democratisation Processes in Africa: Problems and Prospects*. Dakar: Codesria, 1995.

Jalali, Carlos. *Partidos E Democracia Em Portugal 1974–2005*. Lisboa: Imprensa De Ciências Sociais (Ics), 2007.

Johnson, Essuman. "The State in West Africa: The Crisis of Production, Democracy and National Identity." In: Fawole, A., and Ukeje, C. (Eds), *The Crisis of the State and Regionalism in West Africa: Identity, Citizenship and Conflict*. Dakar: Codesria, 2005, pp. 45–56.

Lijphart, Arend. *Modelos De Democracia: Desempenho E Padrões De Governo Em 36 Países*. Rio De Janeiro: Civilização Brasileira, 2003.

Linz, Juan, and Stepan, Alfred. "Toward Consolidated Democracies." *Journal of Democracy*, 7(2), April 1996, 14–31.

———. *A Transição E Consolidação Da Democracia—A Experiência Do Sul Da Europa E Da América Do Sul*. São Paulo: Ed Paz E Terra, 1999.

Lopes, José Vicente. "O Estado E A Transição Para Democracia Na África Lusófona." *Revista Annais*, 1(1), 1999, 33–47.

Mainwaring, Scott, and Share, Donald. "A Transição Pela Transação: Democratização No Brasil E Na Espanha." *Revista Dados*, 29(2), 1989, 207–236.

Monteiro, Euridice. "Quem Governa? Da Ausência À Emergência De Mulheres No Campo Político Em Cabo Verde." In Sarmento, Cristina, and Costa, Suzano (Orgs), *Entre África E A Europa: Nação, Estado E Democracia Em Cabo Verde*. Lisboa: Almedina, 2013.

Montero, José, and Lago, Inácio. "*The Electoral Systems of the Spanish Democracies*." In Marcet Et Montero (Orgs), *Roads to Democracy: A Tribute to Juan J Linz*. Barcelona: Institut De Ciencies Politiques É Socials (ICPS), 2007.

Nicolau, Jairo. *Multipartidarismo E Democracia*. Rio De Janeiro: Fgv, 1996.

Nwabueze, Ben. "The Forms and Process of Transition from Authoritarian One-Party Rule to Multi-party Democracy." In: Nwabueze, Ben (Ed.), *Constitutional Democracy in Africa: The Return of Africa to Constitutional Democracy*, Vol. 5. Abuja: Spectrum Books, 2004.

Osório, Conceição. *Género E Democracia: As Eleições De 2009 Em Moçambique*. Ed: Wlsa, Maputo, 2010.

Putnam, Robert D. *Comunidade E Democracia—A Experiência Da Itália Moderna*. Rio De Janeiro: Fgv, 1996.

Rennó, Lúcio. "Escândalos, Desempenho Parlamentar E Reeleição: A Câmara Dos Deputados De 2003 A 2007." In: Messenmberg, Débora et al. (Eds), *Estudos Legislativos: Pensamento E Ação Política*. Brasília: Câmara Dos Deputados, Coordenação De Publicações, 2008, pp. 169–179.

Riley, Stephen. "Political Adjustment or Domestic Pressure: Democratic Politics and Political Choice in Africa." *Third World Quarterly*, 13(3), September 1992, 539–551.

Sartori, Giovanni. *Partidos E Sistemas Partidários*. Rio De Janeiro: Zahar; Brasília: Unb, 1982.

Schmitter, Philippe. *Intermediaries in the Consolidation of Neo-democracies: The Role of Parties, Associations and Movements*. Barcelona: Institut De Ciencies Politiques É Socials (ICPS), 1997.

Silva, Mário. *Código Eleitoral*. Praia: Ed Do Autor, 2007.

Silveira, Onésimo. *A Democracia Em Cabo Verde*. Lisboa: Colibri, 2005.

Soares, Mário. "Democratização e Descolonização: dez meses no governo provisório," quoted in António Caldeira Marques, *Os Bazófios da Independência*. Unpublished, 92.

Van de Walle, Nicolas, and Smiddy, Kimberly. "Partis Politiques Et Systèmes De Parties Dans Les Democracies Non Liberals Africaines." In: Darbon, Dominique (Ed.), *L'Afrique Politique 1999: Entre Transition Et Conflits*. Paris: Karthala, 1999, pp. 41–57.

Chapter 5

Tourism in Cape Verde

Evolution, Risks, and Challenges

Edgar Bernardo

Tourism[1] is today the biggest and most dynamic sector of the economy of Cape Verde. The 2013 report of the World Travel and Tourism Council (WTTC) shows a growing trend in the African continent regarding the direct contribution of tourism to the GDP. The figures point to $168 billion in 2019, about 7.1 percent of total GDP (WTTC 2021). An example of this growth trend is Cape Verde, which has one of the fastest growing and largest tourism services in Africa. Tourism has been generating growth, attracting foreign investments, and creating jobs, but it is imperative to acknowledge the dangers and challenges of the tourism model chosen by Cape Verde and many other countries in Africa.

This chapter presents an overall picture of tourism and its importance in Cape Verde. Specifically, the chapter examines political strategies and development planning toward a gradual tourism-led strategy since its independence in 1975. The analysis and the data presented show the rapid growth of tourism in the country, as well as some of the negative impacts affecting the islands and local communities. The final section of this chapter intends to be a reflection upon the past and present evidence and what the future of tourism may hold.

TOURISM-LED DEVELOPMENT IN AFRICA

The data seems to be clear. In 2017, according to the African Development Bank (AfDB), 2018 tourism employed in Africa about 9.3 million direct jobs (2.5% in North Africa alone), which represents about 2.6 percent of the world's direct tourism jobs, a sum that reaches 22.8 million if we add the indirect and induced jobs (AfDB 2018). Africa had in 2016 about 5.1

percent world tourism arrivals, that is 62.9 million international arrivals, a much higher number than the 27 million in 2001, or 19 million in 1995 (AfDB 2018; WTO 2013). But this is a low number when compared with other regions. Africa, along with the Middle East, is still the region that lags in tourism performance and size.

Nonetheless, tourism activity is growing rapidly in many parts of Africa. The growth of this activity on the continent shows that governments are aware of its benefits at a macro and micro scale. Tourism is recognized to be much more than an economic activity. It requires a variety of services, infrastructure, and investments that generate opportunities. In addition, in the process, it also forces a wide interaction between people.

As a Small Island State, Cape Verde has been an example of a country locked in a model of development characterized by the dependence of migration, remittances, external aid, and a bureaucratic system, the so-called MIRAB model (migration, remittances, foreign aid, and bureaucracy). Bertram and Watters (1986) argue that the MIRAB system is a viable long-term strategy, which aims to use foreign aid, enhanced with the remittances sent by emigrants, to generate growth and socio-economic development. Indeed, after 1975, Cape Verde was heavily dependent on foreign aid and remittances.

In this context, authors like Sarmento (2008) suggest that only an external to the internal dynamic strategy may help overcome the weaknesses of this system and simultaneously maximize the advantages in a sustainable manner. In other words, there is broad consensus that tourism is the ideal strategy to capture the world market competitively. However, it is also agreed that given the serious risks that tourism may impose in the conservation of cultural and natural features, and the pressure it places on resources and infrastructure, it must be properly planned, managed, and implemented.

To transform economic disadvantages into competitive advantages, the key is to find a delicate balance that ensures the success of tourism. Tourism's sustainability demands proper planning and implementation. This sustainability depends in part on the ability to manage the fragile island territories with limited natural capital, focusing on the quality and the professionalization of services, and the diversification of the tourism products. However, most countries fail to plan and manage tourism's development properly. Cape Verde is no exception.

For all this, authors such as Vellas (1997), Kakazu (2007), and Sarmento (2008) argue that despite the recognized risks, the export of services through tourism remains as an ideal strategy. Many argue that tourism can contribute to the preservation of the environment, reduce emigration, and stimulate the diversification and growth of local economies. The government in Cape Verde today identifies tourism as a key element to transform and diversify the economy.

The focus on tourism should not be considered lightly. Tourism brings major benefits, but also major problems that tend to be overlooked. In this sense, it is important to know in advance the potential impacts and consequences of this bet if the sustainability of the affected community, its natural ecosystem, and its economic viability, are a sought-after goal.

Tourism's impact is widely debated. Many researchers have established the positive benefits and contributions of tourism. Among the most common positive impacts, we can enumerate the following: the ability to generate jobs (direct, indirect, and induced), to improve the quality of life in the communities, to support construction, investment, and infrastructure development, to boost economic growth, to diversify the local economy, and to facilitate foreign exchange inflows.

Among other prominent impacts, there is the public and private investment in the creation of protected areas, the development of legislation for the protection of environmental assets, the investment in environmental education campaigns, and the facilitation of entrepreneurial measures for environmental preservation.

Some also argue that tourism has positive cultural and social impacts, among which are the cultural exchange between hosts and guests, the revival of traditional practices, the increase in demand of local art, support for the preservation of the cultural identity of the destination, a growing sense of pride in the visited community, an improvement of living conditions, a positive change in the social structure, an increase in cultural and professional level standards of the population, and development of many useful services to the local community.

On the other hand, negative impacts from tourism include: the rising cost of living for the local population, the rising price and cost of services, the unequal distribution of benefits among the local community (usually favoring only a minority), the loss of rights of residents such as land use and access to beach fronts, the seasonality and temporality of the employment, increased instability of income and prices, the abandonment of traditional activities, dependence exclusively on tourism, and increased pollution (of various types), population congestion and traffic, excessive exploitation of agriculture and fishery, destruction of nature, deforestation, destruction of historic sites or monuments, over-consumption of essential natural resources, such as water and soil, and the pressure on infrastructure sanitation and waste management.

Finally, other negative cultural and social impacts include; a gradual loss of the local language (replaced by the language/languages of tourists), the exponential increase in prostitution and crime, increased alcoholism, destruction of the social fabric with the growth of inter-generational conflict, strengthening of class divisions, a decline in the attitude of the residents toward tourists (sometimes to the point of hostility and conflict), increased stress of living, labor exploitation, gradual loss of authenticity (e.g., through the distortion of craft, cultural manifestations, and local sites), and also change in morality and the cultural identity.

Notwithstanding tourism's potential negative impacts, tourism has been a popular strategy for many countries, especially small island states like Cape Verde. For many small developing countries in Africa and elsewhere, tourism has been attractive and often a favored policy recommendation by international agencies. Given the huge range of advantages perceived in tourism, often undervaluing the disadvantages, choosing tourism as a strategy by both the private and public sector is quite common. Cape Verde is an example of such reasoning. Today the country embraces tourism as its most important economic sector and the basis of its development model.

Tourism began to arouse interest even before independence:

> At the Center of Information and Tourism of Cape Verde, as we have confirmed, arrive almost daily requests for clarification about the possibility of investments in the tourism sector, from all parts of the world. [. . .] In the meantime, there are constant foreigners visiting who go there to personally confirm that the wonderful descriptions are a reality, this serves to show the tourist potential of these islands. (Oliveira 1973, 153)[2]

The next section will provide a short description of the various models and measures adopted by consecutive Cape Verdean governments since independence in 1975. Special attention is paid to the route to international tourism initiated in the 1990s. This section will also identify the major national developments in tourism by analyzing data that is highlighted repeatedly as a successful example, and a few negative impacts of tourism development, particularly on the islands with the highest tourism penetration. The final part of this chapter assesses the successes and failures of tourism development in Cape Verde if future governments are to continue the national tourism project plan.

Development and Tourism Policy (1975–2021)

Cape Verde's small size and lack of natural resources mean that its economy is very limited, and the national productive base is too narrow to generate the income growth, jobs, and living standards needed. Since independence, it has been heavily dependent on outside resources. The MIRAB development model is particularly dependent on revenues and exports of goods and services and unilateral transfers (Sarmento 2008).

Such external dependency ensured a downward spiral in the national economy where expenses kept growing, private initiative was strangled and income was limited by external aid and remittances, disrupting the balance. Such circumstances forced Cape Verde to find an alternative development model or at least a complementary one. The tourism-led model seemed to be the only alternative to this model.

After fifteen years of a socialist development strategy, several national development plans (NDPs) were adopted between 1981 and 2005. The government led by the Party for the Independence of Cape Verde (PAICV) created the 1st NDP (1982–1985). The 1st NDP underlined the difficulties that the country faced, not only those deriving from the recent independence but also recognizing their peripheral position toward the African continent and the barriers created by the geographical dispersion of the archipelago.

The NDP had concrete measures that focused on industry, mainly on the domestic market. This aimed to create basic conditions that would allow the country to escape the MIRAB model, but the plan was not able to reduce the dependence on foreign aid.

The 2nd NDP (1986–1990) had its main goal the creation of a solid economic base to allow the stabilization of production. It had a clear social concern, with goals of social equity, job creation, and the construction of infrastructure. For the political class, between 1975 and 1991, tourism was not a priority area for economic growth. It was only with the first multiparty elections won by the Movement for Democracy (MpD), in 1991, that tourism was seen as the ideal level for the economic and social future of the country.

With the 3rd NDP (1991–1995), there was a bet on the foreign market, seeking to put the country in the global market by encouraging private investment and by liberalizing the economy. An important consequence of the 1991 transition was the introduction of free-market reforms, including privatization, deregulation, and trade liberalization. The state's leading role in the economy was abandoned for a private sector–led growth model. The economy was opened to foreign investments.

In the 4th NDP (1997–2000), there was a strengthening of this liberalization stance (i.e., through privatization of public enterprises) and an increase in the international economic market investment. Reducing state intervention and the development of infrastructure opened the door to private investment.

During this time, the Base Law for Tourism was created as well as a few degrees, such as the creation of "Special Tourism Zones" (ZTE), the "Integral Development," and the "Parks and Tourism Protection Act." These specially designated zones were to be managed by the Cape Verde Investment and Tourism Development Corporation, a newly created government agency responsible for foreign investment. Each type of zone had its rules and regulations toward tourism exploration, the building of infrastructure, and scale parameters for tourism investors. Most of these zones were selected to attract huge investors, namely, mass tourism enterprises. It was the role of this agency to find buyers and manage the development around tourism in the islands.

Recognizing a lack of control in fauna and flora protection, tourism also represented an opportunity to develop the natural resources and channel their protection toward the benefit of tourism by developing quality tourism and consequently ensuring a higher contribution to the economy.

From the start, the focus was placed, not on mass tourism, but on elite tourism, high-quality tourism that attracted the upper-middle and high European classes. For such goals and ambitions, they tried to build new infrastructure, rehabilitate the historic sites and cultural heritage, and promote Cape Verde as a tourist destination.

The 5th NDP (2002–2005), implemented by the PAICV, had three pillars: local equilibrium, good governance, and ethics, and national development goals achievement. This last pillar was a new wager on the guiding principles of the previous NDP, aiming to detect and recognize the advantages and potential of each island, focusing on poverty eradication, national economic and social growth.

The second pillar relates to one of the ongoing issues in power contexts, namely, the fight against corruption, cronyism, and other practices that undermine the country's administrative and economic performance. All this intertwined with the need to balance development and quality of life within each island and across the archipelago.

We must stress the intention to implement the following sub-programs in this 5th NDP: increased efficiency of public administration; diversification of tourism products; training of human resources; tourism development of Boa Vista and Maio;[3] more effective tourism planning in promoting investments; and ensuring a sustainable development of tourism on the island of Sal and the ZTE. Other tourism policies were adopted and intended to promote ecotourism, rural tourism, among other forms of tourism.

Another important tourism initiative was implemented—the creation of a School of Hospitality and Tourism. All these initiatives under the 5th NDP were clear signs that the government was taking tourism seriously, setting up foundations for future employment opportunities.

Tourism became a success. In 2007, because of all these changes implemented by the several NDPs, tourism reached a volume of revenues corresponding to 23 percent of GDP of the country, and responsible for 90 percent of foreign investments (CCIT).[4]

During this year, the country received 333.000 tourists, a long way from the arrivals of the 1990s. In fact, in 1990, little more than 21.000 tourists arrived in Cape Verde, and ten years later there were already 145.000 (INE-CV 2008).

In 2008, the main source of tourists came from the UK, about 77,000 tourists. This was only possible due to the opening of the direct air connection between the UK and Cape Verde (INE-CV 2008).

The growth and development of the country based on tourism was, and is, regarded as a successful political accomplishment. In the words of Cape Verde's prime minister José Maria Neves in July 2010:

> Cape Verde maintained robust growth rates. GDP grew on average 7.3 percent per year between 2006 and 2009. In 2006 we achieved a growth rate of 10.1 percent. The international crisis has countered this expansion. Even so, we continue with good growth rates. (Neves 2010, 2)

The government determined that the next short-term goal would be the enhancement of the tourism sector: "Our vision is to build a tourism quality of high added value; develop a financial center; transform the country into a hub for air and sea transport and create a logistic base to support fisheries" (Neves 2010, 4).

It is important to recognize the key points of the 2011–2016 Government Program. Among these, we underline a continuity in the opening to international markets and the continuation of reforms in the private and public sectors.

In addition, the program also includes measures to respond to the social challenges, such as inclusion and cohesion, and to enhance continuity in the educational commitment and the construction of infrastructure (sanitation, energy, as well as those enabling greater mobility between islands and abroad, to the countries from the tourist market).

The program had a political commitment to build a more sustainable society and economy using tourism as a catalyst it contained concrete measures designed to enhance this "high-value" activity:

> First, how to transition from mass tourism to high value-added tourism. Second, it is imperative to increase its contribution to the national economy. In this sense, it is important that tourism has a much greater connection with the national economy and ensure a Cape Verdean wider participation in the sector. The key is to ensure that, over time, a new tourism sector appears in the content and economic impact locations are much higher than those of today. The agenda is to build a tourism sector that is well integrated in the Cape Verdean economy. This has been difficult and will require a reorientation of policies and incentives. But also the need to diversify offering, to implement a sophisticated and efficient tourism promotion, and to ensure that all the islands are involved in the development of the sector. The Government will seek to establish new routes and attract tourists from new markets. (Programa do Governo 2011, 28–29)

Related to this program are the conclusions of the Strategic Plan for the Development of Tourism in Cape Verde 2010–2013 (PEDTCV 2009). The strategic plan was issued by the Ministry of Economy, Growth, and Competitiveness, specifically, the General Directorate of Tourism. This was intended to make a diagnosis of national tourism. Some of the key findings of this diagnosis revealed the shortcomings of the tourism development process, like the insufficiency of resources, inadequate infrastructure, and price inflation.

This self-diagnosis demonstrates the official concern and interest that the Cape Verdean government has had in tourism. Additionally, it also shows how tourism is the major, if not the only government strategy to tackle the difficult conditions and constraints that the country faces.

The report suggests a set of actions and activities that aim to create sustainable high-value tourism, able to maximize the multiplier effects, with high levels of competitiveness, diversity, and quality (PEDTCV 2009). The plan also recognizes the crucial role of civil society in the implementation and improvement of the strategic plan.

Between 2015and 2016, there was a new national tourism marketing plan that aimed at the product, price, marketing, and distribution elements of the national tourism supply, pushing forward the previous national plan. Following this, between 2016 and 2021, the ninth government developed another national plan where tourism was once more considered the development cornerstone for the archipelagos, and with it plans to improve transportation within and outward, the first national focus on digital tourism, and yet another National Strategic Plan for Sustainable Development 2017–2021 was drawn to consolidate growth. Today is in effect the Strategic Plan for Tourism Development (2018–2030), focusing on public policy strategies, attempts to maintain the set course for national tourism and tourism governance (see Bernardo and Rodrigues 2020).

Considering the course designed and executed to the present day, one must acknowledge the political, economic, and social risks that the various governments encountered as they chose tourism as the national lever. We must also consider the sacrifices, difficulties, and pressure applied by such a bet on the Cape Verdean society and its people.

AN OVERVIEW OF THE GROWTH OF CAPE VERDEAN TOURISM

Now let us look at the results regarding the evolution of tourism in the last decades. An important starting point of international tourism in the archipelago began during the Portuguese government in 1960 when the international airport on Sal Island was inaugurated. In the same decade, because of this investment, the first tourist lodge would be built by a Belgian family (the Vynkier family), which sought to host beach tourists.

Much later, in 1986, the first hotel, the Belorizonte, was built by the Cape Verdean state and operated by a French tourism network. Slowly, over the next decade, more investors came from Italy, Portugal, and Spain thanks to investment conditions offered by various governments. The opportunities for tourism investment are diverse since most islands of this archipelago have huge natural potential.

The island of Sal has natural reserves, protected natural resources, and landscapes that would make it desirable. However, beach tourism is its biggest highlight. In fact, until the opening of the international airport of Boa Vista in 2007, Sal had 51 percent of all beds available in Cape Verde. Now Sal has experienced a diversion of investment and tourist flow to Boa Vista.

Boa Vista is currently the main center of international tourism in Cape Verde with four all-inclusive hotel complexes that alone can accommodate about 5,000 tourists per week. But before 2007, the island was living mainly on subsistence activities, services related to the local governance, and emigrant remittances. The island had a few small hotels and small inns, most of which were built after the opening of the Hotel Marine Club in 1996, at the time the largest in the country. Boa Vista has fourteen of the forty-seven protected areas of Cape Verde, which means it has a touristic potential that can go far beyond beach tourism.

The oldest and still most predominant tourism offering in Cape Verde is beach tourism, especially on the islands of Sal and Boa Vista. In the data we can see the evolution of the number of overnight stays between 1999 and 2017, which confirms the prevalence of these islands. It is undeniably the significant growth of Boa Vista given its very recent mass tourism implementation.

On the other hand, the island of Maio remains on the sidelines of tourism development despite its potential for tourism. Its hotel infrastructure is minimal, and the total number of tourists is only 1,000 per year. Still, its beaches anticipate the viability of a bet on beach tourism if the construction of an international airport becomes a reality.

In Santo Antão, Fogo and Brava, along with ideal natural resources for eco-tourism, their morphology and fauna also favor investment in sports tourism. However, huge gaps in internal access and external communications and the lack of integrated planning jeopardizes any investment, namely, the small number of boats connecting the islands, as well as flights that are both scarce and expensive.

The island of São Vicente merges urban and cultural wealth with a natural landscape that has favored diversified tourism. São Vicente also has a cultural asset—the now famous Baía das Gatas Music Festival held since 1995. Its suitable international airport has also contributed to the growth of tourism and the quality of life of its inhabitants.

In Santiago lies the historical and cultural tourism opportunity, particularly the Old City (Cidade Velha) in Santiago, which since 2009 has the UNESCO World Heritage status. Although the island brings together infrastructure, the largest national market, the largest population, and the central political institutions, Santiago still suffers from inadequate infrastructure and integrated planning.

In fact, all the islands mentioned, as those unmentioned, suffer from deep infrastructure problems, namely, health, safety, accessibility, energy, and other services. The infrastructure missing and the lack of integrated, coordinated, and coherent planning result in the impossibility of a diverse and coherent national strategy and execution. However, based only on mass beach tourism the evolution of supply and demand for tourism has increased dramatically.

The number of guests has evolved significantly, exceeding half million arrivals a year. Growth in arrivals has been pronounced since 2000. Even though the data prior to 2000 is unavailable, the second variable concerning the number of overnight stays, shows a clear upward trend, nearly 700,000 in 2000 and reaching over 4.5 million overnight stays in 2017 (INE 2020). A final note must go to the accentuation of the curve in 2007, the year that the international airport and two major hotels in Boa Vista opened. Finally, another type of tourism, one that is more dispersed and particularly interesting, is residential. More and more tourists are looking to invest in buying a second home, especially retired Europeans.

Ideally, it would be useful to track the rise of tourism in the country since at least its independence. However, the data is not available. As we saw earlier, all these decades were punctuated by events such as independence, adoption of socialist ideologies, then opening to the global market, and the adoption of a democratic government, several advances, as well as reversals. Still, Cape Verde today is already far from a small archipelago unknown as a tourist destination.

Despite all this growth, Cape Verde is still a drop in the ocean in terms of absolute numbers of arrivals or financial receipts. However, Cape Verde ranks among the top fifteen countries in the world in terms of the relative size of tourism to the national economy. WTTC Cape Verde 2019 Report states that tourism is responsible for 37.2 percent of the national GDP, 39.3 percent of all employment, and 50.8 percent of all exports (WTTC 2020).

Regardless, growth is also confirmed by the increasing average stay of 4.4 nights detected in 2000, to 5.9 nights in 2013, and 6.2 in 2017, although some intermediate fluctuations were recorded. Also, one must acknowledge the stable occupancy percentage above 50 percent since 2010. This is a remarkable achievement, especially considering that the percentage of occupation can easily fluctuate with the mere opening of some new hotel establishment.

In terms of the country of origin of international tourists, there is a growing number of British, Belgians and Dutch, French, German, even Portuguese and Cape Verdean nationals. On the contrary, the Italian tourists have been declining despite historically being the main tourists until 2006.

These nationalities found in Cape Verde a service to which they were familiar, provided by large companies and travel agencies, that made this strong growth possible. Particularly the tour operator TUI, from Germany, and the RIU hotel chain, from Spain, both already settled in the country in Sal and Boa Vista. The accommodation with the greatest capacity is by far the large hotels with an average of 6.5 nights per tourist, soon followed by the tourist villages with an average of 5.7 nights, relegating the other types of local hotels to less than 2.1 nights (INECV 2020).

The growth in the number of guests is not only due to the growing number of beds in the mass tourism hotels. If we look at the evolution of the number of guests in the other types of accommodation, we find that the number of guests has grown reaching the first peak in 2006, only to slowly decrease until 2009–2010. Gradually the number of guests grew back, which could be explained by encouraging the opening of tourism in other islands of the archipelago by the various governments.

Throughout the archipelago, we are witnessing a proliferation of different types of accommodation thanks to improvements in communication and transport between islands. However, tourism on most of the islands is limited by the lack of international airports or large hotel projects. As such, its growth is much smaller and its investment riskier.

The large hotels dominate, as illustrated by trends in hotel check-ins. Between 2000 and 2005, the number of tourists overnights did not exceed 200,000. However, they more than doubled in 2012, reaching 476,000 guests in 54 accommodations, and in 2019, 710,000 guests of all the 819,000 total guests (INECV 2020). This value is even more representative if we consider that the remaining 168 accommodations together accounted for less than 106,000 guests in 2019.

Hotel tourism, especially hotel tourism based on an all-inclusive policy, is largely responsible for accommodating most tourists. The latest data on the number of outlets confirm that the hotel establishments increased from 79 in 1999 to 284 in 2019, always in continuous growth, with particular emphasis on the hotels (total of 73). In fact, the last illustration demonstrates beyond doubt the weight of large mass hotel complexes in the evolution of the number of overnight stays in Cape Verde.

These big hotel complexes are located mainly in the islands of Boa Vista and Sal. In 2017, they represent more than 4.1 million overnights a year, while all the other islands together make up just over 420,000. Sal Island, between 2014 and 2017, had an average occupancy rate of 57 percent, and Boa Vista Island had an incredible 81 percent.

According to data from the World Travel & Tourism Council (2018), the direct and indirect employment generated by tourism in the country in 2017 was 93.500 jobs, about 39.3 percent of national employment. Apart from a break in 2009, employment associated with tourism has grown constantly. The variation could be explained by a lack of data or just different criteria in the chosen indicators.

According to the WTTC, both foreign direct investment and gross tourism receipts, including millions in tourist visas, are significant to the national GDP, representing over 49.7 percent of the national GDP in 2018. On the other hand, there has been a tendency for a reduction in foreign investment, from 2009 to 2014, but since then the growth has been clear. In 2018, it was around 25.7 percent of the total investment in the country, which resulted in 14.3 billion Cape Verde Escudos (CVE) or $153 million.

An analysis of total spending within the country by international tourists for both business and leisure trips, including transportation spending, shows a significant increase. The increase was triggered mostly in late 1990, the time of the first political reforms, but they exploded in the mid-2000s as soon as a few new mass-scale hotels opened in Boa Vista. The same is true for the total revenue generated within a country by industries that deal directly with tourists.

As for the domestic spending within Cape Verde's residents, its value is modest. In 1988, spending was shy of $6 million, and in 2013 it reached about $28 million. In 2018, it was estimated to be 12 percent of the $153 million mentioned above ($18 million). Another significant data is the total capital investment spending by all sectors directly involved in tourism and travel in Cape Verde. According to WTTC, in 1988, the total value was less than half a million dollars, but in 1999, it was twelve times higher.

Diverging from the success accountable by hard economic data, in our opinion, the biggest social success of the focus on tourism was the retention of emigration. With the growth of the national economy and employment opportunities, thousands of Cape Verdeans have and may still choose not to migrate. In fact, the archipelago already has thousands of immigrants from countries such as Senegal, Guinea, and other neighboring countries off the coast of Africa, demonstrating that it is becoming a receiver of migration and not only a sender.

One example of this retention is the island of Boa Vista which went from 4.000 inhabitants in 2000 to over 16,000 in 2017. An island with a tradition of emigration for the first time in over 100 years is seen nationally as synonymous with opportunity and hope.

Despite its small size and insularity aggravated by a territorial discontinuity and its geographical distance to other economies and international trade, the archipelago has differentiating elements at its disposal that continue to be channeled through tourism with great success.

Among these we highlight the political, economic, and social stability, good economic indicators, proximity to the main markets (particularly in Europe), and a geographical position with potential to capture new markets in the Americas and Africa, and of course, high average temperatures (25ºC). Another of its strengths is the diversity in landscape and cultural traits of its islands, which allow for various types of tourism that go beyond sun and sand.

The Negative Impacts of Tourism

In search of a process of modernization and revitalization of the economy, numerous countries around the globe, like Cape Verde, have their sights pointed to international tourism. The encouraging early results of this process should be considered. At the same time, we must not lose sight of the less positive impacts in the medium and long term.

Tourism in the archipelago of Cape Verde has also exposed or accentuated the national exposure to some negative impacts and consequences. Many of the impacts and challenges are an obstacle to the sustainability of the national tourism project. Sarmento (2008) examined the internal pressures and external barriers, as well the natural vulnerability as some of the major challenges.

The first barrier is more common in less developed destinations. It refers to the problems associated with lack of capital and investment, which require the usage of available resources as required and not based on a strategy. To some extent, an application of resources aimed at survival more than their sustainability (Gartner 2001). In other words, the capital is invested as needed and not according to a predetermined plan.

The rapid growth of tourism is vital to the fiscal sustainability of the country. But the dependence on tourism brings with it potentially more serious and dangerous consequences than the activity itself. This is particularly relevant if we recognize the considerable leakage of the Cape Verde economy due to imports of goods essential to tourism. Among the essential goods are food and materials imported directly from the countries from which tourists come, which demands an adjustment to the actual benefits of tourism to the national economy.

The tourism resorts also aggravate other leaks. These sites consume as much energy as some cities of the archipelago. The energy is based on fossil fuel that is also imported and then used to produce water via a desalination facility.

Similarly, the management of solid waste and garbage requires the importation of machinery and technical personnel. This is an additional cost that is often overlooked, but which dramatically increases the environmental and economic costs in the long run.

The pressure on the sensitive ecosystems of the island by large hotel complexes that occupy the beaches, jeopardize the survival of species such as the turtle *caretta caretta*, one of the national symbols. The increasingly numerous island tours with pickups and four-wheeled motorcycles damage and pollute beaches and dunes, precisely one of the main tourist attractions of the country.

Tourism may have contributed to the increase in crime, prices, and inflation, evidence that can be seen in official government statistics. More research is necessary in this area, but the experience of other tourism destinations in the world suggests that there is a strong correlation between tourism and these negative social impacts. Such consequences break the motivation and confidence of host communities, often confusing the common impacts of tourism with the weaknesses and shortcomings of its strategic planning.

Another factor that has contributed to the worsening of this feeling is the loss of some rights by the residents of the islands where the tourism bet was higher, like on the islands of Sal and Boa Vista. Among these factors that weaken popular support and confidence, we underline the restriction and even ban of native residents to local beaches which were traditionally leisure and meeting places and are now explored by hotels. In addition, the expropriation and acquisitions of private land for tourism development were controversial; previous owners have not been compensated.

One of the negative results was undoubtedly the emergence of slums on the main tourist islands where labor was insufficient. This happened on the island of Sal, and today in Boa Vista. These slums are neighborhoods without access to clean water, electricity, adequate housing, and sanitation. They are spaces inhabited by thousands of people, most of them employed in a large hotel, construction companies, and related activities to tourism growth. This discussion on the impacts of tourism in Cape Verde is much more discussed in depth by Bernardo and Jorge (2019), specifically in relation to the perception of impacts and governance among locals and other residents.

In the words of the World Bank: "In Cape Verde, development has occurred so fast that regulations and monitoring could not keep up, which has led to ecological and social stress" (World Bank 2013, 82–83). The same report recognizes that such impacts are the result of rapid, poorly planned coastal development.

To be able to control, mitigate, or even eliminate such negative impacts, large public investment is required in infrastructure improvements, social spending, environmental protection, and other areas. This, in turn, requires an increase in external and internal public debt to finance the national treasury to execute such investments. However, such an operation is high risk if we consider that this is an investment that depends on the success and steady growth of tourism and tourism revenues.

This brings us to the challenges associated with external demands. The tourist activity is mainly controlled by large tour operators. Depending on their interests, they may manipulate tourist flows between the available destinations or markets. An example of the ability to quickly manipulate the tourist flows toward destinations is precisely Cape Verde, which benefited greatly from the redirection of tourists from politically unstable countries in North Africa. The political or economic instability of a destination does not affect the overall flow and the increase in the volume of tourists managed by these companies and corporations. They have technical and organizational capacity, as well as viable alternatives to bypass such difficulties.

With the political stabilization of competitors in North Africa, Cape Verde as a tourism destination can suffer from the redistribution of its tourists, inducing tourism demand stagnation or even shrinkage. If this is not prevented or mitigated, it can lead to the collapse of the national tourism project.

The development and planning of the activity is often driven by the public sector. The lack of skills and/or disregard from the public experts and politicians frequently leads to high inefficiency, and even the multiplication of negative impacts (Bernardo and Rodrigues 2020; Helmy 2004; Gartner 2001).

Another crucial issue and serious challenge is presented by tourism is vulnerability to natural disasters. Vellas (1997) highlights how countries in tropical and subtropical areas are permeable to natural disasters that aggravate the construction costs and hinder the global competitiveness of destinations.

In the specific case of Cape Verde, its vulnerability to droughts, volcano activity, sandstorms, and desertification is well-known. We recall the volcano incident in 2014 on the island of Fogo. The volcano eruption led to the destruction of villages, as well as hotels and residential, inns which in turn were unable to ensure a substantial part of the livelihood of these communities; or the fact that sea level is gradually rising due to global climate change, endangering the beaches and other resources of the archipelago as their ecosystems, as well as the increasing water temperature is affecting the survival of some species like the already mentioned turtle *caretta caretta*.

Keeping Our Feet on the . . . Beach

Tourism is far from the magic wand once proclaimed (Brown 1998). Particularly in the most fragile economies of developing countries, these countries must manage the growth and change of tourism to ensure that it does not affect the objectives of sustainable and equitable growth at a local and national level.

The successful implementation of tourism in African countries is debatable given the disparity between the results of the global statistics of these countries and regional consequences and the results for the destination and local communities. The lack of data about the negative impacts, especially the environmental and negative social impacts, should not be considered a sign of successful planning but a sign of concern. It is a sign of concern because no data means no research, and in this case, no research means no political capacity and/or interest to determine all the impacts of tourism beyond economic indicators.

Azarya (2004) infers that only the elites and the middle class, political leaders, and the rich benefit from an increase in their income through this type of development process through tourism. Dieke (2003) labels tourism as a form of exploitation and dependence resembling neocolonialism, as the poor, remote from the decisions and lacking adequate training, prefer immediate economic benefits at the expense of long-term sustainability.

This results in a "selfish struggle for survival" which relegates to the background ideas like altruism or sustainability (Redclift 1992).

> We need to set targets and monitor whether tourism is really doing something about poverty as well as to be watchful about where money from tourism goes to the recipient communities. Benefits in kind can be more certain to meet needs and therefore it is important to have transparent auditing of how money from tourism is being distributed to, and used within, communities. Examining the supply chain to tourism enterprises and seeking changes that will bring more benefits to the poor is essential. (Okecha e Mwagona 2007, 12)

The development promoted by investing in international tourism in Africa should consider the impact on the poorest populations and the best way of involving these same populations in the planning process. Drawing together the roadmap for a more just and equitable society. This could range from a totally open and forward presentation of a tourism business plan investment by an investor to the local community and political institutions, a mid-range strategy, where investor and key local stakeholders are heard and involved in all stages of the process.

When looking to develop human resources including enabling and empowering locals, it is important that investors are not only aware of the consequences of their actions but also the long-term sustainability of the sector. As a result, one strategy is to encourage the

> sound utilization of local suppliers and thus enhance not only their productivity but also intersectoral linkages. In this sense, the spin-off effects are obvious: foreign exchange will be retained locally and further income would be earned. (Dieke 2000, 8)

It is also necessary that local small and medium tourism enterprises can escape this precarious situation, which will reduce the quality of service, and may be able to invest in successful strategies to reach these international clients. The precarious situation in the sense that entrepreneurs and businesses are ill-equipped for the ever-evolving tourism clusters, niches, and, at the same time, entrepreneurs use a similar business strategy as though foreign tourists have the same desires and expectations as the local communities' members. This will be one of the biggest challenges of tourism in Africa, and Cape Verde is no exception.

The Cape Verdean government is attempting to promote greater participation of local suppliers. One could question the efficiency of such measures at a point where mass beach tourism has solidified itself. However, the current situation is also a result of political and social instability in other markets that compete directly with Cape Verde. The current situation is but a short-term "golden age," and the long-term sustainability of tourism in Cape Verde depends on taking advantage of current events to invest in its future—a future desired by locals, governments, investors, and tourists.

In its aggressive pursuit of tourism investment, Cape Verde has created attractive conditions and various economic and financial incentives but also invested in infrastructures, such as in communication and transport. These, combined with its economic and political stability, its natural conditions, and its geographic position, made it possible and desirable to invest in the country.

Policies oriented to the international tourism market, the gradual democratization and transparency of these procedures, and generous incentives made it possible for Cape Verde to capture a huge foreign investment.

Also, national investments in infrastructure and land acquisitions have proved to investors that there was a background of political commitment to tourism development. This was reinforced by the peg of the national escudo to the Euro, which allowed for a strong national currency (Twining-Ward 2010).

However, the current tourism growth is only sustainable if there is a continuing significant commitment to invest in four important areas: workforce training and professional qualification in the private sector, especially for small and medium enterprises, the promotion of local supply to tourism, and increase in investment in domestic transport.

These requirements stem from the need to adapt the national market to the specific needs of tourism, and at the same time ensure opportunities and employability to Cape Verdeans beyond the unskilled labor opportunities already in place.

A major national challenge is focused on the issue of infrastructure. Inadequate infrastructure is undoubtedly the main obstacle to continued growth and sustainability. This calls for an increase in international and internal air connections—which would also represent a cost reduction and increase in destination options for the national consumer. In general, planning needs to be adjusted to the needs and priorities of inhabitants and tourists, when considering the challenge of air, sea, and land transportation.

Governments should continue and accelerate the construction and expansion of basic infrastructure to prevent overload on services and scarce local resources, such as water, electricity, sanitation, health services, and so on. This would indirectly also allow diversification in the local tourism offer as well as increase the quality of life and services for all locals and visitors. On the other hand, the investment in tourism-related infrastructure must be constantly increased and updated to reduce the chance of rupture and abrupt economic stagnation on local tourism companies and businesses.

Even the diversification of supply should not be understood only in the sense of variety at national level but also locally. Support for small local investors is essential for the sustainability of destinations and a much more even balance of economic benefits of tourism in local communities.

These are often disregarded in relation to its turnover compared to foreign investors. However, small and medium enterprises are essential in reducing capital flight abroad. It is the government's job to ensure that these companies can be competitive or at least are not negatively affected by the incentives to foreign investment and, by doing so, allow them to sustain part of expense and profit nationally.

It is therefore vital that the juridical and legal structures of Cape Verde are suited to the demands of tourism and related business areas. Legal mechanisms should be set up to facilitate and accelerate the creation of new businesses for both national and international investors. Namely, the creation of an office specialized in tourism-based businesses with the capability to deal with and solve the barriers that foreign and local investors deal with.

There is also the need for coordination between all stakeholders in the planning and implementation of a national tourism strategy: a coordination that is able to approach NGOs, private investors, local and central government, in its economic, social, environmental, and political objectives. Cape Verde does not have an industry-wide umbrella organization that brings together all stakeholders.

A monitoring framework with indicators that are better able to identify the shortcomings and the potential of tourism is needed for this to work—indicators that collect the satisfaction of tourists, operators, and locals, as well as economic macro data.

Recommendations such as these open the door for a sustainable and structured development that allows for mitigation of many of the negative impacts detected currently in the country and, in the long term, with the expected increasing economic capability, address the major social negative impact that requires a huge investment in infrastructure and education. The fragile economy of Cape Verde may have found a haven in international tourism, but it remains to be seen what answers it will provide to the troubles ahead. The anchor was raised, and the challenges will be greater on the route to the future.

NOTES

1. This chapter is financed by National Funds provided by FCT—Foundation for Science and Technology through project UIDB/04020/2020.

2. Free translation from the author.

3. In 2005 the Tourism Development Society for the Islands of Boa Vista and Maio was also created (SDTIBM).

4. Câmara de Comércio Indústria e Turismo Portugal Cabo Verde (http://www.portugalcaboverde.com/main.php).

REFERENCES

Africa Development Bank Group. *Africa Tourism Monitor. The High 5s—Tourism as a Pathway to Industrialization, Integration, Quality of Life, Agriculture, and Powering Up Africa.* ADBG: Abidjan. https://www.afdb.org/en/documents/africa-tourism-monitor-2018. 2018.

Azarya, V. "Globalization and International Tourism in Developing Countries: Marginality as a Commercial Commodity," *Current Sociology*, 52(6), 949–967. 2004.

BCV. Banco de Cabo Verde, Praia: Cabo Verde. www.bcv.cv. 2014.

Bernardo, E., and Rodrigues, V. "Turismo em Cabo Verde, governação e governança," *Revista de Turismo y Patrimonio Cultural*, 18(1), 27–38. 2020.

Bertram, G., and Watters, R. "'The MIRAB Process: Earlier Analyses in Context'," *Pacific Viewpoint*, 27(1), 47–59. 1986.

Dieke, P. "Developing Tourism in Africa: Issues for Policy Consideration," *DPMN Bulletin*, 7(1), 25–31. 2000.

Gartner, W. "Issues of Sustainable Development in a Developing Country Context," in Whabad, S., and Cooper, C. (Eds.), *Tourism in the Age of Globalization*, 306–318, Routledge, London. 2001.

Helmy, E. *Towards Integration of Sustainability into Tourism Planning in Developing Countries: Egypt as a Case Study*, Faculty of Tourism Hotel Management, Helwan University, Cairo, Egypt. 2004.

INE. Instituto Nacional de Estatísticas de Cabo Verde, Praia. www.ine.cv. 2008–2014.

INE. *Conta Satélite do Turismo em Cabo Verde, 2011–2014*, Instituto Nacional de Estatísticas de Cabo Verde, Praia. www.ine.cv. 2015.

INE. *Estatísticas do Turismo Ano 2019.* www.ine.cv. 2020.

Kakazu, H. "Sustainable Island Tourism: The Case of Okinawa," in Carlsen, J., and Butler, R. (Eds.), *Island Tourism: Sustainable Perspectives*, Glasgow, UK. 2011.

Neves, J. "Estado da Nação—Construindo a Prosperidade para Todos," *Discurso do Estado da Nação na Assembleia Nacional.* Disponível no sítio. http://www.governo.cv/documents/Estado_da_Nacao.pdf. 2010.

Okecha, R., and Mwagona, M. "Tourism Contribution in Local Economies: Focus on Poverty Rediction in Kenya," in *4th IPTT African Conference on Peace through Tourism.* http://www.iipt.org/africa2007/PDFs/Roselyne.pdf. 2007.

Oliveira, H. *Cabo Verde—72—ano quinto de seca*, Lisboa. 1973.

PEDTCV. Programa Estratégico de Desenvolvimento do Turismo de Cabo Verde, Direção Geral do Turismo: Ministério da Economia, Crescimento e Competitividade. https://portoncv.gov.cv/dhub/porton.por_global.open_file?p_doc_id=763. 2009.

Poirine, B. "A Theory of Remittances as an Implicit Family Loan Arrangement," *Two Essays on Aid and Remittances*, Pacific Studies Monograph 19, Centre for Pacific Studies, University of New South Wales, Sydney. 1995.

Programa do Governo VIII Legislatura 2011–2016, Ofício de 14 de Junho de 2011. http://www.governo.cv/index.php?option=com_docman&task=doc_download&gid=123&Itemid=91.

Redclift, Michael. "The Meaning of Sustainable Development," *Geoforum*, 23(3), 395–403. 1992.

Sarmento, E. *O Turismo Sustentável como factor de desenvolvimento das pequenas economias insulares: o caso de Cabo Verde*. Edições Universitárias Lusófonas. 2008.

Twining-Ward, L. "Cape Verde's Transformation: Tourism as a Driver for Growth In-Depth Case Study of Cape Verde's Tourism Sector—The World Bank's African Success Stories Project." 2010.

Vellas, F., and Cauet, J. *Le Tourisme et les Îles, Economia*, L'Harmattan, Paris. 1997.

World Bank. *The World Bank Annual Report*, The World Bank. www.worldbank.org. 2013.

WTO. *United Nations World Tourism Organization.* http://www2.unwto.org. 2012–2013.

WTTC. *Travel & Tourism Economic Impact 2018 Cape Verde.* http://www.wttc.org. 2018.

WTTC. *Annual Report.* http://www.wttc.org. 2015.

WTTC. *Cape Verde Report.* http://www.wttc.org. 2020.

WTTC. *Annual Report.* http://www.wttc.org. 2021.

Chapter 6

Cape Verde and the United Nations

Lessons from the Country's Thirty-Year LDC Experience

Djalita Fialho

PART I: CAPE VERDE BEFORE LDC GRADUATION

Cape Verde's strong social and economic performance since 1975 has been internationally recognized, and the country has become a model case for development agencies. Its strong performance prompted the United Nations General Assembly to graduate Cape Verde from the list of Least Developed Country (LDC) in December 2007. However, Cape Verde's graduation from the LDC group was neither smooth nor widely supported inside and outside the country. This chapter examines Cape Verde's relationship with the United Nations (UN), having as the main angle of analysis the country's thirty-year membership in the UN's LDC category. It explains the background of how, during LDC membership, power networks—supported by factors such as the availability of much-needed foreign assistance and the constellation of interests resulting from that—came to consolidate themselves in Cape Verde. The result, roughly thirty years later, was an opposing stance by the country and by certain UN structures toward LDC graduation. Categorized as an LDC in 1977, Cape Verde retained LDC status for thirty years. In December 2007, it became the second country to graduate from the LDC list of over fifty countries.

This chapter examines Cape Verde's LDC graduation negotiation process.[1] As the analysis will show, this process was different from the decision-making process that led to its LDC admission. This also includes an analysis of whose interests are at stake when countries enter and when they leave the category. Through this, I expect to find elements that can be extrapolated to developing country differentiation in general.

Through triangulation of document analysis, descriptive statistics, and semi-structured interviews,[2] the first part of the chapter closely examines Cape Verde's LDC experience, contrasting admission and graduation decision-making processes. This first part of the Cape Verdean case study focuses on the country's LDC admission process, by exposing the economic and political context at the time and the events that led to it becoming an LDC in 1977. It also highlights Cape Verde's development performance while in the LDC category, showing the relevance of LDC status for the external mobilization of development resources, and its importance for the exercise of political power in the country. The concluding part of the chapter examines the graduation process.

THE SETTING: CAPE VERDE

General Economic and Political Context of LDC Admission

Following its independence from Portugal, in 1975, Cape Verde was going through a particularly difficult period, considering its frail economic conditions, largely driven by persistent droughts. Concern with food security—"haunted by the spectre of the return to the 1940s famines" (Correia e Silva 2001, 56)—seems to have been key in the state-building process in Cape Verde and in devising priorities for action. However, territorial discontinuity and the negative impact caused by the lack of natural resources, adverse weather conditions, and a small internal market imposed serious growth constraints to an agriculture-based economy.

Small, poor, lacking natural resources and a favorable climate, Cape Verde at independence became dependent on the outside world to survive. Growth, jobs, food security, and income-generating activities for people had to be financed from the outside. The state-led economic development model embraced in the post-independence years relied heavily on multilateral and bilateral Official Development Assistance (ODA). Monetary remittances from the country's large diaspora also played a key role in the country's economic development. In the years right after independence, the national productive system remained fragile. Agricultural and industrial production was insufficiently strong to lift the economy from low levels of growth. Lacking the internal capacity to sustain an expansion in production, Cape Verde became reliant on external funding, mainly through foreign aid and remittances.

The fact is that the Cape Verdean economy has always faced problems related to insufficient scale economies, production diversification, and heavy dependence on import products and external capital flows, namely, ODA and remittances. For instance, on average, since 1980 (the earliest available data) imports have represented 67 percent of GDP (World Bank 2013). Being an archipelago exacerbates, even more, these problems due to territorial discontinuity and transport and communication costs. Indeed, "the scattering of Cape Verde's territory over ten islands . . . and its arid Sahelian climate pose a constant development challenge" (AfDB/OECD 2008, 198). In addition, the lack of a production base, that allows capital accumulation and the absence of an economically dynamic regional integration space, represent factors that significantly worsen the constraints associated with a small economy (République du Cap-Vert 2006, 10).

Thus, Cape Verde has always faced important structural handicaps, namely, smallness of the internal market (preventing it from reaping the benefits of economies of scale), high trading costs associated with its insularity, ecological fragility, weak agricultural capacity (only about 10% of its soil is arable), and lack of natural resources. Because it is a ten-island archipelago, consisting of dispersed islands, it is necessary to duplicate the number of key infrastructures, namely ports, airports, health, and educational services, among others. For example, when considering the number of airports needed to promote tourism and facilitate communication within the country and between the country and the rest of the world, it is estimated that at least four international airports are needed, even though one would be enough for a country of 500,000 people living in contiguous territory (République du Cap-Vert 2006). This kind of constraint greatly affects the competitiveness of the economy (Fialho 2008). Hence, after independence, the country was able to survive on account of two international programs funded through emergency food aid, covering the 1975–1977 and the 1977–1980 periods.

In general, on the eve of its LDC admission, in 1977, the one-party political system context in Cape Verde was described as follows by a senior member of the first government and subsequently minister and senior diplomat:

> Popular support of the government . . . was still very large; the country was going through a major economic and social crisis caused by the cyclical lack of rainfall and therefore serious shortage of agricultural production; the UN enjoyed an image of ideological exemption and that of a good friend of Cape Verde.[3]

In addition,

> hunger and the inability of the economic system to create new jobs led to mass emigration, which, on the one hand, alleviated the pressure on the labor market and, on the other hand, was, and remains, an important source of income for the country and of income to families. (Querido 2005, 89)

Figure 6.1 shows the importance of remittance in the Cape Verdean economy. Estêvão explains that

> at the time of its political independence in 1975, Cape Verde lived a model of international economic integration that came from the mid-nineteenth century and which was based on three fundamental elements: services, migration, and integration into the Portuguese imperial space. (Estêvão 2004, 1)

This last element enabled "the inflow of transfers from the mainland, mainly to finance operations previewed in the country's Development Plans and to support programs to combat drought" (Estêvão 2004, 3). It was this economic model "heavily based on migration/remittances and public transfers, which was replicated after independence. The key difference was the replacement of public transfers from the metropolis by ODA" (Estêvão 2004, 3).

Cape Verde's heavy dependence on external support, especially donor aid, influenced its domestic decision-making process and its foreign relations. This led to a strategic and pragmatic foreign policy, guided by the interest (and need) to foster relationships that could yield financial flows, which were essential to the viability of the state and the survival of its population. This approach was, in effect, realpolitik at play. The ruling party was known for its "pragmatic and moderate politics" (World Bank 1985, 1). For example, the decision to sell food aid (see discussion below) and the option to join the Non-Aligned Movement during the Cold War are two examples of this pragmatic and moderate stance, both of which have positive implications in terms of improving the prospects for development.

By the end of the 1970s and beginning of the 1980s,

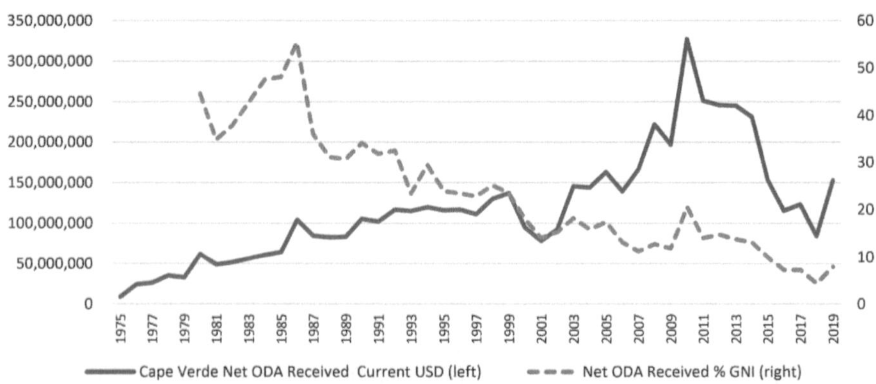

Figure 6.1 Net ODA Received (Current USD) and Net ODA Received (%GNI). *Source*: Created with data from World Bank, World Development Indicators, 2021.

the quasi-totality of production remain[ed] dependent on foreign transfers. Therefore, one should not harbor illusions about the rapid growth of production. . . . This is more of a "blistering," resulting from the multiform recycling of transfers than true progress of production. (Secretaria de Estado de Cooperação e Planeamento 1981, 38)

A former minister and senior diplomat recalls, in the interview, that when diplomatic demarches were being made to have the UN categorize the country as an LDC, "our main problem was to gather statistical data to support what we were saying, namely, that we had received [from the colonial power] a miserable territory." With an estimated per capita GDP of only $267 in 1983, the World Bank (1985, 2) also recognized that

in the absence of official national accounts, it is difficult to measure growth of GDP. According to preliminary estimates, the average annual rate of growth of GDP between 1977 and 1982, in constant dollars, was 2.6 percent per year, or 1.7 percent in per capita terms.

Finding solutions to poverty was indeed a crucial task. Despite the challenging economic situation following independence, the country was able to embark on deep structural reforms. Under a peaceful one-party political regime, economic and social foundations were built with relative success. In the process, considerable international support, notably foreign aid, was gathered. Certain factors were considered essential in promoting the country's development during that period, namely,

developing human resources, halting the ecological and human desertification process in rural areas, international fundraising towards a policy of capital formation, using the country's geo-strategic position to establish industries and services that could allow it to become less dependent from abroad. (Querido 2005, 89)

In such a context, at its start as an independent country, the need to tackle poverty and the constant threat of hunger, and the unavailability of internal resources to do so, created a strategic interest in belonging to the LDC category. The LDC designation was a mechanism that could facilitate access to foreign aid, including much-needed food aid. This interest triggered in the ruling class the need to seek and actively move toward LDC membership.

The LDC category, encompassing a substratum of countries within the larger group of developing countries, was first established as an official UN category in 1971. Countries categorized as least developed are to be prioritized in terms of special international treatment. More specifically, they are to be provided priority assistance and support in terms of development aid and trade preferences. LDC status presently provides benefits in the following areas (UNCDP 2008):

A. bilateral donors' commitment to allocate 0.15 percent of the gross national product as Official Development Assistance (ODA) to LDCs (according to the Brussels Declaration and Programme of Action);
B. several UN organizations target technical cooperation programs to LDCs or earmark a proportion of their budgets for LDCs;
C. Generalized System of Preferences (GSP—non-reciprocal) and Global System of Trade Preferences (GSTP—among developing countries, is a reciprocal scheme available for signatories), granting preferential entry into export markets;
D. special treatment regarding WTO obligations (for LDCs that are WTO member-states) and WTO accession;
E. trade-related capacity-building through the Integrated Framework for Trade-related technical assistance to LDCs; a multiagency, multidonor program to assist LDCs in developing trade-related capacities;
F. financial support provided by the UN (and its organizations) for the participation of LDC representatives in annual sessions of the General Assembly and in other UN meetings;
G. entitlement to 90 percent discount in LDC contributions to UN peace-keeping operations;
H. LDC contributions to the UN regular budget are capped at 0.01 percent of the total UN budget.

Since 1971, the list of LDCs has gone through several periodic updates, according to criteria set by the UN for the identification of these countries.[4] By 2013, the United Nations Committee for Development Policy (UNCDP)—a subsidiary body of the UN Economic and Social Council whose responsibility includes advising on and managing the LDC list, as well as setting its technical criteria—had met forty times since the establishment of the category.

BECOMING AN LDC (1975–1977): WHY AND HOW?

Cape Verde was admitted into the LDC category in 1977, two years after its independence from Portugal and six years after the establishment of the category. In fact, as early as 1975, UNCDP reported having received "a communication . . . by the Secretary-General from the Transitional Government of Cape Verde requesting that Cape Verde be considered for inclusion in the list of least developed countries" (UNCDP 1975, 31). By 1976, UN General

Assembly resolution 31/17 on *Assistance to Cape Verde* requested UNCDP, "as a matter of priority, to give favorable consideration to the question of the inclusion of Cape Verde in the list of least developed countries" (UN 1976, 56). In that same resolution, developed countries and organizations of the UN system are invited "to grant Cape Verde the same benefits as those enjoyed by the least developed among the developing countries in the light of prevailing conditions in Cape Verde" (UN 1976, 56). Subsequently, the 1977 UNCDP Report stated that

> the available data on *per capita* domestic product, the share of manufacturing in total output, and the literacy ratio suggest that Cape Verde and Comoros may be included as borderline cases in the list of least developed countries. (UNCDP 1977, 22)

The context of Cape Verde's admission as an LDC, in 1977, is summed up as follows: "The country's socio-economic situation and low level of development represented great challenges at the time, for both the national authorities and the international community" (Republic of Cape Verde 2005, 1). The former minister and senior diplomat states that Cape Verde's admission into the LDC category did not imply "a negotiation process per se. We had to prove that we met the criteria. . . . Our merit was not to negotiate; it was to capture the moment."[5]

The general gist of the interview with a former president of Cape Verde and prime minister at the time is that the decision to seek LDC membership was essentially a no-brainer; meaning that, to Cape Verdean authorities, LDC admission was the obvious path to follow given the country's extremely challenging circumstances in 1977 and great lack of resources.[6] One former minister of planning and cooperation at the time describes the country's situation right after independence:

> The country had nothing, Cape Verde had absolutely nothing, the boxes were completely empty and at the time it was, I think, a loan of US $500,000 from Portugal, something like that, that was used to buy basic things, because there was no money in the safe . . . it was a country fully assisted, completely so.[7]

A former minister and senior diplomat recalls that in 1977 "the environment was of great patriotism, on the one hand, and of great concern, on the other. We were learning to walk on our own, in the midst of yet another major drought."[8] He adds that

> the hope of the vast majority of the population in the recent national independence contrasted with the consequences of the lack of rain and the opinion of

several personalities who felt that, separated from Portugal or from Guinea-Bissau, Cape Verde would not endure its sovereignty.

Hence, with survival as the very first priority, the country followed what some have referred to as a policy of "national salvation." Basically, LDC admission was approached as "a lifesaver," says the former minister and senior diplomat, considering that being part of the category was seen as a condition that could greatly enhance the country's access to aid.[9]

The former president of the republic believes that, given the country's dismal circumstances right after independence, it made no sense to even promote an internal debate on LDC membership/admission, let alone frame[10] the intention to be categorized as an LDC, considering that:

> Poverty and [the country's] weaknesses were so obvious that one could not dispute that . . . [and in this context] food aid was essential. Nobody could deny the need for food aid. Even though it was a sign of dependence.[11]

In this regard, the former minister and senior diplomat refers to an "apparently full and unconditional agreement."[12] A former minister of planning and cooperation corroborates this view, saying that the decision to seek LDC admission after the country's independence "was an extremely peaceful process for everyone."[13] He adds that

> at the time it was about creating the conditions to maximize foreign aid. And so this [i.e., LDC admission] would be a great opportunity for us to be able to access favorable [financing] conditions. Incidentally, everyone, all of our partners were pushing us to enter this category. . . . So, it was an extremely peaceful process for everyone.

For example, according to both senior officials cited above, UNCTAD was among the international organizations that played an important role in facilitating Cape Verde's LDC admission in 1977. While Cape Verde took the initiative to seek LDC membership, it could count on strong encouragement from organizations such as UNCTAD and UNDP, namely, through the provision of much-needed technical assistance. In addition, support is also reported to have come from "OAU members, the Group of 77, the majority of UN member countries . . . [and from] the ECOSOC and UNCTAD lobbies."[14] He also mentions that he believes that "consistently anti-colonial governments supported the inclusion of Cape Verde in the LDCs, in addition to Scandinavian and central and northern European countries."

To sum up, Cape Verde's LDC admission did not entail a negotiation process. Cape Verdean authorities took the lead to request LDC status, convinced that this would enhance the country's access to international support. This request was encouraged by both internal and external stakeholders and readily accepted by the UN. Overall, there was general agreement regarding Cape Verde's LDC admission.

In terms of power change, independence represented a major shift in the structure of Cape Verde's political power, by transferring it from the colonizer to the local elite, within a one-party political regime (for a thorough discussion on the political transition from colony to independent country, see Évora 2001). The great majority of the new Cape Verdean ruling class was composed of freedom fighters that had been involved in and deeply committed to the struggle for independence on several fronts: armed, diplomatic, and intellectual. To them, this power transfer represented the need to create the necessary material conditions to exercise that power, considering that, as a result of independence, the financial responsibility of the colonizer toward the country should cease. While it was clear that political power had fallen into new hands (i.e., the Cape Verdean independence party), in the aftermath of independence, it was still not so clear on whose hands economic/material power would ultimately fall. In practical terms, and in a context of generalized poverty and much uncertainty, to the new ruling class, exercising political power in independent Cape Verde required being able to carry out a successful external mobilization of financial resources. In light of this, the diplomatic experience of many of the former freedom fighters (who assumed positions of power) proved to be an asset in this context, especially considering that a reasonable international network had already been established during the years of struggle for independence. This fact alone solidified the power position of the new ruling class.

Notwithstanding the dependence entailed in belonging to the LDC category, the route of seeking LDC admission gave the newly appointed ruling elite the possibility to frame the external mobilization of resources within an internationally recognized category of developing countries, enhancing, with this, the chances of success in bringing about economic growth and development. In this sense, LDC membership was also approached as an instrument of power, considering that it allowed easier resource mobilization and facilitated the exercise of political power in a context of extreme poverty where, otherwise, that would have been more challenging. Feeding the starving and meeting the basic needs of a generally poor population was a sine qua non condition for state-building and sovereignty in Cape Verde. LDC membership was instrumental in this regard.

However, it is important to clarify that, as a policy option adopted in 1975, the ruling independence party, while operating a centralized economy, favored foreign aid recycling. This means that the state acted not as a mere recipient and/or consumer of foreign aid, but mostly as a transformer or an investor of that aid, trying to multiply its effects so that, on the one hand, it could be profitable and, on the other hand, it would not create a beggar's mentality in the population. For instance, the policy implemented with regard to food aid was to never freely distribute it to the population. Instead, it was sold at affordable prices by state-owned enterprises and the proceeds were used to create jobs and build public infrastructure, in a centralized economic structure. Notwithstanding its positive aspects in such a context, this type of structural arrangement, when in place for a long time, creates a web of networks and stakeholders, along with a constellation of interests that tend to solidify over time and whose disintegration is never easy. The possibility of change is, therefore, not always welcome for actors such as state bureaucrats (from Cape Verde and its bilateral partners) and representatives from international organizations who have contributed to putting those networks in place and who, over the years, have become accustomed to collecting advantages from them.

BEING AN LDC: GROWTH AND DEVELOPMENT PERFORMANCE AS AN LDC (1977–2007)

Before addressing Cape Verde's growth and development performance during its thirty years as an LDC, it is important to contextualize this performance by highlighting four important changes that marked the 1977–2007 period: (a) the political system changed from single to multiparty in 1990, (b) the liberal party assumed political power in 1991, (c) the economic model changed from centralized to liberalized, (d) the independence party reassumed power in 2001, keeping in place a liberalized economy. Despite these changes, a general policy of foreign aid–led development was kept in place.

Since independence, the Cape Verdean economy has functioned with the support of private and public international capital flows which, by reducing the trade gap, assist private consumption and investment, increase public financing capacity, and ensure the availability of international reserves, guaranteeing access to both consumption and investment imports. Emigrant remittances and ODA represent the two most important international resources made available to the country: (a) allowing equilibrium of the balance of payments, despite high and persistent trade deficits (see table 6.1) and (b) guaranteeing part of the resources necessary to finance the public deficit (République du Cap-Vert 2006, 10). Throughout the country's LDC days, this was the case, with foreign aid and remittances helping to reduce the trade gap.

In the 1980s, the country was much more dependent on foreign finance, considering that the difference between imports and exports was larger

Table 6.1 Cape Verde's Trade Gap

	1980	*1985*	*1990*	*1995*	*2000*	*2005*	*2010*
Exports of goods and services (constant 2005 million US$)	97,752	169,441	171,242	216,297	392,821	367,187	749,500
Imports of goods and services (constant 2005 million US$)	135,642	188,360	231,107	323,439	452,265	647,010	981,579
Trade gap (constant 2005 million US$)	-37,890	-18,919	-59,865	-107,142	-59,444	-279,823	-232,079

Source: Created with data from World Bank, World Development Indicators. Washington DC: World Bank, 2013.

(roughly 60%). Starting in the 1990s, structural changes (namely, economic liberalization) brought the level of imports down and increased exports (part of which due to services exports), which together decreased the trade deficit (to roughly 30%).

Specifically, in terms of exports (which include goods, services—specifically, tourism, and re-exports—namely, fuel sales), it has been concentrated on the European market and based on a narrow range of goods and services, given the country's limited industrial and agricultural capacities. In 1985, the World Bank (1985, 3) reported that Cape Verde's trade account showed "a large and growing deficit. In 1983 merchandise exports represented only 2 percent of imports. The main exports were bananas and fish products, which accounted for more than 60 percent of the total." More recently, the country has somewhat diversified its exports, but food products (mainly fish) still represent the country's main export, particularly to Europe, its main commercial market.

1982–1985: The First National Development Plan

In the context of a state-led, centrally planned economy, where key enterprises were state-owned, the first National Development Plan (NDP) would only be devised for the 1982–1985 period and its implementation resulted in an average real per capita GDP growth of 4 percent for the triennial. The World Bank (1985, 4) considered that "the fact that the Government delayed preparing a first Plan until seven years after independence is an indicator of the prudence with which it approaches the problems of development, given the country's human resources, institutions and physical resource limits."

According to the World Bank (1985, 8–9),

> Cape Verde is an unusual case among developing countries. It is a small economy with a poor resource base, experiencing a prolonged drought, with

large deficits in the overall budget and resource accounts. However, largely due to the substantial inflows of emigrant remittances and foreign aid in the form of either grants or concessionary loans, the country has been able to maintain a positive real growth rate, a surplus in the balance of payments, and a reasonable level of foreign reserves. Economic management has succeeded in preserving a fragile external equilibrium, while an overall strategy of economic and social development is pursued.

1986–1990: The Second National Development Plan

Implementation of the second National Development Plan started in 1986 and aimed essentially at decreasing Cape Verde's international dependence. This called for greater investment in the internationalization of the economy. To achieve this, the plan previewed a greater role for the private sector in boosting national productive capacity and export level. Between 1986 and 1990, the economy presented an average growth rate of about 3 percent;[15] indicating a slight slowdown compared to the 1982–1985 period. However, economic transformation toward liberalization was already in progress, considering efforts toward economic openness, focus on institutional reforms and efforts to build public companies (banks, postal and telecommunication services, and others), which could serve as important pillars of the economy.

All-in-all, the two national development plans implemented at the time (1982–1985 and 1986–1990) were "concerned with valuing indigenous resources . . . , with external solvency, with the unification of the internal market, with satisfying the needs of the populations (production for the internal market)" (Reis 2000, 102). These development plans prioritized infrastructure building, focusing on the implementation of sectoral programs aimed at promoting rural development, fisheries, energy, tourism, education, health, housing, and trade.

1991–2001: Multiparty System and Economic Liberalization

Following the end of the Cold War, the fall of Communism, and the fall of the Berlin Wall, Cape Verde opted for a democratic regime and implemented a multiparty political system—a shift that demonstrated convergence with the emerging new world order. Hence, geopolitics and shifts in the international structure of power motivated an internal political structural rearrangement and important changes in terms of power-sharing within the country. The transformations that took place since then include successive and peaceful political change and economic liberalization. The independence party (PAICV), in power since 1975, lost the country's first multiparty elections to *Movimento para a Democracia* (MpD), who assumed power in 1991 and liberalized the economy. By 2000, the country had met graduation criteria three times (i.e., 1994, 1997, and 2000).

In a nutshell, (a) from independence (1975) to the instauration of democracy (1991) the state played a decisive role in conducting the country's economy and (b) from 1991 on, it transferred part of its economic development responsibilities to the private sector (Reis 2000, 98). In fact, in the Third National Development Plan adopted right after the 1991 elections, the state maintained its responsibility in terms of infrastructure building and human capital, and the private sector started operating as a direct economic agent (Pais 2012).

Being an open economy and very dependent on external flows, the need for economic growth and better integration in the world economy motivated, since 1998, the establishment of a fixed exchange rate regime linking the national currency to the Euro.[16] Considering that the Euro zone has always been the country's main commercial market and home to a considerable share of the Cape Verdean diaspora, this currency peg, by strengthening the country's foreign reserve position, has, evidently, many economic benefits. According to Braga de Macedo and Pereira (2006, 20), Cape Verde has "got it right when it comes to its currency peg, as the peg apparently reflects the [. . .] credibility of Cape Verdean economic policy and so has successfully withstood the scrutiny of international markets." Even before 1998, during economic centralization, the national currency was "pegged to a basket of nine currencies, which in broad terms, is appropriate to Cape Verde's circumstances. The escudo exchange rate has been adjusted to maintain a stable real exchange rate" (World Bank 1985, 3).

As with the general policy option favoring foreign aid–led development (which persisted through single and multiparty political systems and through centralized and liberalized economic models), also in this case, a structural change—namely, change in the domestic power structure—did not result in a complete policy disruption. All-in-all, the new liberalized economic model implemented in the 1990s did not represent a true paradigm shift in terms of ODA.

2002–2007: The Inevitability of LDC Graduation

The 2002–2005 National Development Plan stated the intention to proceed within the framework of an integrated development strategy based on the promotion of a private sector–led economy (Ministério das Finanças, Planeamento e Desenvolvimento Regional 2002, 10).

The 2002–2005 National Development Plan preceded, and overlapped with, the *Agenda for Transformation and Modernization of Cape Verde*;[17] a document that was motivated by the prospect of LDC graduation, and the need to start devising measures to cope with the country's imminent new development status, and aimed at promoting a broad national consensus regarding Cape Verde's transformation. Hence, the need to promote a transformation (i.e., to set up a new development paradigm, considering that, as a result of the impending LDC graduation, foreign aid–led development should come to an end) was only recognized once the negotiations for graduation were close to an end, and not before. Ultimately, this demonstrates accommodation into a long-standing structural arrangement and a lack of long-term planning.

The fact is that this foreign aid–driven structural arrangement was actually bearing fruit. Throughout its LDC days, having gone from a centralized to a liberalized economic model, Cape Verde's growth was clear, especially when comparing its GDP per capita with that of LDCs in general.[18] In effect, the latter shows somewhat of a plateauing trend and little progress since the 1980s, while in Cape Verde GDP per capita grew steadily, following world trends for the most part. When GDP per capita is expressed in index numbers (1982 = 100), Cape Verde's growth is even more evident.

On account of this growth, while still an LDC and running a centralized economy, the country was able to upgrade its income status from low to lower-middle-income country (as measured by the World Bank) since the mid-1980s. However, it is important to keep in mind that—as an escape to unemployment—the informal sector has been an important challenge, considering that it imposes constraints on economic growth, reduces the tax base, and poses serious problems in terms of social protection.

Accompanying Cape Verde's economic growth, other important development indicators also attest to the country's good progress over the years, as seen in table 6.2.

Indeed, by 2011, Cape Verde had achieved a medium human development level of 0.568 (the seventh in Sub-Saharan Africa), compared to 0.523 in 2000 (UNDP 2011).[19] Of the five African Portuguese-speaking African countries,[20] Cape Verde is today the one with the highest human development index, even though at its starting point as an independent country (1975) it was one of the poorest former Portuguese colonies in Africa and the only one with virtually no natural resources.

In fact, the country is well on its way to achieve by 2015, and in some cases possibly earlier, most of the Millennium Development Goals (MDGs) (Pires 2007). According to UNECA (2005, 21–24), Cape Verde will successfully attain the targets related to MDG goals 2 (achieve universal primary education), 4 (reduce by two-thirds the under five child mortality rate), 5 (reduce by three quarters the maternal mortality ratio), and 7 (ensure environmental sustainability). Additionally, poverty reduction efforts have resulted in 27 percent of poor people in 2011, compared to 37 percent of poor people in 2001–2002 (Ministério das Finanças e Administração Pública 2008, 70). These are remarkable achievements, particularly when taking into account the country's economic vulnerabilities, geographic constraints, environmental adversities (e.g., prolonged droughts and deforestation), and lack of natural resources.

However, it is also true that, notwithstanding its relatively good performance and high per capita income, Cape Verde is still: (a) vulnerable to external shocks, (b) limited by its insularity and the aridness of its soil, (c) restricted by the lack of natural resources, and (d) still dependent on variables it detains little control over, namely ODA and remittances (Fialho 2008, 62–63). Although at a clear decreasing trend, in 2007 (upon its LDC graduation), ODA and workers' remittances—which can be considered the country's two main development pillars since independence—accounted for around 13 percent and 11 percent of Gross National Income (GNI), respectively.

Remittances from the country's large diaspora (which is roughly two times greater than the resident population), although not currently the main source of financing of the economy, still show an overall rising trend and are significantly responsible for availability of international reserves, reduction of persistent balance of payments' imbalances and do play an important role in promoting development and alleviating poverty, as they have always done during the country's thirty-year LDC trajectory.

In the past more so than now, emigration has allowed a certain control over population growth and, consequently, has somewhat reduced demographic pressure over the already limited amount of internal resources. For instance, it is estimated that "between 1970 and 1980, the net demographic outflow attributable to emigration corresponded to 15 percent of the population" (World Bank 1985, 8). In light of this, the interest to keep strong ties with the country's diaspora is clear and it is, to an important extent, an economic one. Politically, the relevance of the diaspora in the country's economy has been recognized and transposed to the constitution, by giving emigrants the right to vote in parliament and presidential elections, on an equal footing with citizens residing in the country.

Additionally, as ODA and workers' remittances lose some ground in the economy, tourism emerged as an important source of revenue. The latest available data shows that it accounted for 28 percent of GDP in 2007, compared to 6 percent in 1995, and less than 2 percent in 1980 (World Bank 1985, 6). The increasing weight of tourism in the Cape Verdean economy is also attested by its growing weight in the country's total exports and even more so by the exponential growth in tourism revenue in the 1995–2011 period.

Table 6.2 Selected Development Indicators

	1975	*1980*	*1990*	*2000*	*2010*
Life expectancy at birth	57	60	65	69	74
Infant mortality rate (per 1,000 live births)	87	69	45	32	19
Primary school enrollment (% gross)	97	113	121	124	110
Adult literacy rate (% of people ages 15 and above)	N/A	N/A	63	N/A	84

Source: Created with data from World Development Indicators, World Bank, 2013.

In terms of foreign direct investment (FDI), most of which is targeted at the tourist sector, in the same way that it rose steeply in 2001, it also declined steeply starting in 2008, which demonstrates fragility and the need for economic diversification. However, this decline should also be carefully considered in the context of the 2007–2008 international financial crisis and its negative effects on the tourism industry. Additionally, it is also important to consider that, so far, most FDI in the Cape Verdean tourism sector has privileged the all-inclusive model, which tends to limit positive spillover effects. Yet, the international financial crisis might explain part of the FDI decreasing performance post-2007/post-LDC graduation but possibly not all of it, considering that tourism recovers and FDI does not.

With regard to public debt, it is worth mentioning the considerable increase in external debt following LDC graduation, compared with its steady decrease up until that period. This is an indication of two facts: (a) grants—namely, ODA-related—have lost ground in relation to concessional loans, which now make up most of the ODA received by the country and (b) an increase in international borrowing in order to be able to take advantage of the highly concessional loans that are still made available to the country during this immediate LDC transition period. In fact, this last point—which has raised total public debt to about 97 percent of GDP—has been recognized by several government officials on many public occasions.

In terms of the structure of the economy, all throughout its LDC trajectory, Cape Verde remained an essentially service-oriented economy. While the weight of agriculture in the economy decreased from 19 percent of GDP in 1980 to 6 percent of GDP in 2007, services increased from 65 percent of GDP in 1980 to 78 percent of GDP in 2007. Therefore, the weight of agriculture in the Cape Verdean economy decreased to the same extent that services rose. The industrial sector remained mostly unchanged, accounting for 16 percent of GDP in 1980 and in 2007. Hence, industrialization-focused interventions were certainly not the driving force behind Cape

Verde's economic growth. In this specific case, services—an important part of which is geared toward the tourism sector—stimulated the economy. It is important to stress that during the 1977–2007 period, the Cape Verdean economy remained quite vulnerable and fragile, mainly due to its structural handicaps (Fialho 2008, 63).

For instance, with regard to this last point, a former minister of foreign affairs states that

> Cape Verde's vulnerabilities are manifold. They are energy-based, food-related, and security-related. They are manifold. And islands usually end up having vulnerabilities and costs beyond those of continental countries. And a mountainous insularity is even more costly. Building a 1 kilometer road in Santo Antão is as costly as building a road of 100 kilometers in Senegal. There are clearly costs related to the shape of the terrain.[21]

Overall, political and social stability have been consistently sustained, which contributed to economic growth and development. In fact, the ruling class has, in general, favored good governance practices and efficient use and management of ODA. In 1985, the World Bank (1985, 2) reported that "Public finances have by and large been carefully managed." Commitment toward the well-being of the population has guaranteed a good level of public investment in the social sector; which in 2011 reached 42 percent of annual public expenditures, according to published government budget for that year. Additionally, the European Commission recognizes that, throughout the more than thirty years of its cooperation with Cape Verde, the resources it made available to the country have been managed "in a judicious manner, explaining the fact that successive Cape Verdean administrations have been warranted renewed trust, which they have always known how to build and keep among international partners, among them the European Union" (Comissão Europeia 2004, 10).

In summary, while battling considerable structural handicaps, Cape Verde went through major political and economic changes during its LDC trajectory. Politically, the independence party, in power at the time of LDC admission, went out of power, and was again in power by the time of the country's LDC graduation. Economically, a centralized model gave way to a full-blown liberalized one, as a result of the liberal party's ten years in power, starting in 1991, and the persistence of this model in the following decades. However, a general policy of foreign aid–led development remained in place and throughout the country's LDC period the trade gap was kept manageable largely due to the important stabilizing role played by the same two factors: foreign aid and remittances. All-in-all, this gives a sense of change and continuity over time.

CHANGING TRENDS IN INTERNATIONAL ASSISTANCE TO CAPE VERDE

With insufficient domestic resources to fund its development, a generally positive international image sustained by overall good governance practices and political stability have strengthened the country's bargaining power in dealing with international partners. This has been very important in the mobilization of external resources to finance development, even though such a situation can raise concerns regarding the possibility of perpetuating aid dependence. Indeed, after the country's independence and LDC admission, ODA showed a clear rising trend until 1986. From 1986 to 2007, it presents an overall plateauing trend.

Indeed, for most of the 1970s, 1980s, and 1990s, the country ranked among the largest ODA recipients in terms of GDP.

However, ODA as a percentage of GNI has been clearly decreasing: 45 percent of GNI in 1980 versus 13 percent in 2007. This is an indication that the country is becoming less aid dependent. Yet, this last point is compromised by the fact that foreign aid still finances a considerable fraction of the country's public investments. For instance, while the country has the highest level of education in the Economic Community of West African States (ECOWAS) it has never put its own money, not a penny, to build a school. Cape Verdean schools, all of them, were built with international cooperation money. Only a few classrooms were built with volunteer work in 1975, at the time of independence. The rest was inherited from the colonial system. This is indicative. None of Cape Verdean hospitals was built with Cape Verdean money. And these two facts illustrate great vulnerability.[22]

One deputy minister of foreign affairs considers that Cape Verde might no longer be in need of the aid that it needed in the 1970s and 1980s, "but we are sure still in need of concessional credit that does not penalize Cape Verde in terms of debt, or other financing mechanisms to complete infrastructure building and to create conditions of sustainability."[23]

In fact, the pattern of international assistance in Cape Verde changed over the years (even before LDC graduation), following, for the most part, the development needs of the country and the development of foreign aid instruments and modalities. It has gone from strictly food aid and mostly grants right after independence, in a context of generalized poverty and widespread hunger, to economic cooperation at present (through loans); having included in-between project- and program-funded aid targeted at different social sectors and, more recently, general budget support. Obviously, the order has not been this tidy and sequential and a mix of all these aid modalities has been in place at different times. What seems clear, however, is that the country has surpassed its food aid days, in favor of a somewhat more balanced rapport with international partners (as opposed to a more hierarchical donor-recipient relationship), where economic cooperation has the potential to become the privileged policy route. For instance, the World Food Program discontinued its school meals program immediately after the country's LDC graduation and the World Health Organization no longer offers vaccines free of charge, as it did in the years following independence.

Additionally, precipitated by the news of the inevitability of LDC graduation, the government turned its attention to a more purposeful development policy favoring economic diplomacy. Another former minister of foreign affairs states that LDC graduation "forced us to rethink the development model and that is how the Agenda [for Transformation and Modernization of Cape Verde] was developed, which gives clear guidelines, and we now have a vision, we know where we want to get."[24] Like graduation, he gives the example of Cape Verde's recent WTO membership in 2008, adding that "it is not just for the sake of entering the WTO, it actually served to accelerate modernization, and we can also be aligned with international standards. And [that is important] for a country that wants to attract investment."

The deputy minister of foreign affairs explains that

> our foreign policy continues to advocate an understanding of the dynamics of graduation, in order to mitigate its effects, and we seek new partnerships for development, in terms of aid, credits, FDI, joint ventures. For example, the recent visit that the Minister of Finance made to China, Japan and Singapore was along these lines, with these objectives. We have identified some potential partners for each of the [development] clusters. . . . So, that has been the strategy. And additionally there is an internal response that goes towards internalizing the fact that Cape Verde should innovate in constructing its own development.[25]

Changing policy to accommodate the diversification of partners and the diversification of the country's relationship with them also means that power is more spread out and no one partner is excessively influential, leaving room for the country to autonomously exercise agency in deciding development priorities. According to a former foreign minister, "this transformation will also require redefinition . . . of the [diplomatic] missions."[26]

In addition, budget support became, since 2002, a new important aid modality; so much so that the government promoted the creation of a Budget Support Group (congregating donors currently favoring budget support: the African Development Bank, the European Union (EU), the World Bank, Austria, Luxembourg, Portugal, and Spain). This group meets periodically with the government and follows a coordinated approach by aligning their budget support with the country's Growth and Poverty Reduction Strategy Paper (Austrian Development Cooperation 2010, 6).

Related to this is the fact that motivations for the ODA allocated to Cape Verde are difficult to clearly assess. In this regard, a former chief of staff and senior adviser in the prime minister's office states that

> obviously, we cannot say that all aid received by Cape Verde was due to the fact that it became an LDC, not even remotely. Of course not. What percentage was due to that fact is extremely difficult to determine. We know [LDC admission] had a bearing. Of course it had a bearing. . . . The extent of it . . . no one can tell. But . . . the effort that the country itself makes, the guarantees that the country gives, the strategic considerations also count, of course.[27]

Like remittances, ODA—in its many forms and modalities—has been instrumental in guaranteeing the country's financial, economic, and development viability. Hence, the interest (and policy orientation) to maintain, reinforce, and restructure ties with the country's main partners, to diversify the pool of partners and to extend the donor-recipient relationship to mutually beneficial levels seems obvious. In this sense, for an important period of time, resorting to the country's LDC status did provide a UN seal of approval for seeking and mobilizing external, non-reciprocal support. In other words, LDC status empowered Cape Verde to do so, notwithstanding the dependence entailed in the resulting donor-recipient relationship. However, such a seal of approval becomes inadequate (and, to some extent, weakens the country's bargaining power) if, having achieved a certain level of development, the goal is now to establish and sustain relationships based on more egalitarian and mutually advantageous economic exchanges with former donors, now potential business partners.

At the same time, internally mobilized resources should assume a more prominent role in revenue creation and development financing (see Neves 2010). Graduation from the LDC category should push Cape Verde in that direction. In the same way that independence meant the relocation of (political) power from the colonizer to Cape Verdeans, LDC graduation should signify transferring resource mobilization power from external to domestic sources or, at least, reducing the weight of the former in relation to the latter and being able to reap all the benefits that this can bring in terms of lessening such a long-lasting external dependence.

However, it is also true that a thirty-year-long dependence on international resources, motivated and justified by LDC status, is a situation that creates a constellation of internal and external vested interests and results in deeply ingrained power networks, and these are not easy to counter. It is in this context that the news of Cape Verde's LDC graduation—representing a considerable structural change in terms of the country's development paradigm and gap financing model—can be demotivating to some and originate bureaucratic resistance. Additionally, Cape Verde's LDC graduation also represented a change within the UN, with bureaucratic implications in terms of interests and power rearrangement.

CAPE VERDE'S LDC ADMISSION IN A NUTSHELL

At independence, the population's basic needs were not being met and, in light of Cape Verde's lack of resources, LDC admission was considered an important means to facilitate access to international support. In fact, on the eve of its admission as an LDC, the country was going through quite a challenging economic and social situation. It faced several serious development hurdles, including mass emigration prompted by recurrent droughts and, consequently, widespread hunger. Food security was indeed one of the country's greatest concerns at the time. Because of its lack of internal resources, the country's survival and viability as a sovereign state rested, essentially, on international support measures. To an important extent, so did the possibility of the new ruling class actually exercising power and autonomously steering a viable political project in the country.

Thus, in such a circumstance, how was Cape Verde's LDC admission process characterized? Document analysis and semi-structured interviews provide five main findings:

(i) LDC status was proactively sought by Cape Verdean authorities following the country's independence
(ii) Although the decision to seek LDC admission was not framed (given its unanimity among the ruling elite and the population at large), it was part of an emerging general long-term strategic plan to mobilize external resources
(iii) The intention/decision to become an LDC was not contested domestically
(iv) Admission into the LDC category did not demand a negotiation process with the UN, and the country's request was readily accepted
(v) Cape Verde's LDC admission process was strongly encouraged by international partners, including UN structures, and the process was formalized fairly quickly

All-in-all, it can be concluded that Cape Verde's development since independence is one of a country overcoming extremely adverse circumstances through overall good governance practices and sensible management of international support measures while going through structural political and economic changes. In effect, evidence shows that, after gaining independence from Portugal and becoming an LDC in 1977, the country has been politically stable and has performed relatively well economically and socially, notwithstanding its many vulnerabilities. Remittances have played an important part in this. Most importantly, good performance was essentially made possible and fueled by internationally mobilized resources, specifically ODA; which did increase after Cape Verde's LDC admission, albeit the progressive reduction of its importance when measured in relation to GNI.

However, it is also important to enquire on the impact of development aid and the interests it serves. Eradication of recurrent famines, good human development ranking, poverty reduction, status upgrade from low-income to lower-middle-income country, and LDC graduation itself are clear empirical indications that, given the country's dire point of departure, significant investments were made toward Cape Verde's development. Ultimately, this shows that, through development aid, the interests of the poor were attended to and their basic needs met, in sheer contrast with the performance of the colonial administration on the eve of independence. Concurrently, at the state bureaucracy level, the long-term availability of foreign aid fueled the establishment and the solidification of a bureaucratic structural arrangement that, although successful in financing the country's development, also represented individual interests and power networks that have gained strength over the years and, because of this, are not easy to dismantle.

PART II: CAPE VERDE'S LDC GRADUATION NEGOTIATION PROCESS

Cape Verde's graduation from the list of LDCs became effective on December 20, 2007. In 1994, seventeen years after its admission, the country met for the first time graduation criteria (CNUCED 2003, 8). According to UNCTAD, "this context was seen as resulting largely from the positive socio-economic impact of external funding received by Cape Verde" (CNUCED 2003, 9). In the 1997 triennial review of the LDC list, Cape Verde again surpassed the exit threshold for per capita income and the exit threshold for human capital. According to UNCDP rules, it should have exited the category at this time. However, "as there was no framework for graduation . . . the international community did not push too hard at the time. It was postponed"[28] and UNCDP considered that "Cape Verde [should be] removed from the list if it continues to satisfy the exit criteria at the next revision of the list in 2000, provided a more detailed assessment of its situation" (CNUCED 2003, 9).

In 2000, the country met, for the third consecutive time, two of the three LDC graduation criteria: per capita income and human capital (CNUCED 2003, 10). In April of that year, UNCDP noted that Cape Verde "appeared as one of the most vulnerable developing countries according to the Economic

Vulnerability Index (EVI), as the country stood at only 54 percent of the output threshold under this criterion" (CNUCED 2003, 10). Taking this into account, UNCDP once again refrained from suggesting its graduation and recommended that Cape Verde's graduation be re-evaluated in the 2003 triennial review of the LDCs list. In 2003, having met yet again (for the fourth consecutive time) graduation thresholds for per capita income and human capital (CNUCED 2003, 12), the country was finally considered apt to graduate by UNCDP—a recommendation endorsed by UN General Assembly resolution A/59/210, of December 20, 2004. Following a three-year period, the country effectively graduated from LDC status in December 2007.[29]

Part II of this study explores the question of how Cape Verde's LDC graduation negotiation process characterized and compares this to the process that led to its LDC admission. Emphasis is put on the country's LDC graduation negotiation process, including main decision points, key actors, and other determinant factors of the graduation decision-making process. The focus, however, is much broader than the specific case of Cape Verde. This part of the chapter deals with both LDCs' and the UN's resistance to graduation and with how this resistance is eventually overcome. Therefore, going beyond the case study, part II shows what the Cape Verdean LDC graduation case reveals about the LDC category, in general, as well as the lessons that this particular experience can represent for future graduation cases.

Heavily based on primary data collected from semi-structured expert interviews, this chapter shows how power struggles and the negotiation of deeply seated interests tend to impede potentially overhauling transformations, such as that represented by the LDC graduation. It is possible to understand that the likelihood of change, both at the organizational (UN) and at the country level, creates conflicting interests. This feeds into a contradictory dynamic that leads to dysfunctional behavior by certain structures within the UN and by the graduating country itself. Part II analyses these dysfunctionalities and under which conditions key actors, essentially moved by self-interest, are able to surpass this dysfunctional stage and reach a new level in their relationship. Unlike the only previous LDC graduation example (Botswana) and the LDC graduations that followed Cape Verde (Maldives and Samoa), in the specific case of Cape Verde's graduation, a structural rearrangement within the UN is responsible for triggering and setting in motion this process of change. Therefore, this second part of the chapter documents and analyses Cape Verde's and the UN's move from opposition toward LDC graduation to its acceptance and support, as well as the broader organizational implications of this change.

The remainder of part II is structured as follows: Section 2.2 explores secondary and primary data collected from documents and semi-structured interviews with representatives from international organizations, governmental and non-governmental organizations, academia, public and political institutions, diplomatic missions, as well as representatives from Cape Verdean trade associations, workers' unions and the media, in order to understand the country's main motivations to graduate from LDC status. Section 2.3 concludes, while relating the main findings of part II with those of part I, bringing together the two parts of the Cape Verdean case study by comparing the processes of LDC admission and graduation and by synthesizing the main implications of the latter for the LDC category as a whole and for the UN in general.

MOTIVATION(S) TO GRADUATE

How was the national decision-making process that led to Cape Verde's LDC graduation managed or characterized? This question is particularly important when considered in a context where, for Cape Verde, exiting the LDC category also meant abandoning a thirty-year development model/paradigm heavily based on international support measures, along with well-established and long-standing networks sustained by a web of interests that do not always coincide with what is best for the country. Evidence collected from document analysis and expert semi-structured interviews puts forward four main findings:

- External push vs. bureaucratic pull
- Lack of framing in the national decision-making process
- A new LDC transition framework
- LDC-inspired advantages persist

External Push versus Bureaucratic Pull

External push to accept graduation (and overcome initial reluctance to graduate) is counterweighted by a pull from national and international bureaucratic forces supporting Cape Verde's continuity in the LDC category. These push/pull dynamics is most clearly stated by one of Cape Verde's former ambassador and later minister of foreign affairs:

> UNCTAD was adamant that we should not proceed [into graduation]. The change of perspective came from the time when I was . . . in Washington. I felt the pressure from the US. They had the view that it does not make sense . . . after so much effort from the international community, that no country exited [the LDC category]. I had many discussions with them to clarify all our doubts, but

> they always insisted that there was a need to show the example. I was eventually convinced, in fact, that it was time to walk with our own feet.[30]

A former Cape Verdean ambassador to the UN (2001–2004) corroborates:

> Industrialized countries defended the thesis that LDCs that met graduation criteria should leave the group. . . . In this respect, the most intransigent were the US, but the same position was advocated by the EU, although bilaterally we could count on the understanding of some EU countries (Portugal, Luxembourg) . . . the US was very reluctant to give up the opportunity to reduce the number of LDCs. It did not refrain from reiterating its opposition to the postponement of Cape Verde's exit [from the LDC category], both during negotiations and through their diplomatic representatives in the capital and at the UN.[31]

In search of an example that could (a) contradict the evident stagnation of the LDC category (considering its dismal graduation track record: only one case (Botswana 1994) in over thirty years) and, hence, (b) deflate increased criticisms of the category's futility (especially when we know that other categories that could replace it have emerged), developed countries supported and encouraged Cape Verde's graduation from the beginning. Another one of Cape Verde's former ambassadors to the UN made a similar point. She remembers that: "For some [developed countries], the credibility of the category depended on the application of the criteria, so Cape Verde should move forward towards graduation."[32] The other ambassador also recalls that

> the feeling on the part of industrialized countries was that the group of LDCs eternalized in time and if there were no signs that these measures were being efficient, leading some countries to leave the group, to be "graduated," the conclusion would have to be that the UN had failed in the objectives of creating the group. Cape Verde and Maldives were thus the "trophies" to present to the international community that the policies were working for the LDCs. Hence the enormous pressure exerted particularly on Cape Verde, not only at the negotiating table but also bilaterally, to accept leaving the group.[33]

According to the former ambassador and minister of foreign affairs:

> We always had this question of vulnerability, which was Cape Verde's main argument, and the fear of exiting this category, considering that Cape Verde depended on foreign aid. And being an LDC allowed access [to funding] under extremely favorable conditions. And UNCTAD helped to maintain this position. UNCTAD was always on the side of Cape Verde's fear to graduate.[34]

Regarding this last point, one former ambassador to the UN confirms "UNCTAD's sympathy" and "AOSIS'[35] unreserved support" toward the country's initial position to postpone graduation as much as possible. Another diplomatic colleague also mentions that UNCTAD "was not favorable of graduating countries like ours, with a high level of economic vulnerability, even if they fulfil the other two [graduation] criteria."[36]

A former *Chargé d'Affaires* of Cape Verde in Geneva states that "even when the government decided to accept graduation, [UNCTAD[37] officials were] still trying to get the government to go back on its decision."[38] Another diplomat and director general in the Ministry of Foreign Affairs considers that initially "UNCTAD demonstrated some apprehension [toward graduation], given the nature of the organization. But afterwards they were very engaged, alongside the Cape Verdean government, to assist in this process of graduation."[39] Questioned about the U.S. position regarding Cape Verde's graduation, he confirms that

> the Americans were among those who supported graduation; hence the MCA[40] program which is based on that perspective. . . . No wonder Cape Verde was one of the first countries to be elected to the first MCA package. This clearly demonstrates that the US wants to change that paradigm: support development but based on merit.

A former director general for planning in the Ministry of Finance also recalls that when first confronted with the possibility of LDC graduation, the Cape Verdean government drafted "with the help of UNCTAD . . . a strategy to exit the group of LDCs, *but* this strategy was, in effect, to maintain LDC status," given that "the initial objective was to study . . . how to justify [Cape Verde's] continuity in the [LDC] group."[41] Indeed, the government "was fighting not to exit [the LDC category]."[42]

The G77 was also arguing for the continuity position and

> when Cape Verde began to manifest itself in favor of graduation, there was indeed a kind of uneasiness [within the G77 and] although that was not expressed, the proponents of maintaining Cape Verde [in the LDC category] were a bit taken aback.[43]

One former minister of foreign affairs corroborates, recalling that, among other LDCs, there was "some amazement regarding Cape Verde's position [favoring graduation]."[44] For another minister of foreign affairs, some LDCs were

> "afraid that the example of Cape Verde could lead to more pressure for them to exit the group. There was some uneasiness. But we had an idea of what we

wanted and we moved on. . . . Even with the pressure from UNCTAD, we moved forward.[45]

Cape Verde's former ambassador to the UN confirms, stating that

G77 and China supported the position that LDCs should not move forward to graduation, thus avoiding setting a precedent. This particular position was very marked in the group of Small Island Developing States (SIDS), since three of the countries eligible to graduate, Cape Verde, Maldives and Tuvalu, were SIDS.[46]

However, at initial stages of negotiations

the Ministry of Foreign Affairs was also afraid of losing ODA. At the time I was Minister of Economy and believed that investment should be our objective and it was time, in fact, to switch models. . . . I felt that the ODA model was ending. It is a model that I helped create, as the country's first Minister of Cooperation, but came to the conclusion that this model was exhausted.[47]

In fact, an anonymous informant (Anonymous 2)[48] mentions letters sent by Cape Verdean ambassadors and ministers to UNCDP and to the UN secretary general, opposing LDC graduation. Journalist José Vicente Lopes also recalls that at first the gist of the discourse of main Cape Verdean decision-makers was a bit plaintive: "What will become of us poor devils? . . . but the authorities came to their senses . . . and the most that they could do was postpone the decision until a little later."[49] In fact, in 2004, in a local newspaper article, Lopes reported that "Cape Verde's stubborn attitude received criticism from diplomatic circles" (Lopes 2004, 3).

The aforementioned former deputy foreign minister affirms that

there were two kinds of feelings. On the one hand, people feared that with LDC graduation we would immediately lose advantages in terms of access to funding, grants, and in terms of market access. . . . But early on there was the idea that graduation should be seen as a window of opportunities, considering that analyses made to the development of Cape Verde had shown that the aid recycling model was exhausted. It was necessary to find other ways of developing Cape Verde in the perspective of sustainable development.[50]

Cape Verde's former *Chargé d'Affaires* in Geneva also recalls that, after some time, the understanding was that it was no longer worth fighting to stay in the LDC category,

because there was a [graduation] rule and the great powers encouraged the country to exit the list. So we had partners who advised us to quietly accept that

> there would be no great danger . . . there was this awareness within the Cape Verdean diplomacy. And from 2000 to 2003 this idea was consolidated . . . and our concern changed . . . [and] the diplomats began designing a new strategy. That is, not to insist on LDC status, because it was impossible. We had to exit [the LDC group]. . . . And from 2000 on we tried to negotiate the exit.[51]

Also, despite assurances given by major donors regarding continued support in the post-LDC phase, in order to avoid a fall back into LDC conditions, the fact is that while "the [Cape Verdean] government was trying to get some hard commitments between trading partners and donors [they were] not too willing to do that" (Anonymous 2).

On the whole, evidence suggests that major donors did favor Cape Verde's graduation, while national and international bureaucratic forces strived to maintain the *status quo*, at least initially, playing with the country's uncertainty regarding a future outside of the framework of special and differential treatment promoted and facilitated by LDC status. This does reveal a thug-of-war-like setting of opposing/conflicting interests. While there were clear and major differences of interests between major donors (particularly the United States) and the UN; G77's, SIDS' and AOSIS' opposition can be understood in terms of a perceived need to self-protect against LDC graduation. This also raises a broader question: why are all these countries so afraid of graduation?

Table 6.3 synthesizes the positions of major actors at different periods of time. When referring to the UN opposition, I mean certain UN structures, considering that the decision to recommend graduation comes from within an advisory body within the UN, that is, the UNCDP. The decision is taken by UNCDP, recommended by ECOSOC, and endorsed by the UNGA, but has found some opposition from UNCTAD (or from certain bureaucratic structures within UNCTAD). In a sense, this can be seen as cannibalistic behavior and proof that bureaucratic interests drive the process, considering that it demonstrates that organizational structures within the UN are at odds with each other.

Ultimately, these conflicting interests, as revealed in the interviews conducted, indicate three important dysfunctionalities:

(i) UN bureaucracy's incongruous behavior: by acting as an autonomous agent, the bureaucracy served its immediate interests, instead of safeguarding the long-term interests of LDC member-states. Indeed, this UN dysfunctionality can be explained by the principal/agent dichotomy. By resisting Cape Verde's graduation, certain UN bureaucrats contradicted the purpose of a development instrument (e.g., the LDC mechanism) that the organization itself created precisely with the intention to boost the development prospects of its most vulnerable member-states. This behavior instills or reinforces a sense of dependence and entitlement to international support in those graduating countries, to the detriment of true LDCs, at the same time that it calms down the bureaucracy's apparent fear of change and it serves its interest to keep intact the organizational structure that supports its delegated, moral and expert authority[52] and policy-making power in this area. This functions as a stimulus for the perpetuation of the category. Additionally, UN bureaucracy's reluctance toward Cape Verde's LDC graduations also denotes the organization's lack of long-term planning with regard to the desirable evolution of the LDC category; i.e., the graduation of its members. Possibly due to the stagnation of the category for many years, some of the UN bureaucracy took it for granted and did not foresee its organizational role, nor planned its intervention, in a post-LDC scenario. As a result, it approached Cape Verde's graduation defensively; seeing it, at least initially, as a threat to the survival of the bureaucratic apparatus devoted to managing the category.

Table 6.3 Evolution of Positions regarding Cape Verde's LDC Graduation

	Cape Verde	*UN*	*G77/SIDS/AOSIS*	*Developed Countries*
1994: CV meets graduation criteria for 1st time	opposition	opposition	opposition	overall acceptance
1997: CV meets criteria for 2nd time	opposition	opposition	opposition	overall acceptance
2000: CV meets criteria for 3rd time	reluctance	opposition	opposition	overall acceptance
2003: CV meets criteria for 4th time and UNCDP decides to recommend its graduation	acceptance	acceptance	opposition	overall acceptance
2004: UN General Assembly endorses decision to graduate CV	acceptance	acceptance	opposition	overall acceptance

Source: Author's illustration.

(ii) Cape Verde's paradoxical behavior toward its own development: by first opposing LDC graduation, the country also demonstrated fear of change. This was not just any change but a change that represented (and was a recognition of) the country's positive development performance. With its reluctance toward graduation, the country implicitly rejected this recognition and contradicted both the purpose of development and the wish to overcome foreign dependence, which was the ultimate driver of the struggle for independence. The prospect of graduation represented not just the need but the imperative for Cape Verde to start functioning within a different development structure; which the country's initial opposition revealed that it was not yet prepared for. This different structure involved abandoning, or considerably reducing the weight of, highly concessional and non-reciprocal international support measures and devising more autonomous ways to capture national and international resources to fund its development and stimulate economic growth. In effect, there was a considerable cost to this change: implementing a new development structure also meant tinkering with vested interests and rearranging and investing in the restructuring of well-established power networks.

(iii) G77's, SIDS' and AOSIS' inability to overcome a position (i.e., opposition to graduation) that indicates international dependence and counters the very purpose of development. While Cape Verde was able to eventually surpass its initial opposition to graduation, these three groups of developing countries persisted in their conviction that LDC graduation should be regarded, primarily, in a negative light. Influenced by the strong lobby of their members, the stance of these groups showed that developing countries were not able to consensually see in this status change a catalyst for developing countries to start thinking and acting outside of a framework of foreign aid dependence and, ultimately, an opportunity for emancipation. This contradicted the very purpose of development and showed accommodation to the *status quo*, even if it meant surrendering to a dependent situation.

(iv) Lack of Framing in the National Decision-Making Process

At the country level, the graduation decision-making process was not framed. Lack of framing[53] can be identified in two fronts: (a) stakeholders outside of central government were not actively involved in the decision-making process and (b) most of the decision-making process was predominantly reactive, as opposed to proactive. On the one hand, while some believe that the contribution of stakeholders not directly involved in the negotiation of the country's LDC graduation (such as the parliament, trade and workers' union and other civil society organizations) was not sought by decision-makers, others think otherwise.

For example, former president of the National Assembly states that "the issue did not have formal treatment in Parliament. I do not remember that there was an agenda item on graduation, for example. I do not recall of there having been a debate or an interpellation on graduation."[54] However, one former foreign minister recalls having

> suggested to the ex-President of Parliament [Aristides Lima] a small gathering to share information . . . at the Specialized Committee on Foreign Relations. I went there and said "I think it [LDC graduation] is a serious challenge, I am ready to come back to Parliament." . . . but I have no memory of having gone a second time.[55]

In fact, one former ambassador to the UN mentions a specific parliament session which focused on this matter, on March 28, 2005. Indeed, according to Assembleia Nacional de Cabo Verde (2005), the parliament did discuss the issue of Cape Verde's graduation but this discussion took place a posteriori, that is, after the UN General Assembly's endorsement of UNCDP's recommendation to graduate the country.

A former president of the country's main chambers of commerce recalls that government officials did share "a lot of information" with the business sector.[56] Conversely, one secretary general of UNTC-CS,[57] one of the country's main workers' union, states that

> officially, we were not involved in this process, we were not even heard . . . what we knew is what came out in the media . . . we were never formally invited to analyze the issue, so that we could share our opinion.[58]

Likewise, a president of another important workers' union seconds this view stating that representatives of the union did not know what the consequences, advantages, and disadvantages of graduation were, adding that the issue was not even brought to the Council for Social Dialogue, which sits employers and workers. In the same line, former head of the Cape Verdean NGO Platform, states: "We had no intervention. Not even . . . information from the government on what was happening, much less any request for an opinion . . . we were basically a passive subject, an observer in this process."[59]

Although not at all mandatory, promoting a more purposeful engagement of all those other stakeholders since earlier stages of the graduation negotiation process (e.g., through regular information-sharing sessions) could ease the internalization of changes in policy measures resulting from LDC graduation. In fact, former president of the National Assembly criticizes the way that the graduation process was managed, calling attention to what he considers to have been

> the omission of the internal aspect. For example, the need to appeal to people's, businesses', enterprises' and citizens' particular commitment to the new phase [post-LDC]. So I think there was a failure in communication, because it [graduation] could have stimulated self-accountability much more, if there had been more of an appeal to this domestic policy aspect, if the issue had not been seen mostly from the external point of view. Because there was more concern with "how do we bring more external resources?" and not with "how do we maximize our internal contribution?"[60]

On the other hand, the reactiveness with which the LDC negotiation process was approached is explained by one of the former ambassadors to the UN:

> My understanding is that one of the weaknesses of the process was that negotiations started without there having been a solid preparation of the positions and strategies to be fought for, and of alternative scenarios. The team that coordinated the negotiations was competent, well advised and could have ensured that the initial government positions were more successful, but it was building its position as negotiations progressed and under the pressure of negotiations.[61]

Additionally, the former director general in the Ministry of Finance recalls that "the Prime Minister made an announcement that we [at the Ministry of Finance] did not foresee in the short run and the decision to graduate caught us by surprise."[62] This denotes either lack of coordination among the different government structures directly involved in the negotiations or a negotiation tactic. One former ambassador to the UN claims that

> the position of the Prime Minister's Office evolved much faster than it could be accompanied by the Foreign Affairs Ministry. A few days after the [Foreign Affairs] Minister tried to make the case, at an AOSIS meeting, in Trinidad, for the continuity of Cape Verde in the LDC group, we [Cape Verdean diplomats] were informed of the decision to accept graduation.[63]

Hence, to a certain extent, the foreign affairs minister at the time was "overridden by the Prime Minister's decision [to no longer postpone graduation], since [many of us argued] that we should try to prolong Cape Verde's stay in the LDC [category]."[64]

In the end, (a) the overall reactiveness of the national decision-making process and (b) lack of long-term policy planning by central government decision-makers reinforce the understanding that fear of change, motivated by long-standing bureaucratic interests, was indeed driving the graduation process in Cape Verde, at least initially. Foregoing a deeply rooted thirty-year-long development structure based on international support, along with power connections and all the bureaucratic interests that that structure enclosed, and having to set up new arrangements and build up new networks, proved a challenging task to the country. This was probably precisely because there had been no prior planning in the direction of a development paradigm shift. Instead, this shift was precipitated by the news of LDC graduation. Because of this, resistance to graduation (and the wish to maintain the *status quo* and continue functioning within the same foreign aid–led development structure) was the country's first reaction. Hence, the lack of framing in the national graduation decision-making process is either a reflection of that resistance or a negotiation tactic.

However, this resistance also needs to be analyzed in relation to the UN bureaucracy's contradictory behavior toward the possibility of LDC graduations in general. Indeed, the organization's complacency, and to some extent encouraging behavior toward LDCs' fear of graduation, does contribute to and reinforces the dysfunctionality of perpetuating a category of countries forever in need of international support. For instance, the criterion change from EDI to EVI in 2000, proposed by UNCDP and endorsed by ECOSOC, can be seen as a UN decision against graduation.[65] The introduction of the EVI criterion (which exacerbates the vulnerability aspect and makes it harder for countries to reach graduation point) was essentially a positive response to Vanuatu's and Maldives' objection toward graduation, legitimizing a behavior that supports the perpetuation of foreign dependence and setting a defensive precedent for all future graduation cases. Essentially, the rules were changed to suit the wishes of certain countries, so that they could profit longer from the benefits associated with being an LDC. However, one should be aware that ECOSOC is an intergovernmental body and not an internal body of the UN bureaucracy. Thus, ultimately, it was both the UN bureaucracy (through UNCDP) and member-states (through ECOSOC) that listened to these countries' views and decided to allow them to remain in the LDC group. The UN as a whole, bureaucrats and member-states caved to the lobbying pressure of countries that did not want to let go of the LDC special and differential treatment. Ultimately, this behavior ends up perpetuating foreign dependence.

A New LDC Transition Framework

Cape Verde's LDC graduation negotiation process proved key in contributing to the formulation of an UN-supported LDC transition framework, non-existent until then. At the country level, initial reluctance to accept LDC graduation when that possibility first emerged was primarily justified by the lack of a UN-backed post-LDC framework that could allow decision-makers to, at least, anticipate the country's development financing future outside of

LDC special and differential treatment and, with this, avoid a fall back into LDC status. Chief of staff and senior adviser at the prime minister's cabinet, explains that, initially, the country's stance was as follows:

> There are no conditions for Cape Verde to exit the LDCs. A country that has been so attached to the exterior in terms of development inflows, cannot, from one day to the next, see its development framework changed without knowing where it is going.[66]

He adds that it made no sense for the UN to graduate an LDC "without saying how it works. What is the graduation framework? In fact, there was no graduation framework, nothing! That is why everyone legitimately feared graduation." Former deputy foreign minister considers that Cape Verde's lesson is that the graduation process was not sufficiently prepared by the UN. In effect, the country managed to play a bit with this lack of post-LDC definition to try to impose its strategy. In a newspaper article published in February 2004, Cape Verde's prime minister is quoted explaining that national authorities were well aware

> that exiting this group is inevitable. We are just calling the international community's attention to certain aspects that may affect the survival of the country in a highly competitive context and for which we are not yet ready . . . we must ensure a transition period. (Lopes 2004, 3)

In the same vein, and calling attention to a tactic of negotiation, one former minister of foreign affairs considers that

> to exit or not to exit the LDCs is a false issue. The matter is that accompanying measures must exist to ensure that transition is a success. There is an apparent contradiction between countries wanting to develop while not wanting to exit the group of LDCs. . . . If the objective is development, the aim should be to exit the group of LDCs. I always thought there should be nuances between our principle stance and our negotiation stance as a strategy to avoid adverse consequences resulting from a graduation process dealt with according to a purely bureaucratic-administrative approach, which tends to be the logic of the UN.[67]

In overcoming the initial lack of enthusiasm regarding LDC graduation and openly acknowledging its inevitability, as another head of foreign affairs recalls:

> I realized that we could negotiate the transition period. That was the agreement we reached with the US: we will graduate, and this is good because it gives an

> example . . . and we can negotiate a transition agreement. From there we started to negotiate the conditions of transition. . . . I must say that opposition continued in UNCTAD . . . completely against it, and when we started to negotiate . . . [UNCTAD believed it] was a mistake on our part to do this.[68]

To the former chief of staff:

> This was the innovative vision of Cape Verde. Departing from [the principle of] rewarding merit . . . first, you cannot penalize a country for good performance; second, you cannot abandon a country without telling it what the [post-LDC] framework is.[69]

Eventually, this led to a new concept within the LDC mechanism: that of a *smooth transition* for countries graduating from the LDC list (UN 2004). While it is not clear how exactly this new concept was introduced, Cape Verde's former UN ambassador is "certain that the proposal did not come from . . . our Permanent Mission [at the UN], absolutely not. Most likely it resulted from a UN effort to convince reluctant beneficiaries."[70] His assertion might also be an indication that the UN saw the new transition framework as an opportunity to safeguard the long-standing bureaucratic structures created to manage the LDC category, by structuring it according to its interests. However, a former senior member of the cabinet argues that the idea of a smooth transition was always in the Cape Verdean authorities' mind, taking into account Cape Verde's vulnerability. The fact is that this new framework—which lacked before and motivated the indispensability of an LDC transition strategy for all graduating countries—moved Cape Verdean negotiations forward and, although not specific for the Cape Verdean case, assisted in helping the country overcome its initial reluctance to let go of the LDC status.

However, in the case of Cape Verde, the lack of definition (or the lack of a consensual understanding) regarding the exact extent of the transition period seems to have played in favor of the country's continued access to certain LDC-specific benefits, even after its status upgrade. In fact, according to the director general in the Ministry of Foreign Affairs:

> Until now there is no clear definition [of the transition period]. . . . I think it was a political strategy not to set a date. . . . We are saying it is by 2015, which is the UN deadline for the MDGs. But that's it, there is no date. I think it was a bit deliberate.[71]

The prime minister himself recognized that: "We cannot say how long the transition phase will last" (Neves 2010, 281). The deputy foreign minister states that "it was unclear what the timing for transition would be" and

> without having it written down, we ended up saying that graduation should possibly go until 2015, which is the MDGs horizon. . . . There are theories that defend this, and they are written down. But it is not written as a decision.[72]

Others argued that there are several readings regarding the transition period of three years. According to one former minister of foreign affairs, national authorities accepted the 2015 deadline

> because there was no other solution. . . . The UN insisted on 2015 because of the MDGs, but I did not want to set a deadline. I wanted to establish indicators related to economic vulnerability to determine the transition period . . . to ensure that there would be no fall back in the development process.[73]

While, in a letter of intent to the International Monetary Fund (IMF) dated July 2011, the Cape Verdean government guarantees: “We have been assured by our partners that concessional financing will be maintained and the partners showed willingness to extend concessional financing until 2015” (IMF 2011, 4), a recent study commissioned by UNDESA states that “no formal and public statements have been made thus far by the donors in that regard” (UNDESA 2012, 23).

Chief of staff and senior adviser to the prime minister spells out his understanding of the extent of the transition period, mentioning a grace period, a transition period per se, and an undefined deadline for the total phasing out of all LDC benefits granted to Cape Verde. According to him:

> The transition period did not begin in 2004, it began in 2008. Many people were confused, even Foreign Affairs staff, even [people] in the government. . . . There is a grace period, which is 3 years, 2008, and from here on starts the transition period . . . no deadline. The transition period is variable; it depends on a lot of things . . . this transition period is a period of variable duration and . . . during that period there should be a follow-up. . . . We have adopted the principle that LDC advantages will not be suspended until the country has reached a stage that can allow it to forego these advantages. So that is why it [transition] is variable. It depends on negotiations.[74]

What is clear is that there is an obvious lack of clarity regarding the exact extent of the transition period. All-in-all, the institutionalization of the new transition framework responded to two factors that were impeding change:

(i) It calmed down the UN bureaucracy’s fear of losing control over the bureaucratic apparatus that supports and is supported by the LDC category, with this, putting at risk well-established power networks and ingrained vested interests. In essence, the new transition framework renewed UN organizational structures, particularly those connected with the LDC mechanism, without upsetting individual bureaucratic interests.

(ii) It also helped Cape Verde overcome the incongruence of wanting to develop and not wanting to exit the LDC group and, with this, reduce the dependence that pertaining to the LDCs entails. The smooth transition framework provided a new structure within which the country's future development financing did not seem so uncertain, and this eased most of the initial concerns. It is also worth mentioning that the framework is a product of Cape Verde's agency in wanting to negotiate and determine the conditions of its LDC graduation. The circumstances allowed it to make use of its increased bargaining power, and the country's graduation (on which the credibility of the whole LDC category rested) became conditional on the establishment of this new instrument. For Cape Verde, it is important to consider that, on account of its LDC graduation process; this small and otherwise powerless country, at a certain moment in time, found itself in a circumstance that considerably augmented its power position to the point that it could promote change within the LDC mechanism. Not only that, but it could promote change within an influential organization such as the UN, and this change served its individual interests.

LDC-Inspired Advantages Persist

Following graduation, Cape Verde continued to benefit from LDC-inspired advantages despite the formal loss of LDC status. This is coupled with access to additional international financing mechanisms, namely, budget support. Hence, the country continues to enjoy advantages designed for the LDCs, notwithstanding having exited that category. This is possibly due to the lack of concreteness regarding an exact transition period and/or to the international community's hesitation regarding the country's precise placement within the general developing country differentiation landscape. An example is the fact that, three years after Cape Verde's LDC graduation, a UN General Assembly resolution, adopted in June 2011, still deliberated that

> the long standing benefit of travel-related support that has been made available by the United Nations to the least developed countries will be extended, if requested, within existing resources, to Cape Verde and Maldives for a period appropriate to the development situation of the country and for a maximum of three years, beginning immediately after the adoption of the present resolution. (UN 2011c, 2)

Furthermore, following graduation, two LDC-specific instruments were not discontinued (UNCDP 2011, 5):

- Cape Verde was granted an additional three-year access (and a further two years subject to approval) to the Enhanced Integrated Framework for trade-related technical assistance;
- The EU extended its *Everything But Arms* (EBA) trade preferences initiative to Cape Verde, for three years, which was later extended until January 2012 (figure 6.2).

In fact, according to several of the accounts collected through semi-structured interviews, after graduation the country continues to have access to considerable sources of financing. "Graduation was very positive," according to one former minister of foreign affairs, "because since exiting the LDC, we receive much more funds." Not only the World Bank and the African Development Bank, but bilateral partners, such as Luxembourg, Spain, also increased their support, according to him. Officials in the Ministry of Finance added that "graduation was something positive for Cape Verde in terms of access to financing, except that, in fact, we started to borrow more." UNDESA reports that

> partners responded to the graduation in several ways. Some discontinued their assistance (financial assistance: Austria, Germany, Netherlands; trade preferences: Japan and Russia), some moved to concessional credit while keeping a smaller or larger grant component (World Bank, African Development Bank, Portugal), others maintained the same orientation (Luxembourg, US, Spain), while others re-oriented it towards other forms of political and economic cooperation (EU, France). (UNDESA 2012, 27)

For instance, another former minister of foreign affairs states that: "The Netherlands considers that with graduation there are no conditions for traditional aid and so they entered into a phasing-out process."[75] Indeed, this last point was confirmed by Maarten Gischler[76] and Erik-Jan Oosterhout;[77] both officials at the Netherland's Ministry of International Trade and Development Cooperation and former Chargés d'Affaires based in Senegal whose duties included overseeing Dutch bilateral relations with Cape Verde.

In addition: "Overall, the amount of financial resources externally mobilized by the government (current and capital transfers as well as loans) increased remarkably over the period 2005-2011, from €73 million in 2005 to €220 million in 2011" (UNDESA 2012, 33). In effect, argued the director general in the Ministry of Foreign Affairs,

> some countries continue aiding Cape Verde, in the smooth transition spirit, keeping all the instruments and arrangements previously agreed to LDCs, and very few others said "no, you have graduated and are no longer part of the aid priority list." I mean, you cannot withdraw all the aid suddenly, when the development process is taking off. It makes no sense. If [the graduated country] is unsuccessful, it would be bad for the international community. It would not be very encouraging.[78]

The structure of the international financial support that now reaches the country is changing. Given the lack of more suitable data, we use net bilateral aid flows from DAC donors as a proxy for bilateral assistance and net official flows from UN agencies as a proxy for multilateral flows to conclude that: (a) despite increased levels of bilateral assistance after LDC graduation (reaching the highest levels ever), these flows decreased in 2011 and (b) multilateral flows have remained rather stable since graduation. It is, however, important to bear in mind that the decrease in bilateral assistance might be a short-term event, considering that the trend has been upward since Cape Verde's graduation in 2007.

Additionally, FDI has gained some ground but is yet to pick up speed. Nevertheless, the behavior of FDI also needs to be carefully considered in light of the 2007–2008 international financial crisis and its negative implications on these flows. The foreign affairs official explains that

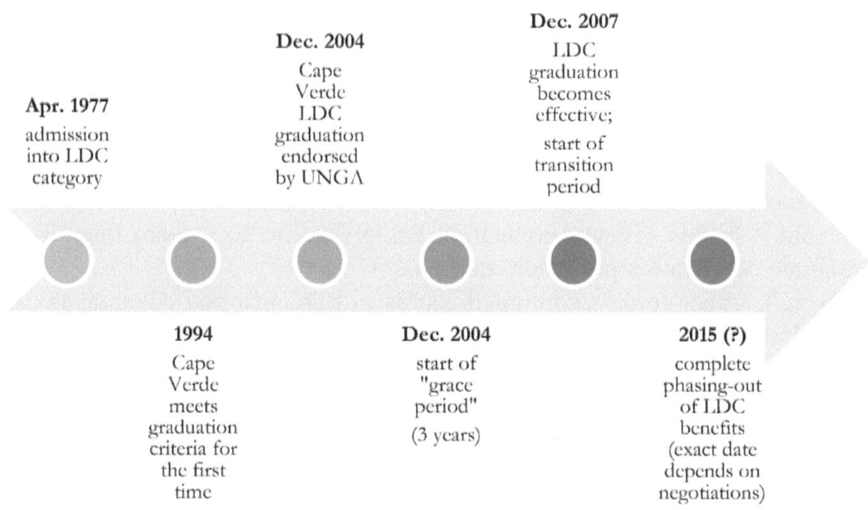

Figure 6.2 Cape Verde LDC Admission/Graduation Timeline. *Source*: Author's illustration.

> some [countries] continue to support Cape Verde as before and others have upgraded their relationship with Cape Verde. The Netherlands was one of the pioneers in helping Cape Verde make this transition from public assistance by favoring other cooperation instruments, especially economic cooperation . . . or win-win cooperation. Austria followed this model and China also privileges this.[79]

Contrary to ODA, where, following the country's graduation, bilateral decisions have been more discretionary, the loss of LDC status did imply a more by-the-book loss of free, non-reciprocal access to markets. For example, one former minister recalls that

> if our graduation was very positive in terms of access to financial and technical resources, we cannot say the same about the issue of market access, which is a prerequisite for a structural response to the problem of uneven development, especially in such an unequal world. Being competitive requires time and the transition period that we had was not enough. For example, in terms of our main partner's market, the EU, transitioning from the *Everything But Arms* program to the GSP+[80] starting January 2013 is insufficient and hinders our ability to attract export-driven investment.[81]

To his colleague and successor at the Foreign Ministry: "Before, we had a diplomacy to mobilize [funds] for development, fund raising, the so-called ODA, beyond classic diplomacy. . . . Now it is for investment, for the internationalization of our companies."[82] In effect, among interviewees, there is the general feeling that LDC graduation—which can also be seen as a seal of quality attributed to the country—has created a more favorable environment for the attraction of FDI. José Miguel Lafuente, Spanish Ambassador in Cape Verde, corroborates this view and states that Spain's relationship with Cape Verde has evolved to a more business-driven approach, as opposed to donor-recipient.[83] In this respect, graduation has given rise to a more intentional economic cooperation policy orientation.

Overall, Cape Verde's continued access to LDC-inspired advantages can be an indication that, also on the part of donors, changing deeply rooted structures is not an easy task. It might also be a manifestation of the new transition framework, whose implementation means that the cessation of these LDC advantages should be done in a gradual fashion, so as not to interrupt the country's development progress. Additionally, and most importantly, the lack of a clear post-LDC structure or the inexistence of a clear label for newly graduated LDCs is not easy to grasp by all. In fact, in terms of policy options, some donors are reported to not be so clear as to where to place these countries and how to restructure their cooperative relationship with them. The fact is that, from 2008 on, a tremendous confusion in the international community was noticeable, as one Ministry of Finance official put it; they could not understand where the country fits. The deputy foreign minister adds: "what we find is that partners do not have a homogeneous behavior. Some continue to support Cape Verde, and even increase their cooperation. . . . Others use the pretext of graduation to withdraw," which has been attributed to the fact that, in general, the international community has "no comprehensive, consensual strategy on how to deal with countries graduated from the LDC list."[84]

Seen as an opportunity, however, this lack of clarity presents considerable room for agency (notably on the part of the graduated country) in triggering negotiations to set up new (and possibly equally advantageous) networks and cooperation modalities. This is an especially important opportunity (and challenge) for Cape Verde, considering that it is the first country to graduate under these transition conditions and, hence, it can set a precedent for all future LDC graduation cases.

CONCLUSION

The main differences between Cape Verde's LDC admission and graduation processes are as follows:

(i) graduation demanded a long negotiation process while admission did not (demonstrating graduation's higher potential to disturb vested interests);
(ii) on the part of Cape Verde, admission was framed and proactive (demonstrating long-term planning), while graduation was not framed and a predominantly reactive process (issues denoting the country's accommodation in the foreign aid–led development structure implemented since independence and reinforced with LDC membership, and lack of future planning outside of that structure); and
(iii) developed countries supported admission and graduation, while certain UN bureaucratic forces supported admission but not graduation, at least not initially (which, ultimately, demonstrates that the UN's role in the category's establishment and in its management was much more planned than its role in the event of its dissolution).

In fact, internal and external bureaucratic forces—that is, Cape Verdean government structures, UNCTAD, G77, AOSIS—were the most reluctant to unambiguously accept, from the very beginning, the inevitability of Cape Verde's LDC graduation. Graduation did threaten a long-standing *status quo* and many vested interests. The need to negotiate LDC graduation indicates its possibly overhauling nature, notably in terms of the need to rearrange interests and power relations. More specifically, unconditionally accepting graduation meant different changes and consequences to different groups:

- The Cape Verdean government feared the loss of LDC advantages and the abrupt fall of a thirty-year-long development financing model heavily based on international support measures.
- UNCTAD (more specifically, certain bureaucratic structures within UNCTAD) demonstrated uneasiness regarding the loss of a constituent, after such a long time working with and toward a stagnant category that represented somewhat of a captive audience for its development policy prescriptions. The fact is that this was not just any constituent, but the first graduation of an island LDC: historically, the type of LDC most likely to reach graduation or near-graduation point.
- The G77 feared that Cape Verde's graduation could open a precedent that would undermine the reluctance already voiced by many of its LDC members who were possible future graduation candidates.
- AOSIS was afraid of "betraying" the solidarity that links LDC island countries, particularly considering that many of them had expressed unwillingness to accept LDC graduation, alleging extreme vulnerability.
- Bilateral donors accepted the change considering that Cape Verde's graduation represented an important example to other LDCs: it showed that special and differential treatment could actually work. Additionally, this example also conveyed an important subliminal message against the perpetuation of foreign aid and the responsibility of donors in this regard.

In trying to understand the reasons behind the bureaucratic pull for Cape Verde to remain as an LDC (or at least to postpone exit from the category as much as possible), it is in fact quite telling to realize that over the years a considerable bureaucratic apparatus devoted to the LDCs has emerged within the UN:

- the UNCDP (and its triennial reviews of the LDC list, for which a group of experts is periodically summoned)
- the UN Office of the High Representative for the LDCs, LLDCs, and SIDS (UN-OHRLLS)
- UNCTAD's Division for Africa, LDCs, and Special Programs
- UN Conferences on LDCs[85]

Ultimately, this also means that the life of these bureaucratic structures greatly depends on the existence of the category. If, by an absurd event, all LDCs were to suddenly graduate, resulting in the dissolution of the category, these structures would, essentially, be left without (one of) their main constituencies, emptying some of their core purpose and reducing their authority and policy-making power. So, there is indeed a bureaucratic interest to keep the category alive.

My evidence suggests that both (a) UN structures directly involved in managing the LDC category and (b) certain Cape Verdean government structures wary of possible disadvantages resulting from LDC graduation (notably the loss of LDC benefits) did have self-interested reasons to:

- resist the country's status change, and
- succumb to strong incentives to hold on to the *status quo*.

In fact, former head of the Ministry of Foreign Affairs recognizes that Cape Verde "could be accommodated in a model and [graduation] forced us to rethink it."[86] Mentioning as an example the government's adoption, in 2008, of the *Transformation Agenda*, another former minister corroborates this, stating that graduation ended up contributing to "the acceleration of measures necessary for the transition of an ODA-based economy to an economy driven by investment and, therefore, more sustained development."[87]

Considering that graduation interfered with all these long-standing interests and power relations, this push/pull dynamics that initially characterized the Capeverdean graduation negotiation process contributed to somewhat of a stalemate, which favored the postponement of a decision (from 1994, when Cape Verde met graduation criteria for the first time, until 2004, when the graduation decision was finally taken). Eventually, this ten-year negotiation period led to innovation in three particular fronts, ultimately contributing to the formal recognition by the UN that (a) LDC graduation should be preceded by a transition period, (b) formulating a country-specific transition strategy is key, and (c) ensuring a UN-based follow-up mechanism to monitor the progress of graduated countries is also key. This innovation succeeded in helping both the UN bureaucracy and Cape Verde to accept the new reality imposed by LDC graduation, overcome their reluctance (motivated by different reasons) toward graduation and reach a new level in their relationship with each other.

While these procedures or instruments (non-existent until then) intended to guarantee the irreversibility of graduation and did advance the category (because, in the end, they allowed change), the new transition framework does play double duty: (a) by providing a platform that stimulates reluctant LDCs to graduate and, at the same time, (b) by revamping the mandate of related UN bureaucratic structures, considering the additional work it entails, especially considering that it previews a new follow-up (bureaucratic) mechanism for newly graduated LDCs.

In practical terms, this last point indicates the genesis of an implicit category of "graduated LDCs-in-transition" within the UN, which justifies the continued existence of the LDC bureaucratic apparatus already in place, favors the bureaucratic *status quo*, legitimizes certain Western-inspired preferential treatment/interventions and perpetuates dependence and a sense of entitlement to international assistance on the part of these countries. In this sense, the establishment of the LDC transition framework took away the disincentive from the bureaucrats (at the UN and in Cape Verde). Hence, the LDC category is much more than objective criteria as it also represents different interests.

NOTES

1. This study draws on data and information collected in my earlier research in Fialho (2008).
2. All interview citations were translated from Portuguese. The names of all interviewees are withheld to protect their confidentiality.
3. Interview, former minister and senior diplomat, 1 March 2013.
4. See Guillaumont (2009) for a thorough discussion of the changes in eligibility and graduation criteria over the years.
5. Interview, former minister and senior diplomat, 1 March 2013.
6. Interview with former president and prime minister, 14 March 2013.
7. Interview with former minister of planning and cooperation, 3 April 2013.
8. Interview, former minister and senior diplomat, 1 March 2013.
9. For a discussion on the benefits associated with the LDC status see Fialho 2015.
10. In this context, framing essentially means prior planning and preparation.
11. Interview with former president and prime minister, 14 March 2013.
12. Interview, former minister and senior diplomat, 1 March 2013.
13. Interview with former minister of planning and cooperation, 3 April 2013.
14. Interview, former minister and senior diplomat, 1 March 2013.
15. World Development Indicators, World Bank, accessed 17 July 2013.
16. The Cape Verdean Escudo (ECV) was first pegged to the Portuguese Escudo and later to the Euro.
17. *Agenda Estratégica de Transformação e Modernização.*
18. $2,986.67, GDP per capita in 2012, constant 2005 US$, based on World Development Indicators, World Bank, 2013).
19. According to the 2011 Human Development Report life expectancy in Cape Verde is 74.2, education index (expected and mean years of schooling) is 0.425, and GNI per capita (PPP US$) is 3,402.
20. Angola, Cape Verde, Guinea-Bissau, São Tomé and Príncipe, and Mozambique.
21. Interview, former minister of foreign affairs, 14 May 2012.
22. Interview, former minister of foreign affairs, 14 May 2012.
23. Interview, former deputy minister of foreign affairs, 22 May 2012.
24. Interview, former minister of foreign affairs, 29 May 2012.
25. Interview, former deputy minister of foreign affairs, 22 May 2012.

26. Interview, former minister of foreign affairs, 29 May 2012.
27. Interview, former chief of staff and senior adviser, 26 April 2012.
28. Interview, former chief of staff and senior adviser, 26 April 2012.
29. While, in terms of economic vulnerability, it still was considered the most unstable among 128 developing countries (CNUCED, 2003: 13).
30. Interview, former minister of foreign affairs, 24 May 2012.
31. Interview, former ambassador to the UN, 3 July 2012.
32. Interview, former ambassador to the UN, 16 August 2012.
33. Interview, former ambassador to the UN, 3 July 2012.
34. Interview, former minister of foreign affairs, 24 May 2012.
35. Alliance of Small Islands States.
36. Interview, former ambassador to the UN, 16 August 2012.
37. For a thorough discussion on UNCTAD's role in LDC admission/graduation criteria see Fialho 2015.
38. Interview, former *Chargé d'Affaires* of Cape Verde, 5 July 2012.
39. Interview, diplomat and Director General in the Ministry of Foreign Affairs, 30 May 2012.
40. The Millennium Challenge Account (MCA) is part of the Millennium Challenge Corporation; a U.S. foreign aid agency that selects beneficiary developing countries based on their performance in policy indicators measuring good governance, economic freedom and investments in citizens. It provides "large-scale grants to fund country-led solutions for reducing poverty through sustainable economic growth."
41. Interview, former director general in the Ministry of Finance, 10 May 2012.
42. Interview, former *Chargé d'Affaires* of Cape Verde, 5 July 2012.
43. Interview, former director general in the Ministry of Finance, 10 May 2012.
44. Interview, former minister of foreign affairs, 14 May 2012.
45. Interview, former minister of foreign affairs, 24 May 2012.
46. Interview, former ambassador to the UN, 16 August 2012.
47. Interview, former minister of foreign affairs, 24 May 2012.
48. This informant only agreed to be quoted directly if unidentified.
49. Interview. 7 May 2012.
50. Interview, former deputy minister of foreign affairs, 22 May 2012.
51. Interview, former *Chargé d'Affaires* of Cape Verde in Geneva, 5 July 2012).
52. Delegated authority from member-states, moral authority based on its role as guardian and diffuser of all-things-LDC, and expert authority based on the accumulated knowledge and experience in dealing with LDCs.
53. In this context, *framing* essentially means prior planning and preparation.
54. Interview, former president of the National Assembly, 23 May 2012.
55. Interview, former minister of foreign affairs, 14 May 2012.
56. Interview with former of president of the Câmara de Comércio, Indústria e Serviços de Sotavento, 21 May 2012.
57. *União Nacional dos Trabalhadores de Cabo Verde—Central Sindical.*
58. Interview, Secretary General of UNTC-CS, 25 May 2012.
59. Interview, former head of the Cape Verdean NGO Platform, 16 May 2012.

60. Interview, former president of the National Assembly, 23 May 2012.
61. Interview, former ambassador to the UN, 3 July 2012.
62. Interview, former director general in the Ministry of Finance, 10 May 2012.
63. Interview, former ambassador to the UN, 3 July 2012.
64. Email correspondence with former ambassador to the UN, 2 February 2012.
65. For a thorough discussion on LDC criteria see Guillaumont 2009 and Fialho 2015.
66. Interview, former chief of staff and senior adviser, 26 April 2012.
67. Interview, former minister of foreign affairs, 14 May 2012.
68. Interview, former minister of foreign affairs, 24 May 2012.
69. Interview, former chief of staff and senior adviser, 26 April 2012.
70. Email correspondence with former ambassador to the UN, 15 January 2013.
71. Interview, diplomat and Director General in the Ministry of Foreign Affairs, 30 May 2012.
72. Interview, former deputy minister of foreign affairs, 22 May 2012.
73. Interview, former minister of foreign affairs, 14 May 2012.
74. Interview, former chief of staff and senior adviser, 26 April 2012.
75. Interview, former minister of foreign affairs, 14 May 2012.
76. Interview. 28 May 2013.
77. Interview. 29 May 2013.
78. Interview, diplomat and Director General in the Ministry of Foreign Affairs, 30 May 2012.
79. Interview, diplomat and Director General in the Ministry of Foreign Affairs, 30 May 2012.
80. Set up in 2005 by the EU, the Generalised System of Preferences Plus (GSP+) is a special incentive arrangement to support sustainable development and good governance, offering additional tariff privileges to support vulnerable developing countries in their ratification and implementation of relevant international conventions.
81. Email correspondence with former minister of foreign affairs, 6 August 2012.
82. Interview, former minister of foreign affairs, 29 May 2012.
83. Interview, 17 April 2013.
84. Interview, former deputy minister of foreign affairs, 22 May 2012.
85. UN Conferences on the Least Developed Countries have been held in 1981, 1990, 2001 and 2011.
86. Interview, former minister of foreign affairs, 29 May 2012.
87. Email correspondence with former minister of foreign affairs, 6 August 2012. The *Agenda* is a policy document based on the assumption that consistent and durable unemployment and poverty reduction demands profound transformation and modernization efforts, by changing the production structure.

REFERENCES

African Development Bank (AfDB) and the Organization for Economic Cooperation and Development (OECD). *African Economic Outlook 2008*. Paris: OECD, 2008.

Assembleia Nacional de Cabo Verde. *Reunião Plenária do dia 28 de Março de 2005*. Praia, 2005.

Banco de Cabo Verde (BCV). *Relatório Anual 2012*. Praia: BCV, 2013.

Comissão Europeia. *25 Anos de Cooperação UE/Cabo Verde*. Brussels: European Commission, 2004.

Conférence des Nations Unies sur le commerce et le development (CNUCED). *Profil de vulnérabilité du Cap-Vert,* July 2003. Geneva: CNUCED, 2003.

Correia e Silva, A. L. "O Nascimento do Leviatã Crioulo. Esboços de uma sociologia política," *Cadernos de Estudos Africanos,* Lisboa, December 2001, pp. 54–68.

Downs, A. "A Theory of Bureaucracy," *The American Economic Review*, Vol. 55, No. 1/2, 1965, pp. 439–446.

Estêvão, J. *O desenvolvimento de Cabo Verde e o modelo de integração económica internacional*, Instituto de Estudos Estratégicos e Internacionais (IEEI) Working Paper, 2004.

Fialho, D. *Status Upgrade: The Case of Cape Verde's Graduation from the Least Developed Country (LDC) Category*, Master's Thesis (Unpublished), Instituto Superior de Economia e Gestão (ISEG), Universidade Técnica de Lisboa, 2008.

Fialho, D. *Slicing Up the Developing World: Differentiation in the Special Treatment of Developing Countries*, PhD Thesis, Eramus University, International Institute of Social Studies, The Hague, 2015.

GAT. *Declaration sur la sortie effective et durable du Cap-Vert du Groupe des Pays les Moins Avancés adoptée par le Gouvernement du Cap-Vert et le Groupe d'Appui à la Transition*, 12 June 2007, Praia, Cape Verde, 2007.

Guillaumont, P. *Caught in a Trap: Identifying the Least Developed Countries*. Paris: Economica, 2009.

International Monetary Fund (IMF). *Cape Verde: Letter of Intent, Memorandum of Economic and Financial Policies, and Technical Memorandum of Understanding*. Washington, DC: IMF, 2011.

International Trade Centre. *Cape Verde LDC Graduation: Implications on Preferential Market Access*, August 2010.

Jain, A. "Using the Lens of Max Weber's Theory of Bureaucracy to Examine E-Government Research," in *Proceedings of the 37th Hawaii International Conference on System Sciences*, 2004.

Lopes, J. V. "Cabo Verde sai mesmo dos PMA," *A Semana Newspaper*, 13 Fevereiro 2004. 2004.

Ministério das Finanças e Administração Pública. *Documento de Estratégia de Crescimento e Redução da Pobreza—II*. Praia: MFAP, 2008.

Neves, J. M. "Cabo Verde no Mundo," in *Uma Agenda de Transformação para Cabo Verde*, Letras Várias, Lisboa, 2010.

Pires, P. *Speech by the President of the Republic of Cape Verde, Pedro Pires, at the Annual General Assembly of the African Development Bank,* 15 May 2007, Shanghai, China, 2007.

Querido, C. M. *Estabilização Macroeconómica e Financiamento do Desenvolvimento em Cabo Verde*. Lisboa: Instituto Português de Apoio ao Desenvolvimento (IPAD), 2005.

Reis, V. *Principais estratégias de desenvolvimento em confronto na República de Cabo Verde após a Independência*, Dissertação de Mestrado em Desenvolvimento Social e Económico em Africa: Análise e Gestão, Instituto Superior de Ciências do Trabalho e da Empresa, Lisbon (ISCTE), 2000.

Republic of Cape Verde. *Implementation of the Brussels Program of Action in Favour of the Least Developed Countries for the 2001–2010 Decade*. New York: UN, December 2005.

República de Cabo Verde. *Primeiro Plano Nacional de Desenvolvimento 1982/85*, Secretaria de Estado da Cooperação e Planeamento, Volume I, Relatório Geral. Praia: SECP, 1982.

République du Cap-Vert. *Rapport D'Information sur le processus De la Sortie du Cap-Vert de la Catégorie des PMA Au Secrétaire Général des Nations Unies*. New York: UN, December 2007.

Schlesinger, S. "Can the United Nations Reform?" *World Policy Journal*, Fall 1997, pp. 47–52.

Secretaria de Estado de Cooperação e Planeamento. *Plano Nacional de Desenvolvimento 1982/85—Esboço "Zero,"* Volume I—Estudo Global: Análise das Tendências. Praia: SECP, Março, 1981

United Nations (UN). *Resolution 31/17 on Assistance to Cape Verde*, 24 November 1976. New York: UN, 1976.

United Nations (UN). *Resolution 59/209 on Smooth Transition Strategy for Countries Graduating from the List of Least Developed Countries*, 20 December 2004. New York: UN, 2004.

United Nations (UN). *Resolutions and Decisions Adopted by the Economic and Social Council at its Resumed Substantive Session of 2004*. New York: UN, 2004a.

United Nations (UN). *Resolution 59/210 on Report of the Committee for Development Policy on its Sixth Session*, 20 December 2004. New York: UN, 2004b.

United Nations (UN). *Resolution 65/286 on Implementing the Smooth Transition Strategy for Countries Graduating from the List of Least Developed Countries*, 29 June 2011. New York: UN, 2011.

United Nations (UN). *Programme of Action for the Least Developed Countries for the Decade 2011–2020*, Istanbul. New York: UN, 2011a.

United Nations Committee for Development Policy (UNCDP). *Report on the Eleventh Session.* Economic and Social Council, Official Records: Fifty-Ninth Session, Supplement No. 4. New York: UN, 1975.

United Nations Committee for Development Policy (UNCDP). *Report on the Thirteenth Session*, Economic and Social Council, Official Records: Sixty-Third Session, Supplement No. 4. New York: UN, 1977.

United Nations Committee for Development Policy (UNCDP). *Handbook on the Least Developed Country Category: Inclusion, Graduation and Special Support Measures*, Department of Economic and Social Affairs. New York: UN, 2008.

United Nations Committee for Development Policy (UNCDP). *Monitoring the Progress of Graduated Countries—Cape Verde*, Committee for Development Policy Expert Group Meeting Review of the list of Least Developed Countries. New York: UN, 2011.

United Nations Committee for Development Policy (UNCDP). *Report on the Fourteenth Session*, Economic and Social Council, Official Records 2012, Supplement No. 13. New York: UN, 2012.

United Nations Department of Economic and Social Affairs (UNDESA). *Graduation of Cape Verde from the Category of LDCs: Lessons and Challenges Ahead*, February 2012.

United Nations Economic Commission for Africa (UNECA). *The Millennium Development Goals in Africa: Progress and Challenges*. New York: UN, 2005.

Weber, M. "Bureaucracy," in *The Anthropology of the State: A Reader*, edited by Aradhana Sharma and Akhil Gupta. New York: Blackwell Publishing, 2006.

World Bank. *Cape Verde Economic Situation and Prospects*, Report No. 5 446-C, Western Africa Regional Office. Washington, DC: World Bank, 1985.

World Bank. *World Development Indicators*. Washington, DC: World Bank, 2013.

World Bank. *World Development Indicators*. Washington, DC: World Bank, 2021.

Chapter 7

Relations between Cabo Verde and Europe

Victor Borges

This chapter was written to be part of a collection organized by Bridgewater State University to provide university students with a reference document on Cape Verde, particularly in the fields of economics, politics, foreign affairs, migration, and culture.

This theme, as formulated—Cape Verde's relations with Europe—undoubtedly entails a trap.[1] A chapter on Cape Verde's relations with Africa is part of this volume. Fully understanding the logic of the editors in structuring the collection, assigning tasks and assigning themes to the different collaborators, I would stress, however, the inherent risk of the choice of treating Cape Verde's relations with Africa and Europe in separate chapters: it reinforces the perspective of antagonistic and self-excluding choices in Cape Verde's relations with Europe and Africa. This perspective is based on a selective amalgam of elements of history, geography, geopolitics, economics, ideology, culture, and political-diplomatic practices. It quietly assembles unquestionable truths, half-truths, historical circumstantial and convenient interpretations, incongruities, states of soul, and identity-affirmative discourses (reactive and affirmative!) that leave most people with a distorted grasp of Cape Verde's essential challenges. At one end or another, it usually takes the form of an incoherent tangle of political choices laden with eclectic psycho-affective and historical-cultural elements. Of course, leading to absolute conclusions, based on abusive and simplifying generalizations that disagree with the complexity and diversity of Cape Verdean society and relations within and between countries, continents, and peoples.

Having agreed to treat relations between Cape Verde and Europe, I resent the need to emphasize the fact that I do not subscribe to the "antagonistic and self-excluding perspective!" That is why I will not resist the temptation to comment at the end of the chapter on West African regional integration (the Economic Community of West African States, ECOWAS).

This text is organized around topics that I consider striking and structuring the understanding of relations between Cape Verde and Europe, which will certainly facilitate reading and/or consultation by students. This is a generic chapter that addresses some aspects of Cape Verde's relations with Europe, without detailed specifics. To a certain extent, its reading is the starting point for specific inquiries and surveys that may possibly confirm or disprove my analysis and clues.

In addition, the chapter does not constitute formal academic work resulting from the application of scientific methodologies. It is a testimony that mirrors my perception, understanding and, probably, expectations concerning "relations between Cape Verde and Europe." It is based on personal reflections, readings, observation, discussions, experiences, and knowledge that I accumulated throughout my personal, social, professional, and political life, with particular emphasis on the period 2004–2008, during which I assumed the ministerial responsibility for foreign affairs, cooperation, and communities.

CAPE VERDE AND EUROPE IN HISTORY

Cape Verde's relations with Europe, specifically with Portugal, the former colonial power, were born with the "discovery" in 1460 and subsequent settlement and continued to this day without interruption. Isolation, communication, and transport difficulties, persistent droughts and political-economic abandonment have given dynamics and facets specific to the process of settlement and configuration of Cape Verdean society. The great famines following the droughts that scar the history of Cape Verde illustrate well the situation of abandonment. In this context of isolation and socio-economic decadence, European settlers and African slaves entered a process of shortening social distances and miscegenation that shaped and produced present-day Cape Verdean society. The history and empirical observation of today's Cape Verdean society show that together with African elements, Europe, particularly Portugal, contributed to the constitution of Cape Verde's human and cultural substratum. It is an initial relationship that has lasted in time and lasts until today.

That said, miscegenation did not completely nullify the original "racially marked" power relations and the socio-political and colonial contradictions inherent in a settlement. Nor did it endanger the long system of colonial domination that would only be extinguished in July 1975 after decades of political and military action in the jungle of Guinea-Bissau, following a radical change of regime in Portugal on April 25, 1974.

Not wanting to enter into the debate on the hypothesis of a pre-colonial population in Cape Verde, I do not think it is abusive to consider that the current Cape Verdean society results from the long relationship between alien and human elements of different origins (African and European), since the time of discovery in 1460.[2]

Human Aspects and Emigration

The absence of natural resources, droughts and cyclical crises, and the situation of political and economic abandonment by the colonial power quickly created migratory dynamics toward Africa, particularly for the former Portuguese colonies, the Americas, and Europe. Emigration and Cape Verdean communities in European countries are certainly one of the most striking aspects of the continuity of human relations between Cape Verde and Europe.

From Portugal, where many Cape Verdeans emigrated under the freedom of movement of the colonial empire, Cape Verdeans followed the paths and destinations of Portuguese emigration in the 1960s and 1970s (Portugal was not yet a member of the European Community). In the history of Cape Verdean emigration to Europe, emphasis should be placed on the role played by Porto Grande in Mindelo, which served as a starting point for many Cape Verdean emigrants, especially for European ports, namely, Rotterdam and Marseille and Africa (Dakar and former Portuguese colonies).

Long before and after independence, some countries of the present European Union (EU) were the privileged destination of the majority of Cape Verdean students with high school and higher education (scholarship students as well self-supported). This individual and group experience, in addition to having created strong networks and relationships (friendship, family, and social), unquestionably influenced relations between Cape Verde and Europe and, in particular, bilateral relations with some EU member-states. Many of the trained cadres did not return to Cape Verde, imparting to the profile of the Cape Verdean communities emigrated in Europe varied nuances of academic and socio-professional qualification. Prolonged labor migration and the non-return of many cadres contributed to the formation/expansion of large Cape Verdean communities in some European countries, including France, Holland, Belgium, Italy, Germany, Luxembourg, Switzerland, Sweden, and Spain.[3] These communities continued to grow even after independence with the arrival of new immigrants.

Many of the children and grandchildren of these emigrants are now EU citizens with strong, affective, family and economic ties with Cape Verde. It is impossible to determine the demographic weight of Cape Verdeans in the world, and particularly in Europe, since many have maintained Portuguese nationality and/or opted for the nationality of the host country. Indeed, many citizens who consider themselves, or who are considered Cape Verdeans, and who maintain intense effective, economic, and political ties with Cape Verde are legally foreign or perhaps binational. A quick observation of the queues at the border customs at Cape Verde and European airports at times of arrival or departure from Cape Verde or to Cape Verde clearly illustrates the diversity of situations and criteria involving Cape Verdean status.[4]

The human capital—scientific, technical, professional, business, associative, sporting, artistic, and political—developed or installed in Europe, and the potential for the creation of networks of dissemination, sympathy, solidarity and influence in favor of Cape Verde, constitute another important dimension of the issue, from my point of view, strategically as important as remittances. Contrary to the thesis that blames skilled individuals living abroad, and the loss of national capacity (brain drain), I believe that the most intelligent strategy for managing this situation would be to raise awareness and mobilize these capacities for the realization of initiatives in Cape Verde, either in occasional or seasonal form. From my point of view, this is the best strategy to reconcile the irrefutable individual freedom to choose the country of residence in order to take advantage of existing capacities.

Cape Verde has been developing numerous attempts and projects to mobilize skilled Cape Verdeans living in Europe, for exchanges with residents, specialized interventions and short-term technical assistance. I believe, however, that there is scope for improving strategies, widening the areas of intervention, and increasing projects. In fact, Cape Verde's capabilities in Europe provide an opportunity and a privileged vehicle for technology transfer and modernization of the Cape Verdean society and economy and the decisive importance of promotion of secondary and higher education and vocational training of Cape Verdean emigrants, in collaboration with the governments of the host countries, with particular emphasis on the so-called "second-generation" emigrants and/or descendants. This is unquestionably a critical factor for the bottom-up socio-economic and professional integration and affirmation of the Cape Verdean communities in the host countries and for Cape Verde.

It is not by chance that during the national liberation struggle the liberation movements of Cape Verde, particularly the African Party of Independence of Guinea and Cape Verde (PAIGC), created and maintained within the different Cape Verdean communities of Europe (and not only there!) political cells of support and mobilization for the ideal of independence. It is no exaggeration to say that the ideal of democracy and the very democratic regime in force in Cape Verde were, *avant l'heure*, defended by Cape Verde emigrants and cadres from abroad, particularly in Europe. After independence, the first opposition party was born within the Cape Verdean community in Europe.

Cape Verdean music, which is now an inescapable centrality of the national cultural scene and an undisputed factor in the country's dissemination throughout the world, makes great use of the European market and the communication channels and circuits of European art centers to make themselves known in the world. Indeed the first Cape Verdean producer (Morabeza) was created in the 1960s by a Cape Verdean emigrant in Rotterdam, the Netherlands. The great Cape Verdean singer Cesária Évora, known and recognized worldwide for her talent, had Europe as a point of fame, concretely, Paris.[5] Cape Verde's national soccer team, elevated to the number one ranking in Africa in the FIFA ranking (March 2016), owes much to the athletes born, raised, and/or professionally trained in Europe.

Cape Verdean emigration has always had a financial and development dimension for Cape Verde.[6] Remittances are sources of income for many families in Cape Verde. In the context of poverty and the great social vulnerabilities that characterize the country, they have functioned and function today as a "social cushion," allowing the financing of basic needs for survival and improvement of living conditions (housing, health, education, etc.). In the same way, the national economy (trade and consumption) and the state itself benefit greatly from remittances. They have also contributed to strengthening national foreign exchange reserves and gross domestic product.

The data from *Boletim de Estatísticas* of the Cape Verdean Central Bank (BCV), in November 2015, on remittances from Cape Verdean emigrants demonstrate the importance of Cape Verdean communities to the national economy, to the state, and to families. For example, in 2012, remittances totaled 14,423.3 million escudos, representing about 10 percent of GDP.[7] The weight of remittances in the national economy and in households is certainly higher, as there are still practices and informal circuits of remittances and consumer goods that completely escape the formal financial system.[8] The choice of the channel seems to depend on the emigrant's level of education, mastery, and/or familiarization with banking services by the emigrant and family members in Cape Verde, facilities, and networks of traveling friends and, of course, transfer expenses which are not trivial.

According to the Bank of Cape Verde, of the top ten countries of origin of the consignments, only two are not European (Angola and the United States). The case of the Cape Verdean community residing in the United States, commonly considered the most numerous, deserves to be emphasized here, but in terms of remittances, it appears third, steadily, from 2012.

A number of factors point to the medium- and long-term in remittances, among them the decrease in emigration departures due to multiple political and administrative constraints on destination countries of Cape Verdean emigration (EU and the United States), family reunification that diminishes or breaks the line of family solidarity that is the basis of remittances, the defense/promotion of integration in the host countries by the Cape Verdean authorities, the aging of the first- and second-generation emigrants (who are the main carriers of values and high standards of family solidarity), among other data and factors. The higher interest rates on Cape Verde savings deposits and other attractive measures that may be adopted by the government may nonetheless arrest or reduce the risk of a decline in remittances.

This brief evocation of some positive aspects of Cape Verdean emigration in Europe does not mean that, in human and socio-economic terms, the migratory experience is only one of a success story. Failures, omissions, political misunderstandings, and inadequate decisions of the host countries; low levels of education and qualification; past social exclusion in Cape Verde of important segments of emigrant communities; subjective and objective difficulties of integration; deficit of diplomatic consular coverage and of the Cape Verdean authorities' approach; and cases of personal and family misconduct have contributed to the emergence of complicated social situations that fortunately do not constitute a dominant rule or condition. Thus, in some European countries, fringes of Cape Verdean communities have been plunged into difficult family and social situations and, sometimes, outright social exclusion. This situation calls for innovative approaches to remediation and anticipation by Cape Verde and the host countries. This would be for the good of these Cape Verdeans, Cape Verde, and the societies of the host countries.

To conclude this point, I would say that the significant presence of Cape Verdeans, remittances, and the great circulation of people and goods in both directions are a relevant feature in relations between Cape Verde and Europe, despite the growing political-bureaucratic restrictions on the movements of people and some complicated situations of social exclusion. The contribution of Cape Verdean communities to the development, modernization of society, democracy, sport, and the arts clearly explains the choice made by successive Cape Verdean governments that communities are an integral part of the nation regardless of formal nationality that Cape Verdeans and their descendants may adopt.

INDEPENDENCE AND RELATIONS WITH EUROPE

Before independence in 1975, Cape Verde's relations with Europe were almost exclusively with or through Portugal. During the national liberation struggle, the African Party for the Independence of Guinea and Cape Verde (PAIGC) received support from some European governments (not necessarily with those where there was a part of human contact) and from progressive and liberal segments of European societies, including sectors of Portuguese society that stood against the dictatorial and colonial regime.

Independence allowed the establishment of a new relationship with Portugal and the creation of diplomatic relations and cooperation with almost all European countries (including those of the former East Bloc). The relationship with the European countries was built on a bilateral basis with the states and also with the former European Economic Community, now the EU.

Cape Verde has benefited greatly from Official Development Assistance (ODA), loans, and other financial flows from Europe.[9] With the exception of the United States, Japan, China, Cuba, Brazil, and, to a much lesser extent, some African countries (Morocco, Algeria, Senegal, Tunisia, Côte d'Ivoire, Gabon, Nigeria, and Angola), the bulk of the bilateral aid that allowed the country to move out of the situation it was in 1975 came from European countries, EU member-states, the European Commission, and countries of the Eastern bloc.

Facing the structural and socio-economic vulnerabilities of Cape Verde, aid was extremely important for preventing food crises and for financing development (education and training of staff, health, agriculture, water, sanitation, roads, ports, airports, etc.).[10] It must be said that Cape Verde, which is extremely vulnerable in all respects, did not have, at the time of independence, its own resources to guarantee even the food security of the population.

I return to the question of the formation of cadres, mentioned above, to emphasize that with the exception of Cuba, Brazil, and the United States (which was variable in terms of projects and geostrategic moments) and more recently in China, the bulk of Cape Verdean cadres were formed in European countries, including countries of the former Soviet bloc. Portugal has undoubtedly been the preferred destination for Cape Verdean students and continues to be the country that offers more scholarships and university placements to Cape Verde, despite the creation and expansion of university education in Cape Verde in recent years.

Another relevant aspect in these relations concerns the possibility of access to specialized health care. In fact, there is a bilateral Cape Verde/Portugal agreement that provides for the evacuation of 300 patients per year for treatment in Portuguese public hospitals of diseases requiring medical specialties, means, and equipment that do not exist in the Cape Verdean health system. There are also cases of specific and specific protocols between institutions of the two countries.

This component of cooperation, despite its high cost, probably underestimated, is not particularly highlighted in the cooperation reports, but certainly for Cape Verdean families and citizens, it is an extremely important aspect of the relationship between the two countries.

Notwithstanding nuances pronounced from country to country, family networks, in a complementary or autonomous way, have also allowed many Cape Verdeans to access specialized care and treatment they would never have in Cape Verde due to the inadequacies and shortcomings of the national health system. Being powerful human experiences that occur in moments of great personal fragility, they are remarkable for Cape Verdean people and families and reconfigure the personal and collective representation of relations between Cape Verde and Europe.

EUROPEAN PRESENCE IN CABO VERDE

Immigration

Human, cultural, and economic relations between Cape Verde and Europe are visible in the growing circulation of people and the European presence in Cape Verde. According to 2014 data from the National Institute of Statistics (INE), about 16.1 percent of all foreigners in Cape Verde are European. More than half of these Europeans are Portuguese (9%), which is explained by the historical and economic relations that exist with Portugal, which also hosts the largest Cape Verdean community in Europe.

Immigration from Europe is closely linked to foreign direct investment (FDI) and related services, partnerships with European companies, the good image of Cape Verde, and also the economic crisis in Europe. The visa granting facilities of the Cape Verdean authorities, in addition to personal, family, academic, and business networks and the frequency of air connections, make this mobility extremely fluid.

With regard to air connections to and from Cape Verde, it would be interesting to see the connections made during the summer months of 2015, from and to Cape Verde.

Table 7.1 shows the preponderance of air connections with Europe, that is, 78 percent of scheduled flights and 84 percent of passengers, and 100 percent of charter passengers and charter flights. The destinations/origins are also diversified (eleven countries). Behind these linked areas and the subsequent movement of people in the growing tourist activity in Cape Verde.

Tourism

Even before we talk about tourism, we should remember the vulnerabilities of a small developing island state (SIDS) devoid of traditional natural resources. In the specific case of Cape Verde, the climate, richness, and diversity of the natural landscape (beaches, volcanic mountains), historical and cultural

Table 7.1 Number of Flights and Passengers to/from Cape Verde, Summer Months, 2015

Region/Country	*No. Regular Flights*	*No. Passengers*	*No. Charter Flights*	*No. Passengers*
Africa				
Angola	122	14,640		
Senegal	292	25,044		
Morocco	284	27,399		
Guiné-Bissau				
Others				
Subtotal Africa	698	67,083		
Americas				
Brazil	102	19,908		
United States	138	28,980		
Rest Americas				
Subtotal Americas	240	48,888		
Europe	3,301	591,619		
Portugal	1,432	231,103	72	20,592
Spain	166	18,960	66	16,302
France	195	37,494	72	11,688
Belgium	183	34,110		
Italy	247	45,258	18	3,402
Germany	300	56,700	48	7,200
Holland	234	42,768		
Luxemburg	14	2,604		
United Kingdom	530	122,622		
Denmark			5	1,980
Czech Rep.			76	16,020
Rest Europe				
Subtotal Europe	3,301	591,619	357	77,184
Asia				
Total	4,239	707,590	357	77,184
% Africa	16%	9%	0%	0%
% Americas	6%	7%	0%	0%
% Europe	78%	84%	100%	100%
% Asia				

Source: Created with data provided by the Empresa Nacional de Aeroportos e Segurança Aérea de Cabo Verde (ASA), 2015.

particularities and, above all, the proximity of Europe, the largest world market for tourism, imposes on Cape Verde a tourist vocation, which in the recent past has been underestimated or postponed due to the combination of political factors. The permanent worldwide growth of tourism is, in fact, a great economic opportunity for Cape Verde.

The flow of tourism to Cape Verde has been increasing. In 2002, the number of tourist arrivals was 152,000, and in 2014, it was 539,000, almost equal to the resident Cape Verdean population. At this time, the government and political parties involved in the electoral campaign underway for the legislative elections of March 20, 2016, announced the goal of one million tourists per year (twice the Cape Verdean resident population).[11] It is an ambitious objective that requires coherent managerial policies, strategies, and management practices for greater dominion of the tourism industry, its insertion into the national economy, and anticipation and screening of undesirable effects on an extremely fragile and societal environment. Environmental protection arises not as a fad of militants and intellectuals but rather as a requirement of quality and competitiveness of the tourist product.

At present, tourism accounts for 65 percent of the export revenues of goods and services and 20.97 percent of gross domestic product, according to data from Cape Verde's tourism satellite account, published by INE. This tourist flow comes almost exclusively from the countries of Europe, according to INE data. Germany, the UK, and Portugal are the three largest suppliers of tourists to the Cape Verdean market. Among the top ten countries of origin of tourists, only two are not European (South Africa and United States) but with a marginal market share.

Although concentrated in the islands of Sal and Boa Vista, the flow of tourists is a floating and permanent European presence in Cape Verde, whose impact is transversal in society. The underlying investment, human and business contacts, the inherent transfer of technical and business knowledge, among other things, reconfigures Cape Verdean society by strengthening relations with Europe and more specifically with the countries of origin.

Trade

Trade is another structuring aspect of Cape Verde's relations with Europe. In fact, the main trading partners of Cape Verde are the European countries. The percentages of exports to the Euro area vary between 93 percent (2012 and 2013) and 86 percent (2014), which undoubtedly represents a preponderant situation in the external trade of Cape Verde, as shown in the data.[12]

In terms of imports, the scenario is slightly different, but the Euro zone retains the dominant position, between 72 percent and 78 percent of total imports in the same period. Here it is worth again to underscore the insignificant weight of imports from the United States: 1 percent in 2013 and 2014 after the 5 percent peak in 2012. Still more challenging is the percentage of trade with ECOWAS (almost zero export and 1 percent for imports, with a peak of 6 percent in the third quarter of 2015). This economic data does not resonate with the appeal of the political discourse of economic and regional integration.

The framework of EU trade relations with Cape Verde has undergone changes following its Least Developed Country (LDC) graduation in 2008.

Cape Verde will no longer be eligible for the Everything But Arms (EBA) framework and will leave the Generalized System of Preferences+ (GSP+) in the course of this year (2016).[13] In this regard, it is worth mentioning Ms Eveline Herfkens, former minister for Development Cooperation of the Netherlands and former representative of the Netherlands at the World Trade Organization (WTO) in Geneva: "More fundamentally, by limiting this preferential access to LDCs, EBA excludes the countries that are low income or lower-middle income, which are precisely those African countries best placed to take advantage of export diversification preferences."[14] And again, we are faced with inadequate policies and instruments which are the challenges and realities of developing countries.

Then there is the Economic Partnership Agreement (EPA), signed in the context of ECOWAS/EU relations, and which is severely criticized in Africa, and in various sectors of Europe, including the European Parliament, non-governmental organizations, and think tanks in European countries. In accordance with the commitments made under the Cotonou Agreement and with the WTO, EPA negotiations were to be concluded by the end of 2007. With a long delay, ECOWAS and the European Commission signed the agreement in 2014 that Cabo Green is part of. I would point out that in 2006, Cape Verde officially informed ECOWAS and informally the European Commission of its intention not to be part of this process given its specificities, and also because it did not have the technical competence of the process and was not in a position to assess independently the impact of the agreement on the economy and, in particular, on tax revenues. It should be noted in passing that Cape Verde's budget is structurally dependent on customs revenues.[15]

In my view, the technical, legal, and political domain of any subject constitutes and, furthermore, constitutes the basic condition for entry into any negotiation, regardless of the goodness or not of the proposals. Objectively, Cape Verde did not have, at the time, the mastery of the complex and complicated issues underlying the EPAs and knowledge about the impact on its economy and development.[16] With regard to the technical field of complex trade negotiations and the imbalance of the technical capacities of the parties involved in the EPA process, I would like to quote again the position of the former Dutch minister Mrs Eveline Herfkens expressed or discovered by me much later:

> This course of action was unfortunate for several reasons. Given the limited capacity for trade negotiations of most countries in the region, their efforts should have focused on the much more relevant Doha Round and on deeper integration within the African market. Moreover, the requirement of reciprocity and coverage of substantial trade in such agreements are not appropriate given the state of development of most of the region. And the EU included issues that

go beyond trade in goods (services, intellectual property, government procurement, abolishing export duties, etc.).This will create unnecessary burdensome obligations for these countries and may distract from or could be inconsistent with their more immediate development priorities.[17]

I do not say that I agree with Mrs. Herfkens, because it was precisely the position I defended nine years ago within the Cape Verdean Government and that led to the decision to inform ECOWAS of Cape Verde's exit from the EPA process (2006). It was also communicated to the heads of some member-states, officials of the European Commission, and parliamentarians (national and European). I only remember support for the position defended by me at the time. Of course, I am referring to private and off-the-record support.

Investment

Economic reforms initiated in the 1990s, notably the privatization program, have allowed European companies, particularly Portuguese companies, to acquire significant or dominant holdings in several strategic economic sectors for development; others will say for sovereignty, namely, banking, insurance, telecommunications, energy, fishing. It is no exaggeration to say that economic reforms, notable privatizations, have contributed to the consolidation of Europe's position as Cape Verde's main economic, financial, and trade partner. Data on the origin of the FDI confirms trade and tourism data, showing the dominant position of Europe (five countries) as the origin of FDI in Cape Verde.[18]

CAPE VERDE AND EUROPE TODAY

At the time of independence, in 1975, Cape Verde was in a distressing socio-economic situation, with no clear prospects for development, the phantom of droughts and past famines hanging in the air in an insidious and persistent way. Many observers doubted Cape Verde's ability to last as an independent state. The main economic activity was agriculture, an agriculture of mere survival and almost totally dependent on rains, by definition irregular, insufficient, and uncertain. The scarcity of land and arable land (10% of the territory) and anachronistic cultural techniques and practices resulted in low productivity and production. Industry and services were virtually non-existent.

Cape Verde's relations with Europe (and with the rest of the developed world) in the post-independence period were profoundly marked by ODA. Without wishing to make an overall assessment of the first fifteen years of independence and the one-party regime, the remarkable course of Cape Verde in this period, in terms of food security and development, is largely due to ODA and remittances. In the post-independence context characterized by nationalist pragmatism, state-building efforts and the "viability of the country" and the international context of the so-called Cold Car that was unjustly scalding for many countries in the south, it is understandable that other issues of international relations—regional and international security, FDI, trade, loans, and related financial issues—would have been less prominent and visible on the politico-diplomatic agenda of Cape Verde's relations with the countries of Europe.

The end of the single-party regime, the first free and democratic elections, the subsequent political alternation inaugurated in January 1991, the journey made in terms of development, the reinvigorating democratic experience, the political-economic changes implemented after the regime change, and the distancing of the new generations from the colonial past, all created a new political environment at the national level. At the same time, the fall of the Berlin Wall, the immersion of the world (and Cape Verde) in the neoliberal ideas adopted and proclaimed by the World Bank and the International Monetary Fund along the lines of the Washington Consensus, the growing role of these organizations in governance in Cape Verde, have interacted with changes at the national level by creating new visions and alternative approaches to development and governance.

This new national and international context has facilitated the widening of Cape Verde's political-diplomatic agenda with Europe (and other geopolitical spaces). In parallel with the ODA, other topics, such as investment and business environment, public-private partnerships, loans and alternative models of development finance, economic and business cooperation, exchange rate cooperation, tourism, labor and temporary migration, defense and security (national, regional, and international), the fight against organized and international crime, have gained prominent positions in the agenda and political-diplomatic discourse on both sides.

Political relations with the EU and the member-states closest to Cape Verde have gained new impetus, content, and outlines on the initiative of both sides.[19] The signing of the exchange agreement between Cape Verde and Portugal in March 1998 (involving the fixed parity of the Cape Verdean escudo with the Portuguese escudo and later with the Euro) constituted a strong moment of mutual trust. By eliminating uncertainties and currency fluctuations, it has comforted trade and facilitated investment.

During the time I was in charge of Cape Verde's foreign policy (2004–2008), I sought in the dialogue with the European countries, the European Commission, and other EU decision centers to defend the following twofold position: (a) reaffirmation of the importance and role of European (and other) ODA for the post-independence period and the continuation of Cape Verde's development given the country's great vulnerabilities and (b) demonstration of interest and readiness to deepen relations beyond the constrained framework of the donor/recipient logic.[20] It should be recalled that in the same period (2004–2008) the country was engaged, with the United Nations, in the graduation process, that is, the departure from the LDC group. Cape Verde had achieved two of the three graduation criteria, namely, the human development index and per capita income. The third criterion, an index of economic vulnerability, fundamental for the sustainability of development, was not reached. On the contrary, at the time of graduation, Cape Verde was considered one of the most economically vulnerable countries in the world.

There was no weighing of the different graduation criteria—for me, the economic vulnerability index should have a different weight—Cape Verde was qualified for graduation. That is why the challenge was positively addressed, in the hope that the "smooth transition" strategy should allow Cape Verde's fundamental concern to be guaranteed, that is, to ensure access to development finance under acceptable and sustainable conditions. Graduation should not inhibit the implementation of the provisions of the United Nations and the Cotonou Agreement for Small Island Developing States (SIDS). Theoretically, graduation, from a bureaucratic-administrative perspective, implies a loss of access to concessional loans (low interest rates and long repayment periods) and a drastic decrease in donations. Cape Verde has tried to build alliances with European partners (commission and member-states) to define the "smooth transition" and minimize the risks of rising development financing costs inherent in leaving the LDC group.

The position advocated by Cape Verde was for a long transition period, based on economic indicators and not on randomly set administrative deadlines. Partner member-states, including the Delegation of the European Commission, were part of the Transition Support Group (GAT) set up by the government in 2006 to follow the graduation process. In this respect, I am reminded of a comment from a leader of a member-state, today a high leader of the European Commission, regarding Cape Verde's arguments and managing the smooth transition: You cannot cut fuel to a plane at the moment of take-off. And in terms of development, graduation is a take-off for a long-haul flight.[21]

While advocating continuing ODA for the post-graduation period, I also argued that relations with the EU should transcend traditional ODA practices, emphasizing the limits of a donor/recipient relationship. And in fact, there were signs that relations reached new heights and depth in the first decade of 2000.

Among some positive signs, I mention the Cabo Verde–European Union Special Partnership Agreement and the mobility partnership. In this regard, the security issue, one of the six pillars of the Special Partnership Agreement, which most ACP countries (Africa, the Caribbean, and the Pacific) in 2005 did not want to see on the ACP/EU agenda, should be highlighted. Cape Verde had a diverse position due to the threats of international trafficking and organized crime. The security issue, objectively being a common issue of concern, was without a doubt the gateway to the special partnership. Indeed, Cape Verde is geographically situated along the routes of drug trafficking from South America to the developed countries (Europe and the United States). Notwithstanding growing and disturbing signs of consumption, the Cape Verdean market—the sparsely populated population and limited purchasing power resulting from the high level of poverty—is clearly not a priority for the great trade that targets the European market. This is unquestionably a critical and common challenge for both parties. The cooperation initiated in this area is promising but, in my view, we are far from meeting the needs and challenges underlying the growing aggressiveness of criminal organizations. It is also within this framework of looking for partnerships against the threats of organized crime and international trafficking that one must understand the first contacts and discussions with NATO that led to the hosting of the steadfast military exercise in Cape Verde (June 2006).

Linked to the issue of security, we have the issue of the sea. From the outside, cooperation with Europe in this area has allowed sporadic patrol operations, exchange of information to combat trafficking, provision of equipment and materials, and training activities. Also related to the sea, we should mention the fisheries agreements and technical assistance from a member-state (Portugal) and Norway in the preparation of the dossier on the expansion of the continental shelf within the framework of the United Nations Convention on the Law of the Sea.

In addition to the need to intensify ongoing cooperation activities, the parties are challenged to take a holistic approach to the question of the sea, which in turn links Cape Verde to Europe, through the outermost regions, specifically the Canary Islands (Spain), with all that it represents in terms of potentialities, opportunities, and risks. The seas, from the standpoint of more development and more security, should be a strategic line of cooperation between Cape Verde and the EU (including individual member-states).[22] On the part of Europe, and particularly the European Commission, there is also a need for reflection and initiatives that have not been pursued.[23] From my point of view, it would be a serious strategic error to assess the importance of Cape Verde for Europe (and not only), exclusively, on the basis of traditional criteria—physical size and population, gross domestic product, market size, natural resources, and such.

Noises and Dissatisfactions in Relations between Cape Verde and Europe

One of the biggest gains in relations between Cape Verde and Europe is the trust built over the years. I think it was the confidence that allowed me, several times, to say no to my interlocutors and friends, without impinging the quality of diplomatic relations and cooperation programs. Being rich and promising, the political, cooperative, institutional and human relations between Cape Verde and Europe are not free from misgivings which, fortunately, the existing mutual trust allows us to approach and discuss with serenity.

I take the liberty of remembering some moments, processes, and subjects that created annoyances, anxieties, or stress.

i. Programming and implementation of cooperation projects under cooperation programs financed by the agencies and funds of the commission or the member-states. The management of the programming cycle, the negotiation of priorities,[24] the complexity of the rules and procedures (administrative, technical, financial, etc.) of the European Commission and of some member-states,[25] the slow procedures in contrast to the urgency of the needs, the weaknesses of Cape Verdean institutions, including in project reporting activities, have created and continue to create moments of stress, disagreements, personal misunderstandings, relational and bureaucratic misunderstandings that one or more, some more than others, tend to turn into institutional problems and even political-diplomatic problems.

ii. Personal and political misunderstandings of the actors and some lack of communication and diplomatic dexterity on both sides are equally observable. Its potential for political-diplomatic disruption is greater than procedural or operational disagreements. Unpredicted or poorly managed, these situations can quickly slip into embarrassing situations for the actors involved.

iii. The fisheries agreement has provoked many reactions in certain sectors of Cape Verdean society (fishing professionals and operators and some political parties) which invoke the disparity in technical means and gains, and the excessive, uncontrolled, and unsustainable exploitation of the scarce marine resources of Cape Verde.

iv. The readmission agreement signed with the EU, and in particular the readmission of third-country nationals in Cape Verde, has created moments of upheaval in society and in some of the services involved. Regardless of the content of the agreement, there will have been a lack of communication with a society that creates a terrain conducive to speculation and multiplication of false ideas.

v. The announcement and the start of negotiations with the European Commission for visa facilitation created a wave of hopes in Cape Verdean society that quickly dissipated, with some disenchantment. In fact, the issue of visas is a sensitive issue in a diasporic society such as Cape Verde. As a result, there were many complaints and dissatisfactions about the administrative and bureaucratic management of visa procedures. Because there is a lot of erosion of principles and objectives among policy, strategies, administrative directives, administrative instructions, and practices, the system lacks efficient monitoring, evaluation, and corrective measures.[26]

vi. This example brings up another aspect that also disturbs the fluidity of the dialogue, which can create noises and misunderstandings. I am referring to the political, diplomatic, technical, and psychological willingness to welcome initiatives and proposals from partners. This is a problem that pervades the relationship of almost all developed countries (donors) and developing countries (ODA recipients). It can be explained, in part, as follows. Donor cooperation agencies with many financial, material, and human resources have the capacity to theorize about development and produce concepts, strategies, tools, methodologies, and intervention techniques "theoretically well-balanced or considered theoretically perfect" that convey a know-it-all and about all attitude, including the priorities of the recipient countries. When confronted with alternative visions, approaches, and proposals that do not fit into established theoretical frameworks and pre-defined priorities, donors, their intermediaries, and service providers demonstrate a total lack of listening, dialogue, or even comprehension ability.[27] Not wishing to say with this observation that all the proposals of the developing countries are good or better, I have seen myself that many interesting ideas of development go unnoticed and that the failure of many development initiatives and projects is partly related to the personal and institutional attitude of not really listening or considering the alternative visions and approaches that can emanate from developing countries.

DISCONNECT OF GEOGRAPHY, ECONOMY, AND POLITICS IN CAPE VERDE

Regardless of declarations of intent, fairness of positions, value judgments or state of mind, of one or the other, data indicate that Cape Verde is a country extremely connected to Europe (or is dependent?) in terms of emigrant remittances, foreign aid for development, trade, investment, and tourism (investors, tourist flows, operators, etc.).[28]

On the other hand, Cape Verde is part of the Economic Community of West African States (ECOWAS) by the political decision taken in the early years after independence. Despite the fluctuations and personal nuances of positioning in relation to regional integration, the two main political parties in Cape Verde insist on the importance of regional economic integration, emphasizing the need for more active participation in the life of the community institutions.[29] Cape Verde endorsed and ratified the main instruments and decisions of ECOWAS. About two or three years ago, the prime minister announced the possibility of Cape Verde joining the regional single currency project.[30] Many Cape Verdean observers took a stand against but few mentioned the essential and dissonant element of the issue: the mismatch between the intent and reality of economic and trade relations between Cape Verde and the other countries in the region. This issue of the single currency is indeed a reminder of the notorious mismatch between, on the one hand, geography and the dominant political discourse on the necessity (or inevitability of regional economic integration) and, on the other hand, the almost inexistence of economic relations and exchanges with the sub-region.

How to manage this situation with a minimum of political coherence and economic efficiency?

Before presenting my personal point of view on the paths that Cape Verde might, eventually, follow, I venture to recall some elements of analysis to help understand the situation:

a) Prevailing economic relations with the developed countries is not an exclusive privilege of Cape Verde. Unfortunately, more than five decades after independence, the structure of economic relations between African countries and the developed countries, and particularly with Europe, has not changed much. It can be summarized as follows: export of raw materials and imports of manufactured goods. Many authors speak of the persistence of colonial economic relations. Europe receives 28 percent of ECOWAS exports; the Americas (mainly the NAFTA countries) receives 40 percent; and Asia and Oceania (mainly China) 16 percent.[31]
b) Low levels of intra-ECOWAS trade. This is an old finding that has to do with the similarity of national economies (export of raw materials), incipient or non-existent industrialization, and, consequently, absence of complementarities.[32] The main export products of the ECOWAS countries are dominated by raw materials—crude oil (75%), cocoa, precious stones, cotton, rubber, fruit, wood, etc.
c) In Cape Verde, the lack of natural resources and tourism introduces nuances in the structure of the economy and its relations with Europe, making a marked difference with the other countries of the region.

d) Some regional products could be imported by Cape Verde at competitive prices. Civil construction and tourism growth are objectively opportunities for imports of timber, agricultural products, and fish from the region. This opportunity is, however, conditioned by at least two constraints: transport and, where appropriate, the quality, certification and other technical, sanitary, and phytosanitary requirements of Cape Verde and of tour operators.
e) Imports from the region tend to coincide with those of Cape Verde, that is, refined petroleum and oil products, motor vehicles, tractors, machinery and equipment, steel and cast iron, pharmaceuticals, all of which come from developed countries.
f) For Cape Verde, there would be the possibility of exporting pharmaceutical products. Again the issue of transportation resurfaces, among other constraints. Second, the aggressiveness of European and American pharmaceutical industry networks that already occupy the market should not be underestimated.[33] It is necessary to ask whether these theoretical possibilities of trade would be enough to generate lasting and economically viable maritime connections.

When examining the experience of economic integration in the West African region and the specific situation in Cape Verde, one finding stands out: the material impossibility of the region's economy to compete for or replace current investors, suppliers, and commercial clients of Cape Verde. Unfortunately, this is not only a Cape Verde problem. It is, to varying degrees, a problem of all countries in the region. The nature of the economies of the ECOWAS member-states remains disjointed in terms of quality of demand and supply. In my view, intra-ECOWAS economic and trade relations in general and specifically with Cape Verde will only change with the development and, above all, with the industrialization of some of the countries in the group. I will not be exaggerating if I say that Cape Verde's relations with the region would be completely different if, for example, Senegal had the level of industrial development of South Africa.

WHICH ROAD AHEAD FOR CAPE VERDE?

This mismatch of geography, economics, and politics is reasonably complex and entangled to be solved or managed lightly or in a simplistic and definitive way, as some reactions and positions lead us to believe (against or in favor of one or another self-excluding). So what can be or should be Cape Verde's strategy?

For me, the starting point for strategy design is a clear awareness of the challenges of financing the economy and development at this post-graduation stage and the adoption of pragmatic and problem-solving–oriented approaches.

(i) The option of tourism and trade imposes on Cape Verde an irrefutable path and priority: the countries of origin of FDI, the flow of tourists, and the current trading partners. The question remains: will there be immediate and feasible alternative options? I believe that Cape Verde should pragmatically and unequivocally pursue and consolidate its economic and political relations with European partners in order to attract more investment, increase tourist flows and maintain or increase trade, especially exports.[34] Many are invoking and will invoke the economic and political crisis that shakes the EU at the moment to suggest that relations with Europe might be exhausted and that new paths and partners should be sought. I think that would be a hasty and inconsistent conclusion with the data of the current economic reality of Cape Verde. Indeed, the data demonstrate that the crisis did not cause any negative effect on the flow of tourists. This alone not to mention investment and trade impose paths and guidelines that are independent of the will of national operators or the government.[35] The concrete situation of Cape Verde does not rhyme with the illusion of hurried or self-excluding choices. On the other hand, the economic approach must be preceded and accompanied by the political-diplomatic approach. Again some will evoke the crisis of the EU. The reality is often different from the narrative conveyed by the media and by the actors themselves. Without underestimating the complexity and scope of the current crisis, I believe that the EU has always grown in the midst of crises and contradictions. I believe that special partnership, the partnership for mobility, development cooperation, and cooperation in the security sector with Europe still have great potential. Its deepening will require more proactive, innovative, creative approaches from beyond the formal or routine diplomatic practices and rituals on Cape Verde's part, today more than ever. The reactive subculture of the Cape Verdean public administration is certainly a major constraint for deepening relations with the EU and for identifying and exploiting new opportunities in other geoeconomic and strategic spaces.

(ii) Cape Verde must accompany this "European orientation" by a simultaneous and huge effort toward other "economically dynamic and safe spaces," which are not part of its traditional area of affinity or belonging. The diversification of relations for a small island country is an economic, political, and strategic need. This is the most prudent way to prevent, disarm, manage, and protect against the risk of over-dependence on a single market and the pressures of international (economic and political) relations. Work must be done to identify and explore new niches and opportunities for mobilizing investment and cooperation. It is in Cape Verde's interest to diversify its trading partners, the tourism market, operators, and the origin of investments, also looking to Africa, the Americas, and Asia. Otherwise, the concentration of economic relations with Europe will translate into total dependency, adding yet another topic to the country's list of vulnerabilities.

(iii) Tourism is associated with FDI. Many observers and government officials argue that so far, FDI has been the result of the initiative of investors who accidentally discovered Cape Verde as a business opportunity. The new approaches mentioned above will require renewed (human and institutional) capacities to identify and mobilize more investments, their framing, and management, so as to reconcile, in a more coherent, consistent, and creative way, the legitimate interests of investors with those of Cape Verde and the requirements of sustainable development. Capacity-building for the sectors related to external relations, investment, and tourism (among others) is a requirement for the effectiveness of new initiatives. Governments' strategies and good intentions know immediate and silent death in the absence of human and institutional capacity for programming, implementing, and monitoring policies, programs, and projects.[36]

(iv) And what about ECOWAS in this strategy, some will ask? The answer I give today is no different from the position I have tried to defend within the government and with some circumspection in institutional spaces and the public arena to avoid provoking premature and sterile debates. First, and again, I believe that Cape Verde does not have to make self-exclusionary choices in economic and political terms. If economic activity and probably survival of the country point in one direction, geography still matters! Having said that, the economic data presented above and the prospects for economic transformation in the region in the short- and medium-term cannot be ignored. In this sense, I reiterate the position that I defended within the government for a "selective, solidary and progressive participation" in the process of regional integration. A selective and negotiated participation with the commission and the member-states. Cape Verde should, under Article 68 of the Abuja Treaty, open a window of exceptionality and opportunity for island states and landlocked countries, to negotiate in depth with ECOWAS special status and/or treatment.[37] This position is much more nuanced than the proposal for greater involvement in regional integration processes, without further consideration. It is quite different from the unplanned, naive, and illusory thesis of some friends and partners who tell us that Cape Verde, because

> of its developmental and governance trajectory, should "be an example" and have a mission to influence the governance and the development process of ECOWAS partners. I have never endorsed the thesis of "example for Africa" whose perverse effects on Cape Verde seem suspect. On the other hand, the physical, demographic (0.15% of the population of the ECOWAS, equivalent to a neighborhood of Lagos) economic dimension (almost 1% of ECOWAS GDP) and the resulting lack of political and diplomatic weight (real and resented by the member-states) of Cape Verde demonstrate the absurdity of such a proposal. In this regard, I remember saying repeatedly, to the displeasure of some former colleagues in the government, who are excited by the risky, eccentric, and almost messianic theory of "Cape Verde, an example for the region and for the world," that we are one "marginal insularity in ECOWAS," in contrast to "unavoidable insularity" of a Madagascar in Southern Africa or the UK in the EU.

As I said at the outset I return to some reflections on regional integration in order to facilitate understanding of the complexity of the situation for Cape Verde. West African regional integration raises many questions that are obfuscated by the political euphoria and voluntarism, the quality of state governance, organizational mimicry, the power play, and certain views and practices of "African solidarity" that become institutionalized taboos. For me, the ECOWAS strategy should be reviewed in the light of recent experience and progress, taking due account of national and regional contexts, the pace and quality of growth of member-states, the diversity of national governance practices, and the institutional and financial weaknesses of ECOWAS.[38]

The idea of being everything, for everyone and at the same time, which seems to be the ECOWAS motto, being seductive by the values it conveys, is nevertheless a complicated and laborious bet. The political and administrative management of the integration process by the regional institutions requires profound strategic, organizational, and priority changes and improvements. There are objective limits to excessive voluntarism or the imponderable mimicry of the experience of others, in disregard of the surrounding reality and context. The success of integration depends on peace, security, stability, respect for human rights, and (at least) democratic governance at the member-state level, which is considered to be the sine qua non for a dynamic, profitable, and durable integration. A real and consistent political will for integration should be reflected first and foremost in internal policy and automatically translate into new governance practices, a sense of purpose, and coherence in the design and implementation of coherent development strategies at the national level. Without consistent national development policies and practices, the discourse of integration is mere rhetoric. It is very likely that these considerations and concerns led the former ECOWAS executive secretary Abass Bundu (1996, 43) to make the following statement (1996): "It is evident that the countries of West Africa have not internalized or been sufficiently aware of the demands and sacrifices demanded from Partner countries to ensure the success of integration."

CONCLUSION

I would conclude that relations (political, economic, and cooperation) with Europe are fundamental to the development and security of Cape Verde and facilitators of the integration of the Cape Verdean communities in the different countries of Europe. The geographical proximity of the three outermost European regions of the Atlantic (MAC—Madeira, Azores, and the Canary Islands), the physical proximity with the EU through Spain (the Canaries), the increasing geostrategic importance of the Atlantic basin and common concerns about the fight against trafficking in narcotic drugs and other illicit drugs at sea reinforce the importance of these relations and point to their intensification and densification. Cape Verde's relations with the EU are also important for ECOWAS, as Mr. Pierre Somda, the former vice president of ECOWAS, said in Praia in 2007 about the special partnership.

In my view, relations with ECOWAS should be renegotiated with a view to "selective, supportive and progressive participation," leading to a special status, in the light of Article 68 of the Abuja Treaty. Contrary to the discourse and dominant positions, based on political voluntarism and abusive generalization that tends to reduce Africanness to participation in regional organizations (or vice versa), I would say that the future of Cape Verde in ECOWAS in economic terms does not depend on itself.[39] The industrialization and development of ECOWAS (hopefully this will happen as soon as possible), particularly in some countries (Nigeria, Ghana, Ivory Coast, Mali, Guinea Conakry, Guinea-Bissau, and Senegal) will dictate the size, depth, scope of integration, and the possibilities of deepening Cape Verde's future relations with the region. As in other places, the regional economy will speak much louder than any speech, decision, or intention, no matter how legitimate and well-founded it may be.

Existing economic relations with Europe and the political and geostrategic need for participation in the life of the region illustrate the situation and the need for creative management of dual and/or multiple ownership, which are at the heart of Cape Verde's history and society. Certainly, this position does not fit into certain approaches and visions of the world. From my point of view, the paradox does not come from the multiple choices and options that Cape Verde can and should do but from the persistence of Manichean visions of the world and of international relations. Between the persistent binary view of the world that declines with the disjunctive proposition "either or," I still consider the copulative "and and" as the fittest and most fruitful for the development and security of Cape Verde.[40]

I do not remember where and when I will have read this sentence, whose idea I reconstitute without guaranteeing the accuracy of it, much less the name of the author. "Those who think that everything must be white or black should know that societies and the world have long been invaded by the gray of multiple tonalities!"

Praia, Cabo Verde, March 16, 2016

NOTES

1. In this text, the word "Europe" is not restricted to the countries of the EU, as is this expression is commonly associated in certain political and media circles.

2. As in other experiences and spaces of colonial domination, this coexistence was fraught with contradictions, conflicts, paradoxes, ruptures and continuities. Forty years after independence, Cape Verdean society still shows subtle but indisputable sequels and traces of its colonial past and the entangled mix of race, class, and power and its socio-economic legacy.

3. Due to its original specificity, I make note of the destination of Cape Verdean migration to Italy, primarily female, in its origin. It was promoted and / or facilitated by Capuchin missionaries to respond to the domestic service needs of well-to-do Italian families.

4. Some say that the Cape Verdeans and / or Cape Verdean population in Europe corresponds to more than half the population living in Cape Verde. This is a resource that Cape Verde has not yet known how to use or has not valued consistently for the development and deepening of its relations with Europe. I think the data on Cape Verdean in the diaspora visiting Cape Verde are important. And I do not think it is difficult to create efficient and speedy mechanisms for collecting this particular data at border customs.

5. The fact that Cesária Évora was known in Africa from France illustrates well the structure of commercial, economic, political and cultural relations between African countries and Cape Verde with Africa.

6. Decades later, development theorists in research centers in developing countries "discovered" the connections between emigration and development. For emigrants, families and countries of origin, emigration and development have always been faces of the same currency. The real issue facing Cape Verde, and certainly other countries of origin, is related to the strategy and approaches to the framing and channeling of savings for productive investments and of great socio-economic impact. The tragedy is that certain financial products, of greater economic relevance and efficiency, require a level of confidence "between the parties involved" which, of course, does not exist. The past of administrative neglect, the absence of the state

in the provision of basic services and social exclusion that fills the (conscious and unconscious) memory of emigrants prevents the creation of the confidence necessary for a new "financial reengineering" around the emigrants' savings. The challenge is enormous and transcends the beautiful theories, power point presentations, colorful charts and graphs of financial flows and more or less technocratic and abstract recommendations produced by theorists to demonstrate the potential of remittances in development finance. The optimization of savings in Cape Verde requires, first and foremost, consistent strategies and innovative approaches to "building and strengthening trust among stakeholders." On the other hand, the implementation of the strategy is linked and conditioned by the management of financial institutions and governance (leadership practices and styles, human and institutional capacities of coordination of the actors involved, communication and quality of service, social negotiation, credibility and security of financial products, etc.). From my point of view there will be no financial reengineering for remittances without a political-social, administrative and bureaucratic reengineering in the management of relations with emigrants.

7. The comparison is made in relation to 2012, since the GDP data for subsequent years do not appear to be consolidated and are not presented in the same Bulletin of the Bank of Cape Verde.

8. Regarding the use of informal channels to send remittances and goods, a study of the past decade reports that "It is actually the channel most used by the oldest (emigrants) with a frequency of 44% for those who send / receive over ten years more, 41% for the six to ten years category, and 15% for the 5 years or less category," in André Corsino Tolentino et al., *A importância de o impacto das remessas dos imigrantes em Portugal no desenvolvimento de Cabo Verde*. Lisbon: ACIDI, IP, 2008.

9. The overall negative assessment, and the anti-ODA view (without rigorous evaluation of the donor's policies and ulterior purposes, recipient country contexts, management systems and practices, etc.) promoted by certain neoliberal sectors of the developed countries (and their mimetic reverberations in the countries of the South) is not applicable in the case of Cape Verde. Not that APD has been managed perfectly—much more and better could have been done with the same resources—but, definitely, Cape Verde does not fit in this judgment that can not hide political-ideological and discursive convenience. Even in countries and cases where empirical observation undeniably points to failure, there is a lack of rigorous and neutral assessment of the practices of ODA partners, donors, intermediaries, and service providers. I speak of this aspect not to defend or condemn ODA but to emphasize the need to uphold judgments in rigorous analysis. In this and other matters, speech is loaded with conveniences, skewed, unidirectional and monopolized by some!

10. It is worth recalling some of Cape Verde's vulnerabilities: scarcity of land and arable land (10% of the territory); absence of natural resources; irregular and insufficient rainfall; laughable agricultural production (15% of cereal requirements in years of good precipitation and good production); cyclical droughts, desertification and other manifestations of climate change with an impact on the life and survival of populations; great dependence on fossil energy; incipient or insignificant industrialization; need for multiplication of certain infrastructures resulting from archipelagic insularity, exorbitant costs and low level of return; smallness and fragmentation of

the market with impacts on economic activity (diseconomy of scale); weak attractiveness for FDI; persistence of high levels of poverty and social exclusion, excessive exposure to external shocks, growing threats of international trafficking networks and organized crime, etc. etc.). Today we could add that restrictive immigration policies in Europe and the United States increase internal pressure and social vulnerability.

11. Perhaps more important than announcing the number of tourists, it would have been preferable to define concrete objectives and economic results (number of jobs, direct and indirect income, participation of the national business, etc.).

12. See BCV data, published in the monthly *Boletím de Estatísticas*. The trade data tell us that exporting to the United States is insignificant, countering the excited political discourse on AGOA of some Cape Verdean politicians. Petroleum products and raw materials constitute the bulk of U.S. imports under AGOA, according to information from the U.S. Department of Commerce, U.S. Trade with sub-Saharan Africa, January-December 2014 http://trade.gov/agoa/pdf /2014-us-ssa-trade.pdf. In that regard, it is worth quoting an extract from that note: "AGOA imports totaled $ 14.2 billion, 47 percent less than the previous year, due mainly to a 55 percent decrease in petroleum product imports. Petroleum products continued to account for the largest portion of AGOA imports with a 69 percent share of overall AGOA imports. With these fuel products excluded, AGOA imports—almost exclusively dominated by raw materials—were $ 4.4 billion, decreasing by 10 percent as compared to 2013. AGOA imports of transportation equipment decreased by 34 percent and imports of energy products decreased by 55 percent. However, imports of minerals and metals increased by 17 percent, imports of agricultural products increased by 5 percent, and imports of textiles and apparel increased by 9 percent. Finally, the top five AGOA beneficiary countries were Angola, Nigeria, South Africa, Chad, and Gabon. Other leading AGOA beneficiaries included Kenya, Lesotho, and Republic of Congo. The key issue that remains is the mismatch between developed trade policies and instruments developed by developed countries and the real challenges of development. This inadequacy is also found in relation to other European and American instruments."

13. The unilateral decision to exit Cape Verde from these preferential arrangements is yet another reminder of how the management of the "smooth transition" by the partners, notably the European Commission and probably Cape Verde, has fallen far short of the expectations created during negotiations related to the graduation process.

14. Cited in: Daniel Hamilton, *Atlantic Rising, Changing Commercial Dynamics in the Atlantic Basin.* Center for Transatlantic Relations, The Paul H. Nitze School of Advanced International Studies (John Hopkins University, USA, 2015), 64.

15. I am reminded of the report by Mr Jean Claude Lefort, Member of the French Parliament, in 2005, which is extremely critical of the EPAs and which points to the risk of negative impacts on the budget, balance of payments, industry and agriculture. The precautionary principle has led me to believe that Cape Verde should be removed from the case.

16. The same thing—absence or poor national dominance of the processes—will have happened in connection with accession to the World Trade Organization, WTO. It was supported by assistance from developed countries. Without wishing to doubt

the good faith and professionalism of the technical assistants, it seems to me legitimate to think that the perspective which the assistant gives to the positions will not in any case be that of the assisted country. And when this country is an atypical micro state such as Cape Verde, at least the risk of a mismatch between the proposed / retained solutions and the requirements of development is enormous.

17. Cited in Hamilton, 2015, 65.

18. The data of the Bank of Cape Verde are not clear in relation to the rubric of "Others." Does it simply want to highlight the top five? There will be other European countries included in the category "Others." Indeed, tourism in Cape Verde, particularly on the islands of Sal and Boa Vista, was preceded and carried by FDI from Europe and with a single operator occupying about 70 percent of the market.

19. Contrary to what many national politicians believe, Cape Verde is not the only African country with such an exchange arrangement with an EU member-state. The currency zone of the CFA franc was long before Cape Verde, the same type of currency agreement with fixed parity with the French franc that was later also extended to the Euro. In the CFA franc zone this agreement has been severely criticized because of the "high financial costs (deposit of 50% of the foreign exchange reserves in the French Treasury), monetary and political dependence on France, negative implications on export competitiveness due to overvaluation of the CFA, etc."

20. Cape Verde's foreign policy, and particularly relations with Europe, should be the subject of some explicit understanding among Cape Verdean political actors. I think there is a "tacit understanding" about the main issues. From my point of view, "tacit understanding" does not and cannot mean, in the context of democracy, "uniformity of perspectives and analysis." It is a recurrent and vain illusion that does not take place even within the same governing body. For me it should only mean permanent spaces for information sharing and consultation, avoiding the use of relations, contacts and results of diplomatic action for electoral battles, some caution in the dialogue with partners on possible internal differences and, certainly, explicit solidarity in issues and positions essential for the security and development of Cape Verde. However, the unstoppable temptation to translate any initiatives, projects, programs, contacts and / or international agreements into political-electoral gains disturbs the existing "tacit understanding," creating noises and unnecessary moments of mismatch between national political actors.

21. The political and technical management of the transition, and in particular the Praia Declaration, on the smooth transition (MNEC, June 2007), endorsed by all the members of the GAT, did not seem to me to be consistent with the discussions and with the text on the part of the United Nations and many partners, including Europeans, as evidenced by their hasty disengagement and phasing out. The dominant discourse of the time about ODA, the financial crisis of 2008, the temptation to consider FDI as an antidote and substitute for ODA, the political-electoral treatment given to graduation by the government, some diplomatic passivity on the part of Cape Verde may have contributed to the merely bureaucratic management of the challenging "smooth transition" process by the United Nations and development partners. Years after graduation, Cape Verde is more than ever confronted with the challenge of financing the economy and development that many political and electoral

discourses by all sides tend to ignore. The coming years will be difficult and crucial for the future of this country! The United Nations will certainly underestimate the impact of a Cape Verde denunciation on the practical inconsistency of the "smooth transition" on the objective of reducing the number of countries in the LDC group from forty-eight to twenty-four Istanbul for the LDCs (2011–2020).

22. Each day, more and more the word "strategy" and its adjectives and derived adverbs, fill the political and economic discourse, in clear counterpoint, with many decisions, movements and acts of the same actors, which seem determined almost exclusively by reactive logics and short-term objectives, if not merely operational. In fact, when analyzing many of these acts one can not glimpse defining elements of strategic action and thinking.

23. As an example, I recall my old position on the European "near abroad," or European Neighborhood Policy (ENP), which, in my view, is still impregnated with the logic of the Cold War and security concerns toward the former Soviet bloc, the Caucasus, the Middle East and the Mediterranean, excluding the Atlantic side with all that it currently represents in geostrategic terms, security, trade and shipping, environmental protection and marine resources. I used to say to my European friends and interlocutors using the French expression "il faut boucler la boucle." In this respect, it is worth recalling the European Parliament's resolution of January 19, 2006 (point 7) on the ENP in which it "urges the Commission to propose and develop specific policies aiming, as far as possible, to extend the ENP to the neighboring island states of the outermost regions of the EU bordering the European continent, where particular issues of geographical proximity, cultural and historical affinity and mutual security are topical". There can be no better definition of Cape Verde. Especially at a time when many actors start talking about "wider Atlantic." And for me, this line of cooperation does not imply, in any way, the departure of the ACP group.

24. In this respect, it is often impossible to distinguish the priorities of institutions (Cape Verdean or European) from the preferences or obstinations of the intermediaries (officials, consultants, service providers, companies, etc.).

25. My experience has made me realize that some are more flexible or more rigid than others (states and intermediaries). The temptation to replace national decision-makers and the micro-management trap in the implementation of programs and projects increases the possibilities and opportunities for conflict.

26. Because my name is associated with the Mobility Partnership, I am often called on the street by people who have seen their application refused. Conscious of the legitimate right of the EU and the Member-States to control migration flows and to prevent irregular labor migration, I would have some difficulty in justifying many denials and protests that I am aware of. Complaints have to do with excessive administrative complexity, slowness, apparent subjectivity of criteria, unpredictability of response and quality of care. I give some examples which are illustrative in my opinion. Cases of secondary school teachers and public servants with multiple visits and holidays in Europe who suddenly saw their visa application denied without plausible explanations or bureaucratic justifications without substance. Cape Verdean citizens with visas to spend holidays in the United States and that because of the decrease and / or provisional suspension of direct flights Praia-Boston from the company

Cape Verdean area (TACV) tried to travel, via Lisbon, and they did not succeed because they were denied a transit visa. This is an urgent question because mobility is an important milestone in Cape Verdean society and the image of the European Commission and the Member-States will be a matter of individual, family and collective experiences in granting and obtaining visas. As I once told an European diplomat friend, Europe will have to pay attention to this matter because it runs the risk of losing friends as the squad of enemies increases and without resolving the challenge of irregular immigration.

27. Robert Chambers of the Institute for Development Studies (Sussex University, Brighton, UK) has a much more elaborate and critical explanation of the mismatch between experts from international agencies and national and local development actors. *For the convenience and control of normal professionals, it is not the local, complex, diverse, dynamic and unpredictable reality of those who are poor, weak and peripheral that counts, but the flat shadows of that reality that they, prisoners of their professionalism, fashion for themselves . . . the vertical transfer of reality occurs with development bureaucrats and professionals through their education, training and socialization; and many then seek to transfer their reality in turn to the poor and weak.* In "Whose reality counts? Putting the first last" by Robert Chambers, Intermediate Technology Publications, 1997, London.

28. Again I avoid the unstable arguments of history and culture to focus on the issues of economics and politics that give substance and perenniality to any integration project. Having said that, I do not want to ignore the importance of history and culture for the understanding of men, societies, the development process and governance practices.

29. As I mentioned in my introduction, I invoke the issue of regional integration (ECOWAS) as it tends to appear, rightly or wrongly, in the debate on Cape Verde's relations with Europe. And the emotionally charged debates are articulated around (pre) positions "for or against" which are almost always presented as excluding opposition and linked to an inextricable and selective mix of historical, cultural, societal, economic arguments and politicians who, for the most part, overshadow the understanding of the essential issues.

30. This complex dossier is far from being consensual within ECOWAS. Specifically, Nigeria, the putative engine of integration, would be against the single currency.

31. These exports are dominated by Nigeria and Ivory Coast that carry between them 87 percent of these transactions. Nigeria provides 77 percent of regional exports and Côte d'Ivoire 10 percent. For their part, Ghana and Senegal are placed third and fourth with 4 percent and 2 percent respectively. Mali follows the traditional leaders with 1.7 percent of regional exports. Five Countries (Benin, Burkina Faso, Guinea, Niger and Togo) each carry 1 percent of regional exports.

32. "Unfortunately, the different trade arrangements defined by ECOWAS and WAEMU do not advance the integration of markets at the official level. In trade as a whole, the share of intra-State trade continued close to what it was before the creation of such institutions." John O. Igué, former Minister of Benin and former Director of the West African Institute (Praia) "Etats-Nations in the face of regional integration

in Afrique de l'Ouest," Karthala, Paris, 2006. Unfortunately, the 2006 is still topical. Exports represent 9 percent and imports 10.5 percent of intra-ECOWAS trade. In *Accords commerciaux et flux de commerce dans la CEDEAO (UNECA).*

33. With regard to the aggressiveness of developed countries' interests and networks in protecting the market segment already occupied in the region, it would be edifying to assess the failure of the Cape Verdean airline's attempt to penetrate the West African Following the bankruptcy of Air Afrique in 2002. Failures are opportunities for learning without which future attempts and practices are hardly improved.

34. Contrary to the prevailing discourse that tends to consecrate the idea that Cape Verde would be in a weak position vis-à-vis the tourist industry and investors—this discourse sometimes takes the form of rough economic manipulation. For me, the climate (and microclimates), the natural beauty of the landscape, beaches and mountains, social and political stability, geographical proximity, the aging of the European population, the growing fascination with travel, leisure and *dépaysement*, the saturation of direct competitors (Canary Islands) and the persistent insecurity and political instability in North Africa and the Middle East put Cape Verde in a strong position.

35. We must be aware of the limits of any political statement or decision, however justified or just, to change or neutralize the strength of existing economic and trade relations with Europe. Such a decision of this nature to function must be preceded by having safe, credible and more advantageous alternatives.

36. Strategic human resource management practices in the vital sectors of the economy and development (particularly the recruitment and appointment of managers on the basis of bureaucratic, academic, political, and accumulated experience) have already shown their limits, perversions and negative impact on the life of organizations (public and private) and on the economy and development. While there is a notable gain in recruitment, competitive hires do not solve most of the problems of development management and governance. Competitive recruitment do not generate competences. The market gives what it has! Since spontaneous generation of skills does not occur—the permanent training of human resources (strategic, intermediary and operational) in critical sectors is an urgent need for development management in the near future. Building up an organizational culture that encourages learning requires more than just changing regulations and policies. It should include motivating staff, nurturing leaders and champions and developing a vision for the agency or Ministry that can inspire and drive forward efforts to improve results. See: *Evaluating Development Activities, 12 lessons from OECD*, DAC, Paris, 2013.

37. This position was presented and defended by me in at least two ECOWAS statutory meetings in 2006 and 2007. The last one was at the Council of Ministers and Summit of December 2007 in Ouagadougou. Cape Verde's initiative and arguments were accepted without any challenge or resistance from the Council Members. And if memory does not betray me, it was recorded in the final communiqué of the Summit. Taking advantage of the presence of ECOWAS ministers in Ouagadougou, I took up the matter in private with several former colleagues and with the former ECOWAS Commission President, Mr. Mohamed Chambas, in detail to explain the reasons, motives and vulnerabilities of Cabo Verde and the need for a "special status." Following the positive reaction from the Council, I tried to agree with President

Chambas on a mission to Abuja, scheduled for February 2008 to open the negotiating process with the commission and to initiate information to Member-States. This mission should also serve to relaunch the process of setting up the Western Africa Institute (IAO) sponsored by UNESCO and Cape Verde. In order to prevent interpretations and speculations that such an initiative would normally provoke in the Cape Verdean and African contexts—international relations are always loaded with pre-judgments, perceptions, emotions and inscience—the government persuaded that we should close the diplomatic mission in Addis Ababa and open a diplomatic mission in Abuja. This option was intended to defuse possible perverse interpretations of the exclusionary logic while at the same time favoring relations with ECOWAS and Nigeria, which in my view deserved priority over the African Union. Subsequently there was to issue a circular to inform the missions in some Member-States, primarily Senegal, Guinea-Bissau, Côte d'Ivoire, Ghana and Mali for information. Until the date of my leaving the government (June 2008) and despite repeated insistence and successive reprogramming, unfortunately, the agenda of the President of the ECOWAS Commission did not allow me to accommodate my mission to Abuja.

38. Indeed, the success of regional integration will depend on the development dynamics and governance practices of Member-States. In 1996, the former executive secretary of ECOWAS, Abass Bundu, wrote: "The poor economic health of West African states remains a major obstacle to integration efforts since the early 1980s." In "Intégration et coopération régionales en Afrique de l'Ouest," Karthala-CRDI, Paris and Ottawa, 1996. Author's translation. Fourteen years later, UNDP's Human Development Report (2014) reports that, with the exception of Cape Verde and Ghana, all countries in the region remain in the category of low human development country. The development balance is far from meeting the aspirations of the people, the commitments made under the Millennium Declaration and the demands of economic integration.

39. According to this reasoning scheme, one might ask whether some Member-States suspended from ECOWAS because of coups d'état or other abuses of EC rules lose their Africanness.

40. At the II Cape Verde Transformation Forum 2030 (Praia, May 2014), the executive secretary of the United Nations Economic Commission for Africa (UNECA), Mr. Carlos Lopes, made a speech, with consistent facts and arguments, challenging society, political parties and the Cape Verdean government on governance options and practices. I believe that the Cape Verdean political actors should take due account of these reflections. However, listening to him speak about the potential and prospects for the rise of the African economies, something everyone wanted, and Cape Verde's relations with Europe, I had the strange impression of hearing / seeing, in the effluvia of the applause and in the absence of consistent contradiction, the failure to take into account (or be unaware?) of the structural economic factors linking Cape Verde to Europe and the lack of immediate and viable alternatives on the part of African economies to respond to the demands of consumption, investment and of Cape Verde. I emphasize an even more disturbing detail in the speech by the UNECA executive secretary. It is the resuscitation of the specter of disjunctive logic in Cape Verde's relations with Europe and Africa that he had considered dead and inhuman! I have been

disturbed by the halo and features of an Africanism typical of authoritarian regimes that build and use the "nationalist / pan-Africanist fog" to obfuscate the understanding of the problems and to neutralize the just claims of populations to democracy, democratic alternation, respect for human rights, security, accountability, satisfaction of basic needs and improvement of conditions and life framework. I will probably have poorly decoded the tone, words and message of Mr. Carlos Lopes, whose attachment to the values and principles of democratic governance is well-known to all.

REFERENCES

Banco de Cabo Verde (BCV), *Boletim de Estatísticas*, Novembro 2015, Praia: BCV, 2015.

Bundu, Abass, "La CEDEAO et l'avenir de l'integration régionale en Afrique de l'Ouest," in *Intégration et coopération régionales en Afrique de l'Ouest*, Paris: Karthala-CRDI, 1996.

Chambers, Robert, *Whose Reality Counts? Putting the First Last*, London: Intermediate Technology Publications, 1997.

Hamilton, Daniel, *Atlantic Rising, Changing Commercial Dynamics in the Atlantic Basin.* Center for Transatlantic Relations, The Paul H. Nitze School of Advanced International Studies (John Hopkins University, United States, 2015).

Igué, John O., *Etats-Nations in the Face of Regional Integration in Afrique de l'Ouest*, Paris: Karthala, 2006.

Organization for Economic Cooperation and Development (OECD), *Evaluating Development Activities, 12 Lessons from OECD*, Paris: OECD/DAC, 2013.

United Nations Development Program, *Human Development Report 2014*, New York: UNDP, 2014.

Chapter 8

Where Are the Women?

The Cabo Verdean Diaspora in the Context of African Development

Terza Alice Silva Lima-Neves

Cabo Verde's diaspora has been a vital factor in the country's social and economic development historically. This chapter examines the role of the Cabo Verdean diaspora in the country's development. Broadly, the Cabo Verdean case is a window into the patterns, limits, and possibilities of global migration, diaspora, and African development. Specifically, this chapter draws attention to an overlooked but critical dimension to the role of diaspora communities in development. This chapter makes the case for gendered perspectives and analyses in the study of Cabo Verde's diaspora and development.[1] Although there is a wide range of research on the role of the diaspora in the development of this small archipelago of ten islands located on the West African coast, as a unique and fascinating case, most discourses have focused on the diasporic population in its entirety. Limited attention has been given to the impact gender plays on migration, diaspora community building, and development at home.

Cabo Verdean women make up half of the country's population and have been emigrating at a faster rate than men. When we consider the large numbers of female-headed households, the predominance of women in transnational economic activities, the higher rates of savings and remittances by women migrants, any understanding of the role of the diaspora in Cabo Verde's development—but also the impact of migration on social relations, family structures, and local communities—is incomplete without a gendered perspective. However, the plight of women is viewed as an afterthought in scholarship, as well as government development policies, as subjects rather than active agents of social, economic, and political change in both the homeland and host country.

The discussion in this chapter has two objectives: first, to stimulate critical reflection on the existing mainstream "diasporas and development" paradigm which offer gender-blind analyses in the Cabo Verdean case study, and second, to make the case for serious state-level gendered policies in order to fully consider the role of the diaspora on development at home. I argue that the absence of gendered policies in engaging the diaspora has limited the development goals of the Cabo Verdean government. I claim that Cabo Verdean women have been marginalized by the state in key decision-making processes. The state's neglect, in turn, has led to the creation of women's strategic social and economic informal diasporic networks. Gender equity and equality policies at home and abroad must mirror each other if sustainable development is to take place. By situating Cabo Verde, its diaspora, and development processes within the larger African context, I call for a critical look at all national and international actors who are designing Cabo Verde's development plans, which may include neo-liberal gender and development policies that attempt to render African women invisible in their communities and often do not reflect the economic, cultural, and environmental realities of this small archipelago nation.

WOMEN, MIGRATION, AND DEVELOPMENT

Why is gender perspective important in the study of diasporas and homeland development? Gender affects all aspects of the migration experience for women and men, the reasons they migrate, the decision of who will migrate, the network of individuals they will use to migrate, experiences of integration and finding work in the new country and the relationship they maintain with their homeland. A gendered perspective highlights important information about the frequency and quantity of remittances that are sent, how the remittances are transferred, and the level of impact the remittances will have on the development of the homeland. There is a consensus on the importance of gender considerations in the policies and research on migration but it continues to be ignored, leading to ineffective policies that do not reflect the realities of migrant men and women. Migrants are human beings and not just remittance senders. Many face harsh living and working conditions in their host countries which make their ability to send remittances to their homeland a challenging process. Very often conditions in the host country and household hierarchies such as who gets to work and control the family income affect the way men and women migrants interact with their homeland.

According to World Bank reports, the population of international migrants is an estimated 247 million and was expected to surpass 250 million in 2015 (World Bank Report 2015). Women make up for half of the world's migrant population and at least half of the remittances sent through formal channels. Migrants' remittances to developing countries reached an estimated $436 billion in 2014, an increase from 2013. The top five immigration destination countries are the United States, Saudi Arabia, Germany, the Russian Federation, and the United Arab Emirates. The largest group of migrants remains Mexicans going into the United States. Cabo Verde's per capita remittance flow of $352 (USD) makes it one of the world's highest recipients of remittances, along with states such as El Salvador ($664), Guatemala ($349), Philippines ($258), and Nepal ($187). Cabo Verde's remittances per capita are the highest in the West African region. Since independence, remittances accounted for 40 percent to 50 percent of the country's national income up until the 1990s. Remittances have declined in more recent times, accounting for only 9 percent of the gross domestic product (GDP), but still higher than other Sub-Saharan African states (Resende-Santos 2015). However, these numbers do not account for the informal channels through which unreported remittances are sent and received.

Theories on international migration and development have shifted over the years between negative and positive outlooks of the linkage between the two variables (De Haas 2010; Faist 2008; Portes 2009). In the 1950s and 1960s, during the post-war and decolonization periods, remittances were viewed as a way for developing countries to take off. Strict immigration regulations were imposed in the 1970s in Europe, due to the economic recession while at the same time there was a shift in development theory with a new focus on dependency and structuralist approaches. In 1979, the United Nations adopted the Convention for the Elimination of All Forms of Discrimination against Women (CEDAW). National governments were asked to accept the convention and commit to implementing measures to end discrimination against women in all its forms by incorporating the principle of equality of men and women in the legal system, abolish all practices that discriminate against women, establish institutions that protect women against discrimination, and work to eliminate all acts of discrimination against women by individuals, organizations, and institutions. Similar to other development agendas and policies, CEDAW has compelled member-states to make substantive changes in improving the lives of women. However, critics argue that it is part of the larger vision of pushing liberal policies in the developing world, with no regard to the country's cultural and traditional realities.

In the 1980s, migration was connected to dependency, brain drain, and increased socio-economic inequality in the homeland and viewed in a pessimistic way. However, in the last ten to fifteen years, migration and development theories and policies have yet again altered, and there is an optimistic outlook on the role of migrants in the development of their homeland, leading to poverty relief and economic growth via investments. For policymakers at the international level, migrants were seen as key actors in the development of their homeland, sending monetary remittances, as well as transferring knowledge (social capital) back to their homeland to support not only their families but also their entire communities. The current discourse on development theory calls for the diaspora population to be fully involved in development processes, beyond economic remittances but also to contribute new ideas, expertise, skills, and networks they have gained while abroad (Akesson 2011). These various policies which call for an optimistic outlook of migration and development cooperation are published by institutions and countries in the "North" or developed states, such as the World Bank and the European Union (EU), attempting to address increased pressures of international migration and national security, with little input from the local governments that are supposed to implement these policies. The level of discourse on gender in most migration and development studies have included a "throw women in and stir" paradigm, separating statistics on men and women and not including gender as a variable to be studied in determining the factors that impact migrants' decisions and realities.

The migration and development optimism, however, is challenged by De Haas (2010) who argues that the idea of migrants as agents of development from below is largely based on ideology rather than empirical studies and evidence, driven by neo-liberal positions on development and immigration control. De Haas cautions against this and calls for in-depth discussions on the real political, social, and economic constraints of positive human development. Furthermore, the critique argues that this optimism plays down the role of the state in development processes and plays up the role of individuals and communities in development. For example, it makes the general claim that if a migrant comes from a poor country, she has the moral obligation to support the development of the homeland. However, remittance-based development ignores the often challenging working and living conditions of some migrants. Remittances are seen as unethical because migrants often work in deplorable conditions and are forced to send money back home. Diasporas are often seen as heroes and agents of development. This optimism puts an emphasis on national rather than local development, which in the case of Cabo Verde's diaspora is problematic because as an island nation, individuals are more likely to remit to their island of origin, particularly their local communities rather than the government (Gamlen 2014).

The migration and development model proposed by liberal institutions also does not take into account the diverse factors that affect diasporas' ability to advance in political, social, and economic ways in the host country. In a previous study, I argued that given its history of strict racial stratification, the Cabo Verdean community in the United States faced the harsh realities of racism thus leading to social, economic, and political marginalization

(Lima-Neves 2009). Consequently, it would take one or two generations for the diaspora to move from unskilled or labor to skilled diaspora by acquiring formal education and entry into fields that had once been denied to blacks, non-whites, and most immigrants. Thus, in this generation, we see an increase in the number of Cabo Verdeans who are formally educated and skilled professionals, especially in Portugal and the United States which are the main destination countries for this diaspora group.

In her study on Cabo Verdean returnees and development, Akesson (2011) makes similar conclusions in the optimistic link between diasporas and development, in that migrants from the developing world may not have the opportunity to acquire skills that they are able to use in development processes, that "methodological nationalism" is responsible for creating the notion that migrants have a moral obligation to support their homeland, that it takes a long time to accumulate enough resources for a successful return and lastly, that often the skills of the returnees are not adaptable to local realities. In terms of gendered perspectives on migration and development, there is limited information detailing the factors that impact the decision-making process and different ways in how migrant women and men remit to and support their homeland.

Until recently, women remained invisible in migration and development studies. In the United States, in particular, there was an interest in ethnic and identity studies following increased migration in 1965. New feminist movements in the 1960s and young white women attending graduate school called for an increase in the interdisciplinary study of women's work, particularly immigrants from Asia and Latin America to the United States. Thus, work on non-white women, foreign-born, and working-class challenged the existing norm of only studying white middle-class women. With the United Nations focusing on women and gender equality in the mid-1970s and a more global approach to migration, studies moved beyond the North American context. In the 1980s, scholarship in the fields of sociology and anthropology called for an analysis of gender as a system of power relations instead of just a focus on women. Feminist theory calls for the study of the social construction of masculinities in regard to migration and gender identities. Migration can have different effects on different women. It can emancipate some or perpetuate existing traditional norms from the migrant's homeland.

Current literature calls for the position of gender as a major concept in migration theories beyond the family and household and into economic analysis, cultural society, and state/political institutions. The destination of migrants also affects the way migrants behave. When women were introduced to the scholarship on international migration studies, it was to highlight the predominance of men in migratory flows. Women were simply added to the literature as an attempt to address male bias. In the 1960s and 1970s, migration theories often assumed that most migrants were male and that women were merely wives and dependents who followed their husbands. Consequently, migration was portrayed as purely a male phenomenon. Yet, women have always been present in migratory flows, traditionally as spouses, daughters, and dependents of male migrants. The past decades have seen an increase in women's autonomous migration, including the case of Cabo Verdean women and their transnational practices spanning several countries such as Portugal, Brazil, and the United States, as the main economic providers or breadwinners for their families. Men and women show differences in their migratory behaviors, face different opportunities, and have to cope with different risks and challenges, such as vulnerability to human rights abuses, exploitation, discrimination, and specific health risks. Therefore, migration is not a gender-neutral phenomenon. From the moment they decide to migrate, women's experiences as migrants are different from men's experiences. It wasn't until the early 1990s that scholars brought to light the connection between gender and migration. Previous discourses were simply to highlight the differences between women and men migrants. Future scholarship on migration and development should not only consider additional factors that impact the experiences of the sexes but also consider sexual orientation as a main indicator and the experiences of the Lesbian, Gay, Bisexual, Transgendered community.

In the Cabo Verdean case, sex and gender were introduced as a central category of migration analysis by Grassi and Evora (2007). In this study, women's transnational economic activities were seen as central to their survival and that of their families in Cabo Verde. Grassi and Evora analyzed the complex but strategic transnational nature of these women known as "rabidantes" and their activities, some who lived in Cabo Verde, others in Italy and Portugal but traveled to Brazil to purchase merchandise and sell across the diverse diasporic locations, as well as in Cabo Verde (Fikes 2000). Men, on the other hand, as highlighted in this study, did not see these practices as "appropriate" for them as men. In addition to holding other jobs, this informal economy helped women support their parents and oftentimes the children they left behind in Cabo Verde who were in the care of their parents.

Cabo Verdean immigrant women have been the pillars of their communities, helping newly arrived Cabo Verdeans, educating their children about their culture, forming organizations, and helping their families and communities back home. In the absence of infrastructure in their homeland and limited access to formal structures in their host countries due to language or other socio-economic barriers, Cabo Verdean women in the diaspora have found ways to connect with their communities at home, via strategic informal networks which include family and friends relationship, as well as hometown associations. These networks have given women greater autonomy in navigating their new communities as well as homeland, away from non-government partners, which do not benefit the women's strategic goals and objectives in supporting development projects in Cabo Verde, more often than not, in their specific hometowns. Shifting the ways we analyze and define political, economic, and social agency, as well as community-building practices, and allowing individuals to determine for themselves the ways they organize can provide better insight into the lives and practices of women in their immigrant communities. The existing literature argues for the improvement of homeland policies and infrastructures such as ease of money transfers and shipping of goods as well as increased business investment possibilities and cheaper airlines prices, as a way to increase diaspora engagement with the homeland (African Development Bank 2011 and 2012; Resende-Santos 2015). I argue, however, that Cabo Verdean women will still choose informal ways to engage with their homeland. Recent diaspora polls show that a continued lack of trust in the Cabo Verdean government hinders the diaspora as a whole from wanting to formally engage with the homeland (Melo 2008). This last point will be discussed in greater detail later in the chapter.

There is an expectation that Cabo Verdean emigrants will either return home to live after spending years abroad; or for those who choose to stay abroad, will invest from afar in the development of their beloved homeland. However, careful attention is not given to whether or not conditions at home and abroad are favorable to this dream of return. To this end and as pointed out earlier, there is limited research that addresses the different experiences of migrant men and women, as well as a myriad of factors that impact their status in the host country and the decision to return home.

CABO VERDEAN WOMEN IN THE CONTEXT OF AFRICAN DEVELOPMENT

In this section, I turn my attention to the status of women in Cabo Verde in the context of African development to shed light on diaspora and development policies. Why is it important to analyze domestic government policies and initiatives when we discuss diaspora and development policies? I argue that if domestic policies are not strategically designed to intentionally improve women's lives such as equal pay, access to political participation, legal protection against domestic and sexual violence, then it is less likely that diasporic women will want to permanently return home after living abroad. Additionally, if there are existing patriarchal structures, as well as bureaucratic challenges, then formally educated women who are skilled professionals will not feel compelled to engage with the state in investment and other projects for the benefit of their homeland.

Noted African scholar Ifi Amadiume argues that the main factor affecting African women today is the development policies that are designed abroad and seen as mere continuations of foreign interventions in state economic planning and budget allocations. This is exemplified in the continued role of the International Monetary Fund (IMF) and the World Bank, who have had negative effects on local communities and gender relations by promoting policies, such as austerity measures and privatization, that have reduced public services for women and children, reinforced existing gender income inequalities, and marginalized economic sectors heavily represented by women, such as agriculture and the informal sectors. Development planners have left out women's work, particularly those in agricultural and rural settings where they are the heads of households and they have also ignored poverty.

In the context of development, Cabo Verde is well on its way to achieving its target United Nations Millennium Development Goals among others, eradicating extreme poverty and hunger, achieving universal education, promoting gender equality and empowerment of women, and reducing child mortality. The country is still plagued by poverty leading to growing crime rates and class divisions. While data shows little difference in unemployment between men and women today, Cabo Verdean women continue to suffer a higher rate of poverty, 33 percent according to 2007 data. Women are especially hard hit by both urban (19.6%) and rural (48%) poverty rates.

In post-independence Africa, we witnessed a rise of international economic partnerships and aid from the west and more recently, China. Foreign intervention in the likes of powerful agencies like the United Nations, World Bank, and the IMF was actively involved in determining the path of Africa's future via structural adjustment programs. The United Nations Decade for Women (1976–1985) coincided with the rise of development theories and mirrored the development policies driven by Western institutions like the World Bank and IMF. This resulted in development theories that focus on gender—women in development (WID), women and development (WAD), and later, gender and development (GAD). These theories designed by Western thinkers made general policy recommendations and did not account for the cultural and socio-economic realities of African women in their own environments. WID, WAD, and GAD measured development on economic indicators, depicted the lives of women in the developing world as uniform, and failed to recognize the unique realities, opinions, and world views of these women. Western feminism argued for equality between men and women while in the developing world women's lives are interwoven with their family and community, as central systems of social and economic support. Demanding that women abandon the very system of support that had sustained them for the sake of development is not only unrealistic but results in the dismantling of the family as a central institution in most developing states. However, given that most policies on women's lives are carried out by researchers, the educated and elite populations, women are often seen as incapable of making their own decisions and understanding their own situations with the objective of articulating them coherently. Similarly in Cabo Verde, there is the presence of non-governmental organizations that lead several projects on behalf of international agencies and institutions for the purposes of development. There are limited studies that report whether or not Cabo Verdean nationals are at the forefront of creating and implementing policies as well as whether or not these policies benefit the citizens or have the citizens' input, particularly rural women in all the islands.

In his critical essay on democracy in Cabo Verde, Amado refers to Cabo Verde as "West Africa's Democratic Potemkin Village" where he argues that "the institutional mechanisms that were intended to buttress participation by ordinary citizens are either lacking or have simply become part of the Pays Legal (Legal Country) without any repercussion in the Pays Reel (Real Country)" (Amado 2015). He argues that Cabo Verde has become "two-faced," one that exudes democracy and sound governance toward development with the intention to attract foreign donors and investors in the international policy community and another where the country's citizenry only demonstrate active electoral participation every four years during the legislative and presidential elections with little to no civic engagement in policy-making processes on a regular basis. Amado goes further to make the case for the "Super Cape Verdean" who uses political power for personal gain with no consequences or penalties, an elite class that has constructed a democratic Potemkin Village in exchange for development assistance. Amado's critique stands in contrast to existing reports such as those published by the African Development Bank, EU, and the United Nations which offer praise to Cabo Verde's economic and political progress.

Roselma Evora also points to the disconnect between a commendable representation of women in appointed executive positions in government and a low number of women in the parliament, which are elected positions as well as low numbers of women as chief executive officers in companies. Women have made significant gains over the years in the sphere of political participation. There was a considerable increase in the numbers from elections in 1991 to 2011. In executive positions of leadership, women made up 49 percent, and currently, women make up 55 percent of all governmental positions. In the 2016 legislative elections, women made up 30.5 percent of all candidates, with 17 elected (9 for MpD; 7 for PAICV; and 1 for UCID). The current percentage of women in parliament is 23.6 percent, an increase from 2011 (20.8%) and a record for Cabo Verde, surpassing the world average for women in parliament (22%). In terms of judicial power, the number is very low as it pertains to women as members of the Supreme Court (one of four), judges (ten of twenty-three), prosecutors (five of nineteen), and assistant prosecutors (one of six) (INE 2008).

Although these numbers are encouraging, national statistics mostly focus on formal political participation, women who are either elected or appointed to political office at the national level, and not on the trends of the electorate. Evora (2011) offers a quantitative account of democracy and the participation of Cabo Verdean women and men in both local and national politics, highlighting that women have been systemically left out of the positions of power that make the most impact, namely, as mayors of specific islands, members of municipal assemblies, judges and state/local attorneys. She points to the existing limitation of Cabo Verde as an African success story of consolidated democracy and good governance and the portrait of lack of gender equality and equity in decision-making processes, essential components of any successful democratic state. Suzano Costa (2011) also argues for a more nuanced discussion of additional government policies on women's political participation in the democratic process via the introduction of quotas for women in key political positions.

Cabo Verde's Constitution is one of the most advanced on the African continent, guaranteeing civil and political rights to the citizenry, which for the most part are respected in practice. However, there is still concern over the legal rights of women in the areas of equal pay for equal work, domestic violence, and protection by the state. Although a two-year national plan was launched in 2009 to fight gender violence, and a law was passed in 2010, criminalizing gender-based violence, beating by a male domestic partner and sexual violence is still a major challenge to women's and girl's advancement and is widely blamed on cultural and traditional habits. The Penal Code was revised to include a more comprehensive definition of sexual abuse and strengthened the penalty against perpetrators. However, women will still not go to the police due to a lack of knowledge about their rights, the legal process, or they do not feel protected by the authorities. There is still a stigma that domestic issues should not be made part of the "public sphere." Maritza Rosabal's research (2011) highlights violence against women and the imbalanced power relationships between men and women in Cabo Verde both in the public and private spheres. Women face the double burden of caring for themselves and their families and are underrepresented in the public decision-making processes.

In Cabo Verde, women face extreme poverty in the predominantly rural areas where female households constitute the great majority of single-parent homes. Reports by national and international institutions claim that the Cabo Verdean state has met or is well on its way to meet all of its Millennium Challenge Goals. However, these claims do not take into account the conditions of women and girls in extremely impoverished conditions, particularly in the rural areas. In most instances, women will engage in local economies or go abroad, if they can, to look for better economic and social opportunities. In Cabo Verde, environmental concerns have impacted women's lives. The eruption of the Pico de Fogo Volcano in 2014 led to the destruction of nearby communities and the displacement of families. Rebuilding efforts have not taken into account the role of women in this process and resettlement of these internally displaced peoples. Additionally, in the case of the Ribeira da Barca community in Santiago Island, women spent countless hours in the ocean, digging and carrying sand for construction companies. Not only did the digging of sand lead to environmental degradation for the locality but also to health problems for the women such as vaginal infections, deafness, blindness, arthritis, and hair loss (InforPress 2016). Recent implemented environmental laws put a stop to the digging of sand in this area, leaving the women in this industry jobless. Consequently, women are now relocating to the island of Boa Vista looking for employment in the tourism industry. These accounts of complex internal migration warrant attention from the local and national governments because they affect both sending and receiving islands which face their own challenges as it relates to growing populations, employment opportunities, and poverty.

Women's rights activist Zezinha Chantre calls for national attention to the women in the coastal communities, who make up the majority of the workforce in these regions, have lived from the extraction of sand, and find themselves without employment and facing major health risks. Cabo Verdean gender and development expert Adelsia Duarte calls for United Nations and international conferences on gender equality to pay close attention to island nations where equal opportunities and representation for women may be quite difficult in local and national governance. She highlights that it is important that the process of decision-making be as participatory as possible. Besides involving the governments of the different island states, it should give a special emphasis to civil society institutions that work on gender issues. She has called for special attention to the environmental and economic vulnerabilities facing these states and how these vulnerabilities impact women (United Nations (UN) Women 2014). In addition to being impacted by environmental degradation, economically poor women may also seek sex work as a way to make money for personal and family survival. There is no evidence of efforts by the government to address the growth of tourism, sex workers, and prostitution in Cabo Verde, which often impacts not just women but young girls and boys. Future policy studies should explore these factors that are becoming a cause for concern in Cabo Verde, particularly those islands that experience higher levels of tourism like Sal and Boa Vista.

In addition to national efforts, the Cabo Verdean state has signed on to several regional and international agreements for the empowerment of women and to combat gender inequality. As a member of the African Union and Economic Community of West African States (ECOWAS), it adheres to the organizations' regional agreements on gender equality. The African Union has various agreements on gender equality and women's rights such as Protocol for Human Rights and People, the rights of African Women, Declaration on Gender Equality in Africa, in which all heads of states agree to submit national reports on the achievements of their respective states in achieving gender equality goals. It ratified the United Nations CEDAW in 1980. Although policies and projects are in place as mandated by CEDAW and other international and African gender equality agreements, Cabo Verde still has much work to do in the areas of gender mainstreaming in rural areas, especially given the issues of climate change and food security for women, preparation of a second national plan of equality and gender equity, mainstreaming of gender issues in various sectors, such as education, health, justice, and police, through staff training, empowering women for their participation in politics through the same training, and inclusion of gender concerns in water and sanitation issues (UN Women 2014).

This chapter is not arguing that the role of women has been disregarded since the inception of the Cabo Verdean state. There are documented accounts by noted scholars of the role of women in the making of the Cabo Verdean state via armed struggle as well as social and political participation (Gomes 2011; Monteiro 2009). However, I do make the claim that there is limited evidence of current strategic government outputs, inclusive of gendered perspectives especially given the large size of the female population on the islands (Ministry of the Communities ENED Report 2014). I argue that from the position of formal structures, gender and women appears to be a "side discussion" of development policies often left to the hand of international organizations that operate locally, with limited voices from the local rural population and more often than not, only inclusive of the voice of the elite and formally educated. In reaction to this, diasporic Cabo Verdean women may consider how their lives will be impacted, when thinking of a permanent homeland return, especially in the face of limited government policies that intentionally address and improve women's lives, if they are coming from a host country where they have enjoyed considerable socio-economic and personal freedoms.

AN OVERVIEW OF THE CABO VERDEAN DIASPORA

I situate the Cabo Verdean diaspora within the larger African immigrant community and as a modern diaspora, defined as an "ethnic minority groups of migrant origins residing and acting in host countries but maintaining strong sentimental and material links with their countries of origin—their homeland" (Sheffer 1986). We often hear that there are more Cabo Verdeans living abroad than on the islands, allowing for the space to tell the unique story of a West African Kriolu island nation and former Portuguese colony that has experienced a massive exodus of its people since the mid-1800s as a result of extreme poverty and long periods of drought and famine.

The current Cabo Verdean diasporic community, however, is very diverse in terms of geographical location, as well as socio-economic realities. This community constitutes populations living in mainland Africa, North and South America, as well as Europe. It includes formally educated and skilled professional men and women doctors, social workers, lawyers, professors, business owners, entrepreneurs, community advocates, politicians, judges, actors, and artists, as well as non-specialized laborers, factory, domestic, and construction workers. Although socio-economically and phenotypically diverse, this diaspora is unified in their understanding of what it means to be Cabo Verdean or Kriolu (Pilgrim 2015). This sense of unified ethnicity and love for their homeland allows them to maintain diverse levels of connections with Cabo Verde. The intensity of this connection has been historically impacted by the working and living conditions they face in the host country. The connections take several forms such as listening to Cabo Verdean music, eating traditional foods, attending cultural events and religious festivals, traveling back home, sending monetary and in-kind remittances to family members, hospitals, and community organizations. In any given Cabo Verdean immigrant community in the world, one will find hometown associations and clubs, cultural centers, radio programs, restaurants, night clubs, as well as the only existing academic center outside of Cabo Verde, the Pedro Pires Institute for Cape Verdean Studies at Bridgewater State University in the United States.

As mentioned above, since the formation of the Cabo Verdean community abroad, members have supported their families, friends, and communities back home. In moments of famine, drought and everyday hardship Cabo Verdeans abroad have organized to send money, food, and other goods to the different islands. Numerous organizations in the diaspora have supported these efforts, as well as to preserve cultural connections and educate younger generations. Cabo Verdeans also travel back to Cabo Verde on vacation adding value to tourism, the country's leading industry. Although the level of remittances has fluctuated over the years, in more recent times, they have accounted for roughly 9 percent to 20 percent of the nation's national income. The diaspora enjoys political rights, which include citizenship to all people who can prove that their parents and grandparents were born on the islands. Moreover, similar to Haiti and the Dominican Republic, Cabo Verdeans abroad also enjoy the right to vote in parliamentary and presidential elections.

The diaspora is now viewed as a major contributor to the development of their homeland, often called the "eleventh island" of Cabo Verde.

Migration is an important part of the formation of Cabo Verdean society, and it continues to shape the islands' development in modern times. Opportunities and desire for migration arose from Cabo Verde's strategic location in the geography of trade and empire building as well as the lack of natural resources and agricultural base. It is estimated that between 1774 and 1975, 120,000 Cabo Verdeans perished as a result of drought and famine (Almeida 2007). Previous detailed studies by noted Cabo Verdean scholars offer accounts of the harsh conditions of Cabo Verdean life on the islands under the Portuguese colonial regime and patterns of migration (Carreira 1982). Today there is an estimated population of 500,000 Cabo Verdeans living throughout the world, exceeding the domestic population. However, it is important to note that we do not know the exact number of the Cabo Verdean diaspora.

The dispersion of native Cabo Verdeans began in the fifteenth century, through forced migration of the slave trade which was replaced by spontaneous forms of migration in the eighteen and nineteenth centuries, when slavery was abolished. Cabo Verdean migration throughout the nineteenth and twentieth centuries assumed different routes, as Cabo Verdeans searched for new destinations. Because of its archipelago-form, Cabo Verde's migratory process had specific features with different migration flows and destinations by islands of origin (i.e., Santiago Island to Lisbon and São Vicente Island to Rotterdam). Cabo Verdean emigration is divided into three migratory cycles: From the end of the nineteenth century to the first decade of the twentieth century, Cabo Verdeans migrated to the Americas, mainly to the United States. During this time, there was also substantial migration to São Tomé and Príncipe and other parts of the Portuguese colonial empire, such as Angola and Guiné-Bissau. This cycle was thus divided into two migratory flows: North to the United States and South to São Tomé and Príncipe and Angola. The second cycle took place from the 1920s until the end of World War II. Two major trends occurred: a reduction in the number of exits and shift in migratory destinations to Brazil, Argentina, Senegal, and Gambia. Migration within the Portuguese colonial empire continued to be significant for Cabo Verdeans. The period following the end of World War II to present time marks the last of the migration cycles. In this cycle, the main destinations were Holland, Portugal, France, Luxembourg, Italy, Switzerland, Spain, and Germany. During this period, migration to the United States was also reactivated. This migration cycle has different features: A first flow toward Holland; a second flow toward Portugal; a third flow toward Italy; and a fourth flow toward other European countries (Grassi 2006).

Europe has been the main destination for Cabo Verdeans since 1960. The 2000 census highlighted that between the periods between 1995 and 2000, 50 percent of emigrants were destined mainly to Portugal. The United States was the second major destination of choice, followed by France and Holland. There were also significant flows to Italy, Spain, and Luxembourg. Economic growth in post-war Europe as well as the need for labor attracted Cabo Verdeans to the continent. In Portugal, for example, there was a flow of Portuguese workers to more industrialized parts of Europe (Germany, France, Switzerland, and Belgium), thus prompting the demand for unskilled labor in Portugal. The port city of Rotterdam in Holland was an attractive destination for workers. Toward the end of the 1960s, 9,000 documented Cabo Verdeans lived in Rotterdam, a few thousands in Lisbon and Paris, a few hundreds in Italy (mostly women living in Rome, Naples, and Milan). Rotterdam and Lisbon were the main destination cities for Cabo Verdean emigration to Europe (Carling 2008). Currently, Cabo Verdean migration is relatively high in migrants who hold tertiary education and are highly skilled.

CABO VERDEAN WOMEN IN THE DIASPORA

The desire to emigrate has been a constant in the Cabo Verdean's imagination. Some desire to go abroad, work hard, and come back to their homeland. Cabo Verdeans cite unemployment, having relatives abroad and recurring remittances as factors in their desire to emigrate, while others desire to go abroad, work hard, and come back to their homeland. However, easy access to social media makes Cabo Verdeans at home less enamored with the dream of going abroad as they see their fellow compatriots abroad often suffering in deplorable socio-economic conditions. In terms of gender, there has been a balance in emigration flows. The shift changed from individual labor to family-related migration. In contrast to previous times where men migrated leaving the women behind to care for the home and raise the children, present-day Cabo Verdean women are more independent and also exercise their desires to migrate and find opportunities for economic freedom and educational advancement. The current generation of migrant Cabo Verdean women sees migration as an opportunity to escape patriarchal norms such as domestic abuse and dependence on their male partners, as well as poverty. Migration allows women the agency and freedom to seek education, professional training, and financial freedom, as well as define their own future. Highlighting that not all development is positive, women's rights advocate Zezinha Chantre asserts that with the departure of the women, Cabo Verde suffers a loss of the educator who is responsible for the preservation of the cultural fabric of the Cabo Verdean state. Women teach their children and other community members the significance of Cabo Verde's history and culture (Nos Genti 2013).

Cabo Verdean men settled in northwestern Europe during the 1960s and 1970s and brought their wives and children in the 1980s. During this period, single women also migrated. While men migrated to the Netherlands and Portugal, women tended to choose Italy, although not exclusively (others still migrated to Portugal). These places were major destinations for Cabo Verdean domestic workers, both documented and undocumented. The number of women migrants to Italy tripled that of men. Women in Italy were employed as hourly domestic workers instead of live-in domestic workers (Grassi 2007). Research points out that although the domestic sector wages were higher in northern Italy, this did not lead to Cabo Verdean women's increased internal mobility due to strong family ties in the cities they predominantly resided (Grassi 2006).

The migration of women to Italy also forged a new level of transnationalist networking. Cabo Verdean males in Holland often vacationed and visited the women in Italy. This relationship between Cabo Verdeans in Holland, Portugal, and Italy formed the Cabo Verdean European community. They came together during social events and exchanged economic and cultural goods. The regional integration of the European community, the EU, has made it much easier for the formation of a stronger community of Cabo Verdeans in Europe. It has facilitated migratory circulation in Europe. There are several actors responsible for building the transnational nature of this relationship. Women have been important actors in this process. They bring the different diaspora communities together and also connect them with the homeland. Female entrepreneurs in the informal market carry traditional Cabo Verdean products to be sold to the diaspora, and in turn, bring back to the islands consumer goods, such as clothes, shoes, domestic appliances, foods, as well as other products otherwise inaccessible to the poor.

The accelerated nature of the process of globalization has reduced the distance between emigrant communities and the homeland or among emigrant communities. Communication has become easier and more consistent. These links are much stronger compared to previous periods of migration. Even those who have been fully integrated or assimilated into their respective host country are never disconnected from their country of origin, as in the cases of Cabo Verdeans in the Netherlands and Portugal since the 1960s. Cabo Verdeans who migrate from outside of Cabo Verde transfer traditional practices of the homeland from their previous country of residence to the new host country. For example, instead of traveling home, Cabo Verdeans in Holland and Italy visit their friends and relatives in Portugal because it is less expensive or they no longer have any relatives living in their homeland. This trend does not affect the connection they may have with the homeland.

Diasporic Cabo Verdean women's commitment to community activism and development at home has taken different forms, often impacted by the socio-economic realities of their particular host countries. The feminist and black power movements in the United States in the 1970s coincided with the Cabo Verde independence movement. In the Cabo Verdean case, local manifestations of these global trends resulted in social movements and the launching of women's organizations both government and non-government led by Zezinha Chantre, Crispina Gomes, Paula Fortes, Isaura Gomes, and others. In the diaspora, women were also actively supporting the recognition of Cabo Verde as an independent state. Romana Ramos, for example, led initiatives to create spaces in the wider New England region of the United States where the Cabo Verdean immigrant community could express cultural pride and maintain connections with the homeland. Her efforts resulted in a radio program that discussed politics at home and the Cabo Verde independence celebration which took place in the Fox Point neighborhood in Providence, where a predominantly Cabo Verdean community resided. This event is the longest running Independence Day celebration across all diaspora locations. Past scholarship have documented the strategic ways Cabo Verdeans, both men and women built community, navigated questions of identity and ethnicity within the context of a strict U.S. racial system and black identity politics, as well as how they supported the independence movement in Cabo Verde (Pilgrim 2015; Pires-Hester 1994).

As highlighted in gender, migration, and development theories, remittances sent by women are, in nature, more diverse than men and often include individuals and groups beyond their immediate families. Women are more likely to help causes that are social in nature such as education, health, and anti-domestic violence initiatives. They are also less likely to engage directly and formally with government officials for diverse reasons such as high import fees and lack of confidence in elected officials. As discussed previously, in her study on gender and Cabo Verdean women in Portugal, Marcia Grassi highlights the predominance of women in the informal transnational economy known as "rabidantes" as a means of helping their families back home, as well as personal survival. Highlighted below are a few of the many examples of the ways through which women support their communities, both in the diaspora and in Cabo Verde.

In the United States, there are several organizations led by women whose mission fulfills goals in their immediate communities but also in Cabo Verde. For example, Criolas Contra Cancer (Cabo Verdean Women Against Cancer) raises awareness of cancer and other illnesses, removing the community taboos about not discussing illnesses in the public sphere. This organization raises funds to help Cabo Verdean men and women who face debilitating illnesses both in the United States and in Cabo Verde. Our Children Our

Future Organization serves impoverished children in Cabo Verde and helps them with school fees, materials, and uniforms. The Battered Women of Cape Verde Island, launched by a Cabo Verdean-American woman, located in the island of Fogo provides an emergency shelter for women and children. Sabura Youth Camp founded by Aminah Fernandes Pilgrim and Anita Monteiro serves the youth population in the city of Brockton and surrounding areas by teaching them about Cabo Verdean culture. Additionally, Pilgrim and Lima-Neves founded the first International Conference on Cabo Verdean women in the United States. Most organizations whose mission is to support Cabo Verde point to lack of support from the government and complex bureaucratic processes as challenges in reaching their desired goals in supporting the homeland. In addition to formal hometown organizations, there are several women who strategically choose to operate in informal settings in offering support for communities in Cabo Verde. For example, some women hold fundraising events for specific goals such as sending supplies to their island of origin for a particular school while others may do the same for a hospital in need of materials such as beddings, gloves, and needles. Some women who strategically operate in these networks cite bureaucratic institutional challenges and high costs in shipping and receiving as reasons why they choose to navigate the process in their own ways. Lastly, informal research also points to several diasporic Cabo Verdean women business owners in the United States who have expressed interest in offering entrepreneurial training and business education for women in Cabo Verde and have not received any response from government officials.

Pojmann's (2007) research on women migrants in Italy offers great insight on Cabo Verdean women as domestic workers and their formal networks in Rome. What was once a male-dominated phenomenon, migration in Italy became female-oriented. Large numbers of women, including Cabo Verdeans, Filipinas, and Moroccans began arriving in Italy in the 1960s and 1970s. According to Pojmann, the formation of women's associations in Rome was largely due to the lack of assistance these women received from the Italian government, unprepared to handle the massive migration of female domestic workers. The Cabo Verdean Women's Association in Italy was founded in 1988 because the women wanted to self-organize and create awareness on being part of a predominantly female migrant group. While a Cabo Verdean community organization existed, Pojmann emphasizes three factors that motivated the women to launch the women's association: (a) The women developed a consciousness of their gender-based needs. They wanted more detailed and practical solutions to their problems. (b) In 1986, Law 943 was passed in Italy, recognizing the rights of immigrant communities to organize. This law opened the doors to immigrant groups' full participation in the political process. (c) And lastly, an Italian women's trade union supported the Cape Verdean Women's Association with "office space as well as with a model for organizing on behalf of women's interests."

The case of Cabo Verdean women and their networks demonstrates a grassroots level of political and social consciousness. They demanded their rights not only as members of the immigrant community but also as members of the larger Italian community. These women are mostly from São Nicolau, Santo Antão, São Vicente, and Sal and Boa Vista Islands. Figures from 2003 and 2004 highlight the population at around 1,249 Cabo Verdeans, 923 women and 326 men, and 923 women and 331 men, respectively. However, this does not account for undocumented immigrants, placing the figure at a higher number. More up-to-date research and statistical data are necessary for an in-depth understanding of this Cabo Verdean population in Italy. The Italian government and the International Organization on Migration established the Migrant Women for Development in Africa (WMIDA) program with the objectives of engaging women from West African countries like Cabo Verde, Mali, Nigeria, Sierra Leone, and Togo in development projects, by using their remittances to establish small or medium enterprises in their homeland. In the Cabo Verdean and many other cases, the extent to which this program has been successful is not yet fully measurable given that women, for the most part, choose to remit directly to their families, friends, and immediate communities due to existing bureaucratic challenges in establishing businesses in these countries.

Cabo Verdean women in Portugal face numerous challenges in settling and acculturating in their new country. They cite hard working conditions and discrimination in the job place as major challenges to their livelihood. As mentioned before, the majority of women work in the private domestic and cleaning sectors, which are the lowest paid jobs requiring little to no qualifications. Women with children, in particular, find it very difficult to navigate the working hours, securing care for their children, and actively participating in their children's academic progress. The long working hours do not allow women to attend conferences with teachers and other academic activities so that their children are well integrated into the social and academic systems. Women often have to make the difficult decision and forgo involvement in their children's academic progress in fear of losing their jobs. Another obstacle to the settlement process securing legal immigration status, which can take a very long time depending on the employer's willingness to provide paperwork for the process. The legalization process also affects the unification of families and the integration of children in the Portuguese society. Many mothers who do not have family or social support have to hire someone to help them care for their children as they work long hours in these low paying jobs. Becoming accustomed to a new society is very difficult for women. In the Portuguese and broadly speaking Western contexts, the family consists of the nuclear members (mother, father, and children), while in the (African) Cabo Verdean context, "family" consists of the extended members who often live together and offer social and economic support. To this end, the women interviewed in this particular study revealed that their immigration experiences have been filled with loneliness and alienation due to being away from their families and lack of social support.

Detailed studies about the status of women in diaspora locations such as Holland, the United States, and particularly Italy given that the Cabo Verdean population is predominantly female, would shed light on the needs of this sector of the Cabo Verdean diaspora, as well as their desires, if any, to engage with the homeland. Although diaspora communities face many socio-economic challenges, they still remit at a high rate and have more than half a billion dollars saved in Cabo Verdean bank accounts. They find value in supporting their families and communities in the homeland, which support the country's development, more often than not in informal ways.

THE CABO VERDEAN STATE AND DIASPORA ENGAGEMENT

This section focuses on the Cabo Verdean state and its interaction with the diaspora community. It will focus particularly on the political participation of the diaspora in general as well as policies and projects specifically created to address the socio-economic realities of diasporic Cabo Verdean women with some attention to gender equality initiatives. Previous studies have included extensive and commendable analysis of diasporas' economic and investment policy initiatives and will not be discussed in my analysis (Resende-Santos 2015). I focus on diaspora political participation, an understudied area of the diaspora's involvement in homeland development because this is a significant indicator in whether or not the diaspora community will engage formally with the Cabo Verdean state. If the diaspora lacks confidence in elected government officials and the electoral process in its homeland then it is less likely to vote in elections and invest in state-led development projects. Consequently, the diaspora, particularly women, will continue to resort to informal economic activities and development projects, as it has in the past.

From the time of independence in 1975 until 1990, Cabo Verde was governed as a one-party state, led by the PAIGC, later renamed PAICV. In 1991, with the introduction of the multiparty system, MpD won the parliamentary and presidential elections and remained in power until 2001. MpD secured public support in the 1995 legislative and in 1996 for the presidential elections. However, President Monteiro could not run again because he had already served the maximum of the two terms guaranteed by the country's constitution. The Movement for Democracy party was defeated in both the parliamentary and presidential elections, demonstrating the public's loss of confidence in the party that had been in power for nearly a decade. Consequently, PAICV took political control of the National Assembly and candidate Pedro Pires beat Carlos Veiga in a second round runoff by a very close margin of twelve votes. Both candidates accepted the results. In 2006, Pires won yet again, although the voter turnout was the lowest it had been since the first multiparty elections in 1991. In 2011, PAICV won control of the parliament but failed to secure the victory in the presidential elections. MpD candidate Jorge Fonseca defeated PAICV candidate Manuel Sousa. In the latest legislative elections in March 2016, MpD returned to power, securing 53.9 percent of the national votes. The voter turnout was 70.1 percent. For the past five years, Cabo Verde's government has experienced a peaceful "political cohabitation," as the president and prime minister have been from opposing parties. The fact that there have been very close elections with both candidates accepting the results and the non-conflictual nature of the political cohabitation in the legislative and executive branches are the main factors in Cabo Verde being called a stable and peaceful African democracy leading to attention from the international community of donors and investors. However, one of its biggest external supporters, its diaspora, has remained merely a spectator of the political process. Although the Cabo Verdean state has worked diligently to engage its immigrant community via numerous policies, as well as citizenship and voting rights, statistical data demonstrates that the diaspora is not an active participant in its homeland's political process.

In the 1980s, the Cabo Verdean government improved relations with its immigrant communities. The government includes a secretary of state for immigration affairs, as well as ministries of culture and education, that specifically deal with issues pertaining to the immigrant population. Founded in 1986, the *Instituto de Apoio e Protecção ao Emigrante*, Institute of Emigrant Support and Protection, renamed the *Instituto das Comunidades*, Institute of the Communities in 2001 and now, a full Ministerio Das Comunidades (Ministry of the Communities), symbolizing the growing importance of the role of the diaspora in homeland development. It seeks to reinforce ties with the Cabo Verdean diasporic community and also assists the organizations of migrant communities in need. The Cabo Verdean Constitution established in the early 1990s, after the multiparty system was introduced, allowed Cabo Verdean citizens to retain their citizenship even after obtaining citizenship in their new country of residence and granted them a vote in Cabo Verde's elections. The diaspora was allotted three seats in parliament in 1991 with an increase to six seats in 1995: two for the Americas, two for Europe, and two for Africa. The African Party for the Independence of Cabo Verde (PAICV) presidential candidate Pedro Pires won a majority of the votes over the Movement for Democracy (MPD) candidate Carlos Veiga.

In the 2011 legislative elections, from 34,347 registered voters in the diaspora, only 20,650 actually voted. The 2016 legislative elections highlight a significant decline in the number of registered voters from the 2011 elections. From the 44,847 registered voters, only 15,972 casted a ballot. For example, the community in the United States which is said to be the second largest outside of Cabo Verde with over 200,000 members, only 9,265 were registered to vote in Cabo Verde's parliamentary elections, while Portugal, the second largest group, registered 15,077, 6,104 in France and Italy, 6,104. There has been a decline in the number of active voters in the diaspora population since the 2006 elections and a discrepancy between the number of individuals who are registered to vote and those who actually go out to vote. The Cape Verdean elections board numbers revealed that although the diaspora community may be large in numbers, they are not active in the political process of Cabo Verde.

There has been continued support for the PAICV in the Americas and Africa diaspora locations while Europe and the rest of the world demonstrating allegiance with the MpD. However, there has been a lack of representation of diasporic women in the Cabo Verdean parliament. The data also suggests that the diaspora community, although large in number, does not engage in the political process in Cabo Verde. These numbers can be interpreted in several ways: that there is a lack of voter registration and low level of outreach by the Cabo Verdean government or that the diaspora is politically passive, have busy work schedules and do not have an interest in political participation or perhaps they have strategically exercised their right not to politically engage with the homeland for diverse reasons such as lack of trust in the political process at home or political officials. For women, pressures related to family and child care responsibilities as well as societal norms and family expectations of married women, single mothers, and unwed women are all factors that may prevent or discourage women from running for political office. For migrant women, it can be that added pressures of a harsh work schedule and patriarchal barriers keep them from pursuing political aspirations. It is also important to note that there is also low political participation by the Cabo Verdean diaspora in the host countries.

Additional data on the political attitudes and choices of the diaspora population, inclusive of data on gender, are extremely significant in determining the ways that the government and elected political officials engage them for development projects in Cabo Verde. More often than not, citizens may choose to abstain from voting or will vote against a particular party based on how they feel about personal experiences they may have had during a return trip back home, ineffective investment opportunities or other types of business transactions they have encountered in their homeland. The reality is, and based on the limited studies that do exist, most Cabo Verdean immigrants are politically passive and choose not to engage directly with the governments of their homeland and host country.

In a study conducted on the Cabo Verdean diaspora in the United States, where a majority of the respondents were women, Cabo Verdeans demonstrated an unwillingness to be officially attached to any political party (Lima-Neves 2009). The U.S.-based diaspora has historically been a major supporter of PAICV, since the struggle for independence and continuing on in the most recent elections.

Data has demonstrated that the diaspora is ambivalent about its relationship with the government while being critical of the way that the government engages with them. Strategically engaging the diaspora and learning about the ways they wish to engage with their homeland can be beneficial for an improved reciprocal relationship.

Although respondents were ambivalent about the nature of the relationship between Cabo Verde's government and the immigrant community in the United States, they strongly agreed the government could do more to improve ties to the diaspora.

As it relates to a permanent return to Cabo Verde, a large number of respondents revealed that they owned or were working on building homes in Cabo Verde, but in this study, more than 30 percent revealed that they were not sure whether or not they would permanently return. Further studies should highlight the socio-economic realities and gauge the level of political, social, and economic involvement of this group in their destination and country of origin.

In recognizing the diaspora as a key in the development of the homeland, the Ministry of the Communities created the Comité Nacional de Emigração e Desenvolvimento, CONED, (National Committee for Emigration and Development) in 2013. This committee's objective was to bring together national institutions whose programs and initiatives impact the emigrant population in various capacities. Consequently, in 2014, the Ministry of the Communities also published a comprehensive plan for action entitled, National Strategy for Emigration and Development, recognizing the importance of state intervention in the relationship between Cabo Verde's diaspora and the state's development (ENED 2014). The plan calls for increased institutional cooperation between institutions and organizations that carry out similar work in order to have better communication in serving the needs of the populations.

Through this publication, the state recognizes the condition of the most vulnerable members of society, namely, economically poor women and rural populations, in general, who do not benefit from remittances from family members or friends who live abroad. This comprehensive plan includes progressive and detailed perspectives of the role of gender in migration and the realities of men and women both at home and in the diaspora and how emigration affects them, paying close attention to the political, economic, and social realities of their destination countries. The plan includes the following objectives: facilitate and prepare migrants for departure, support the integration of Cabo Verdean communities in the destination countries, get to know the diaspora and its dynamics, reinforce the ties and promote dialogues and information between Cabo Verde and the diaspora, facilitate and attract the transfer of remittances and cultivate the diasporas' philanthropic activities, mobilize the diasporas' skilled knowledge, and improve the reintegration process for returnees. Although the 2014 ENED Plan is very comprehensive, it seems a bit ambitious and unrealistic when we closely examine the socio-economic conditions of the diaspora population. This and other national development plans have intentionally included strategies to engage the diaspora community in more gender-specific ways, accounting for the increasingly present female face of migration, a phenomenon that can no longer be ignored as pressures are placed on sending and receiving countries.

Drawing from previous studies on diaspora enabling, building, and integration (Brinkerhoff 2009; Melo 2008; Resende-Santos 2015), Cabo Verde has historically had a stable and positive relationship with its diaspora communities. Conditions at home, such as political stability, economic growth, and sound governance, have made it possible for Cabo Verdeans to engage with development at home both in formal and informal ways. Reforms in public administration as well as the function of A Casa do Cidadao (House of the Citizen) have been updated and is now remotely accessible via the internet by the diaspora. There have been improvements in the business and investment climate for Cabo Verdean nationals at home and abroad. However, there are still challenges to development and diaspora engagement such as bureaucratic inefficiencies, transportation, and customs administration. Other issues related to favoritism, social inequality, and policy ineffectiveness concerns with increased crime rates threaten the stability and continued growth of this African state (Resende-Santos 2015).

On the other side of the challenges connected to engaging the diaspora are the socio-economic conditions of the diaspora in the host countries. Cabo Verdeans abroad are plagued by a lack of time, long workdays, and lack of trust in the leadership of associations as many of the reasons they choose to not formally engage with formal organizations that benefit the homeland (Lima-Neves 2009). Nevertheless, there are several hometown associations in the various Cabo Verdean communities abroad but they function at lower and informal levels of engagement without any formal presence in lobbying the host country to invest in development projects at home. In the United

States, for example, there is an umbrella federation tasked with bringing all associations and organizations together for collaborative efforts. However, it functions sporadically and with little to no outcome. There are also networks of professionals and scholars which seem to be dormant. Moreover, there are efforts of businesses, non-governmental organizations, and other investment projects to attract contributions by skilled Cabo Verdean professionals but no consistent policy efforts have been made so that these programs are permanent (Resende-Santos 2015). Below, I highlight the activities of the embassies in Portugal and the United States, because these two countries have the largest communities of Cabo Verdeans in the diaspora.

The Cabo Verdean embassy in Portugal does not have programs specifically geared toward women but it works in partnership with local Cabo Verdean organizations that support women by connecting them to necessary resources in dealing with challenges related to domestic violence, access to education for their children, and personal and social freedom. According to the embassy, there are dozens of Cabo Verdean organizations in Portugal that offer training and workshops for women in diverse fields such as cultural training which promotes the preservation of cultural identity. There is one particular organization, the Associacao da Mulheres Cabo Verdianas na Diaspora em Portugal, AMCDP (Association of Women in the Cabo Verdean diaspora in Portugal), whose focus has been in the area of domestic violence, children and youth education, traditional dancing, and professional training. There are no available reports that reveal their level of success in supporting Cabo Verdean women.

The Cabo Verdean consulate in the United States functions as a link between the Cabo Verdean community and services provided by local agencies. It helps the Cabo Verdean citizens identify and seek services based on their needs. The consulate also highlights its success in creating a federation for Cabo Verdean organizations in the United States, where they can work together under one umbrella to effectively address issues of concern to the community, inclusive of the status of women. The consulate has planned several initiatives to engage the community throughout the years such as the Common Threads Conference founded by Cabo Verdeans among them three women, Gunga Tolentino, Claire Andrade-Watkins, and Dawna Thomas, which operated from 1999 to 2006, an effort to bring individuals and organizations together to discuss issues affecting the community, such as domestic violence, deportation, and crime. It included men and women, young people, as well as first- and second-generation Cabo Verdeans. In 2001, an all-day program in Brockton, Massachusetts, entitled, "Dialogos Multiculturais" (Multicultural Dialogues), addressed gender-based violence specifically. The Cabo Verdean consulate in the United States has also sponsored workshops on gender inequality with the presence of key advocates from both Cabo

Verde and the local community in the likes of human rights champion and Cabo Verdean judge, Vera Duarte, as well as historian Aminah Fernandes Pilgrim, political scientist Joao Resende-Santos, and linguist Ines "Nezi" Brito. Consulate administrators, in their capacity, assert that they do not have services specifically geared toward women but that all of their efforts in community engagement are representative of all segments of the immigrant communities based on gender, professional skills and background, education level, and island of origin.

Across the diaspora, the Congresso de Quadros Cabo Verdianos Na Diaspora, a bi-annual conference was established in 1994 with the purpose of bringing the Cabo Verdean diaspora together, particularly the formally educated and skilled professionals to discuss issues and concerns facing the immigrant communities. This organization and its founders saw themselves as key agents in the initiatives launched by the Cabo Verdean government toward engaging and improving the lives of its diaspora. Over twenty years later, the organization finds itself at a standstill. Critics of the founders, namely, a younger diaspora generation of Cabo Verdean professionals, sees the organization as stagnant and unwilling to change with the time, citing among other concerns, a need for updating the way it engages with the communities, particularly young people via internet presence. On the other hand, the wider Cabo Verdean community sees this organization as "elitist," out of touch with the real needs of the community, marginalized from the conversations that impact their lives, and made up of individuals looking to secure free vacations in Cabo Verde and other diaspora locations.

The above accounts and illustrations have highlighted the level of engagement of the Cabo Verdean state with its diaspora demonstrating that there is still a lot of work to be done in improving the socio-economic challenges they face in the host country. Particularly for women, migration and a new life in the host country does not always mean that they cease to encounter challenges. Informal and observational research show that in addition to domestic and sexual violence against women, sexual violence against children, high crime and suicide rates among youth, access to education are issues that must be immediately and consistently addressed in the communities, beyond single projects, workshops, and symposiums (Rosa 2015). Cabo Verdean embassies and consulates exist in most diaspora locations. For the most part, diaspora organizations are not well organized and when they do, members of the community operate based on fundraising events for specific causes such as collecting school supplies and hospital needs, as well as clothes drives. There are very few formal organizations across diaspora locations that specifically cater to the needs of women and geared toward improving the lives of Cabo Verdean women, both in the diaspora and in the homeland. On the government side, there are various organizations in Cabo Verde tasked with similar initiatives in improving women's lives, particularly in preparing women who show interest in emigrating. However, research points to a lack of inter-agency communication and bureaucratic inefficiencies as some of the challenges they face in operating effectively.

In the presence of a weak state apparatus, low level community participation in electoral politics both at home and in the host country, diaspora distrust in the political process, harsh socio-economic conditions, and continued gender inequities, the Cabo Verdean diaspora, particularly women will continue to use informal ways to find support and engage with the homeland. However, this does not absolve the state of the responsibilities toward providing formal spaces where the community can seriously address cultural and socio-economic issues that affect women's lives such as physical and sexual violence against women and children.

CONCLUSIONS

This study has made a case for the inclusion of gendered perspectives in the study of the Cabo Verdean diaspora and development in the homeland, with a focus on state policies on diasporas and development. I have argued for the following: (a) nuanced and strategic gendered analysis in national policies which have rendered women's participation invisible in the context of development; (b) critical assessment of whether national development policies mirror the realities of the Cabo Verdean population both at home and abroad and within the context of African development, particularly women's realities, and not driven by the agendas of international institutions or the Cabo Verdean state; and (c) that development policies at home must mirror diaspora policies, with particular focus on the role of women in the process given that women make up half of domestic and diaspora populations.

Since its independence only forty-five years ago, Cabo Verde has made tremendous social, political, and economic progress. The state's constitution is one of the most advanced on the African continent, securing equal rights for men and women, at least by law. As it pertains to the incorporation of gendered perspectives in the discourses on development, nongovernmental organizations, national reports, and strategic plans point to a commitment of the inclusion of both men and women. Nevertheless, the rights of the (LGBTQ) community continue to be marginalized from research, policy studies, and within national, regional, and global migration and development discourses.

In the past decade or so, academic scholarship, international institutions, such as the United Nations, the World Bank, and the International Organization on Migration, have pointed to the importance of gendered analysis in the studies of migration and development, forcing developing states like Cabo Verde to address these issues. As a small island nation, Cabo Verde is in the unique predicament of having as many or more of its population living outside of its borders. The Cabo Verdean diaspora population has significantly contributed to its development via remittances and informal economic activities. However, research calls for states to look beyond economic remittances as a means of diaspora involvement. What this means is that the diasporic individual, her skills, educational background, and professional knowledge should be considered in the development of her homeland. In the Cabo Verdean case, women make up half of the national and diaspora populations. The state can no longer afford to ignore the Cabo Verdean migrant woman and must actively and strategically create policies that positively engage her. Informal and observational research shows that formally educated and professional women want to engage directly with the homeland's government in support of long-term initiatives that promote the advancement of women's rights and services that support women such as professional training, creating domestic violence shelters, and educational opportunities for young girls. I am not arguing that women will always choose to invest solely on women's initiatives. However, women are more likely than men to invest in projects that impact the lives of women and children particularly in their municipalities and island of origin. Consequently, for this to happen, the government must work to eliminate patriarchal, cultural, and bureaucratic barriers that prevent women from investing at home.

An important factor in any successful democracy and diaspora involvement in homeland development is the political process. Additional research on the level of diaspora political participation in homeland elections is necessary. As revealed in the existing electoral data, diaspora's voter turnout in the homeland's electoral process has decreased in the last two legislative elections (2011, 2016). The low voter turnout should be disaggregated by sex and other significant indicators which offer detailed insight into the electorate and its voting behavior. If the diaspora doesn't have confidence in elected officials and state agencies, it is less likely that it will engage in the electoral process and national development initiatives. On the other hand, we must uncover what factors impact the diaspora's political passiveness both in the host country and homeland.

In this chapter, I have argued that the Cabo Verdean woman has been rendered invisible by state development policies, leading her toward strategic informal economic and social activities and networks, circumventing highly ineffective bureaucratic state structures. If the Cabo Verdean state is to truly experience development, it must consider the status of women both at home and in the diaspora, recognizing the existing challenges they face related to adjusting to a new culture and society, immigration status, as well as domestic and sexual violence. Moreover, I have argued that development policies at home must mirror policies in the diaspora, inclusive of women's voices and experiences via sustainable programs and initiatives. Although there have been some recent national strategic plans on migration and development inclusive of gendered analysis they are too recent and it is premature to assess their level of impact. However, if the government is still struggling to prioritize strategic domestic gendered policies, it is less likely to be successful in recognizing the importance of gendered initiatives that target diasporic women to invest in Cabo Verde's state-led projects.

NOTE

1. In this study, gender is defined as socially and culturally constructed differences between men and women, boys and girls, which give them unequal value and opportunities. Masculine and feminine traits are abilities and expectations about how men and women should behave. A gendered analysis allows us to identify how gender influences people, families, institutions and society in general. In this way we can see what may be causing inequalities and potential obstacles to equitable development. Development is then defined as progressive and qualitative changes that occur in society which improve the quality of people's lives and conditions. Within this process the following components must be present: (a) raising people's living standards, including their incomes and consumption levels of food, medical, services, and education; and (b) creating conditions conducive to the growth of people's self-esteem through the establishment of social, economic, and political institutions, which promote and protect human rights, dignity, and respect. Because the process of development is progressive and qualitative, various stages of development are often hard to measure. Gender-blind analysis is when potentially differential policies that may impact women and men are ignored. Gendered policies in state development include promotion of good governance and guarantees human rights of women through democratic institutions, adherence to principle of equality between men and women as well as boys and girls, ensuring that they enjoy their human rights and guarantees fairness and equal treatment for all. Additionally, gendered policies are those that promote equitable access to resources for women and men, knowledge, information and services including basic needs, facilitate implementation of corrective measures to address existing inequalities with regard to access to and control over resources as well as other empowerment opportunities. Gendered policies and programs take into account specific needs of women and men and work to shift unequal power relations to enable full enjoyment of human rights for both sexes.

REFERENCES AND ADDITIONAL READINGS

A Semana. "MCA-CV II Assina Memorandum Com ONU Mulheres e ICIEG." March 4, 2014.

A Semana Online. "Congresso de Quadros Cabo-verdianos na Diáspora precisa de se rejuvenescer." December 4, 2014.
African Development Bank (AfDB). *Cape Verde—A Success Story*. Tunis: AfDB, 2012.
African Development Bank (AfDB). *Cape Verde—The Road Ahead*. Tunis: AfDB, 2012.
Akesson, Lisa. "Making Migrants Responsible for Development: Cape Verdean Returnees and Northern Migration Policies." *Africa Spectrum*, Volume 41, Issue 1, 61–83, 2011.
Almeida, Raymond A., ed. *Cape Verdeans in America: Our Story*. Boston, MA: The American Committee for Cape Verde (TCHUBA), 1978.
Amado, Abel Djassi. "Cabo Verde: West Africa's Democratic 'Potemkin Village'." Political Matter.org, 2015.
Andall, Jacqueline. "Cape Verdeans in Italy." In Luís Batalha and Jorgen Carling (eds), *Transnational Archipelago: Perspectives on Cape Verdean Migration and Diaspora*. Amsterdam: Amsterdam University Press, 2008.
Andrade, Elisa. *The Cape Verde Islands: From Slavery to Modern Times*. Eugene, OR: Third World Students Coalition Press, 1974.
Batalha, Luís, and Jorgen Carling, eds. *Transnational Archipelago: Perspectives on Cape Verdean Migration and Diaspora*. Amsterdam: Amsterdam University Press, 2008.
Brinkerhoff, Jennifer M., ed. *Diasporas & Development: Exploring the Potential*. Boulder, CO: Lynne Rienner Publishers, 2008.
Bruce Baker. "Cape Verde: The Most Democratic Nation in Africa?" *Journal of Modern African Studies*, Volume 44, Issue 4, 493–511, 2006.
Cabral, Amílcar. *Return to the Source: Selective Speeches of Amílcar Cabral*. New York: African Information System, 1973.
Cabral, Amílcar. *Unity and Struggle*. London: Heinnemann. Educational Books Ltd., 1980.
Cabral, Iva. "A Representacao das Mulheres, Casadas, e Viuvas, da Ilha de Santiago nos Documentos dos Seculos XVI-XVIII (Um Estudo Prosopografico)." In Carmelita Silva and Celeste Fortes (eds), *As Mulheres Em Cabo Verde: Experiencias e Perspectivas*. Universidade de Cabo Verde, 19, 2011.
Carling, Jorgen. "Policy Challenges Facing Cape Verde in the Areas of Migration, and Diaspora's Contribution to Development." International Peace Research Institute, 2008.
Carreira, Antonio. *The People of the Cape Verde Islands: Exploitation and Emigration*. London: C. Hurst, 1982. Translation by C. Fyfe of the 1977 Portuguese edition.
Conferencia Das Nacoes Unidas Sobre Comercio e Desenvolvimento (CNUCED). "Quem Beneficia Com a Liberalizacao do Comercio em Cabo Verde?" Uma Perspectiva de Genero, 2012.
Costa, Suzano. "Mulheres e Participacao Politica no Cabo Verde Democratico." In Carmelita Silva and Celeste Fortes (eds), *As Mulheres Em Cabo Verde: Experiencias e Perspectivas*. Universidade de Cabo Verde, 77, 2011.

Coutinho, Ângela Sofia Benoliel. "Mulheres na "Sombra": As Cabo-verdianas e a Luta de Libertação Nacional." In Carmelita Silva and Celeste Fortes (eds), *As Mulheres Em Cabo Verde: Experiencias e Perspectivas*. Universidade de Cabo Verde, 39, 2011.

Curran, Sara R., Steven Shafer, Katharine M. Donato, and Filiz Garip. "Mapping Gender and Migration in Sociological Scholarship: Is It Segregation or Integration?" *The International Migration Review*, Spring, 199–223, 2006.

De Haas, H. "Migration and Development: A Theoretical Perspective." *International Migration Review*, Volume 44, Issue 1, 227–264, 2010.

Evora, Iolanda Maria Alves. *Commissao Consultiva Para as Questoes da Imigracao Cabo-Verdiana Em Portugal*. Praia: Ministério de Negócios Estrangeiros, 2011.

Evora, Roselma. "Um Pais de Mulheres Governado por Homens: Democracia e Processo Decisorio em Cabo Verde." In Carmelita Silva and Celeste Fortes (eds), *As Mulheres Em Cabo Verde: Experiencias e Perspectivas*. Universidade de Cabo Verde, 67, 2011.

Faist, T. "Migrants as Transnational Development Agents: An Inquiry into the Newest Round of the Migration-Development Nexus." *Population, Space, and Place*, Volume 14, Issue 1, 21–42, 2008.

Fikes, Kesha. *Santiaguense Cape Verdean Women in Portugal: Labor Rights, Citizenship and Diasporic Transformation*. Doctoral Dissertation, University of California—Los Angeles, 2000.

Freedom House Reports, 2011 and 2015. Accessed at www.freedomhouse.org.

Gamlen, Alan. "The New Migration-and-Development Pessimism." *Progress in Human Geography*, Volume 38, Issue 4, 581–597, 2014.

Gomes, Crispina. *Mulher e Poder: O Caso de Cabo Verde*. Praia: BNL, 2011.

Government of Cabo Verde, Ministry of Finance. *Cape Verde: Constraints to Growth, Transformation, and Poverty Alleviation*. July 2010.

Grassi, Marzia. "Cabo Verde Pelo Mundo: O Género e a Diáspora Cabo-Verdiana." Instituto de Ciência Sociais, Universidade de Lisboa, 2006.

Grassi, Marzia. "Cabo Verde Pelo Mundo: O Genero na Diaspora Cabo-Verdiana." In M. Grassi and I. Evora (eds), *Genero e Migracoes Cabo Verdianas*. Lisboa: Imprensa de Ciencias Sociais, 2007.

Halter, Marilyn. *Between Race and Ethnicity: Cape Verdean American Immigrants, 1860–1965*. Urbana, IL: University of Illinois Press, 1995.

Ifi Amadiume. "African Women: Voicing Feminisms and Democratic Futures." *Macalester International*, Volume 10, Article 9, 2001.

InforPress. *Mulheres de Zonas Ruras Sao Guerreiras que Precisam de Uma Discriminacao Positiva*. March 28, 2016.

Lima-Neves, Terza. "Beyond Cultural Descriptions and into the New Millenium" An Updated Portrait of Cape Verdean Women in the United States." In Carmelita Silva and Celeste Fortes (eds), *As Mulheres Em Cabo Verde: Experiencias e Perspectivas*. Universidade de Cabo Verde, 2011, 241.

Lima-Neves, Terza. "D'Nos Manera: Gender, Collective Identity and Leadership in the Cape Verdean Community in the United States." *Journal of Cape Verdean Studies*, Number 1, April 2015.

Lima-Neves, Terza. *Diasporic Cape Verdeans and Development at Home*. Ph.D. Dissertation. Clark Atlanta University, 2009.

Lima-Neves, Terza. *The Role of Women in the Development of Cape Verde*. M.A. Thesis. Clark Atlanta University, 2006.

Lobban, Richard. *Cape Verde: Crioulo Colony to Independent Nation*. Boulder, CO: Westview Press, 1995.

Melo, Sonia. *Migration and Development in Cape Verde*. International Peace Research Institute, 2008.

Ministry of the Communities. *Estrategia Nacional de Emigracao e Desenvolvimento (ENED): Linhas de Orientacao Para Accao*. 2014.

Monteiro, Euridice. *Mulheres, Democracia e Desafios Pos-Colonias: Uma Analise da Participacao Politica das Mulheres em Cabo Verde*. Praia: Edicoes Uni-CV, 2009.

Ogundipe-Leslie, Molara. *Re-Creating Ourselves: African Women and Critical Transformations*. Trenton, NJ: African World Press, 1994.

Pessar, Patricia R., and Sarah J. Mahler. "Transnational Migration: Bringing Gender In." *The International Migration Review*, Volume 37, Article 3, Fall 2003.

Pilgrim, Aminah. "Free Men Name Themselves: U.S. Cape Verdeans & Black Identity Politics in the Era of Revolution, 1955–1975." *Journal of Cape Verdean Studies*, Number 1, April 2015.

Pires-Hester, Laura J. *A Study of Cape Verdean-American Ethnic Development: The Emergence of Bilateral Diaspora Ethnicity and Its Impact in a Southeastern New England Locality*. Diss. Ph.D., Columbia University, 1994.

Pojmann, Wendy. "Organizing Women Migrants: The Filipino and Cape Verdean Women's Associations in Rome." *Migration Letters*, Volume 4, Issue 1, 29–39, 2014.

Portes, A. "Migration and Development: Reconciling Opposite Views." *Ethnic Studies*, Volume 32, Issue 1, 5–22, 2009.

Rathgeber, E. M. "WID, WAD, GAD—Trends in Research and Practice." *Journal of Developing Areas*, Volume 244, 489–502, 1990 .

Resende-Santos, Joao. "Cape Verde and Its Diaspora: Economic Transnationalism and Homeland Development." *Journal of Cape Verdean Studies*, Number 2, October 2015.

Rosa, Leila. "This Country Does Not Have My Back!": Youth Experiences with a Parent Threatened by Deportation." *Journal of Cape Verdean Studies*, Number 2, October 2015.

Sheffer, Gabriel. "A New Field of Study: Modern Diasporas in International Politics." In Gabriel Sheffer (ed.), *Modern Diasporas in International in International Politics*. New York: St. Martin's Press, 1986.

Singh, Shweta. "Deconstructing 'Gender and Development' for 'Identities of Women'." *International Journal of Social Welfare*, Volume 16, 100–109, 2007.

Sinke, Suzanne M. "Gender and Migration: Historical Perspectives." *The International Migration Review*, Volume 4, Issue 1, 82, Spring 2006.

Tastsoglou, Evangelia, Valerie Preston, and Brian Ray. "Gender and Migration Intersections: In a Canadian Context." *Canadian Issues*: 91–93, Spring 2005.

Wall, Karin, Catia Nunes, and Ana Raquel Matias. "Female Migration: Immigrant Women in Portugal: Migration, Trajectories, Main Programs and Policies." Instituto de Ciencias Socias, Universidade de Lisboa, 2005.

World Bank. *World Development Indicators*. Washington, DC: World Bank Group, 2014.

World Bank Report. *Migration and Development Brief: Migration and Remittances: Recent Developments and Outlook*. April 13, 2015.

Chapter 9

The United States and Cabo Verde

From Humanitarian Assistance to Security Partnership

Abel Djassi Amado

No other two countries from the Americas and Africa have far deeper and more recognized (and recognizable) historical attachments as in the case of the United States and Cabo Verde.[1] On July 14, 1975, President Gerald R. Ford, in a letter extending U.S. recognition to the state of Cabo Verde, pointed out "the historic ties of friendship and cooperation between the people of the United States and Cape Verde" (United States 1977, 992). A key objective of this chapter is to describe the nature and evolution of bilateral relations between the United States and Cabo Verde.

This chapter also seeks to understand the pattern of relationship between the United States and Cabo Verde in the past fifteen years. Specifically, it studies the securitization of the current U.S.–Cabo Verde relations. It argues that in the wake of 9/11 terrorist attacks, the U.S. policy toward Cabo Verde, as in the case U.S.–Africa policy, in general, has become more focused on security and military issues. The securitization of diplomatic relations, as it will be shown further below, is channeled mainly through two political military institutions, namely, the Millennium Challenge Account (MCA) and United States Africa Command (Africom). These two agencies ultimately serve the objective of securitizing relations with Cabo Verde and with other African states, providing not only the discursive framework but also technical and financial assistance toward that goal.

This chapter consists of three main sections. Following this brief introduction, the following section provides a history of U.S.–Cabo Verde relations from the early 1800s to the period of independence. This section analyzes the main points of intersection between the two states. Then, in the second section, I discuss diplomatic relations between these two states, following the ascension of Cabo Verde to statehood in 1975. This section also critically analyses the independence politics among Cabo Verdean Americans in the first half of the 1970s and how different social groups from the Cabo Verdean community articulated with and/or sought to influence U.S. policy toward Cabo Verde. I also talk about key instruments of the U.S.–Cabo Verde policy. I argue that in the first fifteen years of independence of Cabo Verde, U.S. policy toward the islands was practically dominated by Official Development Assistance (ODA). In the third section, the main corpus of this chapter, I argue that current U.S.–Cabo Verde relations are based on the notions of securitization and militarization. Security concerns now dominate the political relations between the two states. In the conclusion, I critically highlight the major points raised throughout the chapter.

U.S.–CABO VERDE RELATIONS: FROM THE 1800s TO 1975

Long[2] before their political independence, the United States and Cabo Verde Islands shared an intimate history. Early contacts between the United States and Cabo Verde date back to the beginning of the Atlantic World in the seventeenth century. The two territories were intimately linked within the global patterns of exchange of goods, people, and ideas throughout the nineteenth century. Their deep historical connections were multi-level, including diplomatic, commercial, social, and cultural relations. Trade and diplomacy have been vibrant features of their bilateral relationship, but the centuries-long pattern of migration and transnational exchange have been its most salient and compelling feature. By the early twentieth century, the United States became a major center of the settlement of the people of Cabo Verde, which, in turn, has further facilitated contacts and relations between the two countries.

Cabo Verde and the United States are the two examples of modern societies of the Atlantic World. The two countries were for most of the first centuries of their existence critical parts of the geography of the Atlantic slave trade: Cabo Verde as the re-exporting territory and the United States as the endpoint of the Middle Passage. The history of U.S.–Cabo Verde relations dates back to the second half of the eighteenth century when American whaling ships began to call at ports in the islands for victuals, watering, and ship maintenance (Duncan 1972). That the two countries were destined to have their destinies intertwined can be found in the fact that the war of American Independence spilled over in Cabo Verde, with the so-called the "Battle of Porto Praya," a naval battle between French and British naval units in the territorial waters of Cabo Verde (Rodger 2005, 349). These relations were reinforced in the first half of the 1800s, with the development of the so-called legitimate trade with

West Africa. Cabo Verde became the U.S. informal commercial forward operating base to West Africa (Brooks 1970). In order to protect and safeguard Americans and their business interests in the region, in 1818, the U.S. government opened a consulate in Cabo Verde, the first in the Sub-Saharan African region. Following the 1842 Webster–Ashburton Treaty, the United States strengthened its use of Cabo Verde as a strategic base against the Atlantic slave trade. For over two decades, the city of Praia (or Porto Praya, as it was known then), in Santiago Island, became the base for the African Squadron, a unit of the U.S. navy tasked, along with the British Navy, with the control of the Atlantic Ocean against slave trade (Canney 2006, 58).

Throughout the seventeenth century, Cabo Verde Islands were "the crossroads of the Atlantic" (Duncan 1972). This characterization can be well applied to later centuries, particularly around the mid-nineteenth century, when the island of São Vicente became one of the key refueling ports for transatlantic shipping. During its heyday, São Vicente attracted ships from across the globe. The coming and going of ships greatly contributed to the development of a cosmopolitan culture among its people.

In general, the 1800s were one of the hardest and most difficult centuries in the history of the islands. Political crises in Portugal, particularly in the first half of the century, meant that the islands were left almost abandoned. Domestically, economic crises and climacteric calamities took a heavy toll on the people. Social unrest and violent protests were a constant for most of the nineteenth century (Pereira 2014). These facts acted more like a push factor that compelled people to look for better living conditions abroad. By the mid- to the late 1800s, southern New England became one of the major migration destinations for the people of Cabo Verde (Halter 1993). The decades of the 1890s to 1910s were the ones with the greatest numbers of annual migration from Cabo Verde to the United States (Carreira 1982; see table 9.1). Around the early 1900s, there were several Cabo Verdean communities across southern New England, mostly around Nantucket Island, New Bedford, and Cape Cod areas, in Massachusetts and in Providence and East Providence areas. The migratory flux would suffer backlash as a consequence of the passing of the laws that restricted the admission of foreigners in the United States. The immigration laws of 1921 and 1924 took a toll among Cabo Verdeans seeking to move to the United States. The Immigration Act of 1924 restricted the admittance of foreign nationals to 2 percent of the number of people from that country, as counted in the 1890 census. Given the fact that Cabo Verde counted as Portugal—for it was part of the Portuguese colonial empire—Cabo Verdeans had to compete with Azoreans and other continental Portuguese for entrance into the United States.

The restrictions on immigration from Cabo Verde to the United States did not mean the end of bilateral connections between the two sides of the

Table 9.1 Cabo Verdean Immigrants to the United States, 1860–1930

	Portuguese Immigrants	*Cabo Verdean Immigrants*	*Percent Cabo Verdean*
1860–1870	2,658	124	4.6%
1871–1880	14,082	144	1.0%
1881–1890	16,978	571	3.3%
1891–1900	27,149	2,340	8.5%
1901–1910	69,149	6,899	9.9%
1911–1920	89,732	10,825	12.0%
1921–1930	29,994	1,999	6.6%

Source: Created with data from Halters, 1993, 45.

Atlantic Ocean. In order to circumvent isolation in the United States as well as to help family members, friends, and neighbors from the homeland, Cabo Verdeans in the United States developed the packet trade. As noted by Ray Almeida, during the 1930s and 1940s, the height of the Packet Trade, ten or more ships made the trans-Atlantic voyage connecting southern New England and Cabo Verde (Almeida 1978). While statistics on the migration of the people of Cabo Verde are not conclusive, some scholars estimate that from 1820 to 1975 some 35,000 to 45,000 immigrated to the United States (Halter 1993). Through most of the first half of the twentieth century, isolation and invisibility were the two dominant sociological characteristics of the Cabo Verdean-Americans (Halter 1993).

World War II and the transformation of the Atlantic Ocean into one of the important theaters of operations increased belligerents' interests in Cabo Verde. Plans were made by Allied and Axis powers to invade the islands for geostrategic concerns. Hitler and his generals had plans to invade the islands in the northern Atlantic (including Cabo Verde), and the British responded by developing Operation Puma in 1941 (Schreiber et al. 1995, 229; Stone 1994, 173–174). The U.S. government, under President Roosevelt, was also aware of the geostrategic importance of the Atlantic islands. President Roosevelt's War Cabinet also had plans to occupy Cabo Verde and the Azorean islands (Clifford and Ferrell 2010, 15–16). Modern global wars, whether hot or cold, often meant an increase in the geostrategic importance of the islands. The ongoing U.S.-led "global war on terror," as it will be seen below, is just one of the latest "wars" that has highlighted the geostrategic importance of the islands.

ANTI-COLONIALISM AND ANTI-RACISM ON BOTH SIDES OF THE ATLANTIC

The 1960s was the decade of African independence. Contrary to the cases of France and the UK—and to some extent Belgium—who swiftly decolonized in order to neo-colonize, Portugal, under the dictatorship of Antonio Salazar's *Estado Novo*, chose to maintain an archaic colonial system than to give in to the demands of anti-colonial nationalists. African nationalists in then Portuguese Africa had no other alternative than to resort to the armed liberation struggle. While several political organizations were created, and many did attempt to take part in the conflict, by the mid-1960s, only a handful of political movements were actually carrying out the struggle, with different levels of success. The demands for the political independence of Cabo Verde found their ultimate expression with the PAIGC, the African Party for the Independence of Guinea-Bissau and Cabo Verde. The PAIGC, unlike other movements in the former Portuguese colonies, aimed not only at the liberation of both Guinea-Bissau and Cabo Verde but also the institutionalization of a future, post-colonial federation between the two states.

To better understand African decolonization, it is important to grasp the contours of post–World War II global politics. Soon after the war, it became clear that the alliance between the United States and the former Soviet Union was rather fragile. As the epicenter of global power shifted from European capitals to Moscow and Washington, DC, political and ideological competition between the two superpowers, first in Europe and later in other corners of the globe, became the key feature of international politics. This period, which covers most of the second half of the twentieth century, corresponds to the Cold War era. In essence, Cold War politics had a tremendous influence on U.S. African policy. In the late 1940s and 1950s, the United States still clung to the idea that Africa was a reserved sphere of Europeans (Wright 1997, 17). By the early 1960s, under the Kennedy administration, the U.S. government sought to pursue a more pro-African independence policy. Kennedy's political ambitions were built on criticizing Eisenhower's foreign policy. As a presidential candidate, Kennedy shook the establishment grounds by noting that his administration would

> no longer abstain in the United Nations from voting on colonial issues [. . .] no longer trade our vote on other such issues for other supposed gains [. . .] no longer seek to prevent subjugated peoples from being heard. (cited in Rodrigues 2004, 1)

Against this backdrop, in 1961, following the breakout of the Angolan rebellion and the issue was brought to the United Nations Security Council, Kennedy instructed the U.S. ambassador to cast a vote against the imperial power, Portugal.

Geopolitical considerations of the Cold War led the United States to reconsider its position, vis-à-vis, the independence of the Portuguese African colonies. For the military strategists in Washington, the Azorean islands, critical for the defense of western Europe in case of a Soviet attack, deserved far more attention than African issues (Wright 1997, chapter 3). When Lyndon Johnson assumed the presidency, the issue of the liberation war in Southern Africa and Guinea-Bissau was placed on the "back burner." In 1965, the U.S. ambassador to Portugal George Anderson's suggestion that "we let the pot simmer on the back burner until some significant event makes a new approach advisable" was seriously taken by President Johnson (Anderson cited in Wright 1997, 51). Moreover, the Johnson administration became far preoccupied with the debacle of Vietnam to actually be interested in taking a pro-African policy.

The arrival of Richard Nixon in the White House signified a more pro-Portugal policy in Southern Africa. The 1969 National Security Study Memorandum 39 (NSSM 39), commissioned by Henry Kissinger, President Nixon's national security adviser, reinforced such a policy, by putting the United States even closer to the white minority regimes in Portuguese Africa, South Africa, and Southern Rhodesia (Khawas and Cohen 1976). The NSSM 39 basically rested on the two principles: first, that South Africa was and should be Southern African regional hegemon, and, second, white minority rule (Southern Rhodesia, South Africa, and Portuguese colonies) was "here to stay" (Lake 1976, chapter 4; Lockwood 1974).

By the end of the 1960s, the liberation wars in Africa had become a total and internationalized war (Gleijeses 1997). Policymakers in Portugal and in colonies alike came to realize that the war must include political and psychological operations if Portugal wanted to retain her colonies (Spínola 1970). Operations to conquer the hearts and minds of the colonized people were put forth across the empire and other spaces deemed important. Portugal was aware of the relative socio-economic and political significance of Cabo Verdean-Americans. For this reason, through calculated efforts of public diplomacy, the government of Portugal courted the elites of Cabo Verdean-Americans as part of a grand strategy to save the colonial empire. The idea was to use these elites as *interlocteurs valables*, vis-à-vis, both the local and federal governments and, and perhaps, more importantly, to the Cabo Verdean community as a whole. In 1969, the government of Portugal financed a tour to its African colonies (Angola and Mozambique) by a group of renowned Cabo Verdean-Americans. The group, formed by Belmira Nunes Miranda, Attorney Roy Teixeira Sr., and Judge George Leighton, was to use their social positions to facilitate and support Portugal's political position in the United States (*The Cape Verdean* September 1969; Amado 2020, 42). This task was best performed by Belmira Nunes Miranda, who went to write several articles on *The Cape Verdean*, a local Cabo Verdean–owned newspaper, relating the trip to then Portuguese Africa.

While some sections of the Cabo Verdean-American community were deeply influenced by Portugal's public diplomacy, other groups and individuals became fully integrated into the juggernaut of the Civil Rights struggles of the 1960s and 1970s. The Civil Rights Movement of the late 1950s and 1960s ultimately stirred and awoke the Cabo Verdean-American community. As a social movement that sought to elevate the socio-economic and political conditions of African Americans, the Civil Rights Movement had an impact across American society. Cabo Verdean-Americans were in no way immune to the influence of this socio-political transformation. Few young Cabo Verdean-Americans, mostly from working-class families, embraced the ideologies or even joined black nationalist movements. Cabo Verdean-Americans in contact with African American movements eventually became aware of the similar struggle that Africans were conducting on the continent (Matteos 1973). This is in part the consequence of a long history and practice of a transnational black public sphere that linked Africans and diasporic Africans of the Atlantic World since the early 1900s (von Eschen 1997). Few Cabo Verdean-Americans even rose to leadership positions within black radical movements. The case of Frank "Parky" Grace, who became the leader of the Black Panthers Party's New Bedford chapter, is an illustrative example (Lazerow 2006).

On April 25, 1974, the Portuguese dictatorial state was toppled down by a military coup d'état. The military debacle in Guinea-Bissau contributed largely to the military intervention in politics in Lisbon. By July 1974, the new regime in Portugal had conceded for unconditional decolonization of Africa. Through a series of political agreements between the Portuguese government and the mainstream political organizations in Africa, the calendar and the process of decolonization were laid out. Portugal had two agreements with the PAIGC. The Alger Agreements of August 1974 recognized the independence of Guinea-Bissau. The Lisbon Agreement of December 1974 paved the way for political independence in Cabo Verde.

The idea that Cabo Verde would be independent under the PAIGC was not welcomed among some Cabo Verdean Americans, as discussed further below. A similar attitude was also found among the conservatives in Washington. Both disliked the idea of a federation between Cabo Verde and Guinea-Bissau, under the PAIGC. They seemed to agree that a political unity between Cabo Verde and Guinea-Bissau translated into submission of the former to the Soviet interests. For instance, Henry Kissinger, then secretary of state, was quoted to have said that the "United States was not opposed to the independence of Guinea Bissau, but would not stand for the Portuguese giving up the Cape Verde Islands to the Guineans" (Randal 1974). The idea of this asymmetric triple alliance (Guinea-Bissau, Cabo Verde, and the Soviet Union) was something that was fed by the Portuguese government, since the

1960s, in order to gain legitimacy to its military campaign while obtaining military and non-military assistance from Washington (Department of State 2011, 202).

Some sections of the Cabo Verdean-Americans, particularly the educated and fully integrated into mainstream American society or within Portuguese-American communities, the PAIGC and its political platform of Pan-Africanism and socialism were to be blocked at all costs. After Portugal opened the door to independence of Cabo Verde, steps were taken to halt such a political initiative. A political congress called the World Juridical Congress of Cape Verdean Communities was convened in Sheraton Hotel, Boston, on February 22, 1975 (Amado 2020; Lobban 1995; *The Cape Verdean* 1975). For the leadership of the Juridical Congress, the PAIGC was at the same time a totalitarian and foreign political organization: "the PAIGC is juridically and for all legal effects, a *totalitarian and extremist* political party of [a] foreign country [that is, Guinea-Bissau]" (*The Cape Verdean* April 1975, 6). The Juridical Congress went as far as to declare the independence of Cabo Verde and the formation of a government in exile formed among the leaders of the Congress. Needless to say, these two acts failed to concretize.

The Cabo Verdean-American youth and members of the lower classes, the social group who was most touched by the politics of Civil Rights, did not share the same ideas as those of the elites. The surge in remittances sent by emigrants during the early post-independence years suggests strong support for the new fledgling country. In fact, as early as 1973 a political organization, the PAIGC-USA Support Committee, chaired by Salahudin Omowale Matteos, was created in Massachusetts. That political organization, previously suggested by Amílcar Cabral in his last visit to the United States in 1972, had as its main objective "to raise the general level of awareness among the Cape Verdeans in this country" (Matteos 1973). The organizational strength of the PAIGC-USA Support Committee resulted in a grant of almost $20,000.00 by the Episcopal Church's General Convention Special Program. The grant was to be used mostly for information campaigns of the Cabo Verdean-Americans about the liberation struggle that was going on the continent (*Boston Globe* September 22, 1973, 27). By 1975, this political organization was well built and entrenched in Cabo Verdean-American society. Closely related to the PAIGC-USA Support Committee, and yet totally autonomous and independent, was Tchuba, a non-profit organization created in 1975, under the leadership of Ray Almeida. Tchuba was arguably the first Cabo Verdean-American ethnic lobby organization in the United States. Its stated goal was "to increase US aid and expertise to the islands and to drive away any lingering hint of colonialism" (Allis 1976; Almeida 1976). In practical terms, Tchuba functioned as a bridge among several actors that include the governments of Cabo Verde and the United States, governmental agencies, chiefly the USAID, the Cabo Verdean-Americans, and the people of Cabo Verde.

The PAIGC-USA Support Committee and the Juridical Congress were politically irreconcilable. Both parties sought to influence U.S. policy toward Cabo Verde. Thus, the two organizations met with Senator Edward Brooke of Massachusetts on April 18, 1975, where both sought to feed the senator with their own political perspectives on the situation in Cabo Verde and, as a consequence, to influence the U.S. policy (*The Cape Verdean* May 1975). The Juridical Congress sought to lobby in Washington against the government of PAIGC in Cabo Verde. Aguinaldo Veiga, a former judge in Angola, who was elected as the president of the organization trekked to Washington, meeting with staff of several congress people from about April 25 to May 2, 1975 (Amado 2020; *The Cape Verdean* June 1975).

It is quite improbable that the positions of these Cabo Verdean-American organizations had any influence over U.S. policy toward Cabo Verde. Since the 1960s, the PAIGC had advocated for a position of neutrality within the context of the Cold War. Yet, the war efforts of the PAIGC were supported by the communist bloc, particularly Cuba and Soviet Union (Gleijeses 1997). Association with the Soviet Union was a political liability to the party. Naturally, with the independence of Guinea-Bissau, in September 1973, one of the first political positions was to reassure the U.S. government about its non-communist condition. Against this backdrop, Aristides Pereira, then secretary general of the PAIGC, sent an envoy to the U.S. embassy in Guinea, Conakry, to inform that while the party received aid from the communist bloc, it did not constitute a communist bloc (Department of State 1973). Two years later, in April 1975, the PAIGC sent a delegation to the United States, led by Pedro Pires, tasked with a similar task (Vicente Lopes 2002, 473–474). It can be argued that the leaders of the PAIGC in Cabo Verde may well have feared a Bay of Pigs-type of situation, in which a group of nationals residing in the United States, backed by the U.S. government, would attempt against the regime.

U.S.–CABO VERDE RELATIONS, 1975–2001: FOCUS ON HUMANITARIAN ASSISTANCE

The independence of Cabo Verde was challenged by the Ford Administration. As noted above, Kissinger was well-known for his antipathy toward independence under the banner of the PAIGC. In general, U.S. foreign policy during these years was hostile toward nationalist movements and governments, and any regime or leader the United States deemed questionable, in all parts of the world. In the United States, however, political scandals and the Vietnam debacle resulted in a power shift from the White House to the Congress. Arguably the White House was not in a condition to wage a political battle against Congress over the question of independence in former Portuguese colonies. The U.S. recognition of Cabo Verde statehood came on the day of independence. The letter from President Ford to President Pereira, Cabo Verde's first president, not only extended recognition but also noted that the former would thenceforth develop into a close developmental partner of Cabo Verde. The recognition letter added that "the steps already taken by the United States to provide humanitarian aid and technical assistance to Cabo Verde will help alleviate the current hardship and provide a base for economic development and future prosperity" (United States 1975, 992).

Even though there was some initial opposition within the Ford Administration, two reasons ultimately led to the U.S. government to grant recognition of Cabo Verde as a sovereign state. First, Western powers, including Portugal the departing colonial power, were either unwilling to create obstacles or ready to accept the new country. Second, the fact that the PAIGC, since the days of Cabral, insisted on maintaining an open channel of communication with the government of the United States. It should also be noted that in the aftermath of the debacle of Watergate, the epicenter of the U.S. political movement moved away from the White House to Capitol Hill. Congress was more sympathetic to the causes of national liberation in Sub-Saharan Africa.

The process of assistance to Cabo Verde was initiated even before the formal proclamation of independence. In 1975, months before the formal independence of Cabo Verde, the government of the United States responded to the appeal made by the PAIGC for foreign donors to assist the new state in the making, as it was facing terrible climacteric conditions. In March 1975, the U.S. Congress authorized foreign assistance to be distributed to Portugal and her colonies in Africa gaining independence, of which "not less than $5,000,000 shall be allocated for the Cabo Verde Islands and not less than $5,000,000 shall be allocated for Mozambique, Guinea-Bissau, and Angola" (U.S. Congress 1975, 18). With this Public Law in the background, the USAID channeled three million US dollars into Cabo Verde, "to support Cape Verde Rural Works Projects" (USAID n.d., 1). It should be noted that the proposed U.S. assistance to Cabo Verde met strong resistance among the most radical elements of the PAIGC in Cabo Verde. For them, the assistance coming from the United States was a part of a neo-colonial scheme of defrauding Cabo Verde of its actual independence (Lopes 2002, 472).

In the first few years following independence, policymakers in Washington had far more expectations about the merging of Cabo Verde and Guinea-Bissau than the PAIGC leaders themselves. The assumption of the inevitability of a political merger between the two states was dominant in Washington.

This explains why the U.S. embassy and the (USAID) office, established in Bissau, were tasked with serving the two countries. To the U.S. officials, the two countries were treated as one. However, by the end of the 1970s, with the realization that merging between the two is more at the level of political discourse, the U.S. government began to organize its diplomacy toward Cabo Verde as independent from that of Guinea-Bissau. Thus, in 1977, the United States opened an embassy in Praia, and two years later, a USAID office was also created in the islands to deal with the development assistance (USAID 1994, 6); U.S. assistance to Cabo Verde, from 1975 to 2020, totaled $424,485,376.00. Although its partnership with Cabo Verde lasted for thirteen years (2005–2018), the Millennium Challenge Corporation (MCC) contributed close to 50 percent of all assistance dollars.

In the first fifteen years, U.S.–Cabo Verde policy was fundamentally that of developmental and humanitarian assistance. The USAID was the key bilateral agency tasked with the implementation of that policy. From 1975 to 2018, the USAID contributed a total of $59,666,178.00, most of which were channeled in the first twenty years of independence (see figure 9.1). USAID activities in Cabo Verde can be classified in two major stages, defined in terms of emphasis on a given sector (USAID 1994, 6). During the first phase, from 1977 to the end of the 1980s, the key focus of the USAID assistance was toward natural resource management and sustainable agriculture. In the late 1980s and early 1990s, with the end of the Cold War and the subsequent triumph of neoliberalism, the focus of the agency changed to reflect and to adapt to the new international context. USAID became a major tool in the promotion of the spread of the market-based economy and the so-called Washington Consensus. Against the backdrop, USAID bilateral assistance to Cabo Verde shifted to emphasize export-led growth and private sector development. Starting in 1989, USAID, through its Export Development Services Project, played an important role in the creation of the Center for Investment and Export Promotion in Cabo Verde, which became fully functional in 1993.

On November 19, 1993, USAID/Cabo Verde announced to the government of Cabo Verde that it would cease its operation by the end of the financial year of 1996. Such a move was part of a larger plan of reforming and restructuring the agency by closing twenty-one missions around the globe. The missions to be terminated were classified into three major groups: graduates, small country programs, and countries that were inconsistent or unreliable development partners (Martin et al. 1999, 11). Cabo Verde was included as part of the second group. Two major and inter-related reasons dictated the choice to terminate the presence of USAID in Cabo Verde. The first was the political and economic performance of the country. Judged against other countries in the region, Cabo Verde placed among top performers in terms of economic liberalization and adoption of electoral democracy. Second, USAID believed

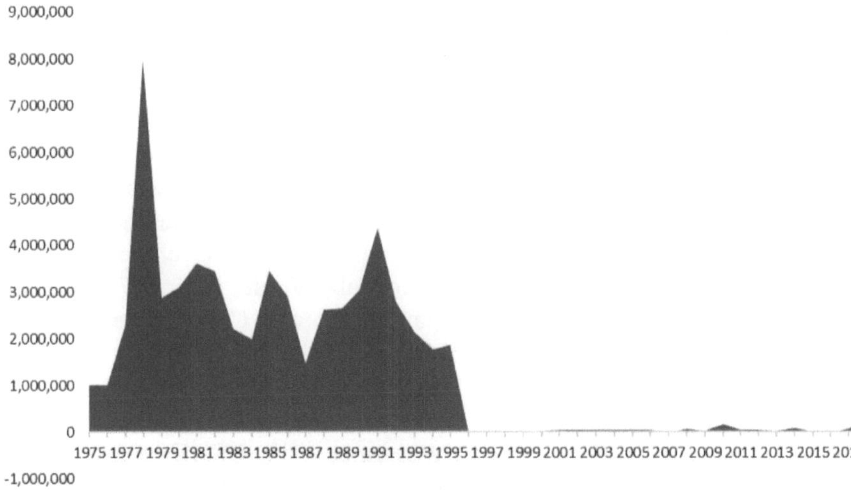

Figure 9.1 Economic Assistance to Cabo Verde, Administered by US AID, in USD, 1975–2018. *Source*: Created with data from U.S. Agency for International Development, US Overseas Loans & Grants (Greenbook), 2016.

that its assistance was not the most appropriate for Cabo Verde, given the latter's economic development and per capita income (USAID 1994).

One cannot talk about U.S.–Cabo Verde relations without referring to the diasporic political economy. Cabo Verde, as a country of emigrants, derives a significant portion of its wealth from the remittances sent by thousands of Cabo Verdeans residing across the Atlantic World. Cabo Verdean-Americans have since the early days of settlement supplied both financial and social remittances to Cabo Verde (Tavares and Monteiro 1997). With independence, Cabo Verdean-Americans took to themselves the task of assisting, materially and financially, the newly created state. It is not the scope of this chapter to describe all different aspects of this assistance. Yet, a few words about the foundation of Tchuba—the American Committee for Cape Verde, a non-profit organization—suffices to shed light about the political-economic importance of Cabo Verdean-Americans in the early days of the country.

Tchuba, created in January 1975, led by active and energetic Cabo Verdean-Americans, operated in different domains of diasporic socio-political life. First, Tchuba basically functioned as an ethnic lobby organization, that is, “a formal organization devoted to promoting group cohesiveness and addressing group concerns” (Ambrosio 2002, 1). In that capacity, the organization lobbied state and federal officials in order to have the U.S. government channeling humanitarian assistance to Cabo Verde. Tchuba was also critical in providing direct assistance to the people in Cabo Verde. In this aspect, Tchuba worked very closely with the Cabo Verdean Institute of Solidarity, a governmental agency created months before independence (November 1974) tasked with delivering assistance to the Cabo Verdean poor with the ultimate goal of social integration (*A Semana* 2005). Tchuba also engaged in providing assistance to other less fortunate Cabo Verdean communities in other countries. Thus, in the second semester of 1975 and throughout the year of 1976, Tchuba, along with other Cabo Verdean community-based organizations, spearheaded the movement to assist Cabo Verdeans residing in Portugal who were going through difficult times (*The Cape Verdean* August 1975; *The Cape Verdean* February 1976, 1–3; *The Cape Verdean* March 1976, 3–4).

In the 1980s, the U.S.–Cabo Verde relations underwent two major developments. First, the use of public diplomacy by the governments of Cabo Verde and the United States in order to reach the other country's public. Second, the two governments made instrumental use of the other party as a trampoline and bridge to reach other states and regions where relations were either problematic or non-existent.

Public diplomacy, as an international political tool at the hands of states, is distinguished from traditional diplomacy (Melissen 2005). The former is basically about the development and maintenance of relationships through the exchange of states' representatives (ambassadors or other categories of diplomatic representation). Public diplomacy, on the other hand, constitutes all the actions taken by the state directed at foreign societies, specifically non-official groups, organizations, and individuals. Public diplomacy is intimately linked to soft power (Nye 2008). Soft power can be defined as the capacity to influence other actors through the attractiveness of one's culture and values (Nye 1990).

Since the early days of independence, the government of Cabo Verde understood that Cabo Verdeans abroad was an important partner for the socio-economic development of the country. As such, the government of Cabo Verde assumed as a political necessity to mobilize and guide the diaspora. Control of Cabo Verdeans residing abroad can be understood as an attempt to minimize or even to uproot all the attempts of dissent against the one-party regime. It is against this backdrop that the government of Cabo Verde called for the First Conference of International of Cabo Verdean Communities. This conference, which took place in 1978, in the city of Mindelo, Island of São Vicente, brought in representatives of community organizations from fifteen states. The government of Cabo Verde invited the PAIGC-USA Support Committee, Tchuba, and American Committee for Cape Verde, Inc., to represent the Cabo Verdean-American communities.

In 1981, following the end of the political dream of unity with Guinea-Bissau, the government of Cabo Verde invited a group of Cabo Verdean-Americans in what was called the Invitational Conference and Tour. For the government of Cabo Verde, these individuals could play the role of "key communicators." They were to serve as intermediaries between the government of Cabo Verde and the public and political audiences in the United States. In other words, the ultimate and long-term objective of the organization of this tour was to provide these key communicators with enough materials that can be further disseminated among Cabo Verdean-Americans, the American public in general, and the local, state, and federal governmental agents. To accomplish such an objective, the group had an opportunity to meet public officials and cultural agents, visit several developmental projects that were carried out by the government, as well as to discover their ancestral villages and islands (Pires-Hester 1999, 494). According to Laura Pires-Hester, the Invitational Tour and Conference met three inter-related short-term political goals. First, the group had an opportunity to learn about the new, post-colonial, and independent Cabo Verde. In a way, this was to reform the image that the immigrant population had of their homeland. In light of the scarcity of information between homeland and the diaspora, the latter's imagination of the former is informed by the older generations' perception. The second major goal was to let the group observe, on their own, the application of the foreign assistance resources in the process of development of Cabo Verde. Lastly, the group was to be used as the government's mouthpiece to be used to spread information about the country's struggle for national reconstruction and development.

Following the conference and tour, in 1981 some of the members of the group, once back in the United States, created the National Coordinating Council for the Development of Cape Verde (NCCDCV). The NCCDCV was to function as an ethnic lobby organization, congregating the forces and strengths of the community in order to properly influence the U.S. economic assistance toward Cabo Verde. Manuel Monteiro, one of the founding members of the NCCDCV, noted that the organization's main task was to "plan specific strategies to involve Cape Verdean-Americans as a group in a process which can generate economic assistance to the Republic and people of Cape Verde" (cited in Pires-Hester 1999, 494). While in its first years the organization had some degree of success, it became non-existent by the end of the 1980s.

On the part of the U.S. government, public diplomacy was carried out with the deployment of the Peace Corps. Peace Corps, created in 1961 by President Kennedy, is an independent program of the U.S. government. The program consists of sending Americans abroad to work with local communities in different areas of technical and socio-economic assistance. The history of the Peace Corps in Africa is as old as the organization itself. The presence of the organization in Cabo Verde dates from 1988 (Peace Corps 2009). In 2011, Peace Corps ceased its operations in the islands. For the officials of this organization, Cabo Verde has reached higher levels of socio-economic development that makes it unqualified for the type of assistance provided by the organization.

The other major diplomatic development in the 1980s was the mutual use of the other party as an intermediary to the reinforcement of diplomatic channels with other regions and/or countries. In the 1980s, the United States counted on Cabo Verde as a facilitator with the Angolan government. Since the independence of the former Portuguese colonies in 1975, Southern Africa had become a major locus of superpower competition. During the Cold War, Africa was a "zone of confluence," where the United States and the Soviet Union fought for control and influence. Places like Angola, Horn of Africa, and Mozambique were the fighting ground of "proxy wars," that is, local wars, fought by local political and military organizations, supported, directly and indirectly, by the two great superpowers.

Given the good relations with the government of Angola and commercial links with the government of South Africa, Cabo Verde became a strategic partner of the United States for the resolution of the conflict in Southern Africa. In fact, since the late 1970s that Cabo Verde sought to bring South Africa and Angola to the negotiation table (Saunders 2011). The geostrategic and political importance of Cabo Verde in the resolution partially paved the way for the meeting of President Aristides Pereira and President Ronald Reagan in 1983.

Cabo Verde, for its part, sought to broaden its developmental partners, away from Western and communist states. Given the status of the United States as the leader of the capitalist world, the government of Cabo Verde hoped to use the United States as a trampoline to the East Asian states. Thus, in April 1989, in a meeting between the presidents of Cabo Verde and the United States, Aristides Pereira asked George Bush whether the latter could act as a facilitator to Cabo Verde's aspirations to reach out to East Asia. President Bush stated that he

> would be glad to help encourage the relationship between Cape Verde, Japan, and South Korea. [The U.S. President] would certainly tell Japan and Korea about Cape Verde's positive role in the Angola/Namibia accords and the excellent bilateral relations that Cape Verde has with the United States. (White House 1989)

The end of the Cold War led to a considerable reduction of U.S. presence in Sub-Saharan Africa. Ian Taylor notes that, for instance, by end of the 1990s, the U.S. presence in the continent had been curtailed: diplomatic personnel in Africa was reduced by 15 percent while intelligence personnel was cut by over 30 percent, military and security assistance was reduced, and several USAID missions were completely closed (Taylor 2010). The case of Cabo

Verde was no different. For most of the 1990s, the U.S. policy toward the islands seems to be based more on disengagement, as the islands were of little geostrategic significance.

THE UNITED STATES AND CABO VERDE: THE FOCUS ON SECURITY

Relations between the United States and Cabo Verde today are characterized by an increasing securitization of bilateral relations. The relationship has evolved away from primarily economic development and humanitarian focus to one where strategic and security issues take precedence. This section first explores the theory of securitization and discusses trends in the securitization of U.S.–Africa relations.

Securitization theory is relatively new in international relations, dating back to the 1990s. The key premise of this theory is that security issues are above all speech acts. This means that to talk about security is to act upon something. In other words, to talk is to act. As noted by Ole Wæver, "it is by labeling something a security issue that it becomes one" (cited in Taureck 2006, 54). This point is further elaborated by Rita Taureck, who notes that "by stating that a particular referent object is threatened in its existence, a securitizing actor claims a right to extraordinary measures to ensure the referent object's survival" (Taureck 2006, 54). This is to say, securitization is politically consequential at the levels of domestic and international politics. It permits the securitizing agent to create "states of exception" that permits exceptional and swift measures.

Regarding the second point—securitization of U.S.–Africa relations—scholars debate about whether post-9/11 U.S.–Africa policy constitutes a rupture or continuity to the policies carried out in the 1990s. Some posit that the 9/11 terrorist attacks on U.S. soil placed Africa on a different level within the framework of U.S. foreign and security policies. For instance, Nicholas van de Walle writes that the "absence of core US interests was an article of faith in the mid-1990s, which probably marked a low point in US-Africa relations" (Walle 2010). In other words, during the 1900s, the dominant tone among policymakers in Washington was that of political disengagement.

On the other hand, other scholars consider that U.S.–Africa policy pre-and-post-9/11 is marked more by continuity. Political discourses and practices of engagement that were emphasized in the years following the attacks could also be found in the 1990s, during the Clinton administration. Basing on the writings of Susan Rice, Clinton administration's assistant secretary of state for African Affairs (1997–2001), Ian Taylor notes that the United States "'crafted and funded innovative counter-terrorism, counter-crime, and counter-narcotics strategies' in Africa, including police training centers in South Africa and American activity in brokering and helping sponsor peace processes in the Congo, Ethiopia and Eritrea, Mozambique and Sierra Leone" (Taylor 2010, 26). Engagement with Africa was characteristic of the Clinton administration.

Whether U.S.–Africa relations before and after the 9/11 attacks are characterized by continuity or rupture is a moot point. Yet, undoubtedly there is an "intensification of security concerns about Africa from Washington's perspective" (Taylor 2010, 27). This state of affairs has led a myriad of authors to characterize George W. Bush and Barack Obama administrations' U.S.–Africa relations in terms of securitization and militarization (Abrahamsen 2005; Walle 2010). This means that security and military concerns are taking the front seat in U.S.–Africa relations. This conclusion is supported by the fact that a myriad of security and military programs, initiatives, and institutions have been created by the United States to be applied in African states.

Following the attacks on the United States in September 2001, a growing diplomatic and military engagement took shape between the U.S. government and African states. A myriad of development and military programs and initiatives were developed by the United States. President George W. Bush's eight years in command of the U.S. government had provided far more assistance dollars than any other president in the past. When President Obama assumed power in 2009, it was expected that the African continent's general importance to Washington decision-makers would be greatly increased (Resende-Santos 2015, 10). Contrary to these expectations, President Obama's first term was characterized by an almost total neglect of the continent. While it has become diplomatically fashionable for major states and organizations to arrange for what can be called "dash Africa summit" (Japan-Africa Summit, India-Africa Summit, China-Africa Summit, European Union–Africa Summit, and so on), it was only in the second half of 2014 that the U.S. government went on to design and implement such a model of diplomatic engagement. For Resende-Santos, the fact that the U.S.–Africa Summit happened that late "was illustrative of the lower policy priority that Africa continent continued to merit in US foreign relations before and during Obama" (Resende-Santos 2015, 10).

This chapter asks whether U.S.–Cabo Verde policy follows the pattern of U.S.–African relations, whose dominant tones, as noted above, are securitization and militarization. It can be argued that, in practical terms post-9/11, U.S. foreign policy breaks down the continent into two major areas: an area of conflict, the hotbed of potential and real international and fundamentalist terrorism, and an area of (supposedly) good governance, where liberal electoral democratic institutions thrive. Such a distinction is verifiable in terms of the key instruments of foreign assistance and cooperation deriving from

Washington. In what concerns the "Africa-circle of conflict and terrorism," different National Security Strategy documents highlight the causal relations between state failure and international terrorism (Bush 2002).

Cabo Verde is included in the second group of African states, that of liberal, electoral democracy, and good governance. Since the late 1990s, the islands have been praised by U.S. officials as an example of electoral democracy in the region. In 1998, President Clinton hailed Cabo Verde as a beacon to Africa (*All Africa* 1998). A decade later, another Clinton (Hillary), then U.S. Secretary of State, while in Cabo Verde, applauded the government as "a model of democracy and economic progress in Africa" (Lee 2009). More recently, President Obama called Cabo Verde an example of democracy in Africa (*A Semana* 2014).

In general terms, post-9/11 U.S. Cabo Verde policy has been conducted through the means of two key agencies, namely the Millennium Challenge Corporation, and the U.S. Department of Defense and its Africa Command (Africom). The distinction between two different types of states in the developing world—and in Africa, in particular—prompted the Bush administration to create a new program, the MCA. Proposed in 2002, the MCA became fully instituted in 2004. This new institution was hailed as a "fundamental change" in the approach to foreign aid (Tarnoff 2007, 1). Yet, critics pointed out that the MCA was no more than old wine in a new bottle (Soederberg 2004).

The MCA can be seen as part of the global strategy of promotion of liberal democracy and free-market economies. According to this initiative, states that fulfill certain liberal-democratic and good governance requirements could apply for developmental grants. The criteria for the selection of the states were first laid out by President Bush, who argued that "Countries that live by these three broad standards—ruling justly, investing in their people, and encouraging economic freedom—will receive more aid from America" (ibid, 294). These three broad criteria further break down into a total of sixteen criteria that states must pass in order to be considered for the MCA grants.

Cabo Verde was one of the first countries to apply to the MCA, a few months after the formation of the MCC. The application for the MCA funds, submitted in the second half of 2004, is an example of a successful history of a close relationship between the homeland and its diaspora. Given the complexity and technicalities of the application to the MCA, the government of Cabo Verde sought assistance from Cabo Verdean-Americans. While a lot can be written about this, two cases are to be emphasized. First, the MCA application's first draft was written at Bridgewater State University, then led by Dana Mohler-Faria, a Cabo Verdean-American, along with a group working in the Cabo Verdean embassy in Washington. Second, Ray Almeida, then a Washington insider, made use of his connections in order to lobby for the Cabo Verdean case.

According to the 2005 Congressional Notification by the Millennium Challenge Corporation, Cabo Verde was awarded a little over 110 million dollars to be "be disbursed in tranches over the course of the Compact's term upon satisfaction or waiver of relevant conditions precedent" (MCC 2005). The MCA-I was focused on three main areas: (a) increasing agricultural productivity in the intervention zones; (b) increasing integration of internal markets and reducing transportation costs; and (c) developing the private sector through improving the private sector investment climate and reforming the financial sector (MCC 2005).

Two critical aspects of the MCA are to be highlighted. First, the program grants the receiving state relative agency is proposing the areas that funding could be channeled. In other words, the receiving state, through its application, establishes the areas that need intervention. Second, it is the relative rapidity and swiftness in reaching a decision, particularly when compared with other bilateral and multilateral assistance organizations. In this aspect, during the MCC Public Outreach meeting, held on June 16, 2005, Ambassador José Brito (cited in U.S. Department of State 2005) noted that

> we presented our proposal in August last year, and we have already, in June, the agreement of the Board. World Bank it is a minimum 18 months generally, normally it is almost two years to have this. And if we have done it, it's because of the spirit of the MCC was totally different from other donors, where we are mainly a team, a joint-team, walking together for the same objective: to reduce poverty.

On February 12, 2012, the government of Cabo Verde made history as it was the first among states with access to MCC money to sign a second MCC compact. This Second Compact established a total value of over $66 million "to increase household incomes by reforming two sectors identified as current constraints to economic growth: the water and sanitation sector and the land management sector" (MCC 2015).

The United States Department of Defense and its Africa Command (Africom) are the second vectors of the U.S. Cabo Verde policy. In 2007, President Bush announced that a new military command would be created, with the focus on the African continent. Hitherto, military and security matters pertaining to Africa were split among three other military commands, namely, Centcom (Central Command), Pacicom (Pacific Rim Command), and Eucom (European Command). The institutionalization of Africom in 2008 meant the submission of all of the missions, initiatives, programs, and exercises to one command (Taylor 2010). The argument of securitization of U.S.–Africa relations is further sustained by what was called a new paradigm (or ideology) of development. Many international commentators have noted a shift from the development/humanitarianism paradigm to the development as a security model (Abrahamsen 2005; Keenan 2008). Until 2007, U.S. military cooperation with Cabo Verde had been rather negligible. Economic cooperation clearly crowded out military assistance (see figure 9.2). Since 2007, the United States has substantially increased its military cooperation with Cabo Verde. The decade of 2010s translated in a 180-degree change in the cooperation between the two states, with military assistance being the dominant tone.

Africom relations with African states, at both bilateral and multilateral levels, have been through different initiatives and programs. While an analysis of these programs and initiatives is beyond the scope of this chapter, it warrants to mention some of the most important security architectural institutions created under Africom: two recently created programs such as the Security Governance Initiative for Africa (SGI), the African Peacekeeping Rapid Response Partnership (A-PREP), and a myriad of older programs that include, among others, Pandemic Response Program, Partner Military HIV/AIDS Program, Partnership for Integrated Logistics Operation and Tactics, and VETCAP.

The government of Cabo Verde has embraced Africom since its inception. In January 2008, during a video conference with Ambassador Mary Carlin Yates, Africom's first deputy to the Commander for Civil-Military Activities, officials from the government of Cabo Verde showed great interest in the new organization (Vicente Lopes 2008). Carlos Reis, then adviser to the Republic

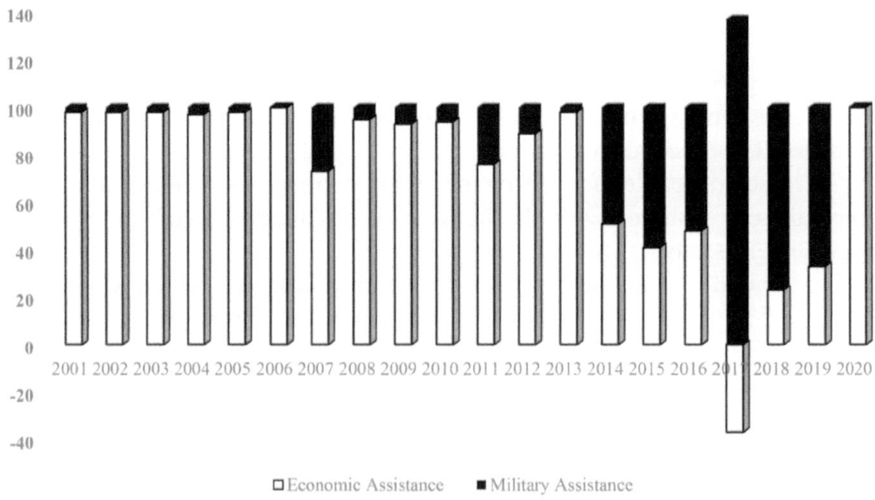

Figure 9.2 Economic Assistance versus Military Assistance, 2001–2018, in Percentage Shares of Total. *Source*: Created with data from U.S. Agency for International Development, US Overseas Loans & Grants (Greenbook), 2020. The numbers in 2017 are negative in relation to the previous year.

of Cabo Verde Ministry of Defense, went further to note that Africom "may help Africa in its new takeoff, to integrate into the global market, to have the necessary security and to tranquilly walk" (ibid, my translation).

The discourses of securitization found fertile ground among Cabo Verdean policymakers. In 2011, for the first in its history, the government of Cabo Verde issued a white paper on national defense and security (RTC 2011). It is beyond the scope of this chapter to fully analyze the document. It is worth noting that the document is a catalog of significant threats, mostly deriving from the new international context. For the government of Cabo Verde, there were substantial destabilizing regional and global risks including "ethnic and racial based armed conflicts as well as those based on religious, political and ideological extremism" (Conselho de Ministros 2011). The same document points out a link of causality from this situation and the rising of "weakened states" (*Estados fragilizados*), taken to constitute "authentic sanctuar[ies] of narco-, arms-, and people-trafficking and organized crime" (Conselho de Ministros 2011).

The document clearly securitizes foreign policy by pinpointing that it "should continue as one of the key sectors of security and defense of Cabo Verde" (Conselho de Ministros 2011). The white paper also signals a rupture with previous governments' position of avoiding strict military and defense cooperation with global powers. According to the 2011 white paper on national security, "The United States are, de facto, a partner in the development of Cabo Verde with whom our country must increment, even more, relations in the framework of security and defense" (Conselho de Ministros 2011, 9).

Africom Cabo Verde relations have taken place through three main levels: (a) meetings at the highest levels; (b) training exercises; and (c) institutional capacitation assistance. Since its inception, several high-level Africom officials have met with the leaders of the government of Cabo Verde. These talks were often around security issues and about ways that the United States could help Cabo Verde in curbing the security threats. While the region of West Africa, in general, has taken stable steps toward economic development and political democratization, the region is still perceived by the U.S. government as one of the hotbeds of several threats such as international terrorism, transnational organized crime, and major disease outbreak (such as the recent case of Ebola in West Africa).

At the same time, as a result of these talks, several agreements were signed between the two parties. As an illustrative example, on March 24, 2014, the city of Praia, Africom, and the government of Cabo Verde signed two major agreements (RTC 2014). The first agreement dealt with the reinforcement of Cabo Verde's capacity in areas of transnational illicit maritime activities, such as illegal drug trafficking. The second accord was called the Acquisition and Cross Servicing Agreement (ACSA), a type of agreement that permits the contracting parts to mutually benefit from the logistic apparatus and services. Cabo Verde has become one of the nineteen African states to have an active ACSA (Africom 2014).

The second level of interaction between Cabo Verde and Africom is through training exercises. Since 2011, Cabo Verde has taken part in the annual exercises of Saharan Express. The program, which falls under African Partnership Station, is a regional exercise in West Africa that brings naval and sea security forces from West Africa, Europe, and the United States. According to Africom, Saharan Express' main objective is "to develop participant nations' capabilities to monitor and enforce their own territorial waters and exclusive economic zones" (Africom 2010).

Institutional capacity-building assistance can be said to constitute the third level of Africom Cabo Verde relations. In this regard, Africom has worked closely with the government of Cabo Verde in terms of providing assistance in the matters of maritime security. It suffices to note that the Counter Narcotics and Maritime Security Operation Center, known for its Portuguese acronym COSMAR, opened in May 2010, was made possible by a $1.5 million grant from Africom (Crawley 2010). Africom has also provided valuable legal and technical assistance in terms of modernization of Cabo Verde's maritime law and the formation of its Coast Guard. Since 2011, a U.S.-funded surveillance operation was based in the old airport in Praia.

Through these three different levels of cooperation and partnership, Cabo Verde has become Africom's one of the most loyal partners. Given the geostrategic position of Cabo Verde—a position that is often highlighted during periods of global or regional conflicts—Africom seeks to maintain the islands within the circle of valuable partners.

CONCLUSION

This chapter outlined a history of U.S.–Cabo Verde relations since the early nineteenth century. Given the history of the Atlantic World, I argued that the two states were inextricably linked—though the relations were stronger in historical periods that highlight the geopolitical position of the islands of Cabo Verde. I noted that this close historical relationship explains why Cabo Verde was chosen by the U.S. government for the establishment of its first consulate in West Africa or as the base for the African Squadron in the mid-1800s.

The second part of the chapter delved into the politics of national independence and political recognition in the mid-1970s. It first emphasized the existence of different socio-political groups among Cabo Verdean-Americans, who formed political and civic organizations with the ultimate goal of the ethnic lobby before the U.S. government. Then I analyzed the development of diplomatic relations between the two states by noting that the major instrument of U.S. policy toward Cabo Verde, from 1975 to the 1990s was the USAID. In the last part of this chapter, I argued that the end of the Cold War meant the change of the U.S. Cabo Verde policy. This was particularly observable by the fact that USAID was eliminated while the Peace Corps, a major instrument of U.S. public diplomacy, became the major instrument of bilateral relations (see table 9.1).

In the last section of this chapter, its main corpus, I argued that a key feature of contemporary U.S.–Cabo Verde relations is securitization. That is to say, the key element that binds the two states together is the discourse on security and the subsequent actions that ultimately seek to create instruments to properly deal with the perceived threats. U.S.–Cabo Verde policy has been dominated by the two main agencies, the MCA and Africom. The rationale of these organizations is that of security as a development issue. Cabo Verde has attracted not only significant amounts of development dollars from the MCA but also has benefited from different initiatives and projects funded by Africom. I also argued that the global aura of securitization found fertile ground among Cabo Verdean policymakers, whose 2011 government's white paper on national security is a clear illustration of such a trend.

NOTES

1. Throughout the paper I use Cabo Verde and not the traditional *Cape Verde* to identify the country. I do so in respect of a Cabo Verdean governmental resolution that asks the name of the country not to be translated. I kept *Cape Verde/Cape Verdean* as found in primary source documents and in the name of organizations.
2. Ideas from this section were drawn from Amado (2014).

REFERENCES

Abrahamsen, R. "Blair's Africa: The Politics of Securitization and Fear." *Alternatives: Global, Local, Political* 30 (2005): 55–80.

Africom. "Cabo Verde Signs ACSA with DoD." *Africom.* April 7, 2014. http://www.africom.mil/newsroom/photo/12009/cabo-verde-signs-acsa-with-dod.

———. "Saharan Express." *Africom*, June 16, 2010. http://www.africom.mil/what-we-do/exercises/saharan-express.

Allis, Samuel. "Politics Deepen an Old Dilemma." *Boston Globe*, March 21, 1976.

Almeida, Raymond. "Boston Crusade for Cape Verde." *Boston Globe*, April 6, 1976.

Almeida, Raymond A. *Cape Verdeans in America: Our Story*. Boston, MA: Tchuba-American Committee for Cape Verde, Inc., 1978.

Amado, Abel Djassi. "*Doz pezôd*, ou o Liliputiano e o Colosso? As Relaçoes Internacionais entre Cabo Verde e os EUA." In *As Relações Externas de Cabo Verde. (Re)Leituras Contemporâneas*, edited by Suzano Costa, José Pina Delgado, and Odair Varela, 477–506. Praia: Edições ISCJS, 2014.

———. "Whose Independence? Cabo Verdean-Americans and the Politics of National Independence of Cabo Verde (1972–1976)." *Journal of Cape Verdean Studies* 5, no. 1 (2020): 36–53. https://vc.bridgew.edu/jcvs/vol5/iss1/5.

Ambrosio, Thomas. *Ethnic Identity Groups and U.S. Foreign Policy*. Westport, CT: Praeger, 2002.

"Barack Obama apresenta Cabo Verde como exemplo de democracia para a África e o mundo." (August 7, 2014). *A Semana*. http://www.asemana.publ.cv/spip.php?article102186.

"[Senator] Brooke Meet with Cape Verdeans." *The Cape Verdean*, May 1975.

Brooks, G. E. *Yankee Traders, Old Coasters & African Middlemen: A History of American Legitimate Trade with West Africa in the Nineteenth Century*. Brookline, MA: Boston University Press, 1970.

Bush, George W. *The National Security Strategy of the United States of America*. Washington, DC: President of the U.S., 2002.

"Cabo Verde Signs ACSA with DoD." *Africom*, 25 April 2014. https://www.africom.mil/article/12008/cabo-verde-signs-acsa-with-dod.

"Cabo Verde e EUA assinam acordos que visam o combate às actividades marítimas transnacionais ilícitas e apoio logístico." *RTC*, 24 March 2014. http://rtc.cv/index.php?paginas=21&id_cod=8062.

"Cabo Verde já tem documento sobre o Conceito Estratégico de Defesa e Segurança Nacional." *RTC*, July 27, 2011. http://www.rtc.cv/index.php?paginas=13&id_cod=11600.

Canney, D. L. *Africa Squadron: The U.S. Navy and the Slave Trade, 1842–1861*. Washington, DC: Potomac Books, 2006.

"Cape Verdeans of the World." *The Cape Verdean*, April 1975.

Carreira, A. *The People of the Cape Verde Islands: Exploitation and Emigration*. London: C. Hurst, 1982.

Clifford, J. Garry, and Robert H. Ferrell. "Roosevelt at the Rubicon: The Great Convoy Debate of 1941." In *The United States and the Second World War New Perspectives on Diplomacy, War, and the Home Front*, edited by G. Kurt Piehler, and Sidney Pash, 20–37. New York: Fordham University Press, 2010.

"Clinton Hails Cape Verde As 'Beacon'." *All Africa*, 28 October 1998. allafrica.com/stories/199810280164.html.

Conselho de Ministros [Cabo Verde]. *Conceito Estratégico de Defesa e Segurança Nacional*. Praia: Conselho de Ministros, 2011.

Crawley, Vince. "AFRICOM Deputy Discusses Maritime Security, Drug Trafficking, Illegal Fishing at New Cape Verde Ops Center." *Africom*, 16 June, 2010. https://www.africom.mil/article/7473/africom-deputy-discusses-maritime-security-drug-tr.

Department of State. Memorandum of Conversation, Washington, February 28, 1969, between Dr. Vasco Vieira Garin, Ambassador of Portugal, Ambassador U. Alexis Johnson, Under Secretary and Mr. Stephen G. Gebelt, Country Officer for Portugal. In Department of State. *Foreign Relations of the United States 1969–1976*, volume XXVIII. Washington, DC: Department of State, 2011.

———. *Portuguese Guinea: Rebels Establish Government*, October 5, 1973.

Duncan, T. B. *Atlantic Islands: Madeira: The Azores, and the Cape Verdes in Seventeenth-Century Commerce and Navigation.* Chicago, IL: University of Chicago Press, 1972.

El-Khawas, M. A., and Cohen, B. *The Kissinger Study of Southern Africa: National Security Study Memorandum 39 (Secret)*, edited and introduced by Mohamed A. El-Khawas and Barry Cohen; pref. by Edgar Lockwood. Westport, CT: L. Hill, 1976.

Eschen, P. M. Von. R*ace against Empire: Black Americans and Anticolonialism, 1937–1957.* Ithaca, NY: Cornell University Press, 1997.

"Fundação Cabo-Verdiana de Solidariedade desenvolve "Projecto Órfão." *A Semana,* 15 November 2005. http://asemana.publ.cv/spip.php?article13318&var_recherche =Procurar&ak=1.

Gleijeses, P. "The First Ambassadors: Cuba's Contribution to Guinea-Bissau's War of Independence." *Journal of Latin American Studies* 29, no. 1 (1997): 45–88.

"Grant Made to Liberation Group." *Boston Globe*, 22 September 1973.

Halter, M. *Between Race and Ethnicity: Cape Verdean American Immigrants, 1860–1965.* Urbana, IL: University of Illinois Press, 1993.

Keenan, J. "US Militarization in Africa: What Anthropologists Should Know about AFRICOM." *Anthropology Today* 24, no. 5 (2008): 16–20.

Lake, Anthony. *The "Tar Baby" Option: American Policy toward Southern Rhodesia.* New York: Columbia University Press, 1976.

Lazerow, Jama. "'A Rebel All His Life': The Unexpected Story of Frank 'Parky' Grace." In *In Search of the Black Panther Party: New Perspectives on a Revolutionary Movement*, edited by Lazerow, J., and Williams, Y. R. Durham, NC: Duke University Press, 2006.

Lee, Matthew. "Hillary Clinton Praises Cape Verde As She Finishes Africa Tour." *Huffington Post*, 14 August, 2009. http://www.huffingtonpost.com/2009/08/14/clinton-praises-cape-verd_n_259442.html?

Lobban, R. A. *Cape Verde: Crioulo Colony to Independent Nation.* Boulder, CO: Westview Press, 1995.

Lockwood, Edgar. "National Security Study Memorandum 39 and the Future of United States Policy toward Southern Africa." *Issue: A Quarterly Journal of Africanist Opinion* IV, no. 3 (1974): 63–72.

Martin, Frank, John Eriksson, Stephanie McNulty with assistance from Steve Metzger. *USAID Graduation Recent Experience and Outstanding Issues.* USAID Special Evaluation Study Report No. 81. Center for Information Development Information and Evaluation, May 1999.

Matteos, Salahudin. "The Cape Verdeans and the PAIGC Struggle for National Liberation: An Interview with Salahudin Omowale Matteos." *Ufahamu: A Journal of African Studies* 3, no. 3 (1973): 43–48.

Melissen, Jan. "The New Public Diplomacy: Between Theory and Practice." In *The New Public Diplomacy*, edited by Jan Melissen, 3–27. New York: Palgrave Macmillan, 2005.

Millennium Challenge Corporation. "Cabo Verde Compact II." 2021. https://www.mcc.gov/where-we-work/program/cape-verde-compact-ii.

———. "MCC Completes First Compact in Africa, $110 Million Compact with Cape Verde," October 15, 2010. https://www.mcc.gov/pages/press/release/release-101510-mcccompletesfirst.

———. "U.S. Department of State," June 29, 2005. http://2001-2009.state.gov/e/eeb/rls/fs/48965.htm.

Nye, J. S. "Public Diplomacy and Soft Power." *The Annals of the American Academy of Political and Social Science* 616, no. 1 (2008): 94–109.

———. "Soft Power." *Foreign Policy* 80 (1990): 153–171.

Peace Corps. *The Peace Corps Welcomes You to Cape Verde*. A Peace Corps Publication for New Volunteers, 2009.

Pereira, Eduardo Adilson Camilo. *Politica e Cultura: As Revoltas dos Engenhos (1822), de Achada Falcão (1841) e de Ribeirão Manuel (1910)*. Praia: Imprensa Nacional de Cabo Verde, 2014.

Pires-Hester, Laura. "The Emergence of Bilateral Diaspora Ethnicity among Cape Verdean-Americans." In *The African Diaspora: African Origins and New World Identities*, edited by Isidore Okpewho, Carole Boyce Davies, and Ali A. Mazrui, 485–503. Bloomington, IN: Indiana University Press, 1999.

"Publisher Interviews Dr. Veiga." *The Cape Verdean*, June 1975.

Randal, C. "CIA Role is Alleged in Portugal." *Washington Post*, October 17, 1974.

Resende-Santos, João. *United States–Africa Relations during the Obama Administration*. WAI Critical Analysis and Action Strategies No. 2, 2015.

Rodger, N. A. M. *The Command of the Ocean: A Naval History of Britain, 1649–1815*. New York: W.W. Norton, 2005.

Rodrigues, Luis Nuno. "About-Face: The United States and Portuguese Colonialism in 1961." *E-JPH* 2, no. 1 (2004): 1–10.

Saunders, C. "The South Africa-Angola Talks, 1976–1984: A Little-Known Cold War Thread." *Kronos* 37, no. 1 (2011): 104–119.

Schreiber, Gerhard, Bernd Stegemann, and Detlef Vogel. *The Mediterranean, South-East Europe, and North Africa, 1939–1941: From Italy's Declaration of Non-Belligerence to the Entry of the United States into the War*. Oxford: Clarendon Press, 1995.

Soederberg, S. "American Empire and 'Excluded States': The Millennium Challenge Account and the Shift to Pre-emptive Development." *Third World Quarterly* 25, no. 2 (2004): 279–302.

Spínola, António de. *Por uma Guiné melhor*. Lisboa: Agência-Geral do Ultramar, 1970.

Stone, Glyn. *The Oldest Ally: Britain and the Portuguese Connection, 1936–1941*. London: Royal Historical Society, 1994.

Tarnoff, C. *Millennium Challenge Account*. Washington, DC: Congressional Research Service, Library of Congress, 2007.

Taureck, R. "Securitization Theory and Securitization Studies." *Journal of International Relations and Development* 9, no. 1 (2006): 53–61.

Tavares, Eugénio, and Félix Monteiro. *Eugénio Tavares. Pelos Jornais*. Praia: Instituto Caboverdeano do Livro e do Disco, 1997.

Taylor, I. *The International Relations of Sub-Saharan Africa*. New York: Continuum, 2010.

United States, and Gerald R. Ford. *Public Papers of the Presidents of the United States, Gerald R. Ford, 1975*. Washington: GPO, 1977.

United States Congress. "An Act Making Appropriations for Foreign Assistance and Related Programs for the Fiscal Year Ending June 30,1975, and for Other Purposes." Public Law 94–11, U.S. Statutes at Large 89 (1975): STAT 17-STAT 25.

USAID. *USAID/Cape Verde Phase Out-Plan*, March 1994. http://pdf.usaid.gov/pdf_docs/PDABM584.pdf.

Vicente Lopes J. *Cabo Verde, os Bastidores da Independência*. Praia: Spleen, 2002.

———. "Cabo Verde Receptivo à Criação do AFRICOM." *BBC*, January 15, 2008. http://www.bbc.co.uk/portugueseafrica/news/story/2008/01/080115_cvusaafricomlc.shtml.

Walle, N. "US Policy towards Africa: The Bush Legacy and the Obama Administration." *African Affairs* 109, no. 434 (2010): 1–21.

White House. *Memorandum of Conversation: The President [George Bush] and Cape Verdean President Aristides Pereira*, April 21, 1989.

Wright, G. *The Destruction of a Nation: United States' Policy towards Angola since 1945*. London: Pluto Press, 1997.

Index

About the Editors and Contributors

EDITORS

Aminah N. Fernandes Pilgrim, PhD, is a faculty member in the UMass Boston Transnational, Cultural & Community Studies MS Program, Africana Studies Department and the Women's & Gender Studies Program. She is also a founding faculty member in the Pedro Pires Institute for Cape Verdean Studies at Bridgewater State University. Her areas of research primarily include late nineteenth- and twentieth-century African American history, African American women's history, African Diaspora studies, and Cabo Verdean studies. She recently coled a historic trade mission to Cabo Verde for the City of Boston Mayor's Office and the Hyams Foundation, where many of the issues presented in this volume were examined in an attempt to connect the Cabo Verdean capital city of Praia to the U.S. city of Boston for the purpose of creating pathways for development in Cabo Verde.

João Resende-Santos, PhD, is associate professor of international studies at Bentley University in Waltham Massachusetts, the United States. He received his PhD in political science from Harvard University. Prior to Bentley, he taught at the University of Pennsylvania and the University of Pittsburgh. From 2009 to 2011, he served as dean of the School of Business and Governance/Escola de Negócios e Governação (ENG), University of Cape Verde (UNICV). His research areas include international relations theory, U.S. foreign policy, development policy, political economy of Cape Verde, diaspora engagement, and Cape Verde foreign relations. He remains actively engaged professionally in Cape Verde, as a policy practitioner and international consultant in the areas of economic development policy, entrepreneurship, and trade policy. He has been a consultant for a number of international organizations and the Government of Cape Verde. He was a member of the task force that prepared the project proposal for the Second Millennium Challenge Account (MCA) grant that the United States awarded Cape Verde in 2012. His first book, *Neorealism, the State, and the Modern Mass Army*, was published in 2007. He is coauthor of the recently published *Innovation Africa: Emerging Hubs of Excellence*, which is part of a broader set of initiatives based on the Africa Innovation Summit. Among his most recent publications are "Cape Verde: Rethinking Diaspora in Development Policy," *International Migration* October 2015; "The Risks of Tourism Specialization: The Tourism Option for Africa's Small States," *Journal of Contemporary African Studies* (2019); and "Cape Verde and the MCA Foreign Aid Program," *Journal of Modern African Studies* (2020).

CONTRIBUTORS

Abel Djassi Amado, PhD, is assistant professor of political science and international relations at Simmons University, Boston, Massachusetts. Prior to joining Simmons in 2016, he taught at various universities in Massachusetts and Rhode Island. He co-directed the University of Rhode Island Summer Abroad study program in Cabo Verde for many years. Amado is an active board member of the West African Research Association (WARA), a U.S.-based non-profit scholarly organization that promotes investigation and study of West African issues and encourages academic linkages between scholars on the two sides of Atlantic. He holds a PhD in political science from Boston University. He resides in Boston, where he teaches at Simmons College, Boston College, and University of Rhode Island. Abel Djassi's research interests include U.S.–African policy, with particular focus on African countries with Portuguese as the official language, diaspora politics, politics of language policy, and the political history of anti-colonialism and decolonization. Beyond academia, Abel Djassi is an engaged member of the Cabo Verdean community in New England. He served as secretary to the *Nos di Tchada i Amigos, Inc.,* and he was a board member of the now defunct *National Alliance of Cabo Verdean Organizations*.

Crisanto Barros, PhD, is full professor of social sciences at the Universidade de Cabo Verde (UNICV), where he served as former provost (vice rector) of the university since its founding. His undergraduate degree in education and social sciences is from the University of Campinhas in Brasil, and he received his PhD in political and social sciences from the Catholic University of Lovaina in Belgium. He is currently professor in the Faculty of Social and Human Sciences of the UNICV, where he teaches courses in sociology and political science. He was former president of the Pedagogical Institute and served as vice president of the Installation Commission that created the UNICV. Currently he directs that Post-Graduate Program in Social Sciences and is a researcher in the Research Laboratory in Social Sciences (LPCS). His areas of research and expertise include the formation and reconversion of the political-administrative elites in post-independence Cabo Verde.

Edgar Bernardo, PhD, is a professor at the University of Trás-os-Montes and Alto Douro (UTAD) in Vila Real, Portugal. A specialist on tourism studies, Bernardo is a research fellow at the Center for Transdisciplinary Studies on Development (CETRAD). He has published several articles in specialized journals and two books. He received his PhD in sociology from the University Institute of Lisbon (ISCTE), Lisbon, Portugal. In addition to his research and writings on tourism in Portugal, Bernardo has also conducted field research in Cabo Verde. His most recent work on tourism in Cabo Verde is "Turismo Insular Africano: múltiplos olhares sobre a experiência Cabo-verdiana," *PASOS—Revista de Turismo e Patrimonio Cultural*, January 17, 2019.

Victor Borges, PhD, is former minister of education and former minister of foreign affairs of the Republic of Cabo Verde. Mr. Borges was minister of education, culture, and sports (2001–2002); minister of education and human resources development (2002–2004); and minister of foreign affairs, cooperation, and communities of Cape Verde (2004–2008), during which he successfully guided the landmark Cabo Verde–European Union Special Partnership Agreement. He served as a member of the Governing Body of UNESCO Institute for Lifelong Learning, in Hamburg (2008–2012). He was the chairperson of the Council of Ministers of ACP Group (2005); member of the Executive Board of the UNESCO (2003–2007); and coordinator of Swiss cooperation office in Cape Verde, SDC (1995–2000). Trainer and resource person for various national and international organizations in Cape Verde, Mr. Borges has two bachelor's degrees in education sciences (University of Paris VIII, 1979) and in psychology (University of Nice, France, 1978) and a master's degree in psychology (University of Paris VIII, 1980) and doctoral studies in education and development (University of Paris VIII, 1981–1983). He was the chief of the technical assistance team for the launching of the vocational school of Praia, IBF, European Union (1995–1997); national director of the project "Training and Information on Environment," PFIE, CILSS/EU (1990–1995); general coordinator of education projects, Bureau of the Ministry of Education, funded by World Bank, and African Development Bank (1988–1990); and director of primary education upgrading project, funded by WB (1987–1988).

Roselma Évora, PhD, is an academic, researcher, and policy practitioner. A highly sought-after public intellectual and media commentator, Évora is among Cape Verde's most renowned political sociologist. She has also served in Cape Verde's public administration, as senior staff in Secretary of State for Public Administration. She holds a bachelor and master's degrees in political science, and PhD in sociology, from the University of Brasilia (UNB), Brasilia, Brazil. She is author of two books and coauthor of four more with themes on the political system and democracy in Cape Verde. She has participated in various national and international seminars and conferences focusing on democracy issues. She is commentator on various radio and television programs in Cape Verde, founding member of LusoForumForDemocracy, independent researcher and consultant, country expert for the Varieties of Democracy Project 2013–2015, winner of the 2008 CES Young Researchers Program Edition and honored by the Brazilian Ministry of Education as a former PEC High-School Student in 2014. Roselma Évora's book, *Cabo Verde: a abertura política e a transição para a democracia* (Praia: Spleen Edições, 2004), is widely regarded as a definitive explanation of Cape Verde's 1991 transition to democracy, the first in Africa during the wave of democratization beginning in the 1990s.

Djalita Fialho, PhD, is a member of the executive board at the Pedro Pires Institute for Leadership (IPP) in Praia, Cape Verde, since 2014. Djalita received her doctoral degree in development studies from the Erasmus University, International Institute of Social Studies, Rotterdam, the Netherlands. She received her master's degree from the University of Lisbon, at its renowned Instituto Superior de Economia e Gestão (ISIEG). She also has a management degree from the University of Massachusetts Boston (minor in economics and concentration in marketing) and a post-grad degree in management from Harvard University. She has conducted extensive primary research on Cape Verde's foreign relations, especially bilateral relations with international organizations like the United Nations. Among her publications on the subject include "The Proliferation of Developing Country Classification," *Journal of Development Studies* (2016) and "Altruism But Not Quite: The Genesis of the Least Developed Country (LDC) Category," *Third World Quarterly* (2012). With sixteen years of professional experience, she was an adviser at the Department of Cooperation at the Executive Secretariat of the Community of Portuguese-Speaking Countries (CPLP), in Lisbon, and adviser in the Permanent Missions of Cabo Verde and Portugal to the United Nations, in New York.

Terza Alice Silva Lima-Neves, PhD, is a wife, mother, educator, and advocate for access to quality education for all. She was born and raised in São Vicente Island, Cabo Verde. As a teenager, Terza immigrated to Pawtucket,

Rhode Island, the United States, with her parents and two younger sisters. Dr. Lima-Neves is assistant professor of political science at Johnson C. Smith University in Charlotte, North Carolina, the United States. She received her MA and PhD in political science from Clark Atlanta University in Atlanta, Georgia, the United States. She teaches courses on African, comparative, and international politics. Her research interests and published scholarship focus on modern African diaspora politics, gender, and development. She's particularly interested in the politics of gender and community building in the Cabo Verdean community in the United States. Terza is also the founding president of the Cape Verdeans of the Carolinas Association, an organization that brings together the Cabo Verdean community in North and South Carolina, their friends and allies via cultural and educational events, highlighting the rich history of their homeland. Terza lives in Charlotte, North Carolina, with her husband Luis and their children Erivaldo, Ema, and Emilio.

Carlos Rocha, PhD, is a senior administrator in the Central Bank of Cabo Verde, and former member of the bank's governing directorate. He received his PhD in monetary and financial economics from the Instituto Superior de Economia e Gestão (ISEG), Lisbon, Portugal, in 2007. He holds degrees in business organization and management economics from the Higher Institute of Labor and Business Sciences (ISCTE), Lisbon, Portugal; postgraduate in small business administration in the European Union, South Bank University in London, United Kingdom; master's in development economics from ISCTE, PhD in monetary and financial economics from Instituto Superior de Economia e Gestão (ISEG), Lisbon, Portugal, in 2007. He was former director of Cape Verde Investments (2009–2014), the investment and trade promotion agency, and director of several departments at the Central Bank of Cape Verde, including the Department of Markets and Department of Statistics and Economic Studies. He has been a senior technician in the following departments of the Bank of Cape Verde: Foreign Department, Banking Supervision Department, and Statistics and Economic Studies Department. He worked as a consultant in Portugal, during which time he advised several institutions and was also a training manager in Portugal. In teaching, he has experience as coordinator of the first edition of the master's degree in public administration at the UNICV in 2008–2009. He has also served as a faculty member and trainer in various other institutions in Portugal and in Cape Verde. Rocha was a member of the national task force that prepared the diagnosis for the Second Compact MCA between the United States and Cape Verde. He was a member of the National Approval Committee (ECOWAS), a member of the PSI Agreement Monitoring Committee with the International Monetary Fund (IMF), and a member of the Coordinating Committee of the Exchange Cooperation Agreement between Portugal and Cape Verde.

Amb. André Corsino Tolentino, PhD, is a former longtime diplomat, former minister, writer, and one of Cabo Verde's best-known public intellectuals. He was a guerrilla fighter during war for independence, participating in the national liberation movement led by Amílcar Cabral. After independence, he served as secretary of state for foreign affairs, Cabo Verde's first ambassador to Portugal, minister of education, ambassador, and later director of the Calouste Gulbenkian Foundation. Tolentino played another historic role as lead negotiator for the ruling party in 1990 during the multiparty negotiations for national elections and the transition multiparty democracy. He received his PhD in education from the University of Lisbon, studied development economics at the University of Minnesota, and management education at Harvard University. He also holds a degree in public administration from the Technical University of Lisbon. Tolentino is author of numerous books, articles, and commissioned studies. In 2007, he published *University and Social Transformation in Small Developing States: The Case of Cape Verde*. In 2008, he coauthored, with Carlos Rocha and Nancy Tolentino, *The Importance and Impact of Immigrant Remittances in Portugal on Cape Verde's Development*. Tolentino was distinguished with the Grand Cross of the Order of Infante D. Henrique (Portugal), the Order Amílcar Cabral, and the Order of Merit by the Government of Cape Verde. Member of the ECOWAS Science and Technology Panel and corresponding partner of the Lisbon Academy of Sciences, he contributed to the establishment of the West African Institute and the Cape Verde Academy of Sciences and Humanities. In 2015, he received from the University of Minnesota the Distinguished Leadership Award for Internationals.

www.ingramcontent.com/pod-product-compliance
Ingram Content Group UK Ltd.
Pitfield, Milton Keynes, MK11 3LW, UK
UKHW041449071026
15587UKWH00010B/712

9 781793 653833